Hin̶d̶sights

the autobiography of an unknown artist

Stan Erisman

Hindsights

Published by Stan Erisman
Publishing partner: Paragon Publishing, Rothersthorpe
First published 2021

© Stan Erisman 2021

The rights of Stan Erisman to be identified as the author of this work have been asserted by him in accordance with the Copyright, Designs and Patents Act of 1988.

All rights reserved; no part of this publication may be reproduced, stored in a retrieval system, or transmitted in any form or by any means, electronic, mechanical, photocopying, recording or otherwise without the prior written consent of the publisher or a licence permitting copying in the UK issued by the Copyright Licensing Agency Ltd.
www.cla.co.uk

ISBN 978-1-78222-864-6

Book design, layout and production management by Into Print
www.intoprint.net
+44 (0)1604 832149

Cover illustration: *Turning*, oil painting #79, by Stan Erisman, 1978

The Foreword to the *Hindsights* series can be found in Book 1, *Natural Shocks*.

A Sea of Troubles

To be, or not to be, that is the question:
Whether 'tis nobler in the mind to suffer
The **slings and arrows** of outrageous fortune,
Or to take Arms against **a Sea of troubles**,
And by opposing end them: to die, to sleep
No more; and by a sleep, to say we end
The heart-ache, and the thousand **natural shocks**
That Flesh is heir to? 'Tis a consummation
Devoutly to be wished. To die, to sleep,
To sleep, **perchance to Dream**; aye, there's the rub,
For in that sleep of death, what dreams may come,
When we have shuffled off this mortal coil,
Must give us pause. There's the respect
That makes Calamity of so long life:
For who would bear the Whips and Scorns of time,
The Oppressor's wrong, the proud man's Contumely,
The pangs of despised Love, the Law's delay,
The insolence of Office, and the spurns
That patient merit of the unworthy takes,
When he himself might his Quietus make
With a bare Bodkin? Who would Fardels bear,
To grunt and sweat under a weary life,
But that the dread of something after death,
The undiscovered country, from whose bourn
No traveller returns, puzzles the will,
And makes us rather bear those ills we have,
Than fly to others that we know not of.
Thus conscience does make cowards of us all,
And thus the native hue of Resolution
Is sicklied o'er, with the pale cast of Thought,
And enterprises of great pitch and moment,
With this regard their Currents turn awry,
And lose the name of Action.

– William Shakespeare, Hamlet's soliloquy
from *Hamlet*, act III, scene I

A Sea of Troubles
Book five in the Hindsights series

Stan Erisman

CONTENTS

Chapter 1: Drowning 1

How I self-destructively attempted to mute my grief with whisky and cigarettes; how Bob pleaded with me daily to avoid self-pity at all costs; how I discovered that my employer (and thus my job) had also disappeared; how I went through with a previously planned vasectomy; and how a visit from my brother and his wife, including a trip to see Bob, gave me some unintentional comic relief.

Chapter 2: Helpers 18

How Bob tirelessly exhorted me to go on; how others got me to try windsurfing and cannabis; how my mom came to visit that autumn and I refused to defer to her; how she got me to continue the work on our almost-finished house; and how, despite my consciously self-destructive path, I began to realize that my libido was not dead, even though my painting and my muse were.

Chapter 3: Amor præcox 34

How I at a party, in a haze of alcohol, saw Sonja, whose striking resemblance to Jeanette threw me into chaos, and how she eventually helped me to see; how mutual friends shortly thereafter threw a party where they introduced me to Lena; how she phoned me and wanted to visit me and spent half the night with me; how I fell madly in love with her and spent most of December and all of January together with her.

Chapter 4: Convulsion and catharsis 59

How Lena suddenly announced she was tired of me and turned away; how desperate I became; how I tried to finish the work on the house so as not to leave too much unfinished behind me; how I knew I could take no more, and for nine days feverishly wrote the story and plan of my own suicide, whereupon I collapsed and woke up a day later to find I'd experienced a catharsis; and how I was offered a job.

Chapter 5: Joie de vivre 69

How I found myself in the bizarre situation of teaching adult Swedes both English and Swedish; how my relations with Lena became intermittent (I came when she called, but went elsewhere when she didn't); how my teaching work blossomed into further pleasures; and how Voltaire's Candide aroused in me the need to paint again.

CHAPTER 6: Making the rounds..91

How I was living for the day more than ever before; how Perstorp, a company from which I'd taught many employees through the language school, offered me a job starting in the autumn; how I visited the States again, this time without the agony; and how a number of attractive women were eager to see me whenever Lena wasn't.

CHAPTER 7: Perstorp 113

How I came to be employed part-time at a chemical company far from home; how my life, libido and painting continued to thrive even though Lena remained frustratingly out of reach; how my work began including translations and editing of texts, and how I started aiming to be able to work solely from home one day.

CHAPTER 8: Through the woods 135

How I began to wonder whether my focus on Lena might be due to a desire to inflict punishment on myself for having failed to recognize and respond to Jeanette's desperate mental state; how I met a second Lena, who nearly rescued me from the first; and how I felt "safer" than before, knowing I not only had limits but also other opportunities.

CHAPTER 9: Trying 155

How the battle between my reason and my unrequited love for Lena frustrated Bob, and how hard he tried to weigh his words; how Sonja gave me sound advice that I failed to heed; how much joy I was getting from painting again and how indifferent Lena was to it; how I chose to ignore that alarm bell as well, and how I convinced myself that Lena was softening.

CHAPTER 10: Attrition 171

How I took Lena to the Canary Islands for a week, and how her fickleness remained; how I finally had enough and left her one evening, and how she coaxed me back under her spell; how I started focusing on my work on restoring another part of the house and on my work for Perstorp; how Bob opened my eyes to science with a book by Dawkins; and how Lena finally agreed to become engaged to me and to share her life with me.

CHAPTER 11: The new life 189

How Lena moved in with me and how we drove down to Switzerland to see Bob; how I was for a time mostly in a state of bliss; how I met Leif, a new client with whom I would collaborate and begin copywriting; how conjugal bliss quickly faded and gave way to screaming whenever I questioned anything Lena didn't agree with; how I buried myself in work on the house; how I got an unexpected offer to show most of my paintings publicly.

CHAPTER 12: The show 216

How I continued to hope that Lena would love me despite her gradually increasing acrimony; how my exhibition only strengthened my disinterest in selling my paintings; how completely I chose to ignore the warning signals of a one-way-street relationship and instead began urging a wedding; how my participation in planning our wedding was marginalized, but how it happened more or less as planned.

CHAPTER 13: Landing 239

How Lena and I spent a lovely honeymoon with Bob in Zuoz and Basel; how Bob absorbed the devastating diagnosis of Parkinson's with equanimity; how Lena was unable to regard my house as her home; how she refused to hear of my past; how I had largely succeeded in my long-range plan to work from home.

CHAPTER 14: Clutching for hope 251

How Lena disallowed the importance of my painting (even its importance to me); how Lena's hostility towards me grew, as did my desperation; how I looked for salvation in the form of a vasectomy reversal; how I learned to ski in Norway; how I learned the importance of confronting my mom; how Lena continued to scream and say vile things to me daily; and how I continued to hope that having a child would make her love me.

CHAPTER 15: The end of an era 276

How we were threatened and attacked by unruly neighbors; how I no longer had the strength to continue painting in the face of Lena's scorn and derision; how we somehow managed, after two vasectomy-reversal operations, to become pregnant; and how, despite my bitter disappointment at no longer having a working environment that was remotely conducive to continuing my career as an artist, I hoped to channel my creativity into writing instead; and how I was about to embrace a new and unexpected role as a father.

APPENDIX 1: LAMINATES 298
APPENDIX 2: PAINTINGS 79-86 302

CHAPTER 1

Drowning

Although it falls no more than a few days after the summer solstice, which even in southernmost Sweden means that perpetual daylight fades only long enough to allow dusk to turn back into dawn, I've always sensed a profound melancholy about Midsummer Day in Sweden. Even if it happens to be as sunny and balmy as can be, there's a national collective realization that the days have started getting shorter again, and will continue to get shorter until the days are entombed in dusk and darkness. Whether cheerful or raucous, Midsummer Eve celebrations mark an end more than a beginning. There won't be another national holiday until Christmas, half a year away into the gloom, when the nights will be as long as the days had been.

I'd drunk as much as I could keep down the evening before. I'd held my seemingly leaky glass firmly, a bastion between my terrifying memories and anything festive, but the amount of alcohol (either by volume or by weight) wasn't nearly enough to make the howling emptiness inside me take a break and let me sleep. I was, however, too intoxicated to know (or care) whether I remained all night on the sloping lawn of Björn's grandmother's home in Skepparkroken – the family's country retreat and venue for their annual *Midsommar* celebration – or whether somebody steered me in under a roof and threw a blanket over me to prevent me from waking up covered with dew. Instead I awoke at dawn (around three AM) immersed in nihilism; I was drowning all the same, in a sea of troubles unlike anything I'd ever known. The only bitter amusement to reach me the evening before was Björn telling me how at family gatherings one of his overly inflated uncles, fairly reeking with a fatuous sense of his self-proclaimed dignity, always dismissed calls to lend a hand with the clean-up with an indignant, haughty and greatly affronted, "*Should one such as I, with my education, wash dishes?!*"

The sun, after briefly ducking into the wings of the northern horizon, resumed control of the stage about four in the morning. Everything was still except for the birds and the raging in my head. I couldn't look at or listen to anything for more than a few seconds before the image of my darling wife's agony swept every other perception from my mind and rendered me incapable of thought or action. I staggered around in search of whatever might help to keep me inebriated, and settled for emptying the dregs from a few mostly empty wine, beer, and schnapps glasses still standing derelict on the long table in the covered veranda where the party had gone on until a few long hours before. No one awake was in sight. I curled up somewhere and wondered how long it would take for somebody else to get up – somebody who could help me get the hell out of Skepparkroken and back to Malmö, back to my home for the homeless.

Nothing meant anything to me. There was no value, no purpose, no point. Everything I'd been doing – my paintings, all that work on the house, all the struggle to make a life and a living, all my joy and ambition, all my love – had suddenly become futile and vain, the vexation of my spirit. It had all been for us, for *her*. Now she was gone, there was no Jeanette, no us, just me – a worthless piece of *shit*. What was I doing here, in Skepparkroken, in Sweden, *alive*? Did I ever *really* understand that she was my *every*thing? Did *she*? Too late now, too gone.

For the past three months, nighttime only meant hoping that my mounting mental exhaustion would allow me a few drunken moments of unconsciousness until anguished memory would again awaken me in disoriented terror. I didn't feel I'd slept at all since I discovered Jeanette hanging from a tie beam in the room at the top of the stairs in our almost-finished house-restoration project at Korngatan 12 in Malmö. The grotesquely twisted expression on her face was burnt into my retinas and had permanently branded my memory, along with an overwhelming sense of guilt and self-recrimination for having failed to recognize the depths to which her mental anguish had slowly deteriorated her lust for life. That indelible sight of her, my *last* sight of her, was consuming my soul. In place of sleep I had only stupor – my vain attempts to numb the pain of consciousness. I hardly dared to close my eyes. *What dreams may come.*

Keep pouring. Not too much, not get sick and throw it all up again. There, by the sofa, in the dark, she'd thrown up, searing her throat, her dear throat, did I ever tell her I loved her throat too. Drink a little more. Why won't it stop. That look, those vacant eyes. I'm so cold. She was cold. NOOOO!! Gone, so gone, so forevery gone, I can't.... Did I lock the door? Do I have another bottle? Oh Jeanette, please, please, pleeease. Why does the wall, why is that wall here when it was there, why's it moving, better lie down, sust one more jip, I can't be here, I can't be anywhere, anyshittywhere, no, no, stop now, another little sip or gulp or whatever the fuck, nothing works, nothing helps, don't turn out the light just,...A few more swallows – till I find you, take my hand and live on, love on, leave on, leave me, DON'T leave me, please PLEASE my love, I don't want, I can't....

That kind of mental ranting and raging would go on for hours, day after day after day – and night – until I passed out a drunken blob only to awaken a few hours later in undiminished pain, then top up my alcohol, smoke a few cigarettes to make sure I wouldn't be OK, work my way towards that elusive, illusory escape.

I kept reliving almost every moment since I first met her, on October 10th, 1964, just four months after my friend Norm and I escaped the perverse but well-meaning oppression and indoctrination of our hyper-religious parents and fled from Chicago to a new life in San Francisco. It took me about six weeks from that first October encounter with Jeanette to realize that I would love her forever. It took about another year for her to believe me and to start to feel the same about me – and for us to begin finally abandoning the religious indoctrination (Roman Catholic for her, Plymouth Brethren – a.k.a. the Meeting – for me) to which we, like nearly everyone else in America (to one degree or another) were subjected since infancy. (Although few people still believed the earth was a flat plane in a geocentric universe, most Americans still clung to equally unfounded but harder-to-*dis*prove theism, that escape-from-reason self-delusion called *faith*.)

My escape from religious indoctrination was only the first step in my total uprooting. The ongoing unholy war in Vietnam had compelled me to recognize another, even more common form of indoctrination into which people all over the world are born – patriotism – and to choose exile over my only other options: combat or prison. In 1968, Jeanette and I thus left the country of our birth for Canada, where I pursued a one-year stint at graduate school at UBC in Vancouver, before Jeanette persuaded me that we should pull up our roots from the entire continent and move on to Europe. Sweden quickly became our process-of-elimination choice. Nearly six years later, we found a ruin of a building – our renovation project – that was to be our home, at Korngatan 12 in Malmö. All the while, as it turned out, Jeanette's mind was undergoing the frightening, growing and hidden convulsions of schizophrenia, of which I remained blithely unaware – or in denial – until everything I cared about came to a cataclysmic end. I *wanted* to drown; my *heart and mind* wanted to drown, but my body just wouldn't stop paddling.

Bob, my best friend (despite being my cousin) was doing everything he could to appeal to my rationality, although the rational side of my mind was in deep paralysis. My mom anguished over me, and her natural, human, emotional support was valuable to me too, but it would have been much more so had it not been contaminated by her own need to proclaim *my* need to turn to the Lord and His mercy. I knew that that was *her* great crutch. And it was one I didn't want to pull out from under her, but I could see no way to get her to back off without pulling that crutch away. I *wanted* to tell her, to challenge her. I wanted to say, "If 'His eye is on the sparrow,' and He's content to simply *watch* the sparrow getting its wings pulled off by the cat that is tormenting it, what *fucking* good is He?" Moreover, my brothers continued to labor under the same indoctrination, which largely prevented them from offering me much real support.

The majority of the neighbors and acquaintances (possibly friends as well, but I am strongly averse to using that word lightly) that I'd spoken with since Jeanette's death were clearly frightened by my tragic circumstances, and consciously or unconsciously shrank awkwardly (and perhaps even unwillingly) from my company. This was understandable; I would probably have done the same.

Then there were Björn and Isobel, providing (not offering) incredible and unsolicited support, a totally unexpected source. Isobel was a Catholic from Derry (Northern Ireland), a slightly younger pregnant colleague of mine at the Interspråk language school in Malmö, with whom I had little in common and didn't even know terribly well prior to Jeanette's death. Her husband Björn was a gangly, two-meter-tall Swede, who'd trained to be a cook in Switzerland but was working as a waiter in Malmö. For no other apparent reason than extraordinary human compassion, they swooped down to pick me up from the hospital to which the ambulance brought me in the evening of the day Jeanette died, March 28th, 1977, and kept me more or less under their wing ever since. This included bringing me along to Björn's family's Midsummer celebration in Skepparkroken, a small suburb of Ängelholm, a little more than an hour's drive north of Malmö.

Early in the morning on Midsummer Day, Sweden's National Hangover Day, the daylight was already becoming almost mockingly, piercingly bright and clear. Midsummer Day is always a Saturday, but it felt like a Sunday to me, *Sunday morning coming down*.[1] It was hours before anyone else began stirring. I had to wait for Björn; Isobel didn't know how to drive. I feared that Björn might be too hung over to drive me anywhere, but there was always a chance that he might

---
1 Cf. the eponymous song by Kris Kristofferson, c. 1969.

have been showing restraint on his alcohol intake the evening before, perhaps due to Isobel's advanced pregnancy, now approaching eight months.

When he finally appeared, fully clothed and looking sober, in the late morning (about half of the others were up by then, and somebody was making breakfast), he seemed to be looking for me as much as I was looking for him. I just wanted a ride out of there. Did he just want to get me out? He said nothing to indicate such a thought; it might have been my low self-esteem at work. My raw grief the day and evening before certainly didn't contribute to anyone's festive mood. Björn said that he and Isobel weren't going back to Malmö "for a while", but that he would be happy to take me to the nearest entrance to the freeway, in Ängelholm, where he thought I could "easily" hitch a ride home. As it was the only option I knew of, it sounded like my best one.

It wasn't. After he dropped me off, I stood there alone, at the beginning of the freeway entrance ramp, waving my thumb at the few cars (possibly five per hour) that were out and about in the middle of that excruciatingly sunny Midsummer Day, when most Swedes either don't want to go anywhere or are still too juiced up to make it legal to operate a motor vehicle. I stood there for hours, becoming lonelier and lonelier. I hadn't felt this lonely since before I met Jeanette. When Jeanette and I were alone, we were alone together, and thus we were not alone, and never felt it. Bob, my only true and close friend, was in Switzerland. Standing by the entrance ramp to the freeway with my thumb out felt pathetic. Even worse, I was becoming sober, more and more sober and thus more desperate, until a driver I don't remember took pity on me and stopped. He wasn't going all the way to Malmö, only halfway, to Landskrona, but I had to get *some*where, somewhere *else*. In truth, I didn't want to *be any*where. This was only about fleeing, hurrying *from*, not *to*.

When I resumed my hitchhiking efforts at a new entrance ramp in Landskrona, I realized that there were even fewer cars to wave my thumb at there, and I began to worry about getting home at all that day. By the time I reached Korngatan 12, the clock indicated it was evening, although the sun was still fairly high in the sky. I forced myself to enter my "home", eventually convincing myself to go in because that was where I'd find the whisky. That and cigarettes had been my principal diet for the worse part of three months now.

Since Jeanette's death, my letters to Mom were few, short and apathetic. I didn't know how to respond to hers. Although it was completely understandable and predictable that her letters would attempt to misconscrew[2] Jeanette's horrific suicide as evidence of God's love, it seemed totally perverse to me – enough to make me gag – and gave me nothing to address other than my own strong desire to lash out at (a) the total lack of any evidence of the existence of any god; (b) the utter incompetence or cruelty that such a god would have to represent if he/she/it/they did exist; and (c) my mom's ignorance and insensitivity in once again preaching her unproven and unprovable nonsense at me under a ludicrous label of Truth, particularly at this time. (Her "ignorance" for at least the foregoing decade was in the sense of ignoring anything and everything I said that should have disabused her of the notion that she was entitled to dump her foolish, unfounded, and superstitious ideas and worldview on me without facing rebuttal.) So instead of lashing out at her for that, I kept my replies short.

I knew, however, that she was planning to visit me in September. She reiterated the notion of our making a trip to Israel together (the one we'd talked about making with Jeanette, just before she died). At this point, I couldn't think of anything worse, but I simply wrote her that I wasn't up to it, adding: *"You are very welcome to come here and stay as long as you like. To be tolerant of our differences is all that can be asked ... Stay as long as you think you'll be able to put up with me."*

Bob, thankfully, used his patient letters and pleading phone calls to me to summon all the strength he didn't have in his ceaseless and valiant efforts to battle my nihilistic wolves, not with false or unfounded promises or premises, but with the voice of reason, as could be expected from someone so heavily invested in me, both emotionally (in my well-being) and rationally (in avoiding any claims of absolute truth). He phoned shortly after my return to Korngatan, in the evening on Midsummer Day, and succeeded once again in persuading me to take a small step back from the ever-present brink.

John and Marj would be arriving from California the next day for their 12-day visit, most of which would consist of a car trip to Basel. I would stay with Bob while they "did Europe." John arranged for a rental car on their arrival at the airport, although we spent the first three days in Malmö. It was their first-ever trip to Europe, a fact that would manifest itself in many strange and mysterious ways. My big brother turned out to provide me quite a lot of unintentional (but desperately needed) comic relief in the black hole that was now my world.

I'm pretty sure they met Björn and Isobel during those first three days in

---

2 Sic

Malmö before we took off for Basel. They may have also met the Saabyes, my helpful Danish next-door neighbors. John and Marj seemed to be awed by the house and all the work that had obviously been done on it. It was nearly finished, nearly ready for moving in. *But she never would.*

All that remained for me to do downstairs was to put up a little plasterboard in the living room, lay the rest of the floor tiles, and tile the walls and floor in the bathroom. Upstairs, I just had to sand the wooden floors and make the built-in cabinets along the eaves on the street-side. But I couldn't face any of it. *Quoth the raven.* John kindly offered to help, to get me started, but I just shuddered.

John did have the good sense (and sensitivity) to refrain from preaching at me (Marj never did) about his God and His mysterious ways – or perhaps John's instincts for self-preservation told him not to open a can of worms like that; it might explode in his face. My brother the Engineer (and highly talented amateur craftsman) did, however, express considerable admiration for skills he'd never before seen or suspected in his kid brother. Then it was time for us to hit the road.

John was a loveable guy with an enormous need to be in as much control as possible of every detail of every situation in which he was personally involved. He, Marj and I all had driver's licenses, yet in the 10 days of our European road trip, only John ever sat in the driver's seat. But neither Marj nor I objected; Marj seemed to be used to it, and I willingly occupied the back seat of the compact car so I could be alone with my thoughts, memories and pocket flask. I did, however, find some amusement in the self-evidence with which John assumed his role as sole driver.

John's original plan was to drive to Basel as quickly and directly as possible, taking the same route Jeanette and I took several times before: through Denmark, entering West Germany by ferry at Puttgarden, then heading more or less due south past Hamburg, Hannover, Kassel, Frankfurt, Heidelberg, Karlsruhe, Freiburg and finally Basel. Shortly after Hamburg, there was a general need for a pit stop to refuel the car and empty our bladders at one of the autobahn service stations. I saw John making a beeline for the ladies room, and asked sharply where the hell he thought he was going. He protested, quite seriously and innocently: "*But it says 'Da Men'! And the other one says 'Her-ren'!*" I laughed out loud for the first time in well over three months.

As we were approaching Frankfurt, John spotted signs for a junction with another autobahn in the direction of München, in the southeastern corner of the country. "*Doesn't that mean 'Munich'? I've heard it's a neat place!*" John exclaimed. He abruptly took the turnoff, thus unanimously deciding that the three of us would reach Basel via the hypotenuse and the longer of the two sides instead of the short one. We found a small hotel in Munich that evening and headed out to the "neat" *Hofbräuhaus* for a meal and huge tankards of beer, which suited me just fine. Although I had both feet on the precipice – the edge of the void – the rowdy singalong atmosphere of the Hofbräu, the copious quantity of good beer and the human warmth of John and Marj were so much more valuable to me than all the foolish attempts to convince me that my despair was being orchestrated (or even permitted) by an allegedly good god.

Due to our merriment the night before, we had a fairly late breakfast. But before heading for Basel, John thought we should make a quick walking tour of the central city, so that we could at least say that we'd "been to Munich". We made our way to the main square, Marienplatz, just before noon. This was the location of the City Hall and its famous *Glockenspiel* – a set of centuries-old handcrafted chimes and figures that would be marching and playing in the city hall belfry at noon, about 10 minutes after we joined the growing crowd. Once we quickly surveyed Marienplatz (for about 10 seconds), John announced that it was high time to be pushing on to Basel, but I urged him to let us wait another 20 minutes, so that we would have time to see what the *Glockenspiel* was all about. While I was looking at the old buildings surrounding the square, John and Marj busied themselves comparing the prices of various goods in the nearby display windows with prices in "real money".

At the stroke of 12, the amazing *Glockenspiel* began – small colorful wooden figures of various kinds marching around in the tower, playing their drums and fifes. I was fascinated, wishing I had Jeanette by my side to share the experience. I asked John whether it hadn't been worth waiting a few extra minutes to see? He snorted. "*We've got a better one in Disneyland!*"

Then we were off, heading almost due west towards Freiburg. When we (i.e. John) had driven a bit more than halfway to Freiburg, I began to recognize – by the terrain, the architecture and the map – that we were entering the outskirts of the Black Forest. I didn't find the outskirts particularly exciting, but John did. "*This is really neat!*" he exclaimed as we were passing though one of the outlying villages. "*We've gotta stop and get some pictures!*" I tried in vain to convince him that what the outlying villages offered was *nothing* compared to those we would soon be coming to, but he ignored me, stopped, parked and leaped from the car, camera shutter blazing. I rolled my eyes.

After some 15-20 minutes, John was suddenly in a hurry to move along again, and we piled back into the car. Within half an hour the villages we were passing through were simply spectacular. John agreed, but felt that we no longer had the time for any further walkabout stops. Instead he asked Marj, sitting beside him in the front seat, to lean over and take the wheel from him while he took picture after picture through the windshield as we "drove" through sensational Black Forest villages. If the sight of my archetypically American tourist of a big brother weren't so absurdly funny, I might have felt embarrassed on his behalf.

We eventually reached Freiburg (without stopping), where we reconnected with our original autobahn, headed straight south, and were soon at the Swiss border. I was able to guide John to Bob's place on Gorenmattstrasse in Binningen without much difficulty. We arrived in the early evening with a couple hours of daylight to spare. All this time I was battling wave after wave of deepest grief, despair and horror, incongruously juxtaposed by brief moments of brother-induced absurdity.

This was the first time John had met our eldest cousin Bob since the late spring of 1949, when Bob was 20 and John was 11; they were, in other words, total strangers, without the benefit of eight months of in-depth correspondence prior to this maiden meeting. And with John and Marj still in the Meeting,[3] Bob was understandably skeptical about their finding any common ground.

Bob had stocked up on enough ingredients for me to put together a meal of sorts for all of us that evening. He'd booked a room for them at the Hotel Drachen in central Basel, the same hotel he booked for Mom and Dad in 1970. The plan was that John and Marj would take a few day trips on their own, with Basel as a base, while I stayed with Bob to try to get some greatly needed therapeutic conversation to help me cope with my grief.

That first evening after a light meal at Bob's place, the four of us spent a couple of hours having some wine (I had whisky) and discussing various excursion options for John and Marj's first outing the next day. Bob and I told them that within about an hour's drive of Basel it would be easy to reach the exquisite medieval walled town of Solothurn. Slightly farther in the same southeasterly direction was Luzerne, with its fabulous old town and breathtaking lakeside setting with views of the Alps. Bob then pointed out that to the west, just across

---

3   See *Natural Shocks*, chapter 2.

A Sea of Troubles

the French border in the province of Alsace, they could explore the charming old city of Colmar with its multitude of timber-framed houses. Back into Germany to the north was the opportunity to do a proper job of exploring the wonders of the Black Forest. Armed with such ideas and a few maps, John and Marj left Bob's place for their hotel, and would return to us the following evening for some post-excursion supper and discourse.

On our own, Bob, his liquor cabinet and I spent that Thursday evening and most of Friday trying to deal with my howling void. Despite the respite afforded by John and Marj's visit, I was being pulled down beneath the waves by the dead weight of utter emptiness, tortuous guilt, bitter self-loathing, raw loneliness, an overwhelming sense of my total worthlessness, and growing cynicism. What did it matter if I did *any*thing or not? What did it matter if I *lived* or not? I was certainly doing everything I could to smoke and drink as if *nothing* mattered.

During the past three months, my cigarette consumption had risen to around 50 cigarettes a day – from a former level that was equivalent to about three a day (mostly in the form of about one pouch of pipe tobacco a month). Bob normally smoked a pipe and had an occasional cigarillo, and I complemented my cigarette smoking by joining him in these as well. If ambient tobacco smoke were capable of killing microbes, Bob's apartment would have quickly attained an impeccable level of hygiene, perhaps sterility.

Bob was alternately growling at me to quit feeling sorry for myself, and pleading with me to realize that life is all there is and that it's worth living *no matter what*, if only because there *is* nothing else. *There are no better options!* He encouraged me to focus on experiencing and learning new things. He didn't tell me to try to meet someone new – I might have punched him for that – but he did urge me to turn my libido loose, especially now that my vasectomy meant that I would be "shooting blanks". I wasn't terribly receptive to that advice either, because what girl in her right mind would look twice at me? Bob groaned in exasperation. And what could I offer a girl in my state of grief, when all I wanted was Jeanette and that was impossible? Bob told me that I could always offer my *cock*! I protested that I didn't want to use girls just for sex. He countered by asking me what made me think there weren't any girls out there willing and eager to use *me* just for sex? Or why did "just sex" have to mean anybody *using* anybody, if that's what both wanted? I told him that "just sex" didn't sound ultimately gratifying either. He groaned again, and mumbled something about why the hell it had to be *ultimate* and how not every pleasant meal has to come with a requirement to get the recipe, and that sex is also a healthy *drive*, for chrissake, and sometimes it doesn't need to be anything more than that!

When John and Marj returned to Binningen on Friday evening to report on their first daytrip, Bob and I inquired whether they'd been to Solothurn? *No.* Luzerne? *No.* Alsace? *No* again. Before we could guess any other attractive destinations, John proudly announced, "*We've been to Italy!*" Bob's jaw dropped. My eyes popped and I gasped a whispered three-word expression that ends in "uck" and starts with "what the f". How on earth did they have time to drive to Italy and back?! And what did they see in Italy in that short time?! John looked slightly sheepish when he told us that they'd driven purposefully to the Italian border, crossed it, got an all-important stamp in their passports, and then had a late lunch at a truck stop on the Italian side of the border crossing. I think Bob and I must have burst into whoops of laughter. We weren't out to deride my brother, but the idea of bypassing all the culture, history, opportunities for tasting experiences and eye-popping short hikes in some of the world's most spectacular scenery in order to visit a truck stop was just so comical, so absurd, that no other response was possible for us. John said, again sheepishly, "*Well, we've come all this way and wanted to be able to say we'd set foot in Italy....*" That set Bob and me going again.

Perhaps John felt chastened by our responses (I guessed that Marj wasn't consulted much about the itinerary, even though she may have been "allowed" to object to it), or perhaps the excursion to the truck stop was a little more mundane than my big brother was hoping for. In either case, I believe their subsequent daytrips were quite a bit more worthwhile. At least I don't remember hearing about any more truck stops just across any of Switzerland's other borders.

John announced his and Marj's intention to take Bob and me out for a fancy dinner in Basel one evening. They would pick us up in the rental car after their daytrip. As soon as we got into the car (Bob and I occupied the back seat, of course), John asked about a place where he could get gas. Bob told him that there was a gas station just about three blocks away, on Oberwilerstrasse, along the way to where we would find a restaurant downtown. John pulled into the self-service station (payment was to be made inside a small station-house), filled up, took some cash from his wallet to pay with, entered the station-house, returned to the car, jumped in, and we took off.

We'd no sooner pulled out onto Oberwilerstrasse again than I saw John's eyes in the rearview mirror, darting back and forth in an agitated manner. Then he nervously asked me, "*What's that guy behind me doing?! He's flashing his high beams at me and waving or something!!*" I whirled around to see the driver of a large Mercedes gesticulating wildly, as if pointing to something on the roof of our car. I told John I thought he should stop to find out. John scowled in great irritation, and was mumbling something under his breath as he pulled over. He leaped out of the car as if to challenge Mr Mercedes, who continued to point, frantically and repeatedly jabbing his index finger towards the roof of our car as he drove slowly past. A moment later, John got back in, visibly embarrassed, clutching his bulging wallet – which he'd left on the roof of the car when he went into the station to pay for the gas. It contained all his travel documents, credit cards, driver's license, plane tickets etc.

As we resumed our journey, I could see through the rearview mirror John's eyes feverishly darting back and forth again, occasionally glancing up and meeting my curious gaze. I suspected that an official statement to the backseat press was forthcoming.

At the next red light, John whirled around, his carefully prepared statement blurting from his lips, possibly constituting a release from the build-up of his self-imposed restraint hitherto on the trip: "*I know how you guys feel about these things, but I'm gonna say 'Thank you, Lord, for letting me get my wallet back!!*"

I didn't hesitate a second, but shot back, "Fair enough, John, as long as you *also* say '*Damn you, Lord, for letting me leave it there in the first place!*" John was utterly blindsided. He was clearly unprepared for any comeback at all to his carefully thought-out argument for God's concern, let alone such a quick comeback, let alone one that made complete sense. He just stared blankly for a second. Then he burst out giggling.

The rest of the way to the restaurant, every time he caught my eye in the rearview mirror, he giggled. At the restaurant, he giggled. When he took out his now-famous wallet to pay, he giggled. I loved him so much for that.

The chagrin he must have felt in not finding a single hole in my impeccable logic – that you can't reasonably give God credit for good things that happen without also blaming him for bad things that happen – must have been powerful, and must have shielded my brother from extrapolating that simple principle of reciprocity into everything that happens in a person's life or in the world. How else could John continue to follow a principle that denied such a self-evident requirement for reciprocity, if it were not for all the years he'd already invested in building a value system, a social system, a career, a family, a sense of safety and eternal security, on a world in which God is always right even when, to any rational mind, He's obviously not?

Reciprocity is the very foundation of the Golden Rule: *Do unto others as you would have others do unto you.* When Blacks voice their legitimate claims of not receiving the same justice as Whites; when Women protest that their pay is unfairly lower than that of men for the same work, maybe it's time for White males to repeat the Golden Rule to themselves, over and over, substituting "others" for "Blacks", then for "Women", then for any other group not getting fair treatment. Then keep repeating it over and over till they *get* it!

The three of us left Basel on July 7th and were back in Malmö the next evening. John and Marj returned to the States the following day, and seemed satisfied with their first visit to Europe, which in fact also did me some good. I'd had some tough talks with Bob – he wasn't about to give up on me – that perhaps helped to wrest a *little* control from my raging emotions and return some of it to my brain. One conclusion I'd drawn, a possible milestone that stood out from the rest, was this: *the worst thing that could ever happen to me had already happened.*

My frequent visits from and especially to Björn and Isobel resumed more or less as soon as John and Marj returned to their home and I to what was left of mine. My residual natural curiosity made me want Isobel fill me in on what she knew about the disappearance of Hamadi, the head of the language school where Isobel worked and where I'd worked until the day of Jeanette's death. Isobel had already told me that he'd simply absconded; the school and our jobs ceased to exist without our knowing it at the time. It turned out that Hamadi and his family were not on vacation after all, she said. The whole story – at least as much of it as any of us would ever know – seeped out over the course of several months.

Isobel told me she'd spoken with Hamadi briefly, when he phoned the school while I was in Switzerland in early April, less than a week after Jeanette died. The call allegedly came from Paris. Isobel said he was shocked to hear of Jeanette's death. He'd instantly become agitated and quickly terminated the call. That was the last she or anyone else in Sweden ever heard from him, as far as I know.

How did they figure out he was gone for good? Isobel said that people began phoning the school more and more frequently during the month of April, looking for him, and wondering about unpaid bills, big bills, growing bills. He hadn't paid the bill to *Pers Krog* (Per's Inn), the school's lunch restaurant, since New Year's (Per himself was Hamadi's pupil in French, and had made an exception for him by extending a long line of credit). That represented something like 40 lunches a week for more than three months. Hamadi also turned out to have purchased quite a lot of exclusive furniture (tens of thousands of kronor worth), on credit, from Silverberg's, for shipment "to his brother" in Tunisia. Silverberg's didn't normally extend credit on purchases for direct shipment abroad, but Mr Silverberg had also been Hamadi's pupil and felt he could trust him. The VAT and other taxes for the school hadn't been paid to the tax authorities for many months, and penalty fees were beginning to amass. There were unpaid utilities, and there was the matter of the rent for the school premises. Pupils that Hamadi booked (and received payment from without having told anyone) were showing up. And the teachers who continued teaching for nearly two months after Hamadi went on "vacation" hadn't been paid since the end of February. (Isobel said that the union representative informed her that the Swedish Government generally covered all or most employees' wages in such cases, but that it could take many months.)

When the landlord at Hamadi's residence on Limhamnsvägen phoned the school concerning months of non-payment of rent, Isobel agreed to come to the apartment building as a witness when the caretaker opened it to see if anything was amiss. The apartment had been completely cleaned out. It was a bare, echoing, empty shell. No further evidence was needed to conclude that this fraud was something Hamadi and his wife been planning for at least half a year. He left an incredibly tangled mess, which was still unravelling, without a clear trail, except that it presumably led to somewhere in Tunisia. And Sweden apparently had no extradition treaty with Hamadi's homeland.

Several things leaped to my mind when I heard all this. First, for several months before he left, I'd been starting to let down my guard and view Hamadi as a true friend, which would clearly have been a mistake. But I didn't want to dwell on that thought – it wasn't as if I needed more fuel for the fires of the somewhat misanthropic cynicism that Bob was trying to help me extinguish. Second, I remembered that just a few days before his departure on "vacation" (and before Jeanette died), when Hamadi and his little family stopped by our place one evening, he'd said he wanted to buy "a few" of my paintings and "pay me later", but I told him that I wanted him to wait a bit. *That was a close one!* Third, I no longer had a job to go back to, even if and when my sick leave came to an end. I would have to start job-hunting, selling myself (and whatever skills I might be perceived to have) to some unknown employer, something I felt entirely incapable of undertaking, given my sub-basement-level of self-esteem. And fourth (and the most chilling of all): I realized that *I'd worked that afternoon for nothing*.

Shortly after my return from Basel with John and Marj, I was informed that my sick-leave (for "mental insufficiency") could no longer be extended unless I were to admit myself to a mental hospital. (Memories of *One Flew over the Cuckoo's Nest* may have flashed through my mind; memories of Jeanette's dealings with the psychiatric clinic certainly did as well.) Instead they "commuted" my status to "unemployed", which meant that I had to register at *Arbetsförmedlingen*, Sweden's official government employment agency. Fortunately, the young clerk I met there (and to whom I poured out my story and my heart) was every bit a human being. He told me that while I would have to report back about once a week to get my official dole card stamped in order to get my unemployment benefits, they would make an exception in my case and not place any demands on me to actively seek employment as a condition for receiving that vital financial support. (In retrospect, I almost have to gasp at the humanity of his decision!) Besides, they had no jobs to offer an uncertified English teacher in the summer anyway.

Sometime during the early part of that summer I received copies of the official police and autopsy reports concerning Jeanette's death, but I was unable to bring myself to read them before John and Marj left in July. The reports were clinical and chilling, as I suppose was to be expected. There was nothing in them about *why*. The medical report from the psychiatric clinic at the hospital brought me back to the diagnosis of schizophrenia and depression, but those words didn't tell me much about *why* either.

I turned to Jeanette's writings – the poems and drafts of playlets she chose not to share with me – for possible insights I might have gained from them. But I realized that my capacity for denial might well have made me impervious to understanding anything, least of all the anguish of someone I loved so much. I found a cassette tape (a fragment of a tape-letter to Bob) with Jeanette's voice on it, and listened to it over and over, and then I listened to it over and over again.[4]

---

4 See the laminated drawing in Appendix 1.

One day in July, Björn dragged me with him to the beach to try out his latest craze: windsurfing. He had his own board and sail, and borrowed one for me (he had a special roof rack on his bright yellow VW Beetle for carrying them). At first, windsurfing seemed physically impossible to me; I spent about 43 minutes of the first hour in the water after having fallen off the board as often as I tried to stand on it, and 16 minutes on the board trying to maintain my balance while struggling to haul the damn mast into a vertical position, only to have the wind blow me off the board again. But that one remaining minute of forceful forward movement (divided into about 30 two-second segments) gave me enough of a kick to keep on trying. After several hours, with my muscles aching, I was at last able to get the mast up, dip it forward and feel the power of the wind as it tugged at me for up to 20 seconds until I again hit the water.

The best thing about learning to windsurf was that it required total concentration; in order to get it to work, I couldn't have my mind on *any*thing else, which was a brief but welcome respite from the deep, depressed rut my brain found itself in. During the remains of the summer, Björn and I would go windsurfing numerous times, eventually using the wetsuits Björn somehow conjured up to add to our gear in the late summer. We made one of those outings in gale-force winds. The ride *with* the wind was intense, but trying to make it back to our base *against* the wind took me a couple of exhausting hours.

Björn's work as a waiter was mostly in the evenings. I had no job to go to. That gave us the opportunity to go windsurfing nearly every day when weather permitted and Björn's coaxing managed to make itself heard over my dark moods.

Nearly everyone I talked to kept telling me I couldn't have known what was going on deep inside her if she chose to conceal it, nor that she would take such extreme action as she did, but everything I kept finding in her writings, every little detail my selective memory kept recalling, contradicted that absolving conclusion. I didn't *care* whether my profound feelings of guilt were rational or not; they were real to me. I was certain that Jeanette's family blamed me and would have liked to see me dead, even though they never expressed a word or an action or a look to substantiate such suspicions. Or maybe because they hardly said a word to me about their own feelings, they left the field open for me to draw my own dire conclusions. I received a printed card from Jeanette's Auntie Jo that summer, informing me that they'd paid for a Catholic mass to be held for Jeanette to St. Jude – "*the patron saint of hopeless causes*". Although I recognized their good intentions, it disgusted me. All I could think was that they really knew how to twist the knife!

The guilt, however, was no match for the incredible howling loneliness, like a concrete cape that dragged along the ground behind me, everywhere I went, pulling me backwards and downwards. Why couldn't it just pull me all the way under and let me drown?

CHAPTER 2

Helpers

Most of the events of that summer of 1977 – at least those that came after my trip with John and Marj – are kind of a blur, not only as to what happened, but in what order. Two of my principal memory-jogging sources in writing this book were the letters I wrote to my mom and to Bob (they saved most of them), but during this period I wasn't writing all that much to either of them (my contacts with Bob were frequent, but were mostly by phone). I do recall, however, that in those July evenings when Björn was working and I was on my own, I continued in my role as the Ancient Mariner (cf. Coleridge's poem of that name), hassling neighbors and acquaintances by dumping my sorrowful story and huge emotional burdens in their laps unbidden. All must hear my tale of woe as I desperately searched further and further afield for human warmth or just ears willing to listen. But many would only feel ill at ease – totally understandable *in retrospect* – which was not my intention at all.

On a couple of occasions, a new dimension arose, probably resulting from Bob's admonitions to me to release my libido, which was unquestionably made less repressible by the nearly constant presence of alcohol in my bloodstream. A young woman or two in the households I'd crashed to tell my story came to visit me that they might express their deep sympathy in a more personal, more intimate way. In my looseness I permitted the animal in me to be aroused and give them what they desired from the depths of their hearts and my loins.

I had mixed feelings about these trysts. Despite the lack of selfish intentions on either part, there was a superficiality that felt a bit raw and too far in the direction of sordid. I deeply desired intimacy, but only found fleeting carnality instead, while fighting not to admit to myself that the kind of intimacy I once had and now sought was lost, perhaps forever. And yet I also recognized an aspect of healing even in that kind of carnal intimacy, perhaps in the form of the distance – the breathing space – it seemed to put between the empty life I was now leading and the full one I used to have.

There were no strings attached in these encounters. The young women in question seemed quite satisfied with the purely animal sensuality of it all and didn't seem to me to be looking for anything beyond the moment, except possibly for a kind of extra satisfaction from having charitably given me a few moments of pleasure in return for theirs. From my perspective, it was mostly about first aid, not about forging relationships, and about my making it through at least a few nights that summer with another crutch than whisky.

On August 3rd, Isobel gave birth to a son they named Patrick, in the best Irish tradition. She was thrilled and nervous, as I presumed new mothers were wont to be. Björn's whacky entrepreneurial spirit – he was always embarking on one or more in a seemingly endless series of get-rich-quick schemes – was given a tremendous boost of energy at the birth of his son, unfortunately not equally matched by an equal burst of business acumen. He'd invested in some sort of machine that was supposed to perform personality analyses based on handwriting samples. Its performance level probably matched that of wheels of fortune or the horoscopes found in magazines and newspapers, but the money he made hawking this service at the summer county fair in Kivik was enough to give him visions of future exponential growth and dizzying fortunes.

He also acquired a small stainless-steel *still*, which he placed in the bathtub in their apartment to distill vodka from mash he made from potato peelings. The problem was that the still made quite a bit of noise, a humming, rumbling sort of noise, which he was afraid might arouse the suspicions of adjacent tenants in the building, so he enlisted my help in constructing a relatively soundproof box of plywood and mineral wool in which to place the still while it churned out its illegal hooch. Björn's moonshine was reasonably potable (at least we both retained our eyesight), although the production volume was too small to exceed an amount I could possibly have consumed on my own (and would have liked to try).

Perhaps this flurry of activity was brought on by Björn's new role as the Family Provider. I think his dentist parents may have had a hand in trying to steer (and possibly bankroll) him into some kind of enterprise that might enable a legitimate and more respectable future for him. I don't remember the circumstances or even the timing, but not terribly long afterwards he opened up his own pizzeria (Pizzeria Viking) in Limhamn. He'd had professional training as a cook in Switzerland, so it seemed reasonable as a career move. And he did make *really* good pizza.

Shortly after Patrick was born, Isobel asked me to be the baby's "godfather"! Patrick was to be christened at Malmö's only Catholic Church, not far from the main public swimming pool, sometime in November. I wasn't quite sure what

A Sea of Troubles

being a godfather might entail;[5] I vaguely recalled having heard that godparents were supposed to pledge to assure that the child would be brought up in the faith of its parents in the event of the parents' deaths, something that I as an atheist was strongly disinclined to assure (and Björn had no discernible interest in religion of any kind). But Isobel told me not to worry. Technically, she admitted, I would only be a *stand-in* for the *real* godfather, Isobel's Catholic brother from Northern Ireland, who couldn't attend in person.

The arrival of Patrick inevitably constituted a sea change in my relationship with Björn and Isobel, although not abruptly. They became less able to visit me at Korngatan, while I felt more in the way at their place; they had other priorities, all perfectly natural and obvious. At the same time, I wanted somehow to express my deep gratitude to them for all their incredible and timely help to me in my darkest hours. I had no idea what monetary outlays they might have had for my sake, but I gave them what for me was a very large sum of money. And to express my gratitude further, on a highly personal level, I gave them my painting *Stranded*.[6] (Many years later, after their divorce, after Isobel's death from cancer, and after Björn's move to seek his fortune first in the US, then in Mexico, I learned that this painting was now in Patrick's possession.)

Somehow I had to find a way to address all the inscrutable, incomprehensible *whys* of Jeanette's death, an awful riddle that could never be solved. One day as I was agonizing through the collection of photographs from our time together – more than a dozen years – it struck me that I could perhaps create a poster-size (610 x 914 mm) collage of the best and most representative photos of her (and us), and perhaps make 10 laminated copies of it, so I could keep a couple and to send one to each member of the immediate families (mine and hers), as well as Bob.

I picked out 13 photos showing Jeanette in various moods, from joyous, loving and sensual to contemplative, argumentative and brooding. Then I made black-and-white versions, cropped them and arranged them in the form of a large question mark – 12 photos for the curlicue and one for the point. I used a wide,

---

5 Jeanette and I unknowingly became godparents to a little Swedish boy within weeks of arriving in Sweden, back in September 1969 (cf. *No Traveller Returns*, chapter 3), but I didn't know what was going on then either.

6 Painting #73.

dark-blue border for the poster, with Jeanette's year of birth (1944) written in the left-hand border, our wedding (1966) at the top, her death (1977) on the right, and "Jeanette" at the bottom. In the lower left-hand corner, inside the blue border, I made a copy of her farewell note to me (in the original Swedish), and in the lower right-hand corner I wrote "*In loving memory of my darling Jeanette,*" and then my signature.[7] The result was raw emotion, primitive; technique played hardly any role at all.

Nearly the whole of Swedish industry traditionally shut down for four weeks' vacation every July; all employees were legally entitled to four weeks' paid vacation annually, even from the first year of employment, one of the many perks of living in a country where social equality was a goal, not a demon. Thus, when I'd finished my collage, I had to wait until the vacation period was over to contact Stig Svensson at Perstorp AB to see about getting it produced.

The village of Perstorp, home of the eponymous chemical company, is about 80 kilometers north-northwest of Malmö. The village grew with the company to become every inch a mill-town: a small, fairly isolated community almost entirely dependent on a single big industry, where everybody knew everybody, and neighbors were colleagues were friends. Hierarchies and pecking orders were subtly hidden in the social fabric, but were solidly entrenched. The town itself – a few thousand people – offered little to do but reside, work at Perstorp AB (or at small supporting businesses) and play golf.

When Stig was my pupil a year or two before, he urged me to let him turn some of my drawings into high-pressure laminates, and then persuaded me to make my own designs for laminated countertops and cabinet doors for our new kitchen. I phoned to ask if he could help me turn my collage into poster-size laminates, 10 copies? He said he'd gladly help out. Stig already knew about Jeanette's death; since Perstorp had for years been Hamadi's language school's biggest customer, there were always people from that company in touch with someone from the school, so the word got around. Stig was clearly upset about my loss and was genuinely sympathetic with my grief.

He sent a car down from Perstorp on Monday morning, August 8th, to fetch me and my original collage. I was taken to the main building, the company headquarters and reception, where visitors were delivered, duly registered, and picked up to be escorted to the appropriate sites on the company's industrial

---

7   See Appendix 1

"campus" by whomever they were to meet. Stig's wife Signe was the receptionist at corporate HQ. She remembered me well from her visit to Korngatan with Stig to see the kitchen laminates shortly before Jeanette died. She was also sympathetic towards me, but almost smotheringly so. She was simultaneously one of the nicest *and* most overbearing persons I'd ever met. When she kept telling me that "Fate is in control of everything" and "It's always darkest before the dawn" and "Everything happens for a reason" and "All will be well in the end," I had to have her show me to the lavatory, where I could hide until I was fairly certain that Stig had arrived to pick me up.

I've often wondered whether people (there are plenty of them!) who try to "comfort" someone's grief with tripe like "*Everything happens for a reason*" don't realize that such drivel only makes it feel *worse*?! Bad things will always happen. If they happen by accident, by pure chance, just because shit happens, then there's nothing anyone could have done about it. But if they happen *for a reason*, can I just punch you in the face and say that it was meant to be?! If they happen *for a reason*, then they must be part of some bastard's immutable plan. And if that plan brings you grief, then it's a sadistic, diabolical, evil plan. And that's supposed to be comforting to know?! Really?!

Stig and I walked from the corporate headquarters across a little river, across the main road into the industrial grounds, and across some train tracks, before coming to the closest building on the sprawling campus: the building where decorative laminates were designed and produced. We entered the department for experimental and small-scale laminating. I unrolled my poster across one end of a huge table. Stig and one or two of his colleagues looked at it and discussed how to tackle it. Since I'd told Stig that eight of the 10 copies were going to be exported, he suggested a thin laminate bonded onto a sheet of almost weightless polystyrene, with a backing veneer (a plain laminate bonded onto the back to prevent the sandwiched board from warping). They had quite a backlog of projects after the vacation period, so did I mind waiting until late September? I replied that I was extremely grateful to get them at all.

In the early part of August, I noticed a discharge from my penis. I thought I might have developed a urinary tract infection. I went to my local clinic, where I was given some tests and a prescription for antibiotics, but after that failed to do the trick, I was referred to the urology department at the Malmö hospital on August 23rd. I hadn't experienced any stinging or pain, and my blood tests showed none of the ordinary signs of infection, which seemed to puzzle the urologist greatly. He told me he couldn't find anything *medically* wrong with me. Then he asked me if I'd experienced any trauma or grief lately, and all the floodgates opened.

He let me talk and talk and talk. I told him of my unfathomable and horrifying loss, my experiences with the psychiatric clinic at his hospital – Jeanette having been sent home, the inane questions I was asked when trying to talk about my grief. When he was finally forced to end our conversation in order to receive his next patient, he offered me an appointment to come back and talk again, if I felt that talking to him was helpful to me. I gratefully accepted. And within days, my discharge ceased without a trace.

In late August I received a letter from some authority or other, informing me that the official proceedings for the inventory for Jeanette's estate had to be initiated without further delay. I knew nothing about such matters, let alone that there had already been any kind of delay. Any previous information on the matter that might have been sent to me simply hadn't registered. She was gone, her stuff had become my stuff, wasn't that all there was to it? Apparently not. I was obliged to contact a certain type of agency that handled such matters so that they could procure copies of bank statements and as many different certificates as possible, and make official notifications to Jeanette's mother using notarized translations and signatures, including the signatures of witnesses of me making my signature, and registrations with county authorities – none of which I can claim to have understood very clearly – all to reach the conclusion, a month or more later, that Jeanette's stuff had become my stuff.

At Bob's urging, I was steering towards or drifting into a new habit of gratefully accepting just about anything that was being offered, including invitations to parties. In late August or early September, another of my former teacher colleagues, an American girl named Lynn, originally from Minnesota, invited me to a housewarming party she and her husband Arne were hosting at their new home on Johanneslustgatan, about a 10-minute bike ride from Korngatan. I accepted, of course; there would be drinks. Arne was a powerfully built hockey player. Lynne was a petite bundle of energy and laughter. I was already fairly juiced up on arrival, and did my best keep that ball rolling. I don't remember a lot that happened during the party, except that Arne and I ended up engaging in arm wrestling, and he beat me easily – when we were using our right arms. But I'm very much a lefty, and I beat him (not at all easily) when we switched arms, to his (and my) astonishment.

I also met Lynn's brother Don, who had come over from Minnesota to stay with Lynn and Arne for a while, since he was having some trouble back home in St. Paul. I don't remember whether it was trouble with the law or with dealers in certain kinds of substances or something else. Anyway, he started talking with me excitedly about how he'd discovered a surprisingly fine supply in the Christiania district of Copenhagen. I didn't have a clue what he meant. It turned out he was talking about hashish, cannabis, and that Christiania was some sort of enclave of Denmark's capital city that enjoyed special privileges: cannabis (using, possessing, and selling) was quasi-legal – at least the police didn't interfere if the residents of that district stayed within the boundaries and didn't let things get out of control. I still didn't know what Don was talking about, since I'd never had any experience of drugs whatsoever, despite having lived in San Francisco at the height (or Haight) of Flower Power. I told him that I had zero experience in that department. His eyes went wide. Don viewed that as a lapse in my upbringing that needed to be rectified forthwith, and told me in glowing terms what an experience I'd been missing, how much better it was than alcohol, how he could get me some good shit and would show me all about how to use it. My drunken answer was undoubtedly along the lines of "*Schurr, why n-not?*"

A few days later, Don knocked on my door. He was carrying a plastic bag that contained a present for me: all the requisite paraphernalia. He first took out a one-liter semi-transparent plastic bottle (no cap) with the bottom cut off. He also had a small rubber eraser about 4x2x1 cm, and a small block of a paste or resin that looked like brownish-greenish-yellowish fish food, wrapped in shrinkfilm. It was like a small cake (about the size of the eraser) of high-grade hash, he explained, and he was going to show me how to get stoned.

I was already slightly high from alcohol, of course (it was past 8 AM, after all), as I looked at him and his paraphernalia with great curiosity. From the small cake of hashish he broke off an even smaller piece, about the size of a pea, and began rolling it back and forth and round and round between his thumb and forefinger, working it and warming it slightly to make it more malleable. He asked me for a pin (the kind used for sewing) or a sewing needle, and I procured a pin. He ran the pin through the rubber eraser, so that the sharp point stuck straight up when the eraser was placed on a flat surface. Then he impaled the "pea" of hashish on the point of the pin and laid the eraser on the table, with the pea and pin upwards. Next he took out a cigarette lighter and lit the hashish. As soon as it caught fire, he blew it out, and as the smoke from the extinguished hashish began billowing forth, he quickly placed the bottomless plastic bottle squarely over it, covering the opening at the top of the bottle with his thumb. He waited, carefully inspecting the bottle until it was full of smoke. Then, in one movement, he exhaled sharply, removed his thumb from the bottle opening, covered the opening with his mouth, and inhaled quickly, forcefully and deeply, struggling to hold his breath, while returning his thumb to the opening. "*Your turn,*" he said, grinning and choking, as he slowly began to exhale. I was fascinated by the procedure, and had no idea at all what to expect when I tried it myself.

The first thing I felt after inhaling was an overwhelming need to cough, immediately and repeatedly. Don laughed, and said I'd probably lost most of it, so I should take another "hit", and this time do everything possible to resist coughing – to hold my breath as long as I could. I did as instructed. Within minutes, or seconds, I couldn't be sure – time had already lost all recognizable properties – I was totally unfamiliar with everything I was experiencing. The room seemed to flow, the walls quivered, colors seemed unable to make up their minds, light was playing tennis, flat surfaces were undulating, my arm was playing music, I was floating up to the ceiling without a care in the world. I have no idea how long those sensations lasted (possibly an hour or two) or in what order they came, or when Don and I eventually came back to what I'd previously referred to as reality. "*That was some really good shit, wasn't it?*" he said, laughing. "*You've got enough left for a few more hits – maybe you can use a little less next time. But now you know how.*" And then he left. I never saw him again.

Knowing that my mom was coming in mid-September lit a fire under me to finish the bathroom in the downstairs of the big house; Mom suffered from severe claustrophobia, and the only functional bathroom – the tiny *en suite* in the tiny bedroom downstairs in the little house – would probably have terrified her. So I worked away feverishly, laying tiles, grouting, putting in the bathtub we'd brought with us from our apartment on Vårgatan. Then I built a storage cabinet under the stairs, with just enough space to fit in a door or hatch between the bathtub and the wall. All the while, my mental state was soaring and plummeting like an out-of-control roller coaster, abetted by my intake of whisky. I kept wanting to show Jeanette every completed row of tiles; I kept thinking of anecdotes to tell her and sometimes I forgot myself and called out for her. And every time, the realization that she was so utterly *gone* came crashing down on me, burying me sobbing in the rubble of my former hopes. The pain was unbearable, but I knew

I had to stay reasonably sober while attempting to lay tiles and especially when using a tile cutter. By the time I finished the bathroom, I was drained.

My 64-year-old mom arrived in the morning on September 12th, the day before my 32nd birthday, bearing a birthday cake for me, which sympathetic flight and security personnel allowed her to bring on board. I met her at the Copenhagen airport. We hadn't seen each other since the summer of 1974, a year after Dad died of Hodgkin's disease. Now it was my turn to have lost my spouse. She tried valiantly to conceal her surprise at how much weight I'd lost, how gaunt I looked, how full of sorrow, how disheveled and listless I'd become. She'd come on a mission of mercy to her beloved son – a human mission of human mercy – and to my great surprise and her great credit, she managed to leave the evangelizing, hellfire-breathing side of her dual personality at the door, at least when she and I were alone, which was most of the time. She only commented once that it was "merciful" that Dad didn't have to experience any of this, since he'd loved Jeanette so much. For me, no mercy at all.

I think we were both apprehensive about this meeting, for very different reasons on similar issues. We loved each other (that was never in doubt), and yet love had often been quite hard to find, particularly in my last years at home, as a teenager, in Oak Park, Illinois. She'd always seen herself as having a God-given role of authority over who I was and who I should be molded to become. When I rebelled, it was against that authority more than against her, but both of us sometimes found it hard to see the difference.

By my reckoning, Mom and I had only met eight times in the 13 years since I left Oak Park, first for San Francisco, then Vancouver, then Malmö, but we corresponded frequently. Or at least we wrote a lot of letters to each other, but so many of them went past each other and failed to correspond much. My views and values had undergone major upheavals and revisions since leaving my parental home, while she'd never permitted hers to be challenged in any substantial way since she was a little girl in Des Moines, Iowa. Consequently, I grew further and further from her on most levels, but our love for each other only grew stronger, and she was beginning to grow a new understanding of our relationship. Perhaps that growth accelerated once it became inescapably obvious that I was no longer under her authority.

The manipulative side of her personality seemed to come naturally to her, so automatically that I doubted that she herself was aware of it. (Wouldn't she have to be aware of it for it to be intentional?) In any case, it was there, all the time: a sharp glare, a swift fixing of the bun in which she permanently wore her long gray hair at the back of her neck. I knew that sign, Dad knew it, my brothers knew it. Mom fixes bun = Mom disapproves strongly. No words were needed. But when I began to rebel, I dared to refuse to be manipulated, I gradually began to ignore her disapproval, even when it assumed more and more histrionic proportions: tears, wailing, even prostration. Learning to parry Mom's disapproval was never easy; my brothers never learned how (as I saw it), but continued to toe the line for years and never fully broke free of her apron strings until those strings morphed into invisible chains of my brothers' own making, their voluntarily unconscious servitude to the ancient lies and myths they'd been told to call Truth.

Each of my meetings with Mom since I left home entailed some further small step on my part to break with the restrictions of my childhood, but we never discussed the ideological core; we'd avoided any confrontation that was direct. She fixed her bun and sighed ostentatiously; I stood my ground, prepared to defend my actions should she wish to take her disapproving body language to something more explicit, such as actual language that included nouns and verbs and adjectives and other such useful tools of communication.

Prior to her visit to me in September 1977, about half a year now since my Jeanette died, I'd never once consumed alcohol in her presence. She undoubtedly knew that I imbibed – I think she'd seen a bottle or two at our place before – but she'd never *seen* me drink. In my present state of grief, I was an emotional cripple and needed a crutch. I was no longer willing to abstain "for her sake". I was going to have my wine with dinner, and she would have to find a way to deal with it. I had all the arguments I needed – including *Biblical* arguments! – to defend my choice of beverage in case she should wish to challenge or reprimand me.

But to my surprise, there was no bun-fixing, no deep sighing, no falling on her knees in tearful and highly audible prayer at her chair at the dinner table. She simply rolled with the punch. I admittedly spared her the sight of my adding an equal amount of vodka to my morning orange juice, or whisky to my afternoon coffee. She didn't even raise an eyebrow when I took out my pipe and lit it, even though I didn't mention that the tobacco in my pipe bowl on one occasion was augmented with a small contribution from Don. *Something* deep inside her must have made her realize that any attempts to manipulate me would be totally fruitless, if not counter-productive. I think that *something* was love.

[*John often told me that he'd never dared to drink wine in Mom's presence, so I told him what happened when I did in September 1977:* nothing. *Mom's manipulation turned out to be a bluff. I tried to encourage him not to be afraid to cross that bridge, but it would take him* 20 *more years, until Christmas 1997, when Mom was 84 and John was 60, for John at last to dare to cross that line, to express his stand-on-your-own-two-feet adulthood, to have a glass of wine in Mom's presence at his own home in Boise. And Mom had no problem with it!*

I wonder how much of the behavior of manipulative people is little more than a big bluff?! They let you know (often very convincingly) that they will be extremely upset – whether hysterically sad or viciously angry – only so they get you to do as they wish. If you call their bluff and refuse to bend? Nothing but a paper tiger!]

All this time, I was still living in the little house. I slept in Jeanette's and my little bedroom downstairs and Mom slept on the sofa upstairs. She claimed that the tiny bedroom would have given her claustrophobia-induced nightmares (although she had no problem with it some years later). I still used the tiny kitchen upstairs rather than the now completely functional and fully equipped new kitchen in the big house. I just wasn't ready to start using that big house, and not because it wasn't completely finished.

But Mom was determined to nudge me, to push me to get back to work on it, and in this mission she for once put her more useful manipulative skills to good use. "*Let's go into the other house and I can do some crocheting while you lay some tiles on the floor in the kitchen,*" she would say. "*Just show me how you can do that!*" Or "*You can just finish that little bit before you call it a day, can't you? It's looking so nice!*"

Henry Carlsson came by one day with some revised drawings. It turned out that my benefactor, having realized back in the spring that there was no way I would be in any condition to meet the two-year deadline to complete the work on the house, interceded with the authorities on my behalf to secure a substantial extension of the deadline (as specified by the building permit, it should have expired in June '77). That thought, like most others that year, hadn't even entered my mind. Mom seemed to be suspicious of Henry's worldly elegance and was compelled to begin sounding him out about his position on the Lord. Fortunately for Henry, my mom's tendency to assume cliché mode as soon as religion was involved made her Elizabethan English all but incomprehensible to poor Henry, whose somewhat limited vocabulary in contemporary English failed to include words like "Lord", let alone "saved" in contexts related to souls.

Björn and Isobel also stopped by to meet Mom. I wondered how that would go – a Roman Catholic and an agnostic would-be entrepreneur. We didn't even make it beyond the introductions, when Björn made the completely innocent and unwitting mistake of commenting to my mom, "*You must be very proud of Stan for what he's done with this house!*" I instantly knew how Mom might react, and she did. "*Oh no,*" she said in protest, closing her eyes and piously wrinkling her brow, then rolling her eyes heavenward, "*I'm not a <u>proud</u> woman. All glory be to <u>Him</u>!*" Björn was totally befuddled.

When I was first learning Swedish, back in 1969-70, I was a bit surprised to discover that Swedish has *two* common words that are normally both translated to the English word "proud" (and two more for the noun form, "pride"), yet those two Swedish words mean quite different things from each other. One is *stolt* (noun form *stolthet*), which designates the kind of pride one might feel in having done one's best and maybe a little extra – or how one might presumably feel on hearing of an accomplishment by one's child!). The other is *högfärdig* (noun form *högmod*), corresponding more closely to the English words "haughty" and "haughtiness". In the King James translation of the Bible (which was the original version of the Bible in my mom's emotional world), "pride" is explicitly referred to as a sin, so Björn's comment was tantamount (in Mom's emotional world) to asking her to commit a sin regarding how she felt about me and my work on the house. The Swedish Bible uses the other word (*högmod*) to describe that particular sin, corresponding to the original Greek (*hubris*). But what do translators know?

I don't remember a lot about how Mom and I ate during her stay. Since Jeanette was such a fabulous and adventurous cook – and baker – I'd never bothered to seek a role for myself in the kitchen, and since I was back on my own, I pretty much stuck with my old one-track repertoire of grilled cheese sandwiches made in a waffle iron. They became more or less the only complement to my diet of whisky and tobacco.

The main things I remember about her two-week stay were that there was a great deal of warmth and affection between us in spite of our differences; that she truly helped me by pushing me to get off my ass and start finishing the work on the house; that she turned out to handle my "vices" astonishingly well; and that I was genuinely sorry to see her leave.

[*Just imagine how differently things might have turned out if Dad had dared to say, "Knock it off, Fran!" every time Mom got going on one of her disapproval crusades!!*]

My work on the house continued after Mom's departure, as did my smoking and drinking, my deep mood swings (from the merely morose to the screaming suicidal), my terrifying memories and my lonely, panic-filled nights. Bob continued to provide moral support by refusing to support my low morale. He chided me constantly for devoting far too much of my time and energy to concocting pseudo-intellectual defenses for wallowing in grief. But he was also encouraged that I was at least back to putting my physical house in order; he knew from experience what that could do.

Fred, a neighbor of mine who lived a block and a half away on Kirsebergsgatan, was a lanky, blond-bearded sculptor who looked like a melancholy vestige from the 1960s hippie movement and whose sculptures I admired greatly. He and his wife were on my increasingly short list of neighbors and acquaintances who seemed willing to hear me out when the spirit of Coleridge came over me (or overcame me). Fred's work included a number of fairly large cast bronze pieces, such as a larger-than-life cow. When making such a piece, he first made plaster-of-Paris molds for casting the final sculpture.

Fred and Margareta had two old adjoining houses on Kirsebergsgatan that Fred was also restoring in parallel with his sculpting. We sometimes exchanged tools, made joint purchases of bulky materials to reduce transport costs or gain economy of scale, and sometimes offered each other a helping hand or a little advice. In my efforts to complete the work on the big house, I faced the daunting task of spackling all the plasterboard on all the walls and ceilings – not a simple, one-step operation. The cracks or gaps between the sheets of plasterboard, as well as all the irregular gaps between the plasterboard and the beams, would not only have to be filled, but also sanded after the spackle dried, then topped up with more spackle, sanded again. And again. And again. [*This was before I'd heard of spray-on plaster that hardly takes any time at all and can be worked to almost any desired finish; perhaps it hadn't been invented yet, or was not available for DIY jobs. Nor had it yet appeared on YouTube, which was nearly three decades away!*] For all gaps bigger than a few millimeters (and there were plenty of them), the procedure would have to be repeated numerous tedious times. But Fred knew a shortcut.

By mixing plaster-of-Paris with an equal part of sand and then adding a little water, the whole thick slurry could be slathered onto the plasterboard with a whitewash brush and it would fill everything in one go – as long as a coarse finished surface was deemed acceptable. (I was lazy, so I accepted.) But because it hardened quickly, I could only do small batches at a time (enough for about one square meter) before plunging the brush into a bucket of water and massaging all the remaining plaster out of the bristles before the plaster transformed the brush into a war club. It was extremely messy, but fast (maybe), cheap (yes) and effective (sometimes), and gave a primitive look (definitely). Once the plaster dried and I brushed off all loose material with a dry brush, all I had to do was give the walls and ceilings a couple of coats of matte white paint, and I could move on to the next room.

But still I couldn't bring myself to move in. The 160 x 200 cm dense foam-rubber mattress Jeanette and I ordered shortly before her death had been delivered a month later. I just laid it (in its plastic cover) on the floor in what was soon to have been our new bedroom upstairs in the big house. I had no better place to put it.

In addition to all the hours I spent in the big house plastering the walls, I would often just stand there, for hours on end, in different rooms or corners of rooms, looking at what a beautiful home we'd created – except that it was never to be *our* home. I imagined what Jeanette's delight might have been like at seeing a wall finished, a room ready, and then my vision would suddenly dissolve into her contorted face, her lifeless body hanging there. I couldn't escape it, couldn't control it, couldn't stand it.

A few times, when I got tired of my whisky highs and tobacco fumes, I turned to my new little helper, the tiny brick of cannabis resin I got from Don. I have distinct memories of three fascinating trips, two of which occurred while I was sitting alone at the table in the future kitchen, by the empty fireplace. In the first of these trips, I was transformed into a Gulliver-like figure, or rather the space around me took on Gulliver-like proportions. One moment everything was *huge*; the ceiling was 10 meters high, the chair I was sitting on would have seated more than 50 people of my size. I was dumbfounded. Then, a moment later, I was a giant and didn't dare to stand up for fear of breaking through the low ceiling and then through the roof. Back and forth it went like that; it was quite thrilling, and I had no hangover afterwards.

On my second trip, also departing from the kitchen table, I was sitting on a swing. It wasn't one of those small playground swings, but the kind sometimes found on farms, with very long ropes from a big and very high branch of a huge tree in the farmyard, thus enabling the swing to trace a long, slow, high arc. The main difference was that my swing wasn't moving back and forth through *space*, but through *time* – past and future. But I wasn't experiencing past or future *events*, not specifically *my* past or future, it was just that I was aware that I was there, existing, in the past one moment and in the future the next. It was also utterly fascinating.

For the third and final trip in my hash memory, my departure point was upstairs in the big house, where I'd set up a table and a chair for plastering and painting the walls of what was to be my studio – if I could ever bring myself to paint again. I also had my stereo there to be able to listen to Bach while working, except this time I was listening to Bach while inhaling the fumes of Don's magic resin. When it kicked in after a couple of minutes, I was no longer *listening* to the music, I *was* the music. That's the only way I can describe it. It felt like Bach's contrapuntal notes were literally coursing through my bloodstream; I was breathing his harmonies. It was more exhilarating than any roller-coaster ride I'd ever been on.

After those three experiences, I decided to take a break from cannabis, for several reasons. One was that I was still determined to keep pushing to finish the house and didn't want to be sidetracked. Another was that my small resin supply was starting to dwindle into nothing, and I wanted to save enough for Bob to try it someday (he'd said he was very curious about it and wanted to give it a try), and I didn't want to start placing orders with Don – or with unknown dealers. And then there was the small matter of it being illegal; I didn't want to take any further risks.

I realize I've had quite a few major upheavals in my life, with potentially disastrous outcomes, but nevertheless I claim I'm not inclined to take risks. I can see how that might sound preposterous, but consider this: Am I taking a risk if I'm unaware of the risk I'm taking because I'm so goddamn naïve? And I'm by no means claiming that I haven't spent much of my life being naïve!

I'd been corresponding about once a month with Jeanette's big sister Marilyn. (I received a note from her mother Rose in June, as well as a birthday card in September.) I don't remember much about what we wrote to each other – we'd never had a great deal to say under the best of circumstances, and my paranoia in thinking that they blamed me for Jeanette's mental illness and death certainly wouldn't have helped make our correspondence easier. [*In retrospect, many years later, I gained some insight into my paranoia about that. After all, I was blaming myself for her mental illness and death, so why shouldn't I presume that they were too? Or were* they *blaming* them*selves?*] Jeanette's twin brother Michael never wrote to Jeanette before, and wasn't about to write to me now; the same went for her kid sister Rosanne.

Sometime in late September, Stig Svensson phoned to tell me he was sending a car from Perstorp with 10 copies of my polystyrene-board-mounted poster. As soon as they arrived, I went out to a stationery store and bought a large roll of brown wrapping paper. I think I must also have bought some sort of corrugated wrapping material to protect the sharp and brittle corners of the posters. Then I wrapped and addressed the posters, and mailed one each to Mom, John, Al, Rose, Marilyn, Rosanne, Michael and Bob. I saved two for myself. It never occurred to me that *nobody* would know what to do with such a poster, that it would become an embarrassing white elephant that they couldn't bear to have on their walls, yet found it hard to throw out. I had no strength to work that out in my mind, so I just sent them.

In subsequent letters to me from Rose and Marilyn, they began urging me to "move on", to think about finding someone new and starting a new life for myself. It sounded like they meant well, but it made me upset. Was it because *they* were the ones who felt in need of "moving on"? Were they intending to *forget* about Jeanette?! A part of me understood that they might be truly concerned about me, about me *also* losing my mental balance. There was certainly much more rational evidence to support that idea. But this wasn't the most rational period in my life. I was a raw, open wound.

One late afternoon in my drunken fuzz of the autumn of 1977, my would-be Elvis neighbor, Claes, asked me to help him with a little job he'd somehow been given. I wasn't sure what it involved, but I accepted. He drove us to a truck depot somewhere down in the harbor area late one evening, there to affix self-adhesive signs on the sides of trucks in a depot for the Coop grocery chain. These signs (as I recall, they were roughly 1 x 2 m) extolled the virtues of Coop groceries. The signs were not terribly attractive, but the self-adhesive glue on the backs was extremely attracted to other parts of the same sign, causing great exasperation until we finally figured out how to make it work. When we were done, I'm pretty sure Claes handed me some cash, or not. In any case, his gesture towards me was kind, and for the hours the work lasted, my mind was off my woes and my hand was off the bottle. Just trying to figure out the Swedish meaning of his distorted chatter took all my concentration, and often provided me some startling amusement when I succeeded.

CHAPTER 3

Amor præcox

In October, with the days growing noticeably shorter and our wedding anniversary – it would have been our 11th – slipping by with all the stealth of a bulldozer in a bathroom, I continued along my self-destructive path to abbreviate my life and reduce my pain by keeping as numb as I could without having to spend my nights talking on the Great White Telephone (hugging the toilet bowl).

I spent my days staring into space, lost, wondering whether *any*thing was nobler in the mind or out of it. I was *not* afraid of death; I longed for it. But I was afraid of *dying* – the pain, the risk of a failed attempt to die and ending up somehow even worse off than before. I was a downright coward when it came to dying. I tried imagining all sorts of scenarios: hanging (what if I only caused severe brain damage but went on living in an institution?), jumping in front of a train (what if I was struck and thrown clear – and left paralyzed?), drowning (what about the instinctive animal impulse to struggle and panic?), an overdose of something (what if I didn't take enough or vomited it up and wound up in an asylum in more anguish than ever?), a gun (where would I find one in Sweden in 1977?).

I'd long ago abandoned the childish, fanciful notion that the process of life that ends in death would somehow not end in death but resume in some other form of life, somewhere (where does the living flame of a candle *go* when you blow it out?). There's *no* proof at all of such a crazy notion, no evidence, nothing convincing except to those who are determined to be convinced without evidence. And it was the *lack* of anything convincing that was, in fact, keeping me alive. How ironic that the lack of a rational reason for believing in life after death was now my main reason to go on living!

Bob continued calling me, at least once a week (depending on how concerned our latest call had made him about the state of my mind) for a long talk, usually an hour or more. He encouraged me to read, made some book suggestions, sent me books, advised me to be open to new social experiences (even though he was disinclined to take his own advice on that point), or he just listened to my ranting and crying and moaning with seemingly endless patience.

By this time I was occasionally being asked to join get-togethers hosted not only by my own acquaintances, but by *their* acquaintances, which gave me opportunities to bend the ears of a few who hadn't yet heard my story (and perhaps thus to give my own acquaintances' ears a rest). At one such "party" on October 14th, in the Sofielund district of Malmö, I was hanging out among a dozen or so people around my age, most of them strangers to me, trying to stay as numb as possible without the risk of getting boorishly drunk, when a new guest arrived. She nearly made me fall off my chair (or collapse into one). At first glance, I saw Jeanette walking into the room.

She had medium-long, very dark hair, fair skin, flashing eyes, and when she smiled I was instantly struck by the fact that she also had a slight gap between her upper two front teeth. Her name was Sonja. [*Do I need to keep reminding readers that the letter 'j' in Swedish is pronounced like the consonant 'y' in English, as in 'you'?*] She was an actress employed by the Malmö City Theater. I was stunned. I got chills. My heart started pounding. I stared at her in disbelief. I couldn't take my eyes off her. I didn't know it at the time, but she had one bad eye, so she turned her head slightly when looking straight ahead, which gave her a coquettish, exotic look. I didn't believe in reincarnation, but I probably gave every impression that I did, except that she was blithely unaware that she reminded me of anyone, let alone someone she'd never heard of, let alone the one I adored.

I *had* to meet her, across that not-too-crowded room. Having quaffed sufficient alcohol to squelch my inhibitions, I walked over to her and introduced myself. I have no idea what I said by way of introduction, but I realized (much later) that I probably came on to that poor pretty girl pretty strong, uncharacteristically strong. I was, after all, thoroughly convinced that I was already in love with her – *or with the one whom she reminded me of* – and I was prepared to let all the similarities with Jeanette I first observed remain intact, long after I got a much closer look that might have dispelled some of them. I was even prepared to find close similarities in her personality, even though that required considerable imagination and denial on my part. I was the drowning man; she was the straw at which I was desperately clutching. (I was also the self-appointed casting director for a play for which she had no intention to audition.)

Since I practically threw myself at her feet, she must have been quite alarmed, even initially. And yet she also seemed to have a certain fascination (as in, "*Is this guy for real?*"). I have no clear recollection of the sequence of events that transpired in the intensive days that followed, probably largely due to my extra-large diet of whisky and cigarettes. We *may* have left the party together, we *may* have gone back to her place (where was that? or was it my place?), I may have spent the night with her (or was it a later night?), but I think I may have been impotent (for how long?). My madness for her increased exponentially (what did I tell Bob?), and soon my desperation for her (little doubt about that!) was scaring her. She moved to another apartment and begged her friends not to let me know where she was (no wonder!).

I remember a couple of details with clarity. In the middle of the night (so yes, I must have spent one of those first nights with her), I woke up to the sound of her voice, quite dramatic. I was out of bed like a shot, and found her in the kitchen of her apartment, reading. She was learning her lines for a play. I asked whether it was necessary to read them out loud, and *so loud*? "*Of course,*" she said. "*If I read them silently, I won't be able to say them when I'm onstage!*"

After only having known her a few days (I think), I gave her one of my paintings, *Blue Room*,[8] on which I inscribed on the back something wildly melodramatic like "*To my darling Sonja – the last meaning of my life*" (or the equivalent in Swedish). I think it was after that kind of high drama from me that she felt obliged to "disappear" from my horizon by going to visit friends in Stockholm. Or maybe her plans to visit friends in Stockholm had nothing whatsoever to do with me. In either case, my panic at her *perceived* total avoidance of me plunged me into deeper depths of despair, intoxication and smoke than ever.

When I told Bob, my only true *confidant*, he was greatly alarmed, with good reason, and phoned me every evening, pleading with me to embrace rationality, in whatever form I could manage it. Slowly he lit the lantern of my realization of what was happening: I didn't know Sonja at all; this wasn't about her, it was a thing between me and me, a transfer of feelings, a last desperate reaching out for Jeanette. He saw right through me, of course; I needed love. Jeanette left a gigantic vacuum, a black hole, a void that I had no idea how to fill, how to live with, or how to live without *her*. He observed that I wasn't much good at being or living alone, and indeed never had been. In that respect, Bob and I were polar opposites.

Bob urged me to come and spend a couple of weeks in Binningen at Christmas; he didn't feel up to making the trip north that year, and he might have supposed (presumably correctly) that Christmas might not be the best time for someone with my emotional instability to risk being on their own, especially

---

8 Painting #65 (see Appendix 2 in *Slings and Arrows*)

in the environment of Korngatan in Malmö

On October 21st, just a week after meeting Sonja, I received a piece of mail from the US Consulate in Gothenburg. It was a form I was asked to fill in: "Registration of the Death of an American Citizen". And Isobel phoned to tell me that there would be a rehearsal a day or two later for Patrick's christening, which would take place on November 5th.

Then I received a formal, businesslike letter from one of Jeanette's sisters (I think it was from Marilyn, but it could have been Rosanne, who otherwise never wrote to me) informing me that she and her family felt it likely that I had in my possession some family heirlooms that had been given to Jeanette. They were anxious for me to return to them. These heirlooms were allegedly in the form of textiles – doilies, runners, small tablecloths, napkins, pillowcases etc – that were woven or embroidered or needlepointed by some older relative from Italy. From that vague and fuzzy description, I had absolutely no idea what textiles they might have in mind. I began searching through everything we'd never gotten around to unpacking for use in our newly restored home, but I still had no clue.

I decided I would take one of the large shipping trunks Jeanette and I bought in Vancouver for storing our things in connection with our move to Sweden, and fill it with all the textiles I could find (so as not to miss an heirloom), as well as a lot of Jeanette's fine, hardly-ever-worn clothes (the majority of which were courtesy of The Emporium), so that they could be put to good use, and also to avoid the mess of a half-packed trunk with its contents sloshing around during transport. Since I'd need some time to get it all sorted out, I wrote to Marilyn that I'd be shipping it all to her address as soon as I could, probably in January to avoid the Christmas rush. (I was still sending birthday and Christmas presents to Jeanette's siblings, nephew, niece and mom. I got none in return.)

In late October I rented a floor sander to finish the upstairs wooden floors. Since I'd bought the boards from a demolition company, they were well-worn, irregular, concave (or convex), coated with layers of old varnish They required hour after hour of dust, sweat, exasperation and futility, changing of abrasive rolls, filling sacks sawdust to dispose of, as I went over the surfaces again and again, diagonally, until I'd finally worn down the peaks to the level of the troughs and until only clean, smooth wooden surfaces were visible. Then I mixed equal parts of linseed oil, acetic acid and turpentine in a jeep can, and applied the mixture to the newly sanded surfaces with a rag. (I got this recipe from a translation I'd done for an interior designer friend of Henry's; the concoction was supposed to penetrate the wood – not just coat it, but make it harder – while giving it a pleasing luster.) I finished the job on November 4th. Now just the living room was left.

Patrick's christening was a sick joke to me. I was prepared for how overboard the Catholics always seemed to go on the pageantry – the robes, the gold, the chants, the smoking censers, the chimes, the liturgical nonsense – but I could only remember ever having attended one christening before in my life, and it was nowhere nearly as pompous as this one. I was expecting, I was prepared, to hear about the Father, the Son and the Holy Ghost a few times. But renouncing the Devil? I suppose that if you believe in the Trinity, you might as well believe in the Devil too.

Then it occurred to me that it might make more sense, given the fucked-up mess the world is, with all its wars, disasters and diseases, to have a *Quadrinity*: God the Father, God the Son, God the Holy Ghost, and God the Devil. Jehovah certainly behaves like the devil most of the time, at least according to the Bible. And He hadn't deigned to offer mankind any other, better account of Himself. The Bible was His Word. On the contrary, He admitted it: "*I make peace, and create evil: I the LORD do all these things* [Isaiah 45:7]."

Anyway, the christening seemed to me like nothing but a masquerade party in order to assure that the little boy would get some extra presents, and to give Björn's family an excuse to convene for a fancy meal. I'm sure it meant something more than that to Isobel, like the fulfilling and continuation of a long Catholic tradition, and traditions tell people what to do and how and when to do it, all over the world, and people hardly ever ask themselves whether those traditions serve any good or useful purpose. Traditions don't *describe* behavior, they *dictate* it.

Everything – life itself – felt like a masquerade to me, a vicious, phony, mendacious, absurd and tortuous masquerade, all moving in its petty pace and leading nowhere but to more of the endless pain that was poisoning everything I saw and touched. I was finding it harder and harder to experience more than fleeting moments when I could think of anything but ending my pathetic existence, once and for all. But now it might have been turning into something more dangerous; my brain was also beginning to get involved in my decisions.

I'd been seeing less and less of Isobel and Björn since the baby arrived – understandably enough, considering all the time a baby demands, and all the priorities that must be adjusted – and since the windsurfing season for Björn and me ended long ago. But some days after the christening, I got a phone call from Isobel. I could hear the excitement in her voice before she'd said two words. A few days later, she said, on Saturday, November 12th, she was going to host a fairly big birthday party for Björn (it might have been his 30th). In view of my joy-killing countenance, I was reluctant to accept. Isobel wouldn't hear of it. She was determined to get me to promise that I'd come, even though her overbearing enthusiasm made me nauseous.

The reason for it, she was quick to tell me (and it was reason enough for her to think that I must be excited to hear), was that their former neighbor, a girl named Lena Johannisson, had recently moved back to Sweden again, a couple of months after having moved to California to marry her fiancé Larry, both of whom used to be Björn and Isobel's neighbors in the apartment building on Munkhättegatan. Isobel got to know them and their venomous shouting matches quite well. (She claimed that Larry once put his fist through an inner door in a rage that made Lena flee to Björn and Isobel for protection – although I later understood that Lena was also terribly impressed that Invincible Larry had a black belt in karate, enabling him to put his fist through doors, as if that were a quality that furthered the progress of civilization.) Isobel was speaking so fast that she was almost out of breath when she told me all this, as if she'd just discovered an extremely short expiration date on my ears.

Björn, as it turned out, had known Lena casually since his childhood or youth, when his parents used to spend time in the summers with Björn's grandmother at her seaside home in Skepparkroken, not far from where Lena grew up (or at least lived), in Barkåkra.

I vaguely remembered that when I was in Skepparkroken for Midsummer Eve, less than five months before, I accompanied Björn to look for Lena in Barkåkra, and that Lena later stopped by the house in Skepparkroken to say hello to Björn (and Isobel). On that occasion, Lena said that she was going to be emigrating from Sweden to Sacramento in September. (I couldn't remember what she looked like, except that she was pretty.) But she'd only remained in the US for about six weeks before returning to Sweden on November 1st.

Since Lena's father Allan used to be the vicar at the Barkåkra countryside church, it is quite possible that he was involved in Björn's confirmation, and since Lena grew up in the next-door vicarage, they might have known each other from there as well. Isobel didn't know such details, and I didn't know or care. Björn would later tell me that he'd always been hot on Lena, including some years later when they both happened to be living in Gothenburg. But he was, as far as I know, always spurned.

What really had Isobel so worked up when she phoned me that day was the prospect of match-making, pure and simple. (Except that it would turn out to be anything but pure and not even remotely simple.) Arranging for me to meet Lena at Björn's party was yet another in that inexplicable series of Isobel's well-intentioned hands-on interventions that she bestowed on me during that horrible year. I suppose she was initially disappointed by my total indifference to the prospect of meeting Lena.

I hadn't even known Isobel that well before Jeanette's death. Sure, Isobel had been a colleague of mine for about a year, give or take. But I hadn't been close to her at all, and in fact found her mildly irritating for her apparent inability or unwillingness to distinguish truth from lies or from wishful thinking and gossip. In my role as the "head English teacher" (talk about being a big fish in a little pond – spawn in spit), I showed her how it's done, this business of sitting down opposite someone for eight hours a day, five days a week, someone who may or may not be able to say "Yes, I don't" and working him or her until, at the end of this time, he or she could say with aplomb, "No, I do!" Language schools! If you've ever worked in one, I don't need to tell you what they're like; if you haven't, I'm actually not sure I can. (And if you can read "actually" as a six-syllable word [I-æ-tʃu-ə-lI-ə] while meeting the morning breeze perpendicular to your nostrils, you already know less than I would never be able to tell you.)

Like many (if not most) modern apartment buildings in Sweden in the 1970s, Björn and Isobel's on Munkhättegatan included a basement "party room" available for renting for a festive occasion for a pittance by any tenant in the building. The concrete walls and lack of windows prevented revelers from disturbing the other neighbors, and it was spacious enough to accommodate some 30-40 guests with undiminished air quality.

There were streamers and balloons. Long tables were set up, with lots of candles, paper plates and plastic cutlery, and plenty of food (probably made by Björn the chef). Bring-your-own wine would have been common practice for that age group then, but I don't remember for sure. Björn may have provided the hard liquor for after-dinner drinks, but it probably was not hooch of his own making (his moonshining days didn't last long past the arrival of Patrick – the fumes in the apartment could be pretty intense, even if the noise level was under control).

Most of the guests were more or less total strangers to me, except for Dave and Christina, two other residents of the same apartment building. Dave, a Scotsman from London, was also a former colleague from the language school (so was Lynn, but she and Isobel appeared to have a real personality clash; she and Arne weren't at the party). I think at least two of Björn's three siblings were there; I'd met them in Skepparkroken at Midsummer (to the extent I was capable of meeting anybody then). Björn's younger brother Anders brought a friend to the party, a girl named Irene, but they didn't seem to be "a couple". I looked twice at her – she was cute and sensual, but I needed a lot more booze before anything like Dutch courage would reach a level of any use or bother to anyone.

And then there was Lena, all dressed in black to match my mind, yet blond as the dawn, beautiful as the day, stunning as a sorceress, with a charming velvety voice. I think Isobel had seated us opposite each other for the dinner. (Swedish parties usually involve a sit-down meal before breaking up into dancing and mingling.) After dinner she came around and sat beside me as people began circulating a bit and getting drinks, coffee and cake at a buffet table off to one side. She started sounding me out, in English, about America and why I didn't want to live there. (What had Isobel told her about me??) I countered by asking why *she* didn't, since she'd seemingly been so convinced that it was the only place one could live less than half a year earlier. It turned out that she'd been back and forth two or three times before her latest move in September, unable to make up her mind about America or Larry or both. She said she came back because she was homesick, and besides, she couldn't get a job in America, and besides, a serial rapist was terrorizing Sacramento that summer – the so-called Golden State Killer, alleged to have murdered at least 13 and raped more than 50. [*Joseph James DeAngelo Jr. was finally arrested in 2018, during the writing of this book.*] So Larry more or less forced her into confinement at home, and besides, he didn't understand her, so she decided to break up with him – maybe – and come home to Sweden for good – maybe. She later revealed that they'd begun fighting with and screaming at each other less than a month after she arrived.

Since she returned to Sweden more than halfway through the school term, she couldn't get a full-time teaching position, but registered with the teachers' exchange in Lund to do short-term, last-minute substitute jobs all over town, which gave her enough work to pay the bills without having to borrow "too much" from her family and friends.

Another thing that happened as soon as the dinner part of the party was over was that somebody turned on a tape recorder in a somewhat smaller, candle-lit adjacent room (empty except for a small table, on which the tape recorder was placed), playing slow and fast songs alternately, should anyone care to dance to them. Those who didn't could remain in the main party room. Lena and I danced a couple of times (her initiative), during which I seem to recall (I wasn't exactly sober) getting a relatively tight-lipped kiss (my initiative, but not the tight-lipped part).

At some point, while Lena was off mingling with others or getting herself a drink, Irene came over and asked me to dance. There was nothing tight-lipped about her kissing – it was all open-mouthed and caressing tongues as she worked the slow, undulating stride of her leg in between mine. I was doing my best to disguise the fact that I'd never learned to dance, and there were distractions aplenty. She was riding me and seemed amused to feel the anatomical changes she was causing. It was good to feel all that blood and warmth down there at the center of mutual momentary attention, away from the depression and blackness and confusion. We continued our same fixed-footed, tongues-entwined dancing into the next number, even though the beat was more like someone using a beehive as a martini shaker. We smiled knowingly at each other from our clench; but that was it. Then the dance was over and we just had a laugh as we returned to separate tables in the main party room. Unlike me, Irene wasn't drunk. She would be driving a full carload home to Lund – including Anders and Lena – and me. Following my slurred directions, she dropped me (and my bicycle) off at Korngatan on the way to Lund, a very small detour. I remember getting dropped off at the house and all the laughter I was causing as I drunkenly dug my bicycle out of the trunk. I'm sure I said goodnight to everyone in a general sort of way, but I don't remember any special good-bye to Lena – nor singing *Goodnight Irene*, no matter how drunk I was.

I'll never know for sure whether it was Isobel who told Lena to call me or whether it was Lena who asked Isobel for my number and approval to call. Neither would ever admit responsibility. (No, that's not true. *One* of them would not.) Regardless of how, it came to pass that Lena phoned me some days after the party. My mind is as blank about what she and I may have said to each other on the phone, other than that it was agreed that she would come to "my place" on

Amor præcox

Friday evening, November 25th, 1977. Neither she nor I had a car, so she would take the bus from Lund. The nearest stop for buses to and from Lund was on Lundavägen – "the Lund road" – the main street three blocks down the hill from Korngatan, a location about as convenient as could be desired for any future trips back and forth either of us might be making.

I wish I could remember what the *stated* purpose of that first visit was. It wasn't explicitly that we should go to bed. It must have been for a meal or something. Or maybe to finish our party conversation in peace and quiet. Or both. Another possible reason or excuse might have been for her to have an American to talk to now that she no longer had Larry the Great. Or maybe it was because she'd met someone sadder than she was. Her relationship with Larry was never a calm one, I'd been was told by Isobel, and the rift left a lot of ragged edges. But whatever the reason, she came. *Veni, vini, vidi, vici.*

It was her first view of the interior of the house, and I think she – like everyone else who'd seen it since the renovation concept became apparent – was a bit impressed. (It never occurred to me that she'd grown up in a large patrician vicarage.) The laminated collage I'd done in memory of Jeanette was hanging in a prominent place next to the fireplace in the dining corner of the kitchen. She stopped in front of it. It seemed to disturb her, but perhaps it also made her feel a bit more sympathetic towards me. Or maybe less. Or maybe just cautious. Or maybe it had no impact at all at the time.

The concrete floor in the living room was still untiled (Björn had some kind of carpentry project going there.) Instead I'd set up a temporary living room upstairs in what would later become my studio, to which I'd moved the black leather sofa, easy chair, and stereo from the upstairs room of the little house (with the help of Allan Saabye). I did this sometime after Mom's visit. (In the adjacent bedroom, I'd also removed the plastic from the mattress and replaced it with a blanket.) It was to this makeshift living room that Lena and I retired after whatever meal I may have managed to concoct down in the kitchen, most likely grilled cheese sandwiches. We listened to some records. I know we talked a lot and drank a glass or two of wine, but I don't recall *what* we talked about. Maybe the "about" part doesn't matter.

Lena was wearing a white blouse with a few ruffles on it, and a flowing dark skirt, very feminine. Her blouse was by no means tight, but her breasts were not easily hidden, which became increasingly apparent to me through a successive mental compilation and superimposition of observations that were causing my mind to reel. Her long, straight yet flowing blond hair and charming smile were doing nothing to lower my pulse rate (except for lowering its main point of activity). She was to me the almost archetypally "Beautiful Swedish Girl", sitting there chatting and charming me in my makeshift living room, lit only by a few candles, just outside my even more makeshift future bedroom, furnished only with a blanket-covered mattress on the floor and a small table lamp, also on the floor next to the mattress. I'd never yet spent a night in the big house.

We were listening to classical music – the only kind I had – which Lena also enjoyed, talking and sipping wine, and she was looking at me warmly, coyly, or maybe I only thought she was because that's what I so badly wanted to think. *We've gotta dance if this is gonna get anywhere!* I put on the most romantic classical pieces I could find: a record of exquisite piano and violin sonatas by Mozart – real mood music! I mentioned that one could almost dance to this, and she said *why not*, so we did. I held her close to me. I could easily feel her breasts, firm and warm, pressing against me, making me dizzy. My right hand slid all the way down her back as I pressed her closer, just as Mozart's piano was teaching the violin what to do. We began kissing – no longer tight-lipped – during this swaying excuse for a dance, as we sank into the armchair, with Lena curling herself into my lap, our kiss uninterrupted. I felt the warmth generated in my lap by her sitting on me, on my own source of warmth, which seemed to transport us into the adjoining room, and kept on going and going and coming and coming until we both lay there naked and exhausted. The exhaustion was only temporary. I'd never felt quite like this before. *It* never felt quite like this before. I could have cried with happiness and relief.

Lena didn't spend the night with me that night (after all, we barely knew each other!!), and neither did I – not in that house, not in that bed. But a few nights later we both spent our first night there, the first night anyone had spent in that house for decades, enjoying each other again and again. I couldn't get enough. I'd glimpsed what I felt certain was the light at the end of the tunnel, the end of my nightmare of misery. Or was I once again being fooled by *thinking* I was seeing what I so urgently and desperately *wanted* to see? *Was what I thought to be light at the end of the tunnel in fact the light of an oncoming train?*

The next couple of weeks were both chaotic and euphoric. I stopped drinking alone. I cut down my cigarette consumption from 50 a day to about 30 (she also smoked, *Gula Blend* Swedish cigarettes, to which I switched from my much stronger *Prince*). I began seeing Lena – spending the night with her – nearly every other day, and greatly looking forward to each new meeting.

I was doing everything I could to learn everything I could about her. She'd just finished her studies at the teachers' college that spring, before leaving for Sacramento, and now that she'd aborted (possibly) her plans to live in California and marry Larry, she was hoping to get a full-time job as a 4th-to-6th-grade teacher in Lund. Since she was still registered as a student at the university, having graduated earlier in that calendar year, she remained entitled to rent a small furnished "dorm" room in one of the top floors (I think it was the 6th) of a seven-storey subsidized student housing block in the part of Lund called Ulrikedal, a short walk from where her sister lived. There were several small student rooms on each floor; each room included a small bathroom, but all rooms on each floor shared a kitchen.

Lena was the youngest of four siblings: her sister Eva, my age, lived near Lena in Lund; and two older brothers, Jan and Lars, both of whom lived in the Stockholm area. Her father Allan had retired from his post as the vicar of the small countryside church in Barkåkra, just outside Ängelholm, which was where Lena went to school. Her mother, Marie-Louise, was a housewife. After Allan retired (a few years before I met Lena), her parents were obliged to move from their stately vicarage to a comparatively humble bungalow next door. Eva was the only family member to whom Lena seemed very close and in whom she confided, she said.

In response to my telling her that I didn't believe in gods anymore, Lena told me her father was also "a doubter", not convinced of the truth of what he preached. (She told me of the *deeeep* discussions he and Larry had had, but nothing about them.) And yet her father was also some sort of "mystic" who wrote some fervently awful religious poetry (she showed me a booklet of it once). Lena seemed both to fear *and* revere him. He apparently set lofty standards for his children and was good at showing his disapproval (but he apparently didn't have a bun to fix!). His word had been Law in the Johannisson household, although Jan, the eldest, broke sharply with his father and from everything religious. If Lena was at all religious, she didn't practice any of it.

I asked her all kinds of questions to gain an understanding of her tastes, likes and dislikes, interests, values. I wanted to know almost everything *except* details about her past boyfriends. But I didn't need to ask about them; I had no choice but to hear far more details than I ever wanted to hear. I guess there are people who enjoy hearing about that kind of thing. I've never been one of them. [*Unless you count this work* – Hindsights – *in which I've felt unable to give a full account of the things that have shaped my life without at least some account of the development of my sexuality.*]

In any case, whether I wanted to know or not (I didn't!), I heard that a boy named Johnny took her virginity when she was in her mid-teens and then she grew tired of him. And then there was Ola, about whom Lena repeatedly (and for years) referred to (to me!) as *"the love of my life"*. She showed me numerous photos of him and them together from her album. (Lena herself was exceptionally photogenic as well – particularly when she was aware of a camera.) But he knocked her up and she got an abortion, against his wishes. He had the audacity to become furious with her, so she left him and the province of Skåne for Gothenburg where she spent a couple of years working as a medical secretary before moving to Malmö to go to teachers' college. (I later learned that Björn pursued her to Gothenburg too, without success.)

I think she met Larry in Gothenburg. He was, like me, a draft-dodger opposed to the Vietnam War. According to Lena, he was super-intelligent, a karate expert, a big guy, a force to be reckoned with – and he had a temper. But at least, as far as I could figure out, he'd never hit *her*. To my utter agony, she informed me that she was still in love with him and might go back to him after all, even though she didn't mind sleeping with me while she made up her mind or waited for him to beg. [*Perhaps she was teaching me how to cope?*]

I did my best to turn some of this superhighway of information into a two-way street, but I was largely unsuccessful. She showed little or no interest in my childhood and youth. I wanted to show her my slides from Oak Park to give her some insight into where I came from, but despite my repeated offers, she never wanted to see them [*and never once did*].

It dawned on me during this chaotic autumn, that if I were ever to be successful in romance, I'd have to expand my cooking repertoire beyond grilled-cheese sandwiches. I was scraping by on my unemployment benefits and had no car. Taking Lena or anyone else out to dinner at a nice restaurant and then taking a taxi back to my place was simply out of the question, far beyond my budget. The answer to that question would be to start learning to make acceptable meals – served with plenty of wine to preclude anyone getting any ideas about driving home that evening. I'd have to get working on that!

Lena *mentioned* that she was having problems getting her alarm clock to work and that she hated alarm clocks anyway. So I gave her one of my two identical clock-radios. [*If I'd had any self-insight at all at this point, I might have noticed the extent to which my will had turned to putty in her hands. She wasn't asking. I simply couldn't help giving.*] Perhaps she was afraid of feeling indebted to me, so she asked if she could return the favor by sewing some shades for a couple of my windows – I may have mentioned my intention to acquire some.

She did eventually ask a few cautious questions about Jeanette. It seemed to bother or threaten Lena that I obviously still loved Jeanette. Lena seemed to wish to equate that with her still loving Larry, even though Jeanette was dead and Larry was very much alive. Eventually I figured out that she'd been the one to terminate every relationship with every boyfriend she'd ever had. None of them understood her. *Give anyone enough time and they'll turn out not to understand.* I told her that I'd had a vasectomy, so she didn't need to think about taking the Pill, but she just sniffed at me, as if we'd been talking about Middle Eastern politics and I'd mentioned the color of milk cartons.

Bob was initially pleased to hear of my latest escapade (he knew *nothing* of the rate of acceleration!), with an almost palpable sense of relief because it indicated to him (a) that I was getting plenty of much-needed exercise for my libido, and (b) that my premature passion for Sonja would probably no longer be an issue he would be called upon to help me deal with. He seemed unprepared to recognize that my passion was undiminished; it had merely been transferred to another young woman. Neither was I prepared – for anything that was to come.

Isobel was also following the development of my relationship with Lena with great involvement, particularly in view of her role in instigating it. (I have no idea what role she might have been continuing to play in sounding out Lena or planting stories or dispensing advice.) Isobel phoned me frequently to check whether the seed she'd so cunningly planted might be showing signs of germination. But after just a few days, when she discovered that her hopes and expectations had not only germinated, but had erupted into unbounded, unbridled passion on my part – bursting from the soil in full bloom, as it were – she was alarmed.

Isobel then began urging me, almost daily, to slow down. "*You can't show Lena you're too interested!! You've got to pretend that you don't care!!*" Such advice sounded insane to me, and I dismissed it as a bourgeois game to which I could not relate. Besides, I'd never been much good at hiding my feelings, and Isobel obviously had no idea what a fantastic altitude I'd already reached with Lena (or more likely *due to* Lena). This wasn't about a mountaineer laboriously scaling some forbidding or foreboding crag – it was a goddamn rocket zooming straight for the flaming sun! It never occurred to me that Isobel's fears might have been based on anything Lena might have told her. After all, I could see nothing in Lena's behavior to support the need for caution or restraint on my part.

After that first passionate encounter with Lena, my relationship with Sonja (who was back in Malmö and no longer hiding from me) instantly transformed into one of friendship – which was what she said she'd been hoping for. There might, however, have been some disappointment in her at how quickly and easily that new status was achieved. Although she didn't know that my libidinous passion wasn't gone, merely redirected to Lena, there was perhaps a slight tone of disappointment or jealousy that crossed her face due to the sudden absence of sex, but she was a good actress. After all, she got what she'd said she wanted.

Sonja and I went to the movies in Malmö one evening when Lena was too busy with other things to see me. There was a new French film playing at the movie theater on Stortorget, one that Sonja thought I needed to see. It was a sad and tragic film called *The Lacemaker*, in which a simple girl, Beatrice (the breakthrough role in the brilliant career of Isabella Huppert), is undone (she ends up as a permanent resident in a mental hospital) by her unrequited love for a man who sweeps her off her feet and then loses interest in her once he's finished sweeping. The film strongly suggests that many people may only want to get laid, but create impossible worlds and expectations in order to justify their lust to themselves and society by insisting that it be called love, driving themselves crazy in the process. Beatrice reminded me a bit of the role Natalie Wood played in *Splendor in the Grass* – a film that moved and saddened me deeply back when I was a lovesick adolescent, i.e. indistinguishable from how I was behaving now. But I wasn't looking for (and absolutely refused to see) any possible parallel to what was going on in my own life. [*In retrospect, it seems a safe bet that Sonja could foresee some risk that I might end up like the Lacemaker.*]

On December 12th, I sat down to write to my brothers. As far as I could remember it was the first time I'd ever been the one to owe *them* letters, let alone multiple letters. For some eight months after Jeanette's death, I found it all but impossible to write anything to anyone, or even to think any thought through to its logical conclusions (because none of my thoughts *had* logical conclusions), I let the mail from them pile up.

I wrote nearly identical letters to them, because I had nearly identical things to say in response to their nearly identical messages to me. I didn't feel up to writing them earlier, when my depression brought me to a new all-time-low in early November, but I didn't tell them about Lena or what my new-found passion for her since then was doing for me. I put it this way:

Although I still get depressed from time to time, I haven't been experiencing those engulfing black waves which had been hitting me for such a long time. I no longer find it necessary to go to bed drunk, having discovered better things than bottles to take to bed. I realize I've got a long way to go, but at least I've made a start, and it feels good.

I also wrote them about how our mom's enjoyable visit to me in September had helped me, about my jobless situation, and other incidental information. But what I needed to get off my chest to my brothers was the real reason for my long delay in replying.

They (especially Al) were writing me about how much I had to be thankful for. In the language of our entire childhoods of indoctrination, being "thankful" *always* meant being thankful to the Lord and His Goodness and Mercy that Endureth Forever. It made me want to puke. So I wrote:

No, I can't say I could find anything to be thankful for, at least not to any "god", although I am thankful to my friends for their friendship and help. I don't feel any particular inclination to thank someone for "help" which involves making the biggest possible wreck my life could have, and intolerable misery for others. I may feel pleasure on smelling a cup of coffee brewing or tasting a fine brandy, but not thankfulness. I feel thankfulness for those pleasures which involve another person to whom I can be thankful. [...]

In your last letter you mentioned that your heart ached whenever you thought of Jeanette. Indeed it should, considering the fact that according to your set of beliefs, your merciful god has her roasting in hell. I know that your defensive response will be that "we cannot know these things," a very necessary response for you in order to keep your distance between your beliefs and their afflicting any of the people you may have personally known and loved. It's much easier to accept the notion of hell where it applies to Turks or Mexicans or criminals or any other anonymous category. The fact is that Jeanette did not hold your beliefs or anything like them, and neither do I, which forces you to believe that she is there and I'm going there. It must be much harder for you to live with your beliefs than you could even incorrectly suppose it is for me to live without them. I might have hoped that if you found it necessary to have some sort of god in your life, you could have found one who was somewhat less barbaric. The fact that you have chosen not to is, as a direct consequence, reflected in your support of capital punishment, tacit approval of slavery, and condemnation of a number of things which make human life more enjoyable, and sometimes make survival possible.

My awareness of what your beliefs entail has somewhat dampened my enthusiasm for correspondence, and if in our correspondence we are to avoid touching on these matters, it would be very limited indeed, given the degree to which you have based your lives on them.

I am glad to say that over the years since then, both of my brothers abandoned more and more of the Fundamentalist aspects of their beliefs (a process undoubtedly accelerated by their leaving the Meeting). Instead they adopted a kind of "Christianity Lite" that used the same barbaric Bible, and worshipped the same psychopathic god, but suppressed most of its nasty contents by drawing a velvet glove over the iron fist, or weaving over them a veil of sweetness and love that so many of their countrymen were finding more palatable.

The euphoria I was feeling from my encounters with Lena was real, as were the vast improvements in my diet, even if the underlying reasons were not the stuff that solid foundations are made on. [*Before you go correcting my choice of preposition, refer to Shakespeare's "such stuff that dreams are made on"* (The Tempest, *act 4, scene*).] I was no longer feeling depressed *all* the time, which in itself was a tremendous relief. My self-confidence was returning, probably too fast for me to handle wisely, and my will to live was visceral.

The extension that Henry obtained for me (on the deadline to have the house ready for final inspection by the municipal and building authorities so that the government loan could be finalized) had been generously postponed nearly a year, until the spring of 1978. And now the energy and strength to finalize it began returning to me. I started laying the tiles in the living room in the early days of December, and I completed packing the big trunk I later shipped to Marilyn, in January.

My original, pre-Lena intention was to spend at least two weeks at Christmas in Binningen with Bob, but the new state of affairs made me want to cut that trip short. One reason was that my top priority was now to spend as much time with

Lena as possible; the other was probably that I began to notice that Lena's charm seemed to work on just about every male she met. I'm not convinced that this was her *intention*; her natural charm simply had that effect (it certainly did on me!), and my self-confidence still had a long way to go. And she was exceptionally photogenic – particularly when she was aware of the presence of a camera.

I told Bob I'd be leaving Malmö and Copenhagen on December 21st (by train; my associations of flying to Basel with Jeanette were still too painful), arriving the next day, and leaving Basel on the 29th, arriving home in the late afternoon on the 30th. Lena said she'd take the ferry over to meet me at the central station in Copenhagen, and I was so thrilled by her offer that I booked a table for two at *Packhuset 71*, a rustically luxurious restaurant in the cellar of a hotel in a converted warehouse in the colorful Nyhavn district, near the ferry terminals. After that, we would go to the nearby Danish Royal Ballet before taking a late ferry home to Malmö. I had to dig deep into my meager savings for that night on the town! I asked her if we could spend New Year's Eve together, and she also said *yes* to that. *What joy!*

On the Friday before I left for Basel, I asked Lena if we could meet that evening, but she said she'd promised to babysit for her niece, Lina. Eva and her common-law husband Jan were going to some big party that would last half the night. But Eva (five months older than me) told Lena that it might be more fun for Lena if I joined her (!) in the baby-sitting, so I went to Lena's place after she got off work in the late afternoon, and we walked together to her sister's place on Mångatan.

I was kind of nervous about meeting Eva and Jan for the first time, but Eva turned out to be a real peach. She made no attempt to hide her open appraisal of my looks, nor her ostentatious, grinning nod of approval to Lena (despite my many months of grief having done quite a bit to recast me either as a hippie or as the Alaskan trapper I'd once aspired to be). Lena tried to ignore her nodding sister. Eva, a registered nurse, was full of warmth, fire, vigor, spontaneity, laughter and curiosity – I liked her instantly.

Jan, a medical doctor (a few years older than me), seemed to be a vastly different sort of person from Eva. I felt he projected a kind of naïve arrogance, while trying hard to be cool; his laughter sounded forced. He seemed to think that I'd be convinced of his skills in English if he frequently and dramatically exclaimed "*Gosh!*" He was extremely near-sighted. There seemed to me to be little spontaneity about him. But at the same time I was well aware of how *very* unreliable first impressions can be.

Apparently Eva and Jan met in Gothenburg, where he came from and where Eva also lived for a few years, concurrently with Lena. I had no idea whether their relationship was ever serious then or not, but it had at least been intimate enough to get Eva pregnant. Jan wanted no part of it, but Eva did, so she went through with the pregnancy and began raising Lina entirely on her own. A year or more later, Jan took a job at the Lund University Hospital and moved to Skåne. Shortly before Lena returned to Sweden, Eva and Lina moved down to Lund and in with Jan under circumstances I knew nothing about. But Lina, who was now almost five, was an absolutely darling little girl.

Soon Jan and Eva were off to their party, while Lena and I began playing games with little Lina, which (and who) was great fun. She was a bit shy of me for the first few minutes, but the shyness melted away quickly. We had dinner together – Lena had been grocery shopping and wanted to cook for me herself – and we had a little wine. When Lina began to get sleepy, we put her to bed, and then we followed suit. I badly wanted this introduction to Eva to mean a new level in my relationship with Lena, closer, more permanent. Maybe the start of a new life in which grief no longer dominated everything?

On December 20th, the day before my departure for Basel, I wrote Mom that I was getting out more and meeting people. I didn't mention any details. Mom said she'd like to crochet something for me, anything I wanted, so I suggested a big bedspread for my future queen-size bed, in various shades of dark green.

I wrote one effusively affectionate letter to Lena on the train, for mailing as soon as possible after my arrival at the Bahnhof SBB in central Basel, where Bob was waiting to meet me, and another the following day, hoping that Lena would receive them both before my return. My arrival at Bob's place was concurrent with a verbal outpouring on my part, in praise of Lena, on the transformation of my soul, on the banishment of my sorrows, on the miracle of love, on carnal pleasures the like of which I'd never known, on my new-found and far-flung aspirations for the future. I couldn't see these reactions as most likely to be expressions of my desperation with my ongoing grief. But Bob almost certainly did. My monologue was so enthusiastic and optimistic that Bob's initial vicarious joy soon turned to alarm.

Make no mistake: Bob was 100% in favor of things going well for me, but he apparently felt there could be some justification for taking a long-term view when considering a long-term relationship, of allowing feelings to develop strong roots and mature with a certain degree of caution, above all taking care to ascertain whether sufficient *reciprocity* might be in evidence. Short-term relationships were another matter; the precautions were more physical; pregnancy – not an issue for me – and STDs were such considerations. Another was, as in all morality as far as Bob was concerned, *never to exploit.*

Bob wanted me to let go, to give my libido free rein, but not necessarily to let it run amuck, into a possible quagmire of *unrequited* love that would lead me into mortal danger. At the same time, he wanted to avoid smothering my resurgent enthusiasm; he could see that my joy was genuine enough, just not as stable or well-directed as he wanted it to be or as I'd allowed myself to be convinced that it was. All his attempts to get me to take a few deep breaths and look at what was going on with a greater degree of rationality and distance only irritated me, however, and made me see him as a killjoy.

I'm sure he recognized my reactions; he backed off as best he could. Behind his ill-disguised troubled countenance, he was thinking, as he later admitted, "*This is a situation that calls for great caution!*"; while I, behind my equally ill-disguised euphoric countenance was thinking, "*This is no time for caution!*"

He did his best to get me to talk about other things – my work on the house, Sonja, music, the Nobel Peace Prize to Amnesty International (an organization whose efforts we both avidly supported), the many post-mortem "sightings" of Elvis Presley – anything to divert me from my one-track conversation. I just couldn't wait to get back, to see Lena, to lie in her arms. All Bob could do was hope that this wasn't going to blow up in my face; all I could do was hope to prove him wrong.

Lena was waiting for me at the Central Station in the heart of Copenhagen when I arrived. I was breathless. Had she received my letters? *Yes.* Was she angry or displeased by them? *No, why should she be?* I trembled with relief, and struggled to avoid bursting into tears of joy – my feelings were overwhelming me that much. I couldn't understand it. [*I couldn't see how much of a train wreck my life remained, and how two massive forces at once – grief and infatuation – were more than I could hope to handle.*]

We had a wonderful meal at the restaurant and talked about many things. As we strolled over to Kongens Nytorv to the ballet, I was so nervous that I had to lean up against a pillar while telling her that I was in love with her. Her brow wrinkled slightly. She said she was worried that I might expect her to feel the same. Although I was grievously disappointed, I fibbed and said I understood that she didn't; it wasn't necessary, so there was no cause for alarm. She smiled. When we returned on a late ferry to spend a passionate night in Malmö, I was convinced that I'd already shattered all Bob's misgivings.

We also spent a quiet and cozy New Year's Eve at Korngatan, and watched some fireworks out the window. Both of us were glad that 1977 was over at last, although we didn't talk about why; our reasons were so vastly different, and we were looking for such vastly different things.

Eating and drinking were merely fuel for our passion. Should I have been asking myself whether there is a distinction between passion and lust? I was trying unsuccessfully, distracted by my exuberant dizziness, to hear a voice of reason from within me. I already sensed a clear distinction between love and lust – not that they are by any means mutually exclusive, but that they are not necessarily interdependent. Maybe passion is the overlap between love and lust? Can passion and love can be the same, and passion and lust the same, but love and lust totally different? So if Lena and I were expressing indiscernibly similar and intense passion, could one of us be experiencing it from the perspective of love, and the other from lust? And what might the consequences be if that were so?

I think I must have *felt* hints of these questions that New Year's Eve, but I certainly didn't *think* of them. Something else I didn't think of was the simple fact that no matter how much you may love someone, it doesn't mean that they love you, nor that they have any duty to love you, nor that you're entitled to any expectations that they will *ever* come to love you. *Love must be given freely to have any value at all*! Why was that so hard for me to see? Love is more than blind, it's also deaf. And unrequited love is probably also dumb.

Lena told me that she'd owned a piano before she left for Sacramento, and had put it into storage until she knew more about her future. Now, in her tiny student room at Ulrikedal, she had no room for it, but Eva was going to keep it at her place so that Lena wouldn't have to pay for storage (and Eva welcomed the chance to encourage Lina to learn). I pointed out that there was plenty of room for it at my place, for example in my living room or in my studio. I suspect that she thought that this eccentric American guy was *already* trying to get her to move in with him. And I suspect that she was right, and that this eccentric American was *already* madly in love with her.

Lena's *apparent* acceptance of my love (I had no interest in further analysis) was enough to start removing my depression, more and more rapidly; I began to sketch again. The month of January 1978 was for me a dizzying ride up a winding mountain road without a guardrail, full of twists and turns, thrills and chills, hope and despair. My exuberant optimism that month fostered my enthusiasm for love and for Lena. It also blinded me to the dangers of being let down, shot down.

Lena and I met every single day in January, by my rose-colored reckoning. If we met on a Sunday, then only met briefly on Monday (before parting early in the morning), and then not again till Tuesday evening and parting early Wednesday morning, I still counted it as four days in a row, using my creative record-keeping.

That same January, I also completed the walls in the living room and laid the tile floor there, which meant that the house was now complete enough for final inspection, even though it was still a workroom. As a result, I formally requested the final inspection. Following Lena's suggestion and example, I also registered with the Teachers' Exchange to take on short-term substitute teaching assignments in Malmö, which in my case I presumed would mostly consist of teaching English at high schools. I needed to get myself off the unemployment benefits I'd been subsisting on and start earning some money, and I felt that my mental balance had pretty much returned – not that I was by any means qualified to be the judge of that! I and the other teachers from Hamadi's defunct school were still waiting for the promised reimbursement from the government for the salaries that Hamadi made off with nearly a year earlier, so a cash injection of any sort would be most welcome.

It seemed to take forever before I got my first lousy assignment: to teach a few lessons for a high school class at Latinskolan. It was not an English course, to my surprise, but one in *religion*! It would just be for the one day (the ordinary teacher had an emergency visit to a doctor, or something like that). I found myself facing 25 Swedish youngsters (they were around 17 years old), and I had no intention of spending half the lesson learning from them what their assignments were, and the rest of the time acquainting myself with their textbooks, and trying to come up with what a certified religion teacher would or should have been doing.

Since religion was always a topic of exceptional interest and relevance to me [*this information may come as a surprise to my most inattentive readers!*], I decided to find out what my students truly thought about the subject as a whole, not what items of information they could cough up about what their textbook said. So I conducted a poll (easy enough with 25 students; each one represented 4%). *How many of you go to church every week?* 0%. *How many go once a month?* One student, 4% *How many of you go more than once a year?* 8% (including the one who went once a month). *How many of you believe in god?* 4%. *How many of you have been confirmed?* 92%. *How many of you would have your child christened?* 96%.

I was flabbergasted by the last two answers – particularly in view of the first four. I asked them if they didn't see an element of hypocrisy in being confirmed into church membership or having their child christened if it entailed a solemn promise to raise their child to believe in and worship a certain god, even if they didn't themselves?! That launched a long discussion on how religion in Sweden was nothing more than tradition (for all but one of them), and was almost entirely limited to christening and confirmation *gifts* and get-togethers, not faith or superstition. It revealed an aspect of Swedish society that I found both positive and deplorable, both honest and hypocritical, and I wasn't able to get my head fully around it [*and I still haven't as I write this*].

Some small part of me was occasionally willing to admit that I had a long way to go to overcome my anxiety and insecurity. I was all too willing to overlook or dismiss such concerns if given any excuse at all (like when Lena *returned* my embrace). I flatly refused to notice that *all* our embraces were instigated or initiated by me; my joy always came from having them *returned*, never from being given them. [*In hindsight, I realize I'd lost sight of Bob's admonition always to make sure there was evidence of sufficient* reciprocity *in trying to build any kind of long-term relationship.*]

Some things, however, were becoming more difficult to overlook, even for me. She told me, on several occasions (including both shortly before and shortly after making love with me) that she was ready to go back to Larry. It seemed that all he had to do was say the word, and she would be off (so I have to presume he never did). It was a subject so painful to me that I didn't want to dwell on why he didn't, nor on why she still felt that way about him, nor least of all why she was telling *me* about it! I paid no attention to the possible implications of the fact that she and Larry always spoke English with each other, but with me she clearly preferred to speak Swedish. (Was he such a linguistic chauvinist that he lived in Sweden for years without bothering to learn the language fluently?)

One day Lena announced that she had a problem with my laminated "question-mark" collage of Jeanette. What did I do? I removed it from the kitchen wall.

Then she told me she had a problem with the inscription on the fireplace about me and Jeanette having rebuilt the house. What did I do? I plastered it over. Was she consciously trying to get me to expunge Jeanette from my life? And why, *why* did I accept it? Why was it OK for her to tell me about the time she forgot to remove her tampon and one of her boyfriends drove it up into her uterus during coitus, but it was *not* OK for me to revere the memory of my darling wife, which as far as I could see posed no threat to my love for Lena?

Somewhere in the deepest recesses of my consciousness, I sensed that there was no balance here, no reciprocity. Despite the frequency of our meetings and the love or lust associated with them, all was not well. I'd let my feelings run away with me prematurely, before I'd healed, before I was ready to face life again, before I was equipped to take on such a dangerous game. There was no evidence that Lena's reciprocity applied to anything but the lust part. She told me about herself but didn't want to hear about my life, and never expressed any interest in my paintings beyond acknowledging their existence. That was a great disappointment to me, but I convinced myself that the fault was mine in expecting anything else. She did, however, express a great deal of interest in getting to know the three Norwegian students living above her – three guys – and I couldn't understand that she couldn't understand how jealous that might make me feel. Or maybe she did.

The point I'd missed completely, the only point that could make sense, was that from her perspective she was merely out for a little adventure, not love or a relationship. She, at least at that point in her life, wanted to be needed and loved without needing or loving. Lust was all we had in common.

On January 26th, I got a call from Isobel saying that she and Björn had signed the papers to buy a newly built terraced house in Oxie, on the southeastern outskirts of Malmö, and would be moving there on June 1st. This would further limit my visits to their place – Oxie was on the far side of town, beyond my cycling range.

On the Saturday morning two days later, Lena and I were awakened at her place in Lund by a phone call from her mother; her parents were just about to leave Barkåkra for Lund, to visit her and Eva, and would be arriving in just over an hour. This sent Lena scrambling to tidy up. I was looking forward to the opportunity to meet them at last, but Lena said there was no way that was going to happen. I had to clear out immediately. She wasn't about to suffer any possible scorn from them at finding her with "another American", and she seemed terrified about how her austere father would react. So I was soon gone, booted out, evicted.

During the day on Sunday, Rob and Chris phoned from London and urged me to come and visit them. I said I might. Lena phoned me in the early afternoon to let me know that the coast was clear again – her parents had returned to Barkåkra. She laughed a bit nervously, and said it was a shame she'd had to kick me out so unceremoniously, and would I like to come back that evening? When I got to her place, she received me with more warmth and affection than ever before. I was euphoric when I took the bus home the next morning.

When I returned to Lund that evening, however, an icy barrier had fallen over her. I was confused, and asked her what was up. She said she'd been thinking about it and decided she didn't want *any* involvement with *any*one on an emotional level for a *long* time. To underline this, she said she was going to phone Larry in the States.

Her coldness towards me grew, and with it, my depression began returning from wherever it had been hiding for a couple of months. Then she told me couldn't see me "for a while" (undefined), that she suddenly felt that the great amount of time we'd been spending together was all a bit too much for her; she needed a cooling-off period; she wanted to start "seeing" some other boys too (I knew the euphemism – she also said she'd start taking the Pill again the next day). Just like that. And I started falling apart.

CHAPTER 4

Convulsion and catharsis

I'd failed utterly to heed Isobel's persistent advice that I should play hard-to-get with Lena. I screwed that up completely. I was going for a life-long relationship of love and harmony (not her fault – it was *my* wish), and she was going for transient fun and adventure (not her fault that she didn't want more). My aims were thus entirely at cross-purposes with hers, however much the physical expression of those contrary aims may have been difficult to distinguish, at least for me. I was the one who was completely fucked up by her sudden and inexplicable rejection. I was in free fall, plummeting, backwards into the abyss, back to drinking and smoking to get there faster, as if there were no tomorrow, or at least no tomorrow that I wanted any part of.

This turn of events was Bob's worst nightmare, and would have been mine if my own rosy dream world hadn't made it impossible for me to perceive any need whatsoever to tread carefully. Far worse than that, I couldn't see how perilously fragile I still was, how much grieving I had left to do. I had no prior experience of deep, bottomless grief! I knew nothing of how harrowing and judgment-obliterating it could be. I knew nothing of its course, its time, its rules and chaos. I desperately wanted to be whole, and yet was so unready to live again, so out of balance in myself that any bump in the road would send me careening into the nearest ditch – or over the nearest cliff.

Lena had never asked me to be the love of her life. She'd never asked for *love* at all, nor did she give me the slightest indication that she was offering me anything but a good time with uninhibited sex – at most a few random hours or weeks of affection and intimacy – in other words, a transient fling. Had I been at all rational, I would have realized that my desperation wasn't her *fault*. All the intensity, the despair of unrequited love, was coming from *me*. I had no reason to presume that she'd signed up for anything beyond animal desires and rapturous orgasms. Could I then in any way hold her responsible for what was happening to me? Did I? I don't think I did, it just hurt like an open wound not to have her.

I *did* see that I couldn't help how *I* felt, any more than she could help how she *didn't* feel. She didn't "make me" love her; that was my own responsibility. [*In so many aspects of human life and relationships, it's so easy – far too easy – to say that "he or she hurt me." That is not quite true, unless it was the other person's* intention *to hurt you, which it seldom is. So why don't people take at least some of the responsibility for their own hurt and stop seeking to blame it all on others?!*]

But I couldn't see quite that far then. From my tortured perspective, it was easier for me to think it looked like this: if only she behaved the way I wanted her to, I wouldn't be hurting, would I? *Ergo*, it was her fault that I was hurting. There was nothing to stop me from conveniently piling the blame for *my* hurt on her – apart from the fact that I had absolutely no right or reason to expect her to behave the way I wanted her to.

Bob, my faithful gadfly, was determined not to let me get away with my ambitious attempts to destroy logic and rationality. He saw my "arguments" as yet another of the many guises of self-pity: blaming others for how they "make" you feel, when how you feel is ultimately *nearly* always your own doing and your very own responsibility.

But once again, I was too emotionally crippled to listen to Bob's clear voice of reason. I'd suffered so much in the past year that on some obscene level I welcomed the opportunity to wallow in despair once more.

> *This just wasn't the Lena I had known, it couldn't be, it wasn't possible, I couldn't believe it. Had she just used me to build up her own ego after the trauma of leaving her fiancé? Could she really be that cruelly cold after I had only known her to be warm and affectionate? What the hell was going on? She only seemed to want to finish sewing the shades she had promised to do for me in return for my having given her a clock-radio, and then she would be done with me.*

Such were the agonized thoughts (the above is *verbatim* from notes I made at the time) – no, not thoughts, mere *rantings, whining!* – that were plaguing me day and night. They were adolescent, irrational and unfair. But they were the only activity I was able to generate in my cranium, even though I was capable of expressing them – couching them, dressing them up – in more elegant (pseudo-intellectual) terms, especially when writing about them to Bob.

In early February, I could feel my state of mind shifting profoundly, dangerously. I also had two visits from building inspectors. One was from the government loan office, to see whether the big house met their requirements for approval. This was important to me because it would not only significantly reduce the interest rate and thus my living expenses, it would close the door on the only deadline I had.

(The renovation of the little house wasn't covered by the government loan and thus didn't require this inspector's approval.) In the back of my mind, in this new state of mind, I was starting to go about closing doors, eliminating all deadlines but the real one.

The loan inspector was a friendly, middle-aged man who smiled most of the time, quickly sailed through the house, glanced at the triple-glazed windows, asked about the thickness of the insulation in the walls and roof, told me everything looked great, ticked some boxes and signed a report. As he handed me my copy, he apologized for being in a hurry, but said there was obviously no need to dwell on my dwelling any further. Then he wished me luck and was out the door again.

The second inspector came from the municipal building authority. He was a real clipboard bureaucrat, the polar opposite of the first. Fortunately, I only needed him to approve the big house at this point, even though my application for a municipal building permit applied to both the big house and the little house. Work on the little house was years away from completion, but the municipal permit had a much longer completion deadline, one that I was beginning to feel that I might never be concerned with.

The municipal inspector scrutinized everything, and did his best to find shortcomings in my adherence to the regulations. He started writing down one of them, shaking his head gravely: I'd failed to install a child-safety catch on the knife drawer in the kitchen. I told him I had no children. He said that didn't matter; I might have some one day. Instead of getting him involved in the story of my vasectomy, I merely commented that as a responsible parent, if I ever became one, I would certainly see to that then. I also asked what was to prevent me from having a child-safety catch on one drawer, and then keeping my knives in another. He just shook his head again (without replying) and moved on, pen raised to be ready to document the next evidence of my negligent naughtiness.

He pointed out that the two openable, top-hung ground-floor windows also lacked child-safety catches. I pointed out that (a) the triple-glazed window was far too heavy for a child to open anyway; and (b) that since the window ledge was the same height above the floor as it was above the sidewalk level outside, the non-perilous 65-70 cm height a child would have to climb to reach the too-heavy-for-a-child-to-open window was thus as great as the non-perilous distance said child could fall to the sidewalk; and (c) I had no children. Mr Clipboard found my logic peccable, in the sense that he felt it unacceptable, but he declined to tell me why. Fortunately, he agreed to grant me provisional approval (for the sake of the government loan, which required municipal corroboration), the provision being that I rectify the aforementioned shortcomings in the big house prior to obtaining final municipal approval for both big and little houses when that day arrived. [*When that day arrived, I didn't bother to request final inspection. I did, however, install child-safety catches on two knife drawers – but only years later, once I had children, and only on the drawers where I actually kept knives.*]

One of the many differences I noticed about Swedish universities (compared to the US) was that they had no fraternities or sororities (although I had no recollection of any at San Francisco State, nor at UBC, but then I never looked for them). Instead they had clubs or associations they called "nations" – named after some of Sweden's provinces. These "nations" were established as far back as the 17th century for students coming from the respective provinces (membership back then was often obligatory), but they gradually came to represent various ideologies or other interests, with open membership. For non-members, they often represented nothing more than popular discos.

Lena mentioned several times that she'd visited the disco at Smålands Nation a few times, and although I had absolutely no interest in discos (in fact, I'd never been to one in my life – I wasn't a fan of the kind of music they offered), I was interested in the possibility of a "chance" encounter with her there one Friday evening, so I made my way down to Lundavägen, and waited for the next orange-and-custard-colored bus to Lund. I first walked past her building – a fair detour – stopping to gaze up towards her window, my heart pounding. I stood there for a long time, hurting.

Björn and Isobel told me to forget her. I tried, but I couldn't. Her window was dark. Not home? On to the disco I went, slowly, struggling with anxiety, fear, and anticipation. About halfway there, walking alone in the dark evening along Dalbyvägen, I saw Lena walking towards me, also alone.

At first, I could hardly believe my good fortune. But Lena was *not at all* pleased to see me, and wondered what the hell I was doing there – *stalking* her!? (I wonder if Eliza accused Freddie of stalking her when he sang "*On the street where you live*"....) I said I was just on my way to the disco, and she snorted sarcastically that she didn't realize I liked discos. Then she quickly passed me by and continued heading in the direction of her apartment. I didn't know what to do. I lingered, watching her go, but she didn't look back. I thought I might as well go to the disco anyway, to see what it was like. I soon wished I hadn't. It was full of people at least ten years younger than me. They were mostly in their early or mid-20s, while I was going on 33, which *mattered* – especially to them – at that age. It was so noisy I could hardly hear myself think, let alone hope to have a conversation with anybody, and so dark I could hardly see. Nearly all the girls were painted up ("made up" doesn't cover it, except in the sense of "make-believe"), and everybody seemed to be on the prowl. I guess that was to be expected, but it felt to me like a real meat market, and it sickened me. I doubt that I remained there longer than 15 minutes before plunging back into the stillness of the night alone. I caught the next bus back to Malmö.

With increasing desperation I began looking around for other options (anything but a disco) where I might find someone to hold onto as the storm inside my head and heart was ripping me apart. I'd heard of a dance place in the ground-floor cafeteria of Pilgården, the original venue of Demaret's Language School where I'd worked at my first job in Sweden back in the spring of 1970. It wasn't as bad as the disco in Lund; it was at least possible to have a conversation while seated at one of the surrounding tables, but I couldn't shake my depression; it was coming from within, from some hollow, cavernous fissure opening up.

I was fairly drunk when I slid into a conversation with a few other young people, none of whom seemed to have known each other before. Most of my conversation was with an American guy named George. We were soon joined by a fairly pretty, extremely big-busted Swedish girl named Marie, who seemed eager to catch every word of English George and I were saying. We lost track of time discussing long-forgotten topics, until someone from the staff pointed out that it was closing time, so the three of us continued dredging words at Korngatan for another hour or two. (I think we all cycled there.) But nothing more came of that.

My weight was plummeting again (not eating can do that), and I'd become pretty unstable mentally, like a time bomb that might explode at any moment, unless it imploded or just fizzled. It's possible that I was given a few hours of substitute teaching at a couple of schools around Malmö during this time, but by now I had so much chaos, despair, apathy, sorrow and rage within me that little registered. All my possibilities for new feelings were blocked by a kind of human bondage (cf. Somerset Maugham's novel of that name): my inability to get Lena out of my head.

A Sea of Troubles

I heard from her about once or twice a week; it was as if she wanted to make sure she was keeping me "on the hook". She agreed to let me take her to the movies once, to see *Looking for Mr. Goodbar*, a film with Diane Keaton about a schoolteacher who spurns love in favor of wilder and wilder sexual adventure and ends up being murdered. Lena didn't like it at all; I saw a lot of Lena in it and ached to be wrong, but I said nothing. She must have sensed the parallels I saw, because she said, "*You know, I'm not like her at all!*"

I continued to feel hopelessly at her beck and call, or like a mouse in the clutches of a cat not sufficiently hungry to deliver the *coup de grâce*. I had no idea for how long that might continue. I recalled that she said she was always the one to break up whatever relationships she'd had. I also knew that those were seldom clean breaks; she seemed to like keeping a guy or two (like Larry) on the back burner, and now one of those sorry guys was me.

The transition to mere friendship in my relations with Sonja might have gone smoothly if she hadn't been roped into a terribly demanding assignment as a last-minute stand-in for the lead role in a production of *Katerina Blum* at the Malmö City Theater. The role itself was tough enough, but the short notice she was given caused her unbearable stress. Sometime in mid-February, she more or less collapsed during a rehearsal. When some of her friends and colleagues took care of her, she told them that she wanted to see me, so they bundled her into a taxi bound for Korngatan at 10 PM. And I was the one she could turn to?! Talk about the blind leading the blind! She stayed with me until I had to leave for London on the 19th; then she went to Stockholm instead. From Lena, only silence.

Rob and Chris said they didn't miss Sweden at all – they were emphatic about that – in spite of the high cost of living in London. My instability was rampant during my stay with them, which probably alarmed them quite a lot. I have a vague memory of unintentionally waking them up in the middle of the night one night with my uncontrolled and drunken sobbing on the middle of their living room floor (where I was supposed to be sleeping on the couch). And then I would have a few moments or hours of relatively normal behavior.

On Monday, February 27th, the day after I got home from London, I wrote Bob about it:

> *I've never felt so lonely in my life walking through the crowds of London. It really got to me. I had to go and sit in Hyde Park and count trees and look for a crocus. My*

nerves are getting frazzled. I'm jumpy as a cat. I've been feeling so damned depressed and, in spite of my best efforts and intentions not to, downright suicidal. I think this business with Lena has really fucked up my head. The shitty thing about it: I don't hear mewling violins and see soft petals falling on wet misty streets when the notion of my own death pops into my head, i.e. no Byronic bunk; but the notions come anyway, like big electromagnets suddenly switching on, and you find you've been welded into a suit of armor.

I know these thoughts are a pile of garbage, and I do my best to drive them away or strip them of their vestiges of logic or pretend they don't exist or plead with them to leave me alone or ridicule them or bash them in the teeth. They still LURK. So what in the name of DNA do I do?

The next day I shipped the big trunk to Marilyn. I was told it would arrive in late March. How fitting. My weight was down below 70 kg, as low as it had been since I was a scrawny kid trying to gain weight so I could play high school football. I had to make new holes in my belts. Sending off that trunk and getting the house inspected relieved me of all the remaining obligations I could identify. My work was done, finished, complete. *It is enough.*

February was about to pass into March, and all my old depression had returned, not just in full force, but in double strength, engulfing me like a landslide of mental garbage. For days I ingested nothing but alcohol. I had a cigarette going from the time I woke up and for as long as I remained conscious. Life was more than I could cope with. I had to find a way to stop the pain, the gnawing, devouring agony. A way out. Like a lightning flash through the mountain of shit that was my life, I got an idea; I would make a plan.

On March 1st, I worked out that Jeanette was 32 years, 8 months and 6 days old when she died. Then I calculated that on May 19th I would be exactly the same age as Jeanette was when she died. *That would be the day.* It would give me just over two and a half months to tie up loose ends, or at least to minimize the chaos I would be leaving behind for my brothers – and Bob! – to deal with. But I couldn't tell them, not even Bob. I didn't want to have to deal with efforts to dissuade me.

The house had been inspected. That was taken care of. The trunk had been sent. I could consolidate my bank accounts into a single account. I could review and consolidate all the bureaucratic things that had been involved in settling Jeanette's estate in order to simplify the proceedings for whomever would take it upon himself to deal with them (Al?). *It's hard enough without all that, too.*

It had always been so wrenchingly hard *not knowing why*, never being able to understand what drove her. I didn't want to put anyone through that, the endless wondering that tortured me, the unquenchable feeling that there must have been <u>something</u> I could have done. So I decided to sit down and write my explanation, my story, and make it completely clear that I was making a decision – my final decision – with eyes wide open, without hesitation. I would leave no unanswered questions apart from those I couldn't answer about Jeanette.

I wanted my story to be (or at least to sound) rational, level-headed, not like some treatise written in a state of wild-eyed agitation. Somewhat to my surprise, my decision to write my story, all the way to the end, to the very last second, brought me an unexpected sense of inner calm. At last I knew where I wanted to go and how I wanted to get there.

Thus, on March 2nd, early in the morning, with a portable typewriter, a stack of blank sheets of paper, several bottles of whisky and a carton or more of cigarettes, I sat down to write.

Without ever consciously searching for an approach, the complete structure of the story had sprung into my head, all at once (although with an awful lot of strutting, staggering and fretting). Now it was simply a matter of typing it out. My morbid plan generated sheet after sheet of single-spaced text. I wove my story out of my too-brief past and my too-long remaining future. In alternate paragraphs I described how I foresaw May 19th developing, and how my life had developed from my earliest childhood until how I envisaged it ending on that same date. The two story lines would thus slowly converge, meeting on May 19th, at the moment when I hanged myself, exactly where Jeanette hanged herself, after I'd lived the exact same number of days on this planet as she did. I called my story *The Unparallel Lines*.

I worked feverishly – not only on the actual writing, but on reviewing in my mind everything that had happened in my life, picking out whatever things I felt had shaped me more than the rest. But that was just the half of it. The other half was looking ahead to that final day, picturing the letters of condolence/explanation/apology that I would write to Bob and my brothers. I would also write to Björn regarding a few practical matters and to thank him and Isobel for trying. (But I had nothing more to say to Lena.)

I also wrote about all the banal trivia that make up a day of dying hope and shattered dreams, trying to paint a realistic picture of what would happen, what I fully intended to happen – what I had firmly decided to *make* happen – seen through the resignation and pain I was feeling at the time I wrote it. It meant that I spent hours pacing the floor, staring off into space to follow the gaze of my mind's eye, topping up my level of inebriation to bolster my courage to go on and on, while I went on smoking, smoking, smoking.

One thing I did very little was sleep. My mind was racing and wouldn't shut down, wouldn't even slow down. I would feel exhausted one minute, flop down on my mattress, only to jump up wide awake minutes later. In one sense, I didn't even come up for air, since my mouth was hardly ever without a lighted cigarette in it.

I had a desperate, single-minded purpose: to get it all down, the whole story, and then use those two months or so to carefully prepare for that Big Final Day. Nothing else mattered to me anymore. I'd crossed that line and come to the end of my process, one that would also tally 32 years, 8 months and 6 days. And then it would all be over. The English language has many words and euphemisms for "die"; so does Swedish. But Swedish has one tender and compassionate word that is particularly apt in many cases: *avlida*, literally "to cease suffering." I had applied it to Jeanette. It would now apply to me. Seeing that, understanding it in that way, with that tender definition, strengthened the strange, calming effect on me.

I worked on my story for nine maddeningly intense days and nights, seldom retracing my steps or my words, with remarkable discipline for a drunk. (This was before the age of word processors, so if I forgot something eight pages ago, I'd have to rewrite everything that came after it; I avoided that need by thinking the wording of each part through before typing.) For some reason, I used pseudonyms throughout, but since I made no attempt to change dates and locations, the pseudonyms were quite transparent. Maybe using the real names was just too honest for me to handle at the time. [*But I did my utmost not to lie or distort, even though I was fully aware that I was writing from my own subjective perspective (as indeed I'm doing here in* Hindsights*).*]

In the early hours of the morning on the ninth day of writing, Friday, March 10th, when I came to the final sentence of the final paragraph, the part when I would take my final step forward into the abyss, when my work was done, I collapsed. I instantly fell into a deep sleep until I was awakened just before noon by the phone. The moment I woke up, before I grabbed the phone, I felt that something was different, vastly different. I was a different person, transformed in some way. The raging current of my self-destruction had been turned awry. The gnawing, debilitating, omnipresent background was no longer there. I could breathe.

The caller was the principal at KomVux, Malmö's adult education school. He wanted to know if I could take over a class, starting on Monday morning! I didn't know him at all, a total stranger. We'd never spoken to each other before, so he had no reason to suppose that the shaky, sleepy, confused voice he heard on end of the line was not my normal voice. He asked me if I could please come to the school on Fågelbacksgatan that same afternoon to talk it over. I was stunned, thought I must have misunderstood what he'd said about a job. I was totally disoriented – but I was not in pain. I said I'd be there at 2 PM.

More than a decade earlier, I learned the meaning of "catharsis" from various ancient Greek tragedies I'd read, at least in the academic sense of the word, but I'd never understood it viscerally. Now I did.

CHAPTER 5

Joie de vivre

Powerful feelings of disorientation and newness and *life*, all around me, everywhere I looked and thought and felt. I couldn't grasp what had happened while I wrote, while I slept, when I awoke, what that bizarre, other-worldly phone call was all about. It felt like I'd been through a complete metamorphosis from caterpillar to butterfly, like I'd walked onto a Hollywood set where nothing was what it seemed, nothing was real, and yet it all seemed very real, more real than anything I'd experienced for well over a year. Some of the weirdness stemmed from not being able to identify what was gone. You tend not to notice what *isn't* there (*Hey, look at that moose that isn't there!*), and when something as huge as a deep depression – one that has constrained and tormented and burdened every moment, strangled every attempted thought, and tortured every feeling to an extent you'd never known, never known *possible*, for so long that you've become used to it, like your constant ghoulish companion – is suddenly just *gone*, what remains in its place is like the yellowed grass full of sowbugs under the sheet of plywood that's been left lying on the lawn since last spring. It's nothing you've ever seen before. And it will take some getting used to, to start thinking, reasoning, feeling, growing normally again.

I have to get dressed. Getting dressed had not necessarily been part of my morning (or day) for the past *year. No, first I have to take a shower. And trim my beard, and try to look something like a civilized human being*. None of this had been part of my morning routine for over a month. Once I got dressed, I would find out where exactly this Fågelbacksskolan (the school, my potential new temporary employer) was situated.

I had to look up Fågelbacksgatan (the eponymous street) on a map; I'd heard the name but wasn't sure where it was. The map revealed that it ran along one side of the Kronprinsen complex, close to where Henry and I played tennis and he worked, only a few blocks from the laundromat on Mariedalsvägen that Jeanette and I used to cycle to with our laundry, and a few blocks from Herrestadsgatan and the apartment where we lived for a few weeks while waiting for our work permits to come through. Fågelbacksskolan was marked on the map. I knew exactly how to get there; it would take me about 15 minutes to cycle there from home. There was no time for breakfast – or lunch.

KomVux was currently housed in Fågelbacksskolan, an unimpressive yellowish brick building. It wasn't until I entered the building that I began to wonder about the nature of the job I was being offered. I knew absolutely nothing about it, but presumed it would involve a few hours of teaching English courses to adults during the following week, no big deal.

I spotted a sign pointing towards the principal's office, which I quickly located and entered. There were, if I recall correctly, three people waiting to see me, one of whom was the principal. He said they'd heard I was a good teacher, even though I lacked a Swedish teacher's certificate. (*That* indicated to me they were a bit desperate.) He'd apparently seen the *résumé* I'd filed with the teachers' exchange in Lund in January, and said they were satisfied that I would be right for the job, and that they needed my help most urgently.

The other two nodded occasionally or added a comment or two to the principal's remarks. I just smiled and nodded. My earlier presumptions remained intact. In fact, the whole time they were speaking, I was aware of being unable to suppress a strange smile from taking over my face, a smile coming more from my new feelings within than from my reactions to what was being said in the room. The first wave of the catharsis was still upon me. But since I'd never met any of them before, how were they to know that anything was "different" about me?

The ordinary teacher for this class, he explained, was a young woman who was expecting a baby in the latter half of June, just after the school term was over, but that her baby surprised everyone by arriving yesterday, quite prematurely, so they'd had no time to go through the usual proper channels to hire a qualified and certified teacher. And they needed me to start on Monday. It would be a full-time job, for the rest of the term, until the second week in June!

That information managed to penetrate the fuzzy barrier of my cathartic state. I was shocked. A *full-time* job, just like that?! I hadn't been employed at all for nearly a year, and hadn't worked full-time since 1965, except during a few summers and a full week once in a while at the language school. But never for three straight months! Could I handle this? I asked whether the students were adults. *Yes, from their early 20s and into their 50s*. And this job was teaching English, right? *Well, it's about 50-50, English and Swedish*. I gulped. You mean teaching Swedish to foreign students, right?!? *Uh, no, they're all Swedes*. I gasped. My jaw dropped. I was certain they'd read the wrong *résumé*. I asked whether they seriously meant that I, an American who'd been living in Sweden for just over eight and a half years, was supposed to be able to teach Swedish people Swedish?! "*Yes, it won't be a problem, you'll do fine!*" (So *that's* how desperate they were!!)

Then the principal explained that the Swedish course wasn't about teaching Swedish students how to *speak* Swedish, but was equivalent to when I studied English when I was in school in the US – studying one's native language is part of the standard curriculum nearly every year in nearly every country, nothing unusual about that. One of the others in the room was a Swedish teacher who interjected to tell me that it involved three main parts: Swedish grammar (I knew that quite well; I always thought that one learns more about the grammar of one's own language – and in a way that enables clearer explanations of it – when one learns a *foreign* language); vocabulary (most of the words native Swedes needed to learn in Swedish were borrowed from other languages, and in Sweden most of those came from English, so that would be no problem either); and finally, the third part was world literature (I had a degree in it). These arguments sufficiently convinced me to accept the position, but I pointed out that I wasn't terribly confident about the Swedish part of the job. They said not to worry.

The principal handed me the textbooks my English and Swedish students were using, but he wasn't quite certain how much the class had covered in each so far, and they couldn't phone the regular teacher because she was in the hospital with much more important matters on her mind. I would simply have to ask my students on Monday morning.

Then the Swedish teacher took me to the teacher's room – probably a classroom redecorated as a lounge, with a few sofas, desks, a kitchenette, several bulletin boards full of bulletins and some bookshelves full of books – a room to which teachers could escape during their breaks or when they had gaps due to scheduling difficulties. There were a few teachers in the room when I entered. (The school had a staff of nearly 100, including the teachers.) I made a quick mental note that most of them were casually dressed, to my relief. I always felt more comfortable out of "uniform". I was introduced (to anyone interested) as the sub who would be filling in for what's-her-name whose baby arrived yesterday – *very* prematurely, can you believe it! – and I would be taking over her English and Swedish classes for the rest of the term.

One of the English teachers, a woman about my age, introduced herself as the *head* English teacher, and quickly pointed out that it was *proper* English – *British* English – that was to be used around here. (She was Swedish.) I replied that it made no difference to me. (For years I'd been teaching whichever variant my pupils wanted.) I also mentioned that I'd heard that the position of Sweden's Board of Education was that it didn't matter whether teachers used British or US English, as long as they were consistent. "*Well, here we use English!*" I just winced a smile at her stupid non-answer, and sighed a little, having once again been reminded that the phenomenon of new converts being the most fanatical might also apply to "converts" to a new language.

On my way home I couldn't stop marveling that just a few hours earlier, I'd woken up transformed, redefined, in many ways a different person. Now I was suddenly a newly *employed* person as well. My mind was spinning. I realized I hadn't had a proper meal for nearly two weeks. And I still had a major sleep debt to settle, and textbooks to review. But it was all good. I felt like a newborn calf entering a grassy pasture for the first time ever. I would be getting back some structure in my life and have a real paycheck instead of disability or unemployment benefits for the first time in more than a year. I'd have to phone Arbetsförmedlingen and let them know I'd no longer be on the dole, but would actually be contributing to those who needed help, through the taxes I'd once again be paying.

I stopped at Värnhemstorget and bought some groceries. I was going to start eating again, stop the heavy drinking and kick my smoking habit. I put my perishables in the brand-new fridge in the big house, and made myself a meal on the stove in the new kitchen. I had a glass or two of wine instead of a bottle or two. I intended to return to my pre-depression smoking level (the equivalent of two or three cigarettes a day) as well, but that proved much harder than expected (I'd never before been aware that I had an *addiction* to nicotine). I did, however, manage to smoke only about half a dozen cigarettes while browsing through the new textbooks. Nothing in the course seemed daunting. The parts that would require preparation seemed like they'd be fairly easy once I learned what was next on the list to be covered.

The literature part of the Swedish course would require the most work, in the form of reading. But that would be fun. The reading reference list spanned works from the Ancient Greeks and Romans to Dante and Shakespeare, Victor Hugo, Voltaire, a few of my favorite English authors – most of which I knew pretty well – and of course a great deal of early and modern Swedish literature that I sorely needed to catch up on, i.e. read for the first time ever. It wasn't nearly as ambitious as it might sound; my students weren't required to read *all* these works, nor even any *complete* works. Their textbooks included excerpts from them (all in Swedish

– this was a course in Swedish, after all), but I wanted to make sure I knew the contexts from which the excerpts were taken, so I read as many complete works as I had time to devour.

One thing worried me. My students were all adults, which meant that they were taking these courses *voluntarily*, either because they'd dropped out of their schooling earlier in life, or because they needed to improve their grades after previously having been unmotivated to study. Whatever the reason, they were not studying because they had to, but because they *needed* to – to qualify for more advanced education or a better job or both. And they were depending on me to help them acquire the knowledge they'd missed.

As soon as I thought Bob might be home from work that afternoon – still Friday!! – I phoned him. I didn't get 10 words out of my mouth before he knew there'd been a *profound* change in my life and outlook. I explained to him the astounding effect of having completed *The Unparallel Lines*: the transformation from what was essentially and intentionally a lengthy suicide note into a serendipitous catharsis. And while he was still stuttering in delighted amazement, I told him about the job. He went completely silent, unable to speak. I knew him well enough to know that he was sobbing silently – with joy, relief, nearly a catharsis of his own. I grasped instantly what an awful burden he'd been bearing, yet willingly pushing himself to his own breaking point. Bob was scheduled to arrive a week later and spend two weeks with me, and I realized that he'd been dreading it. Now he could hardly wait for the week to pass.

After we said goodbye, I suddenly felt extremely weary. My many sleepless nights were an unpaid debt that was catching up with me. I went to bed at around 8 PM, but was almost afraid to fall asleep, for fear it had all been a dream, that I would again find the monsters of depression pressing my shoulders down into the darkness. At the same time, since catharsis probably involves a very profound sense of *relief* – the end of a war, a return to the surface of the sea when your lungs are about to burst – I was able to let go and sleep soundly until hunger awoke me close to noon the next day, Saturday. I was almost afraid to wake up, for the same reason I'd feared falling asleep. Instead I was *buoyant*.

I hadn't *forgotten* anything; I wasn't trying to forget or suppress the excruciatingly painful memories of Jeanette. It was more like those memories were softened by other memories *too*, of her smile, of her laughter, of her love, of her joy. Now I *could* remember, could *choose* to remember, *dared* to remember – the horrifying memories didn't come crashing into my consciousness uninvited

A Sea of Troubles

the instant I closed my eyes or heard a certain trigger word or even looked at certain photos. I could and did look at photos of Jeanette when she was happy. I felt *her* happiness then, not just *my* pain now. I could listen to a piece of Mozart that she loved and enjoy the wondrous music, not *only* how much I'd like to be listening to it again with her. I could *cherish* her memory and our love, not just suffer from them. I was not immune to agony, but I was beginning to want to live again. I was feeling truly, profoundly *alive*.

Yes, there was a lingering sadness that I realized would probably never go away. I'd loved Jeanette deeply and naively, during all those formative years when our love was growing deeper and I was just beginning to become a *little* less naïve. There'd been an innocence about our love for each other that was incredibly sweet. But it was also dangerous, because naïveté and clarity of perception are seldom compatible.

I once again got the feeling that *now* I understood the past years of my life, but I hadn't adequately understood my past life at the time I was living it. I thought of Ibsen's last play, *When We Dead Awaken*: do we only understand life when it's over? I still couldn't figure out my inability to see, to grasp the disintegration of Jeanette's mental health. Only in retrospect did I get a glimpse – or imagined that I got a glimpse – of what it all meant. But that glimpse gave me no grounds for supposing I might have been able to prevent her from doing what she'd was determined to do.

That Saturday afternoon I sat down to do my homework, to familiarize myself with the textbooks I'd be using, and to find and reacquaint myself with many of the books on the literature reference list. One of those books was a slender volume by Voltaire: *Candide*. I had a bilingual version in my library. I'd read it years before and enjoyed it, but it didn't make a huge impression on me at the time. Now it made my hair stand on end. The protagonist of the title is an extremely naïve young man born into aristocratic wealth. Candide has his own tutor, Pangloss, whose principal task is to promote the philosopher Leibnitz' favorite thesis (and the object of Voltaire's biting satire): that since God made everything, and since He is all-powerful, all-wise and all-good (omnipotent, omniscient, and omnibenevolent), then everything that *is* must be for the best, in the best of all possible worlds. Well sorry, Gottfried, but François-Marie Arouet wasn't having any of your crap!

As the story unfolds, Candide (accompanied by Pangloss) meets and survives one disaster after another – war, earthquake, shipwreck – in which most or all the people around them are killed, and only the two of them escape. After each escape, Pangloss keeps trotting out his (Leibnitz') thesis. Eventually, Pangloss himself is also among the victims of a disaster, and even though Candide survives, his skepticism accelerates. After further trials, with the idea (that this could be the best of all possible worlds) losing the last of its tenability, Candide finds himself working hard in a neglected garden and turning it into a thing of beauty and value. Reflecting on how Pangloss at this point would have trotted out Leibnitz' thesis, the now-less-naïve Candide finally dismisses it. In the last line of the book, looking back on all that's happened, he realizes the utter cynicism of thinking that all those disasters that killed all those people could represent the best possible world. Instead, he recognizes that *it's up to each of us* to make the world a better place, starting with our own: we must cultivate our garden – "*Mais il faux cultiver notre jardin.*"

This is my interpretation. There have been many other interpretations of Voltaire's conclusion over the years. Some have called it a case for pessimism (!); others claim it's a cynical, nihilistic resignation to apathy (!). To me, re-reading it at that particular moment, it was a sublime affirmation of a life free of magic and superstition. It hit me between the eyes, struck a sympathetic chord that went straight to my heart. None of the shit that Candide endured involved anything he'd ever striven for. It was all shit that was *dumped* on him and came flying at him, unbidden and unwanted, calamities he had to dodge, evade, out-maneuver and survive any way he could. (Did I see a parallel with my unchosen childhood indoctrination, my forced flight from my homeland to escape the unwanted choices of war, and my unsolicited all-encompassing grief? *Oh yes indeed!!*) The good stuff – the lovely garden – was about the only thing that didn't just *happen* to Candide; he had to work for that and *make* it happen. And by striving to make it happen, it *did* happen. And yet he would always have to remain diligent, because the good was temporary, fragile, subject to degradation – but *so* lovely while he *made* it last.

I think I slept another 10 hours or more that Saturday night. I ate more than one meal that Sunday. I fried some chops. I tried boiling some potatoes that turned out awful, so I made some rice instead that turned out well. I'd try adding some different spices next time, and start trying other things. I was able to focus without having my thoughts constantly interrupted by panic. I hoped I would be able to meet the challenge – especially the bizarre challenge of teaching Swedish people more about Swedish – and I firmly intended to give it my best effort. I could think of Jeanette with love and a manageable amount of pain. And I could accept with equanimity the fact that Lena maintained her silence.

I was still in love with Lena, and could find nothing to do about it (I had no experience in how to fall *out of* love). But I knew I couldn't go back to being dependent for my well-being on her every whim, to allow my feelings to be kicked around. So I decided that I would accept the good and avoid the bad, by showing my love to Lena when she would accept it, but looking for (or at least not dismissing) the companionship of others whenever Lena turned away – provided I did not exploit anyone or treat anyone badly. This was my recipe, my tactical defense, for staying sane.

On Monday morning I felt nervous and shaky but determined. I put on a Harris Tweed sport jacket and a Pendleton shirt (both courtesy of The Emporium), and jeans. This job, this new phase in my life, was about to become real. I decided that my first and most important task was to establish contact with my students – my inscrutably unknown students whom I was about to meet for the first time. I had a list of their names that told me nothing more than that they were Swedish. Perhaps they didn't even know they were getting a new teacher, let alone an *American* who was going to teach them Swedish!

There were about 25 of them, already seated and chatting softly when I entered the large, bright classroom and walked to the podium. The youngest appeared to be in her early 20s and the eldest in his 50s. As I opened my mouth to reveal my new role (or possibly even earlier), they gave me the once-over and I noticed a few raised eyebrows, smirks and other indicators of surprise and amusement. I presumed that this was their natural reaction to the somewhat bizarre situation of finding themselves in a course in their native language, about to be taught by someone who spoke it with a highly noticeable accent. I informed them that I'd been summoned on Friday afternoon to be their new teacher for the rest of the term, because their ordinary teacher delivered a very premature baby that day.

After a few seconds of the murmuring and rustling that this news evoked, their eyes and bemused expressions returned to me. I told them that the short notice – and the fact that I didn't know how far along they'd come in their textbooks – rendered me unprepared to start teaching properly that day, but that I was determined to teach them well since I was aware that they'd signed up for the course because they needed it, and that I saw it as my job and my duty to see that they got what they needed to further their education, and that if they felt at any point that I was wasting their time or otherwise in any way preventing them from achieving their goals, I would greatly appreciate it if they informed me, so that something could be done about it!

I asked them specifically about each textbook I'd been given, and they told me how far along they'd come in them. I wrote a quick note to myself about each. Then I said it would be helpful to me if they could tell me a little bit about themselves and exactly why they were taking this particular course. To make it less awkward, I began by telling them a little about myself, where I came from, why I came to Sweden, my Swedish ancestry (must establish those credentials!), my educational background (to give them confidence in me – or to give *me* confidence in having given them confidence in me). I half expected that their bemused expressions would abate once they got used to me, but they didn't. Some seemed to find it difficult to look me in the eye. Some seemed to be wishing for a polite opportunity to burst out laughing.

Feeling we'd come as far as we could for that hour, I told them that I thought it might be best if we finished early that first day. Now that I knew what the next step was in their textbooks and lessons, I needed to go home and prepare. We would all get more out of it if I came prepared, I pointed out with great pseudo-authority. I *would* be prepared the next day, and *then* we would get down to work. They all smiled and nodded in approval (a few may have grinned). I said that class was dismissed, and they all stood up and began filing out of the room, passing right in front of me on their way to the door as they did so, grinning, smiling, smirking and raising their eyebrows. A few were giggling.

One young man lingered behind a little, clearly so that he could be the last to leave the classroom. He stopped to have a word with me, and introduced himself as the class representative, i.e. the student chosen by his peers to represent their interests in case of any discussions or disputes with the principal's office – or with me. He told me that he felt he could speak on behalf of his classmates when he said that they all appreciated my being frank and forthright with them, and that they were certain I would do a great job, and they would be sure to let me know if there were any small problems before they became big ones. "*You're going to be just fine,*" he said, shaking my hand with a smile, "*but when you come here tomorrow, it might be a good idea if you zipped up your fly!*"

Then he walked out, after getting a good look at my appalled, color-drained expression. I wanted to sink through the floor. I stood there for at least half a minute, at first in disbelief, then in order to give my students time to disperse from the area outside the classroom before I showed my face. I felt so idiotic for such a stupid, unnecessary oversight. I had to do something to defuse it.

That evening I worked like hell to prepare a truly interesting lesson for the next day. The first part of the lesson was going to be about adverbs, and I knew from my own experience in learning Swedish how tricky it could sometimes be to distinguish adverbs from adjectives, and how my students were dreading this particular part of the course, not only because they didn't understand the problem, but didn't understand why on earth it should be worth wasting any time on. Who cares about bloody adverbs, anyway? So I thought up a long list of examples where the choice of adverb or adjective form *really does* matter, where the meaning is drastically altered when the wrong form is used, sometimes with absurd results.

[*I should interject here that I realize that it makes no difference to many people whether they speak or write clearly or not. I also realize that language is constantly evolving. My view is that changes that* enrich *a language by making it possible to distinguish between related things are nearly always good changes, while changes that* impoverish *the language by removing such distinctions are bad changes. In response to the question* How are you?, *the reply* I'm good! *(an adjective) uses the word that refers to the assessment of one's moral character: you're a good person, go polish your halo. The reply* I'm well! *(an adverb) uses the word that refers to one's ability to function, i.e. you are healthy, balanced. Unfortunately, when people use* good *in both cases, they contribute to the gradual loss of the ability of the English language to make this distinction. Here endeth the lesson.*]

I made sure I *didn't* arrive early the next morning. My students were already seated when I strode into the classroom, looked them all in the eye, and said, "*Are we ready to begin?*" Then I immediately looked down at the crotch of my own *zipped-up* trousers, then back at my students, and said with a big grin, "*Yes, we are!!*" The classroom erupted in laughter. The ice was broken. And they all learned about adverbs and found it fun doing so.

The English course was a breeze. I'd already been teaching English for more than eight years and was well aware of what aspects of English grammar and pronunciation Swedish people find most difficult, and how to the make them comprehensible. But it was a bit frustrating to have to adjust to the snail's pace. Nearly all my previous teaching was in the form of individual English-only immersion courses, eight hours a day for five days a week (and sometimes two or three consecutive weeks). As soon as I knew that my pupil (singular) understood something, I could move on to the next point, instead of waiting until the slowest ones in the class also understood it. In my immersion courses, *most* of the pupils learned more in a week than my KomVux students would learn in their bilingual classes in an entire schoolyear.

Bob arrived on Saturday morning, five days later, and the Easter break meant that I was off work for the first 10 days of his 15-day stay. He was immeasurably thrilled to see the sea change in my outlook (even though reading *The Unparallel Lines* caused him considerable retroactive distress). He might have felt greater cause for relief if there'd been any kind of balance in the relationship between Lena and me, or if the imbalance weren't continuing to cause me some degree of distress. Whenever I told him that Lena was refusing to see me, he was unable to fully disguise his relief. That he felt the need to disguise it was, I supposed, to avoid putting himself in an awkward position should Lena and I somehow ever achieve a balanced or long-term relationship.

But he was happy to learn that when Lena wouldn't see me, Sonja would, and that I wasn't closing any doors. Whenever Lena turned her back on me, Sonja and I never fully managed to maintain that sexless relationship, but Sonja always assured me that she wasn't looking for anything long-term, no commitment, no strings, just friendship – and a little sex. Thus I felt certain that I wasn't exploiting her, and felt certain that she also felt that way. Her passion was for the theater, she claimed, and nothing would stand between her and the pursuit of her career. I was glad she felt that way, because I *liked* her very much as a person and didn't want to hurt her in any way. Sex between us was never going to be euphoric or even passionate – more like a pleasant way to relieve tension or as a pleasant prelude to sleep.

I was fully aware that I wouldn't be having sex with Sonja or anyone else, if only Lena didn't keep shoving me out. Sonja was an interesting and unpredictable person. Bob liked her too, perhaps recognizing that she helped to keep me in balance whenever Lena disappeared from view (which was most of the time throughout 1978).

There were a couple of other important things going on for Bob. One of his friends from his university days in Rochester in the early and mid-1950s, and with whom he maintained sporadic contact over the years, had been sending Bob family photos on a regular basis, enabling Bob to follow the development of his friend's family. They were now living in Wisconsin. When Jeanette and I were cleaning up Bob's place, I came across some of the photos and asked Bob about them. It was plain to see – and to hear by the change in the tone of his voice – that Bob was particularly interested in his friend's daughter Kathy, now a young woman. He also revealed that he was now corresponding with Kathy intensely, and that she'd accepted his invitation to come and stay with him in Binningen for well over a month starting in late April. But he didn't want to discuss it with me in much detail. Perhaps some irrational impulses were ruling his mind and undermining his position for arguing against my irrational pursuit of Lena.

Another, darker issue I'd begun to notice in Bob during his visit: his increased physical feebleness. He'd never been in good physical shape for as long as I'd known him, but there was now something new. His hand would start trembling from time to time, and he'd quickly grab the trembling hand with his non-trembling hand, perhaps hoping that I wouldn't notice (or that *he* wouldn't notice?). But he said nothing about it.

I still had enough of Don's magic resin left for a couple of hits. Since Bob had said he'd like to try it, we did. Unfortunately, it was a most unpleasant experience for Bob – a bad trip. It made him ill at ease for several hours. My own trip wasn't much of anything, one way or another; I think I was too worried about Bob to be able to let go. [*As of the writing of this book, that was the last time I ever smoked cannabis, and most likely will remain so. I've only ever had one other drug experience – I ate a cannabis-laden "brownie" from a café in Amsterdam in 2005, perfectly legal. But it was also a bad trip.*]

Bob and I did enjoy a lot of music together, drank some good wines over which we solved most of the world's problems, continued our existential probing, and continued finding new reasons to be dumbfounded by how we'd been hoodwinked in our younger years by the all the lies in the huge category of historical mendacity known as religion.

Bob understood better than anyone else I knew what it felt like not only to step away from the brink, but also to turn one's back on it, even to reject it as a choice, knowing that it was an inevitability anyway. "*Having only this*" (from John Fowles, *The Aristos*) was now Bob's mantra, and more or less mine. Bob returned to Binningen on April 1st.

Lena phoned me about a week later, and we met a few times for sex (annoyingly, I always found myself wanting so much more sex, as well as so much more *than* sex than she did), mostly on weekends. The fact that both of us were working full-time, in Lund and Malmö respectively, our schedules weren't terribly conducive to mid-week trysts (her excuse or explanation?), particularly given the painfully obvious discrepancy in the level and nature of the interest we had in each other. Remarkably, she seemed not even to notice the enormous change in me, the disappearance of my desperation and depression. She showed no particular enthusiasm about my having found a job (OK, the job found me). I failed to reflect on how odd all that was.

She was supposed to be sewing my window shades for me, so that might have been as good a pretext as any for us to get together at all. But then she told me that she'd mentioned me to her mom for the first time, which surprised me greatly and of course set my mind, heart and hopes racing, in accordance with reactions I concluded I must have been genetically predisposed to have. But I was not about to abandon my course of tactical defense!

One night in early April at her place in Lund, I was in the process of falling into blissful post-coital sleep when I suddenly experienced a phenomenon that some might call a vision or an epiphany: I saw (very much in my mind's eye and nowhere else) a large painting. (It would take three years to see it anywhere else!) The motif synthesized Voltaire's *Candide* and my own recently concluded year of deep depression and acute mourning. I saw the whole thing, finished (not in every last detail, but pretty close). This kind of "revelation" of a painting had happened to me before, several times, but never involved any painting quite as complex as this. To assure that the image would not disappear like a dream one has failed to relate within minutes of waking up, I quickly slid from the bed, grabbed a piece of paper and a pencil, and made a quick, very rough sketch of the painting I'd just envisaged.

There would be a young man in the center, tilling a garden that is bordered to the left by a hedge. Thorn bushes outside the hedge are encroaching upon the garden, and the man is digging them up from the garden itself. Beyond the thorn patch is the abyss, the void. A large tree in the middle of the garden has lush limbs growing over the garden, while the limb that extends out beyond the hedge towards the abyss is dead.

The moral I perceived in Voltaire's story spoke straight to what I felt upon emerging from *The Unparallel Lines* – a revelation that had required a catharsis for someone as naïve as me to see, but when I saw it, I saw it clearly:

The shit you get in life is for free; if you want something good, you have to work for it, and you have to <u>keep</u> working for it or the shit will quickly take over again.

It only took me a couple of minutes to make the sketch – enough to ensure that I would remember my "vision" the next day. Then I went back to bed and managed to get back to sleep with some difficulty, due to my excitement about the unexpected prospect of painting again.

Lena wondered what I was so excited about. She didn't seem to understand how an idea for another painting could be so earth-shaking for me. The fact that I was inspired to paint again meant more than the painting itself; it also meant that I would be following Jeanette's injunction after all, but I said nothing of that to Lena. The next day she told me – again – that she didn't want to see me, in effect: "*Don't call me, I'll call you.*" But I knew how to handle it now.

A week or so later, Lena did call, agitated, to tell me that her father had been rushed to the hospital following a heart attack. The level of concern she expressed for him came as a big surprise to me, considering the often severely critical way she'd always referred to him earlier (at least to me). But then I reflected on how little concern I'd shown for my dad before his fatal illness was known to me less than five years earlier, and I recognized one of those regrettable aspects of human nature: the failure to show appreciation for the important things one has until one is about to lose them or has already lost them.

Of course it's not possible each time one meets a loved one to treat them as if it were the last time ever; that would make the relationship unbearable. But certainly there could be a way to make a confirmation of love and appreciation more a part of day-to-day life, almost as important as breathing, without anyone having to find it embarrassing, overbearing or awkward? A lot of people seem to have no problem displaying their *contempt* on a daily basis; *why not their love?*

I offered to go with her to the hospital to see him, but she told me she didn't think so. She said, however, that she'd mentioned me to him (or it might have been Lena's mom who did), and that he'd shaken his head (in amusement or disapproval or both?) about Lena having met "*another* American". But the next day Lena went cold on me again and shut me out. Although I didn't spin out of control this time either, I felt it was time for me to get closure. So I wrote about it, this time in the form of a poem, on April 22nd:

Joie de vivre

Sammet	**Velvet**

Ett sammetstyg rörde vid min hy
En kall och stjärnlös natt
Då jag yrade omkring i mörker.

Otaliga nätter hade jag vandrat så,
Saknat ljus och råd och riktning
Vid en gapande rämnas rand.

Ett sammetstyg smekte mitt ansikte
En tröstlös och kolsvart natt
Då jag vacklade omkring i mörker.

Jag häpnade inför dess lena känsla,
Tog i det och drogs in i det
För att värna mig mot kylan.

Ett sammetstyg svepte om mitt hjärta
En bitter och redlös natt
Då jag raglade omkring i mörker.

Längs randen for jag ivrigt
Med dundrande, vilsna, blinda steg
För att komma till dess lenande källa.

Ett sammetstyg grep om min hals
En hopplös och dödstyst natt
Då jag stapplade omkring i mörker.

Dess källa fann jag, den var en sten.
Jag slog mig blodig och föll
Mot den gapande rämna, som jag inte sett.

Ett sammetstyg drog sig tillbaka
En desperat och fredlös natt
Då jag krälade omkring i mörker.

Jag höll i randen med brutna händer
Och ville släppa men drog mig upp
På darrande ben och började gå.

Ett sammetstyg rörde vid min hy
En tidlös och stjärnig natt,
Men jag vandrade vidare.

A velvet cloth brushed my skin
One cold and starless night
As I reeled about in darkness.

Countless nights I'd wandered thus,
Lacking light and air and direction
At the edge of a gaping precipice.

A velvet cloth caressed my face
One disconsolate, pitch-black night
As I faltered about in darkness.

I was amazed by how smooth it felt,
Grabbed it and was drawn into it
To protect myself from the chill.

A velvet cloth enveloped my heart
One bitter, blind-drunk night
As I staggered about in darkness.

Along the edge I hurried
With thundering, lost, blind steps
To reach its soothing source.

A velvet cloth grabbed me by the throat
One hopeless, deathly still night
As I stumbled about in darkness.

I found its source, it was a stone.
I struck myself bloody and fell
Towards the gaping abyss I hadn't seen.

A velvet cloth withdrew itself
One desperate and troubled night
As I crawled about in darkness.

I grasped the edge with broken hands
Wanting to let go but dragged myself up
On trembling legs and began to walk.

A velvet cloth brushed my skin
One timeless, star-spangled night,
But I wandered on.

I wrote this poem in Swedish [*my English translation came years later*] and submitted it to the local newspaper (*Sydsvenskan*). They published it a day or two later. Lena saw it there and phoned me the same day to let me know she'd read it. She seemed to be both irritated and flattered. [*I should point out that the two puns on Lena's name (both quite intentional) found in two words in the Swedish version are unavoidably lost in the English translation, since in Swedish "lena" (4th verse) means "smooth"; and "lenande" (6th verse) means "soothing".*]

On April 26th, Lena's father suffered another massive heart attack and died. Lena was distraught and phoned to tell me. I offered to come to her immediately, or to help in any way I could, but then she suddenly changed her mind again and quickly ended the conversation. I was uncertain whether I should take any action, but decided it wasn't a suitable time to be pushy, so I phoned the hospital and asked if I could make a donation to heart research in Lena's father's name, which they gladly accepted. They said they'd send a letter confirming it if I wished, so I gave them my address, as well as Marie-Louise's address in Barkåkra (but not Lena's).

Kathy's visit to Bob was pretty much of a fiasco, not at all what Bob had been hoping for. According to Bob, Kathy spent her first week in the Canary Islands, together with her sister and an 80-year-old man who was a friend of the two young women. Then, after Kathy had been with Bob for a couple of weeks, the sister and the old friend joined them, to Bob's chagrin. (Bob put them up at a hotel in Basel.) Bob was doing his best to entertain the three of them – as a way of currying favor with Kathy – and took them out for a country drive in his yellow Lancia. I recalled that the Lancia seated two comfortably and three "in a pinch"; now there were four of them (presumably with the two sisters pinching hard in the back).

Bob never fully explained to me the circumstances of what happened on that drive, but the outcome was that when they were approaching a level railroad crossing, there was an incline and Bob gunned it but couldn't handle the responsive power of his sports car and lost control, crashing into a post or a barricade (it might have been a lowered boom; that was never explained either). The Lancia was damaged beyond repair. Some or all passengers were injured, albeit slightly.

Bob was devastated, perhaps more by Kathy's outspoken irritation with him than anything else. He bent over backwards to make amends to all concerned. I don't know how much of the medical expenses were covered by the American insurance policies of the respective parties, but Bob certainly covered anything that wasn't. They left him, licking his own inner wounds as well as his financial ones, to return to the States on May 7th, the same day I finally got payment for my purloined salary from Interspråk.

I'd understood for some time that although Bob's reclusive nature was not watertight, it did include some pretty watertight bulkheads. Now and then he'd mention several of his acquaintances from Roche in friendly terms. A few of them had invited him to their homes for an occasional Sunday afternoon dinner. He'd also begun chatting casually with a couple of his neighbors, and corresponding with a several old friends from the States (including an old flame or two). But none of them – me as well – seemed to know (and definitely never met) each other. Compartmentalization was the way he wanted it, and that was the way he got it.

My work at KomVux was running along smoothly. My students were participating actively, all of them were learning, and nearly all of them were learning well. Our classroom sessions were fun, with lots of joking – which in my experience is always the best way to accomplish almost any serious learning. At the same time, I had little to do with my colleagues and I avoided hanging out in the teachers' room, where office politics and pecking orders and prestige problems seemed to me to prevail. I was made to understand early on that I was an outsider, a bit of an interloper, and that nothing I might have to offer professionally would be appreciated. That included insights about English grammar, which I clearly understood far better than any of them, probably in theory and certainly in practice. The best reaction I could hope for was tolerant silence. Instead of becoming stressed about their lack of positive feedback, however, I took pleasure in the appreciation of my students. After all, they were the ones for whom I was doing my job. I didn't give a piece of fried shit about the pecking order of my colleagues.

I'd learned (perhaps) not to expect any positive feedback from Lena. I tried *hard* not to care. She kept reminding me with her actions that she only got in touch with me whenever she needed to be adored and/or pleasured. Once she'd had her "fix", she was back to "seeing" other boys. I was aware how dangerous a position that might put me in. I was determined not to be driven to the brink again. Since my attempts to resist her charm proved useless, I continued to express my love for her whenever she turned to me, but not to suppress my libido whenever she turned away. It was very much a matter of survival.

Friday, May 19th was a special day for me – an extraordinary live-or-die day. It was the day I'd designated for my own demise in *The Unparallel Lines*, a scenario that now seemed utterly remote from my thoughts and feelings. I thought of Jeanette every hour of every day, but with greater and greater focus on the good memories. I was nearly overwhelmed when I considered the juxtaposition of how I felt when I wrote *The Unparallel Lines* and how life-affirming I'd become since then. Passing the auspicious 19th of May, I felt incredibly, outrageously, intensely, explosively *alive*, knowing that I wouldn't have been if I'd followed through on my ill-conceived plan.

There was such an *intensity* about my feeling of living! I'd never experienced anything comparable before. It would remain at this intense level for months. I was almost radiating energy, like an aura. Others around me seemed to sense it – there really seemed to be an infectious aspect to it – without really understanding what it was. I knew the feeling would gradually fade (cf. *Nothing Gold Can Stay* by Robert Frost), probably even disappear from view, but I hoped I could keep it safely somewhere deep inside me to be retrieved and revived in whatever dark hours might lie ahead in my life.

On Saturday, May 20th, Lena phoned and invited me to come to Lund for the night, which I readily accepted, of course. She also wondered if I'd be interested in driving up to Barkåkra the next day to see her newly widowed mother, Marie-Louise. When I expressed surprise that she would be *driving*, she explained that she'd taken over her late father's small dark-green Datsun – her mom didn't have a driver's license and her siblings already had all the cars they wanted.

I'd seen the house in Barkåkra once before, but only from the outside, when Björn had used his foot to trace out a message for Lena in the gravel driveway. Marie-Louise expressed her sincere warm gratitude and appreciation to me for the donation to the heart research fund I'd made in her husband's name. She said she wanted to thank me in person with a home-cooked meal. Marie-Louise turned out to be one of the relatively few people I've met in my life with whom rapport was deep and instantaneous. She was warm, kind, and laughed easily (sometimes nervously). She was also significantly (perilously?) overweight and as extremely nearsighted as my dad and my brother Al. I could tell she liked me at once, and the feeling was entirely mutual. Her personality was in many ways similar to her daughter Eva's.

Her name was actually Sigrid Marie-Louise, and it was perhaps fortunate for me that she never used "Sigrid", which might have been confusing for Bob as it was also the name of his ex-wife, and would for him have been a constant and painful reminder of that shipwrecked marriage. Apparently Lena's mom truly liked "Marie-Louise", because she also gave the name to her two daughters, Eva Marie-Louise, and Lena Marie-Louise.

The house in Barkåkra where she lived was on the corner of a moderately busy intersection of two small countryside roads, across the road from open fields overlooking the Swedish F10 Air Force base. Next door, to the north, was the grand and spacious vicarage where Lena lived all her young life until she was old enough to move away from home, and where her parents lived for as long as Allan was the vicar at the small whitewashed countryside church, two doors farther north, separated by a well-preserved, timber-framed parish house. I would soon come to learn that when Lena spoke of "home" it would never be where she lived, but only Barkåkra, where she grew up (and to a much lesser extent where her mother now lived).

Marie-Louise's current home, where Lena had never lived, was more or less given to the Johannissons after her father retired from his vicarious (pun intended) position. It was an 18th century cottage with cramped rooms and a small kitchen, a steep stairway up to a small, low-ceilinged open-plan dormer attic in which Marie-Louise slept at one end and where a few single beds at the other end were designated for overnight family guests. They'd built an extension on one side of the downstairs to make space for a dining room and a larger living room, as well as a sauna, Marie-Louise's weekly indulgence in pleasure.

There'd been a small garage outside, along the property line to the vicarage, but it was being used as a storage room and an extra unheated bedroom should the need arise. Around the back and to one side there was a lovely garden. Gardening was Marie-Louise's favorite pastime.

She was eager to take me on a tour past the vicarage to the parish house, which she explained was used for various church functions, wedding receptions (she said, flashing a smile at me – she was *really* on my side!). Surrounding the church was a cemetery – a graveyard or churchyard – with Allan's still-fresh grave just off to the left of the front entrance to the church itself. I'd somehow never made the connection between Thomas Gray's beautiful poem and the fact that most European churches had churchyards that were the burial places. It also struck me for the first time that Søren Kirkegaard's surname means "churchyard" (or "cemetery") in Danish. Marie-Louise didn't need to explain much about the F10 base across the road; it explained itself by occasionally enriching the environs with all the decibels one could wish for.

I took in everything Marie-Louise showed me with great interest, particularly in *her* selective interest in whatever she was showing me. Lena showed more interest in me after seeing her mom's highly favorable reaction to me, which once again boosted my hopes. But that interest quickly waned again as soon as we left. Although we spent Saturday night together in her twin bed in Lund, she was not interested in any affection, let alone intimacy. Sonja was in town from Stockholm, and *she* was happy to spend Sunday night with me.

Mom was ill at ease in her new and unfamiliar surroundings in the countryside outside Knoxville, Illinois. Since Grandma died she was lonelier than ever. She said she'd been hoping I'd come and visit her there ever since Jeanette died, and she intensified her appeals when she visited me in September. My trip to the States the previous summer, just a few months after Jeanette's death, didn't include Illinois. It had been a trip of desperation that I could hardly remember, when I was as low as I felt it was possible to be without being six feet under.

In the meantime I'd learned that although I could never get *over* the tragedy of losing Jeanette, I could occasionally get *beyond* it. I wanted my family – and Jeanette's – to see that I was going to be OK. On a good day, my trove of cherished memories of Jeanette helped to lift me up, not drag me down. I wanted to visit the family and let them see for themselves (and in the case of *my* family to show them that recovery from such an abysmal tragedy could be achieved without the aid of any lords). If they were planning to feed me the lie, á la Pangloss, that *He'd* helped me through it, I was certainly going to point out that if that were so, He would have to take responsibility for having put me and Jeanette there in the first place. It's about *reciprocity!*

I wrote to tell Mom I'd be making the trip, first spending 10 days with her. I didn't mention anything about *The Unparallel Lines*, of course, just that I was finding it "easier to live with scars than with open sores." She was thrilled that I'd decided to come. She was the first and only relative (including Jeanette's family) to ask me about Jeanette's ashes. She offered me to bring them to the States and even to bury them next to Dad's grave. I was well aware of the love behind her offer and was deeply moved by it, but I told her that scattering the ashes at sea was what Jeanette and I had definitely wanted and agreed on. Mom made no further comment and never raised the subject again.

My class at KomVux informed me a few days in advance that in the early evening on Friday, May 26th, they were all going to Copenhagen for a class party. To my complete surprise, they told me they were unanimous about inviting me join them, *insisting* that I come. I accepted instantly. We had a rollicking great time on the ferry (aided by liberal libations), arrived at the terminal at Havnegade in Nyhavn already feeling some of the effects of those libations on board, then headed across Kongens Nytorv to a street parallel with the popular pedestrian street Strøget, and came to a delightful and somewhat rowdy beer hall called Øl og Vingod.

In view of the temporary and short-term nature of my role as the teacher, I felt I could see my adult students as pals, out for a good time (but I still had some inhibitions). Many of them seemed to see that their role as my students had largely disappeared before we ever boarded the ferry in Malmö. Those who didn't feel that way at once soon did, after varying degrees of alcohol and a high dose of merriment. The beer hall atmosphere removed any remaining inhibitions. We sat on long wooden benches at long primitive wooden tables, food was served (it might have been good – or not – at least nobody remained hungry), the strong Danish beer flowed, and *hofbräu*-style singing reverberated throughout the premises. When all the patrons at the restaurant had been given adequate time to finish their meals, the music grew louder and we were all encouraged to move to smaller tables on a mezzanine floor overlooking the long tables that became part of the dance "floor" (dancing *on* the tables *or* on the floor was by choice and level of dizziness).

Several of the girls/women among my students seemed to be champing at the bit to dance with me. I was in that perfect state of inebriation where I found everything incredibly delightful, hilarious, sensual and arousing, and I accepted every invitation to dance. (Some of those invitations were expressed verbally, as actual interrogatory statements, while others merely involved yanking at my arm with a knowing look.) While they took turns whirling me around down below, I could see that many were looking at me from that mezzanine perch with bemused smiles not unlike the expressions they wore on that first day.

One of my students, a girl about my age named Majlis (pronounced MY-lease), certainly lost all her inhibitions (whether due to alcohol or my charms). She was all over me as we danced, apparently determined to let me know in no uncertain terms that she would rather be horizontal with me, and equally determined to ascertain whether I felt the same way, the proof of which soon became apparent to us both. But I was still inhibited enough not to feel right about accepting her proposal to abscond from my class party, so I suggested waiting until we got back to Malmö when the party was over and we could head off for my place. She agreed to the delay, albeit reluctantly.

Somehow word got out that there might be something going on at my place later – an "after-party" at Korngatan. It certainly didn't come from *me*! In any case, about ten of us ended up at my place in the early hours of the morning, with dawn already well upon us, and we went upstairs in the big house to play music and continue to dance and drink. Majlis and I kept shooting glances at each other (neither of us wanted to flaunt our intentions to the others), rolling our eyes, hoping that they would soon leave, but the sun was already up and shining brightly by the time they did. The fact that they left and Majlis did not was not lost on them.

Majlis was about a year younger than me and quite pretty, with long dark-blond hair and a good figure. She wasn't nearly as pretty as Lena (to my mind nobody could be), but she was plenty attractive, as I clearly was to her, and once we were alone it was only a matter of minutes before hours of desire and frustration exploded into hours of unbridled, unchained, uninhibited lust. This *might* have been an emotionally complicated situation for me. I could have berated myself for claiming to love Lena, yet failing to have any reservations about succumbing to raw lust for Majlis. But I knew with absolute certainty and honesty towards myself that if only Lena were willing to be with me, I would never have given Majlis or anyone else a second look. I also knew that if I tortured myself with thoughts of what Lena was doing when she was "seeing" other boys (and it *certainly* wasn't because I refused to "see" her, even just to *see* her visually!), I would only risk sliding back into that awful depression.

So in the meantime, there *were* no complications; it was pure sex, over and over until Majlis and I were both exhausted and reeling with pleasure – a wild hedonistic ride, a lifebuoy of survival, and an exuberant affirmation of life. I tried to think whether the French expression *joie de vivre* should most properly be translated as "the joy of living" or "the joy of being alive" and decided both would do just fine, and the French would do just fine as the title of this chapter because the French expresses both.

And the urge to paint again was now overwhelming me.

CHAPTER 6

Making the rounds

The end of the term – and the end of my employment at KomVux – was rapidly approaching. I didn't have a clue what I'd be doing next. My students seemed more anxious about what I would be doing than I was, and told me they wanted – demanded – that I continue as their teacher in the fall. And I would gladly have done so, but the principal informed me that it was out of the question due to my lack of official accreditation from a Swedish teachers' college, and now they would have plenty of time to go through the proper channels and advertise for a certified teacher to take over the class in the fall, which they were legally obliged to do. Fair enough.

When I informed my students of this sorrowful situation, they were outraged, and within a day or two they'd drafted a petition to the effect that they wanted and demanded me back and nobody else. Every last one of them signed it. I was touched by that, and apparently the school administration felt unable to ignore it completely; they informed me that when the fall term started in late August, there was a *slight* possibility that I could get a short-term, part-time job as a substitute assistant teacher, albeit for another class whose ordinary assistant teacher wouldn't be returning from maternity leave until the second week in October. It was all very vague, and didn't satisfy "my" class one bit, but it was a better prospect for me than any other I had at the time, so I told the principal that I was happy to get anything that would keep me from again having to deal with the specter of unemployment for a while longer.

On May 31st, Björn, Isobel, and Patrick moved into their newly built row house in Oxie, an outlying suburb to the southeast, well beyond my cycling range. In connection with their move, Björn finally collected the cabinets he'd been building in my finished but still-unfurnished living room (Thereafter, the frequency of the visits between us shrank from a trickle to a slow, sparsely spaced drip. Isobel seemed a bit ashamed of the chaos Lena had unwittingly brought to my life because she felt instrumental in having created it with her unsuccessful match-making efforts. (Björn might have been feeling some jealousy about the "success" of those same efforts.)

On the eve of the last day of the school term, Thursday, June 8th, my students decided to have another party, this time at a pub in Malmö. I was not only invited by a class insistent on showing their appreciation of our time together, but most of the girls insisted on taking turns sitting on my lap as the evening wore on; several of them (particularly a girl named Rose-Marie) gave pretty clear hints that I could follow up if I felt so inclined. (It wasn't really a "lap dance" – a term that didn't enter the language until the 1990s – since the girls were far less "purposeful", and no money was involved, just a laugh.) To cap the ribald evening, Majlis returned to Korngatan with me until three in the morning. I was continuing to feel incredibly *up*, living my libido-ruled life.

It didn't stop there. On Saturday morning Sonja phoned to ask if I'd like to accompany her for a weekend at her parents' "country" place in the Råbocka recreational area on the northwestern edge of Ängelholm. I knew that the Sunday was Lena's birthday, but she'd already made it abundantly clear that I was not being included in any plans she might have to celebrate. She seemed not a little puzzled by my shrugging indifference to hearing of my exclusion, as though I'd squelched her intended put-down. She might not have been able to imagine my appealing invitation from someone else. I accepted Sonja's invitation.

Sonja's parents' place was a two-storey house in what seemed to me more like a suburb than the countryside, and the frame house seemed pretty much like a normal house, except that there were more trees and fewer neighbors. The majority of homes in that area were only used in the summer. Sonja seemed more interested than I was in inspecting the upstairs bedroom with little delay. We spent much of our time there, between meals and strolls to the beach, until her brother appeared on his motorcycle on Sunday afternoon to give me a lift back to the Ängelholm train station. Sonja was going to be staying on at the house to spend some time there on her own.

The next day, Monday, Majlis phoned to express her fear that I might be feeling hounded by her, since she was always the one who took the initiative to phone and ask if she could come over to my place. I assured her that the only reason I didn't phone her was honestly because I assumed it would be more prudent for her sake, due to her possible domestic circumstances, if she were the one to phone at her convenience. And, I asked, as long as she'd phoned, would she like to come over right now? She would indeed, so we had another mid-day romp before Sonja came to spend the night.

I cannot account for this confluence of my overcharged libido and the fortuitous availability and willingness of three pretty women to take turns satisfying it. In physical, animalistic terms, I derived great satisfaction from giving them each as much satisfaction as I could, and since they each kept coming back for more, I presumed I was successful in that. I couldn't figure out why or how – my anatomy was quite average – but I didn't dwell on such questions too much.

That is not to say the situation was without complications. But in the case of Majlis, there were none in sight. Sonja was a bit enigmatic; sometimes I got the feeling that she wanted more from me than just sex and friendship, but before I could ask, she would reiterate that her true commitment was never going to be anything but her career, which would eventually take her to Stockholm permanently. I was keenly aware that Lena was the dangerous one for my mental balance. That obliged me to keep a firm grip on the emergency brake of my feelings, knowing that she could and would at any moment turn her back on me, or tell me again that she was still undecided about Larry, or tell me she was going back to him.

As far as I could see (and I can't claim that I could see very far at all in a situation where objectivity was either elusive or a hard-fought struggle), I was doing my not-quite-level-headed best to keep well clear of returning to a horrible situation. My grief was always with me, always there, just below the radar of everyone else, but it was no longer overwhelming my will to live. I'd unwillingly, unwittingly and prematurely fallen in love with Lena, who quite willingly allowed me to make love to her (while she had sex with me), and whose fickleness towards me posed a great risk to the hard-won mental balance I was still striving to maintain as a counterweight to my grief. By willingly accepting the affection willingly offered to me by Sonja and Majlis (or anyone else who might come along), *on their terms*, I could continue to heal while the three of them were making their rounds with me. I wasn't the one pursuing. And I was hardly ever obliged to take matters into my own hands.

The next day, Tuesday, June 13th, I got a phone call from Stig Troell, the education manager at Perstorp AB. He and I had hardly spoken since the spring of 1975, when he offered me a full-time job at the company, just after Jeanette and I started working on our new house. The job he was offering then would have entailed moving to the village of Perstorp – an unthinkable proposition for us – so they therefore hired somebody else, an Englishman named Trevor, who apparently didn't mind life in small-town Skåne.

Three years later, when a Perstorp facility in central England was looking to hire somebody for their personnel department, Trevor applied for and got the job. As a result, Stig phoned me to see whether I might have changed my mind and would consider the job *now*? I remained skeptical. Moving to Perstorp – leaving the house in Malmö – was still far out of the question for me. Commuting daily was pretty much unthinkable (I had no car), and working full-time was not at all attractive either. Stig claimed that they were prepared to be more flexible now. Perhaps I could come up to Perstorp to have a talk about what could be arranged? I told him that I was already committed to another stint at KomVux from mid-August to October 6th, so there wouldn't be much point in hurrying. But since he thought it would be a good idea to get the ball rolling, I agreed to come up for a chat the following week, before Midsummer and before my trip to the States. In view of the fact that I was facing unemployment after October 6th (and possibly as soon as I got home from the States if the KomVux thing fell through), I thought it could be worth looking into.

Sonja was visiting some friends in Malmö for the day, but the next day she dropped by for a long chat. At every mention of Lena my voice must have altered in some subtle way that caused Sonja to roll her eyes, shake her head and sigh, but almost imperceptibly. Was she reading me or vice-versa? I realized that she might have reason to be afraid that Lena still held tremendous power over me and my heart (I *assumed* she knew that I was sleeping with Lena every chance I got, even though I never said so to Sonja directly), and that she was perhaps even more afraid that Lena's power over me might prove hazardous to my health. She knew of my plans to visit my family in the States, and told me she'd be spending most of the summer at her parents' "cottage" in Ängelholm anyway, but would definitely see me again before I left.

Lena phoned the next day and wanted to stop by. But the lack of enthusiasm in her voice made me wonder whether she had an ulterior motive. She did. She wanted to find out whether my Danish auto mechanic neighbors, the Saabyes, could give her a good deal on some necessary repairs to the aging Datsun she'd inherited from her father. They could, and I made a mental note that the condition of her car might run parallel to Lena's future needs to visit Korngatan. She spent that night with me, but her frequent references to Larry were a constant reminder to me not to release my own brakes.

When Jeanette and I first moved to Korngatan, the Saabyes' car repair shop shared a thick mud-brick wall with our future kitchen, with access from a large sliding garage door in the alley (Källargränd). Although they could get up to five cars inside if absolutely necessary, it was cramped, and there was no hoist. During the late 70s (my memory as to the date fails me here), the Saabyes decided to move their workshop to Korngatan 9, the house directly across the narrow street from ours. (After the perfume factory moved out of Korngatan 9, not terribly long after Jeanette and I bought our house, the premises were variously used as a flea market and as a paint-stripping operation, before becoming the Saabyes' car workshop.) It may also have been out of their consideration of our nearing completion of our new kitchen on the other side of the shared wall. In the new location across the street, the Saabyes always remained considerate. Even though their new garage entrance was directly opposite our kitchen windows, they took care never to gun the engines when driving a car in or out.

I told Lena I was going to the States from June 28th to August 3rd, which seemed to surprise her, perhaps because I'd made plans that didn't involve her without informing her of them first?! She suddenly became more interested in me, and complained that she wouldn't get to see me for such a long time. Then she revealed that she'd already signed up to teach a course – in English – for Swedish school kids during the summer, and the course would take place in Eastbourne, along the south coast of England, and she would be away for much of the time I was gone anyway. (Of course she didn't inform me of this before making her decision either, but apparently it didn't matter to her because *she knew!* Why should I?) She was exceptionally affectionate towards me that night, however, which again began to kindle hope that my love for her would someday be requited, but much of her chill was already back the next morning. *Talk about fickle!!* Then she was off, and she made it clear that I wasn't part of her plans for the following weekend's Midsummer celebration. *Still out in the cold*. I just sighed and shook my head. (Unless I shrugged my shoulders. Of course, I might have done both, but in that case probably in succession, not simultaneously.)

On the 15th, I got a phone call from one of the younger students in my former class, Rose-Marie, who wanted to know if I would like to go to see a movie with her. She was in her early 20s, vaguely pretty, long straight brown hair, tall and slender like a model, with exceptionally long and attractive legs. She seemed disappointed that I'd failed to follow up on her "lap dance" at the pub by asking to see her again, so now she was taking the initiative. I had nothing planned for that evening, and we agreed to meet at the cinema near Värnhemstorget. I have no memory of the movie, perhaps because I was distracted by how instantly and intimately she cuddled up to me the moment the house lights went down.

There was still plenty of twilight when we left the cinema, and I casually suggested that we could walk back to my place. She readily agreed. I don't recall her being among those who came back to Korngatan after the Copenhagen party, so it might have been her first visit; at least she demurely accepted my offer to show her around the house. When we got upstairs and I indicated that my bedroom inside a certain open door off my studio, she pulled me inside and started undressing. I knew the drill; so did she.

Once our lust was sated after two or three rounds, a bit sweaty and quivering, we were both in need of a break. She suddenly stopped smiling, gave me a serious look and with a hint of triumph in her voice said, "*You know, I have no protection....*" I was stunned by the timing of her declaration – telling me *afterwards* – but I just smiled and told her it didn't matter, I was sterile, I'd had a vasectomy. Then, to my even greater surprise, she looked disappointed. Not relieved. *Disappointed*! This was way beyond weird to me. She must have been *hoping* I'd knocked her up. I'd never experienced such devious behavior. I'd read about things like that in some novels, but then it was more surreptitious, not revealed until pregnancy (or even birth) was a fact. Self-contradictory as it may sound, this was *openly* devious. Never was I happier that I'd had that vasectomy!

On Sunday, Majlis phoned and asked if she could come by in the afternoon for a while. I was all for it. She arrived looking a bit stressed and hurried, but it soon became apparent that I was the cause; she was no sooner inside the door than she was all over me, although I wasted no time responding in kind. When we got to the bedroom and pulled the rest of our clothes off, I discovered that she'd gone to some extra bother for my sake: her new bra and panties were of burgundy lace that brought out the best in her figure and my lust, which in turn made her eyes glow. Whatever imbalance was building up in me as a result of Lena's emotional jujitsu a couple of days earlier was completely blown away that afternoon. Once again, it was all pure sex, pure mutual lust and pleasure, as much as we could give, with no promises or need for them. She didn't want to talk to me about the relationship she was involved in, and I had no wish to talk to her about Lena.

On Monday, Stig Troell phoned again and said we'd have to postpone our meeting for quite some time, due to business trips on his part and on the part of the personnel manager, followed by the vacation period. I said there was no problem; we could speak again when I got back from the States in early August. Although I realized he might interpret my casualness as indifference, I would in

Making the rounds

fact have preferred to continue at KomVux – *especially* part-time – not considering that I risked ending up with neither.

The next day I asked Allan Saabye if he could give me a hand for a few minutes to move some furniture. Some weeks earlier, I bought a fairly large old oak table from a neighbor and put it in the future living room. There I sanded it down to a smooth finish, then oiled it, but it wasn't going to be part of the living room furniture; it was going to be my painting table, upstairs in my studio. Allan kindly helped me move my black leather sofa and armchair, coffee table, and stereo downstairs, and my painting table upstairs. My studio now contained only the big table, a chair and my easel; I was ready to start painting as soon as I got back from the States. I was getting really eager about it, and had a few sketches gestating in the Petri dish of my mind.

Bob and I were continuing our lengthy weekly phone conversations, but he'd now bought himself a super new typewriter (yes, there were such things!): the latest generation of the IBM *Selectric*. It was about to launch him into a new era of letter-writing unlike any I'd seen before. He also bought himself a used car, a Saab; at least the passengers would now be safe.

I seem to remember that I went to a neighborhood party for Midsummer Eve, held in the yard at Tage Thagaard's house, and that I had a decent time, which I was fully capable of having without the aid of alcohol, which is by no means to say that I left the party sober, which is perhaps why I only seem to remember it.

On Saturday, Midsummer Day, Lena phoned and asked what I was up to. She seemed somewhat disconcerted by how balanced I seemed to be remaining even when she refused to see me. In any case, she readily agreed to come and spend the night with me. But the next morning, after her flames had subsided, she was off again.

Sonja spent Sunday and Monday nights with me and was profuse in her wishes for me to have a safe trip to the States. She said she'd write, so I gave her John's address. Mom would have asked too many questions, and by the time I got to Al's, there wouldn't be any point – I'd soon be home. (I gave Mom's and John's addresses to Lena, but she told me she probably wouldn't write. I could still be pathetic from time to time....) On Tuesday, Majlis phoned and wanted to come over, but I told her that I would be too busy packing and running lots of errands in preparation for my trip the next day, so I'd see her when I got back. Although she was disappointed about having to wait, she wished me a speedy return.

A Sea of Troubles

I flew from Copenhagen at around noon on Wednesday, June 28th, on a 747 Jumbo Jet, with only a single item of baggage for my five-week *tour de force*: a small carry-on that contained two collapsed bags. Clothes were much cheaper in the US then, and I needed clothes, since few of mine fit me anymore after all the weight I'd lost.

The seating on the plane was 3-4-3, and the flight wasn't full. My seat was an aisle seat in a 3-seat configuration on the left-hand side of the plane in the last row before the midsection lavatories; the seatbacks couldn't be reclined. But the flight wasn't full, and there was an empty seat between me and a pretty American girl named Mary Jane in her early 20s who was flying home to Wisconsin for a summer vacation visit from her temporary home in Norway. She told me she was involved in a movement called "Up with People", an American youth organization that was allegedly all about happiness. I'd never heard of it, but was slightly suspicious that it could be about somebody's agenda. She offered no details, but she seemed happy enough.

She and I were preoccupied with our own things for several hours, but since we both found it impossible to get any sleep on planes, we began talking instead, and by talking I mean flirting. The noise level in the cabin was high enough to require my moving to the middle seat in order for us to hear the choice of words we were flirting with, and the cabin temperature was low enough for her to ask me if I could retrieve a blanket for her from the overhead compartment. Since I concurred with her assessment of the chill factor, we agreed that it could be of mutual benefit to drape the blanket over both of us, thereby removing our arms, hands, breasts and thighs from public view. This seemed to have a huge impact on the plane's air velocity, because the previously long, dreary, painfully slow and boring flight suddenly whizzed by and we found ourselves approaching Chicago's O'Hare Airport before either of us could say "*Orgasm*!"

I was supposed to be flying onward to Galesburg via Britt Airways within an hour or so, but since Mary Jane had a few hours before her onward flight to Wisconsin, I managed to rebook my ticket. Since I had no checked baggage and the small airline had plenty of vacant seats, they gladly switched me to a flight in the late evening (I phoned my mom to tell her when, not why). Then Mary Jane and I found a relatively secluded airport corridor where we could continue our erotic game in a more mutually satisfying vertical position before parting, never to hear from each other again. [*I later discovered that "Up with People" was the name of an ultra-clean-cut singing group with roots in right-wing Christian fundamentalism, but nothing she said or did reflected anything like that. Maybe I wasn't the only rebel?*]

On the 50-minute flight to Galesburg, there were only eight passenger seats – fewer than the number of seats *in each row* on the 747. The juxtaposition of the two flights made the small plane feel really weird. The pilot read the identical standard safety announcement as on the Jumbo Jet, but on the Britt Airways flight, he turned around in his seat and looked the passengers in the eyes as he read the out the message from a small card. It was dusk, just getting dark, by the time we took off, and there were numerous highly visible electrical storms flashing on the horizon in every direction. Some of them drew closer as we flew, requiring the pilot to make some tactical maneuvers to avoid them. It felt so much more like flying than on a 747! You could see out windows in three directions at once, and each wisp of cloud we encountered felt like a pothole in the sky.

It was nearly 10 PM when I arrived in Galesburg, where Mom, my Uncle Ralph and Aunt Maxine were waiting to pick me up for the 20-minute drive to Mom's new home in Knoxville. I was glad it was so late – there would be ample reason for heading straight to bed before the three of them could start carrying on about how merciful He was for guiding me (*uh, there was a pilot...*) through the storms (*that He created*) before they would let me sleep.

Although I was exhausted, and the sweltering Midwestern summer heat didn't exactly energize me, there was a stunning contrast between how I felt on this American trip and how I felt on the trip with a similar itinerary the year before. I was no longer an emotional cripple with open sores on my soul. I'd gained a kind of strength I'd never had before – a paradox, since it was a kind of strength I wished for everyone I'd ever cared about, but at the same time I hoped that nobody I cared about or didn't care about would ever have to endure anything like what I'd gone through to get it.

The drive to Mom's place from the airport would have taken me 10-15 minutes. It took Ralf 30. I suspected that Ralph may have been trying to get extra time for himself and Maxine to get some preaching in, but as soon as the conversation in the car turned to religious clichés (almost immediately), I tuned out completely and pretended to doze. At last he pulled his car into Mom's driveway in the darkness, and due to the late hour, he left the engine running, so Mom and I could quickly escape the mosquitoes that wasted no time discovering me as soon as I stepped out of the car. Ralph left his headlights on until Mom nervously inserted her key into the lock, opened the door and turned on a couple of lights inside. We turned briefly to wave Ralph and Maxine off into the night as they drove a few hundred meters down the hill to their own nearly identical new home. I was relieved to find that Mom's had air conditioning.

I looked around me at the many familiar furnishings in the unfamiliar home. Many of the dark-oak pieces of furniture I'd grown up with were there, as were the little copper teapot that was only used for decoration, the framed Bible verses on the walls, a few kitschy paintings (including a couple of mine that I never considered part of the body of my artistic work), the lovely Kay Scott painting from California, the dark green floor lamp with the gold leaf trim, the piano, Bibles and tracts lying about on small tables, as well as things I'd only seen a couple of times at our home on 1231 N. Euclid because they'd been acquired since I left Oak Park in 1964. (But I had seen them when Jeanette and I visited Mom and Dad in 1969 on our way to Sweden, as well as when we visited Mom in 1974.) I was, however, far too tired in so many ways to take it all in that night.

Despite the late hour, Mom had a whole array of snacks and other edibles available should I have displayed the slightest hunger. She also had a variety of beverages (non-alcoholic, of course); I could've killed for a beer, but I gladly accepted lemonade. But before I could take a sip, Mom bowed her head and started audibly thanking her invisible friend for what *she* bought for me. I waited patiently while she gushed on and on.

In my room alone at last, I shut the door and took a couple of big gulps of duty-free whisky, after which I slept pretty well through the night. I woke up earlier than usual due to jetlag. It was only 6 AM, but I could hear that Mom was already up and about, so I went via the hallway to have a shower. Mom must have heard me, because when I turned off the water, I could hear her start playing her hymns on the piano. It brought back many unpleasant memories of the many facets of indoctrination to which I'd been subjected in my childhood. She'd been pretty good about refraining from her preachiness when she'd been to see me in Malmö in September, but I was on her turf now.

She'd delayed her own breakfast so she could join me when I had mine, but I suspect it was mostly to have an excuse to pray aloud (preach) in my presence once again. Mealtime (or snack-time) prayers on her turf were her freebies, I understood, so I tried to be patient each time, looking around the room while she went on and on. But after a few of her endless prayers, I decided that even freebies need limits, so I set one. When she started praying, I started counting, drawling silently, very slowly and unhurriedly. If she was still going on when I got to 30, I started eating. Ready or not, here I come. She quickly learned to keep it short.

Her house made me sad. The house, combined with her looks and subtle comments, made it painfully obvious that it was not her *home*. She showed me the drab room that had briefly been Grandma Erisman's. Everything looked bleak, despite all the familiar furnishings that once made 1231 our home. I could see how lonely, confused and lost Mom was. This clearly wasn't how the dream was supposed to unfold, now that Dad was gone and she was fending for herself out here in the middle of nowhere. She was trying to be cheerful, but her claims that she had "*such joy in the Lord, the only one who can bring true joy,*" rang completely false, both in my ears and on her face.

Stuck out on Swedenburg Road, the house was poorly matched to Mom's fierce independence and strong aversion to having to rely on anyone (except Dad). Ralph told her, quite sincerely and generously, that he'd drive her anywhere she wanted to go, but she *hated* having to ask him. The nearest stores of any kind, in the village of Knoxville (population around 2,000), were small and meant a brisk half-hour walk each way. Although she was still a very swift walker, Mom was very much on the outer outskirts of a village unworthy of any skirts at all. The only familiar sight to her was the white frame farmhouse almost directly across the road, where her father's native Swedish parents once lived (perhaps the origin of the "Swedenburg" name of the road, and certainly the reason for the choice of the location). It was a farm Mom frequently visited as a girl, since Mom's uncle Titus took over it over after his parents. It was also the venue for the local Meeting, scraping by under the Matthew 18:20 rule ("*For where two or three are gathered together in my name, there am I in the midst of them*").

I'd visited that house several times as a child and adolescent, and when I looked at it from Mom's front yard and saw the red barn behind and to the right of it, the sight conjured up an incompletely suppressed memory of the time when my pubertal same-age cousin and I, feeling our hormones, set off towards the barn, having heard that a nice heifer could be worth a try. We never found a willing heifer, and I'd like to think we wouldn't have actually pursued such a cockeyed plan if we had, but who knows what hormones (especially testosterone) are capable of when they course through adolescent brains or groins?

Another unwholesome childhood memory was awakened while I was mowing Mom's lawn. After an hour or so at my task, I felt and saw that my legs were covered with violently itchy chigger bites, just like in the summer of '57, when Little Wolf and Red Eagle played Indians in Aunt Shirley's back yard in Des Moines.

Today the house across the road was occupied by an elderly couple: Clarence Lundin and his wife Barbara. Barbara was the daughter of Uncle Tite (as Mom always called her Uncle Titus), making Barbara Mom's cousin. Before marrying Clarence fairly late in life, Barbara had been inseparable from her unmarried sister Jean. I remembered Jean and Barbara as two lithesome, pretty, coy, chaste, ethereal women who were always giggling softly and looking cautiously flirtatious, but seldom left the farm and never married. [*Decades later, I would see two strikingly similar sisters in the amazing 1987 Danish film* Babettes gæstebud *(Babette's Feast).*] Clarence Lundin, also of Swedish ancestry, was a Laboring Brother in the Meeting.[9] Some years after his first wife died, his eye fell upon the comely Barbara, by that time in her 60s. He wedded and bedded her, to the devastation of the still-virginal Jean, who presumably remained alone for the rest of her life.

While I was laboring in the heat to finish mowing the lawn, it wasn't only the chiggers who were after me that afternoon. I saw someone approaching and instantly recognized Clarence. It came as no great surprise to me, since I'd met him a number of times as a child and his countenance was singular. He was still as lean, wiry and silver-haired as I remembered him, with a sharp, stern gaze and tight lips. What did surprise me was that he began speaking to me in Swedish! I responded in kind, of course. Some of his Swedish sounded a bit old-fashioned to me, but was otherwise pretty good, which impressed me, considering his limited exposure to it. But after a minimum of introductory banter, he turned the subject to religion. (*What else?*) Sweden was once a most God-fearing country, he noted sternly. I smiled and said how great I thought it was that Sweden nowadays was so secular. He looked like he couldn't believe his ears, or that I'd used some Swedish formulations he couldn't quite grasp or that I'd hit him. After a few more exchanges like that, all on his favorite topic, he realized he'd grasped far more than he wanted to. He turned and left and I didn't see him again during my stay with Mom – or ever. On further reflection, I was amazed at how self-evidently he seemed to claim the right to expound his wild beliefs to me (however popular they were in his limited circles), and how equally self-evidently he felt entitled to take offense at my briefly mentioning my own (although far from popular in the Land of the Free).

---

9   Cf. *Natural Shocks*, chapter 2

Making the rounds

In a letter to Bob from Knoxville on July 2nd, I wrote that I found it extremely boring, that there was "nothing to do but watch cows and sweat." I wrote Lena nearly every day during my trip to the States, at first to her address in Lund, and later to the address she'd given me in Eastbourne. I think I got one letter from her during that entire five-week period. I could never learn. But I probably wouldn't have written to her so often if I weren't so excruciatingly bored. Mom sensed my restlessness, and suggested one day that instead of calling upon Ralph's taxi service, she and I might walk to Knoxville to do the grocery shopping. The heat was insufferable and made our feet swell up, and there wasn't even a cold beer to make it more bearable; I feared I was being far too deferential.

Mom went so far as to suggest that she and I take a train to Chicago one day, an offer I accepted without hesitation. Of course Ralph had to drive us to and from the Galesburg train station. I got the impression that I'd managed to make myself pretty clear to Ralph and Maxine; his clichés were directed at Mom only. (Maybe Ralph had had a few words with Clarence? That seems likely.)

The Windy City was a bit outside Mom's comfort zone, but she bravely went along for most of it – except for the elevator ride to the top of the Sears Tower. She stayed below while I went up and got the most wonderful views, from Indiana to Wisconsin. Mom and I went to Marshall Field's in the Loop, which was definitely well within her comfort zone, as long as we took the escalators instead of the elevators. I was constantly joking, and I'm sure that Mom laughed more in that one afternoon than she'd laughed during the past five and a half years. (I spared her my private joking question about whether the Lord would have refused to take elevators....)

During the last days of my stay, I told Mom about my on-and-off relationship with Lena (I didn't mention the in-and-out part), emphasizing the fact that the "off" part of it had nothing to do with *my* wishes. She started asking all kinds of questions, of course, and her interest eerily intensified to blood-in-the-water levels when I told her that Lena's late father had been a vicar for the Swedish Church. But I back-pedaled, explaining that my relationship with Lena was nothing serious yet. That made her happy to drop the subject, or perhaps it was because she realized that she was no longer in a position to command my indoctrination, and that her questions and probings could lead her renegade son to provide answers that she preferred not to hear.

I started doing some probing of my own. She admitted that she wasn't happy being stuck out there on Swedenburg Road, but she was terribly uncertain about what to do or where to go. Apparently Ralph and Maxine were also a bit disillusioned with Knoxville, despite having been so ostentatiously "cast upon the Lord" before making the decision to move there in the first place. They were so convinced that it was His will that led them to Knoxville, so *He* must have screwed up. [*The explanation for my making such observations is simple: there are literally billions of people out there constantly declaring their claims that one or more of their gods is responsible for the good things that happen, but they never blame him/her/it/them for the bad things.* Someone's *got to point that out once in a while!*]

Mom said that Ralph and Maxine were now talking about a move to Florida, which meant that Mom *couldn't* remain in Knoxville, in isolation without her driver. But Mom *certainly* didn't want to move to Florida! Knoxville was already too far from all her kids and grandkids as it was. Yet Southern California (once a possibility) was out of the question. Without a car, it would have been just as isolated, and John and his family had recently moved to Northern California. She also mentioned that she didn't think John would appreciate having her close by (it would take quite a few more years until I realized the necessity of confronting her on matters like this), and besides (and here she lowered her voice to achieve a tone of greatest solemnity), John and Marj had recently committed the most *trying* act, an act that was *"so sad"*, close to apostasy: they'd left the Meeting in Oakland for some local Evangelical church in Santa Rosa. Mom said she wasn't sure about Al (who turned out to be about to commit the same horrendous act as John, but Mom was unaware of Al's intentions at that time). Moving along, she then spoke with emphatic, almost vehement, disapproval of Nancy's working outside the home. (Mom was not a forefront figure in the women's liberation movement.)

Next came a question that took me completely by surprise: "*I don't suppose you're thinking of moving back to the US? Then I could live near you!*" She was deadly serious! She even talked about her and me getting adjacent apartments in the same building somewhere. It was hard not to draw the conclusion that my brothers' leaving the Meeting was far worse in her mind than *my* leaving the entire concept of religious faith and *all* belief that lacked proof, which covered most of it. *Huh?!*

I tried to let her down gently, pointing out that I had a new life in Sweden, that I preferred living in Sweden and didn't feel at home in the US anymore, and that she and I had so many differences on so many issues that it would probably end up causing her way too much distress. I told her I knew that her suggestion was rooted in love, her tremendous love for me, and that I was moved by her plea. But I added that I thought that our history since the early '60s indicated pretty clearly that one of the reasons we now got along so well together was that we didn't get to see each other often, obliging us to make the best of the limited time we had together when we at last did meet.

I asked her whether she didn't think that Seattle might be a better choice for her. She had a few old friends there (unlike in Northern California), and there were direct flights to Copenhagen that didn't take much longer than from Chicago. She said she'd think about it; then she admitted that such a move was already gestating in the earliest stages of her mental and emotional development anyway.

After Knoxville, my next stop was a flight to San Francisco and an onward flight to Santa Rosa. I'd always had good times with John and his family, even in absolute terms, i.e. not only compared to visits with my other family members, which was why I made the California leg of my trip considerably longer than the others. John was by far the least uptight of the rest of my family (extended or otherwise), which is saying a lot about the others. At John's home, we could share a bottle of wine without furtive glances or rolling eyes, and he was proud to offer good wines he knew well. I could tell him dirty jokes (as long as his kids weren't present) and he (and often Marj) would laugh heartily, without any snarling or shaking of the head in feigned disgust. Their walls were not plastered with cherry-picked scripture verses or the need to convince or constantly remind anyone and everyone of their humble piety. And there was the music; John and I had a few enjoyable jam sessions on his guitars (and him on his fantastic banjo), playing and singing some blues and Dylan, and laughing our heads off.

This was our first meeting since their trip to Europe the year before. John looked mighty pleased with himself for having taken what was for him the huge step of leaving the Meeting, but he seemed disappointed that I was underwhelmed by how tiny the step appeared from my perspective. Ever since I'd learned to start questioning what I'd been commanded to believe, I'd seen my big brother as someone doing the splits between two poles: toeing the line of Christian Evangelicalism with one foot and trying to impress me (and himself) with how cool he was with the other. Perhaps leaving the Meeting was the latest example of that split. For him, it was cool enough to be able to say that he was now going to *church*. (Wow.) Defending John to some extent, I wrote to Bob that *"John doesn't allow his beliefs to infringe upon his fun. That he doesn't allow himself to challenge his premises as to the nature and origins of things is more in keeping with the basic inclination of his personality."*

A week into my stay with John and family, I phoned Rose from Santa Rosa and said I'd like to come down to San Francisco for the day. She immediately invited me to spend the night as well, which I gratefully did on July 12th (John lent me a car). Jeanette's mom, big sister and Michael were friendly. (I don't recall meeting Rosanne.) But it was awkward being there, not only because we'd never had much in common, but also because the only one who seemed to want to talk about Jeanette was me. As I recall, nobody said anything about the trunk. (I'd previously received a very brief confirmation that it had arrived, but that was it.)

While at John's, I received a letter from Sonja, as well as one from Lena. Lena told me she missed me (!), and I wondered, in my letter to Bob, whether the barriers were beginning to crack. But I wasn't about to count on anything. *"Although I still love her, I'm not going to get messed up like I did before,"* I claimed.

Santa Rosa was in the heart of California's rapidly growing and increasingly well-reputed wine district. John told me with considerable pride that there was an abundance of wineries nearby offering generous free sampling opportunities, as well as on-site sales of bottles and cases. John didn't even have to ask whether I'd enjoy some outings to visit them, so we took off in their camper late one morning and hit the first of 11 wineries that day at around noon. The next day we hit 10 more (it may have been 10 + 11 instead). John, Marj and I enjoyed plenty of free samples, but Marj was fairly restrictive in her choices. John and I helped ourselves to them all, but John did all the driving, as usual. As I recall, most of the wineries we visited were in Napa County (not so many, if any, in the adjacent Sonoma and Mendocino counties).

The terrain in the wine district was not flat and the roads were not straight and the traffic was not particularly light. Coming around one in a series of tight curves on a steep hillside between two wineries, my less-than-sober brother spotted a hippie-looking hitchhiker on the road ahead. The hitchhiker was clearly growing weary of being ignored by one single-occupant car after another on that hot July afternoon. He aggressively took a step out from the shoulder, which for some reason seriously irritated John. Instead of swerving to avoid him, John swerved slightly in, so as to tap the hitchhiker's extended, gesticulating hand with the passenger-side mirror. There was an audible *thump*. Marj cried out *"John!?!"* And John shot back defensively *"Well, he came out on the road?!"* I looked back to see the hitchhiker wringing his hand a bit theatrically, but John made no move to stop. I was not exactly sober myself and found the situation comically absurd, almost like a continuation of the previous year's experiences in the Black Forest, and I began laughing. But we just pushed on to the next winery and changed the subject. [*Years later I mentioned this incident to John, which I'm convinced I remember with crystal clarity. John denied it ever happened. Lacking affidavits and other instruments of evidence, I can't prove my version beyond invoking the alleged clarity of my memory.*]

Another example of John's desire to impress me with his "coolness" was that he told me he'd seen the scandalously erotic movie *Deep Throat*. The fact was that John had almost *always* impressed me with his coolness, even if my perception of his coolness might only have been in his intuitive selection of what he thought I might find cool. [*But years later he would also categorically deny having seen* Deep Throat. *I can't know whether he did or not (and it makes no difference to me), but I do know that he told me he did, which is what contributed to my perception of him, and makes his subsequent denial curious to me. But once again, no affidavits. Regardless of that detail, his inability and tenacious unwillingness to seriously reexamine and free himself from the fundamentals of his childhood indoctrination – no matter how many Meetings he left – would never be cool to me, and I felt deeply sorry for him that he couldn't or wouldn't see it.*]

Brian and Janet were in their teens now, and since they appeared to me to have few restrictions compared to what I'd had, I was quick to presume that they were able to feel quite free. I never thought to sound them out, if for no other reason than the fact that there were no real opportunities for me to do so – John would have been at my throat like a she-bear. Brian and I played tennis a few times, and we had fun cavorting in the local swimming pool. That was the extent of our activities during our time together

I got a call from Dave Henderson while I was at John's. We talked for about 15 minutes. We'd never had terribly much in common besides basketball, and had very little contact since our Oak Park days, apart from his one bizarre visit to us in Vancouver and another in Malmö. Dave wondered whether I'd been in touch with his cousin (and my former best friend) Norm Denton. I was very surprised that he asked me. I told him I hadn't. I asked Dave if he'd heard from or about Norm, but Dave said he knew very little. Dave had consistently responded to my requests for Norm's address with claims that he, Dave, didn't know himself. I suspected that Dave might be stonewalling me again. But I also found it difficult to comprehend Norm's lack of response the year before, when I'd phoned from Seattle to tell him of Jeanette's death. That and the fact that he hadn't written to me in the meantime led me to conclude that Norm wanted no further contact with me, which I tried not to allow to get me down.

I flew to Seattle's SeaTac Airport on Tuesday evening, July 25th, where Al picked me up and drove me to their home in Bellevue. The same parameters that made John's and Marj's behavior and home environment so "normal" in my eyes, relatively speaking, were involved in making Al's and Nancy's behavior and home so extremely uptight. Tension was omnipresent. While it certainly wasn't for me to tell them how to behave or live, I was nevertheless faced with conditions that tended to make me climb the walls. Once in a while I managed to make Nancy laugh heartily, but any joke with the slightest sexual overtones was met with a scathing "*we are not amused*" glare that made me wish I were somewhere else (as they sometimes seemed to wish as well). So did being in their home, much of the time.

When I asked about the possibility of having some wine with dinner, they looked at me as if I were an alcoholic. They claimed not to disapprove, but they didn't serve any. One day when Al suddenly announced that was going grocery shopping, I insisted on tagging along. (He hadn't asked me to join him any more than I asked if I could.) I took my own basket at the store and picked up a couple of bottles of wine, intending to pay for them myself, but Al insisted on adding them to his shopping cart instead, without comment. There was, however, absolutely no vocalized appreciation or enjoyment involved, and never any initiative to purchase or serve. The contrast with John's home was striking. The main enjoyment at Al's – and yes, there *was* a lot of it – was sports: baseball (playing and watching), tennis and catch (with a football or almost anything else that could be thrown and/or hit).

On Sunday afternoon, July 30th, a friend of Al's came by for dinner. He mentioned that he was going to be driving up to Vancouver the next morning and would come back a day later. I immediately thought of Lee Whitehead, my favorite professor from UBC, and asked Al's friend if I could tag along. He said yes. Then I immediately got Lee's phone number and called him to ask if a visit from me would be desirable and convenient, and he said yes, enthusiastically and without hesitation. He showed me around the university and the burgeoning downtown area, and invited me to spend the night at their place. I was thrilled to see my "old" professor for the first time in more than nine years. It also gave me nearly two days of respite from the ubiquitous and all-too-frequent scowls in Bellevue. The Thursday Night Massacre[10] was still alive and kicking in teeth.

Just before midnight on Sunday evening, August 6th, I flew out of Seattle, heading for home. After a long flight, I arrived in Copenhagen on Monday afternoon. Sonja met me at the airport. We took the ferry to Malmö and then a taxi to Korngatan. Along the way, she told me that she'd be moving permanently to Stockholm in mid-September, and I told her I was happy for her, because it seemed to be what she wanted.

We spent some tension-relieving time in bed until Sonja had to leave. Jetlag caught up with me and I more or less passed out, only to find myself wide awake again in the middle of the night. But I had some accumulated mail to sort through, some bills to pay, and some thoughts to collect.

The day after my return from the States, I wrote to Bob to sum up my trip, claiming that the time I had for reflection enabled me to *"feel much more capable of following my own reactions from a certain distance, of employing my more rational elements in areas where emotions had run wild, of dealing with life with an open mind, a fair amount of courage, and a lot of grains of salt."*

That same day I also started painting *Turning*,[11] a work that started as a sketch done in February 1978 in a state of suicidal misery, in which the man was staring down in front of him, thoroughly depressed. I'd "painted" it dozens of times in my head, at first as a horrendous moan of agony when I envisaged it back in February. After my catharsis in March, it – like me – was totally transformed into something brighter, even vibrant. His face is resting on his hand, in an attitude of *either* sadness, *or* a stifled laugh, *or* simply bored impatience. The bed on which he is sitting has a red velvet bedspread (like Lena's in Lund, and remember my poem!). There is a blue carpet and brown wallpaper (also similar to hers). The blonde girl is lingeringly leaving him, heading towards an open doorway and the void beyond. Their outstretched hands are still touching, while she's pulling away, and he's trying to hold on.

---

10 Cf. *Natural Shocks*, chapter 9
11 Painting #79 (see Appendix 2 and front cover of this book)

And yet it is every bit a painting of resolution (if not revolution), reflecting my metamorphosis from having been deeply and suicidally depressed to now being cautiously optimistic and joyful. The point of contact is one of the lightest areas of the painting, as well as being in the center.

This painting would become one of my personal favorites, because it went so far in helping me to resolve the emotional chaos that Lena unwittingly brought to my life. It thus also helped to prepare me to let go completely if absolutely necessary, whenever that day might come. (But I wouldn't give up easily; my tenacity was also intact.)

Lena only sent me the one letter during my five weeks in the US, as well as a postcard announcing the day of her return from England, August 10th. I'd sent her more than two dozen letters during my absence. Consequently, I wasn't expecting much when she returned from Eastbourne three days after my return from the States. I was thus surprised when she agreed to spend the weekend with me. I finished *Turning* at 3.45 AM on Sunday, August 13th, while Lena was sleeping in my bed in the next room. It was the first painting I'd completed in some two and a half years, and the first ever in my new studio (I remembered with considerable sadness that having a studio was one of the principal reasons Jeanette and I bought the house in the first place). Naturally, I thought again of Jeanette's injunction.

Lena gasped when she saw the completed painting later that day. She knew the woman was her, and she expressed amazement that I'd captured her essence, even though it was abstract. But she didn't go so far as to say how or whether she liked it (I'd learned that her high expectations of and dependence on receiving praise from me were matched by her reluctance to give me any).

I wrote to tell Bob about the painting:

Turning is primarily about Lena and me. She has, in fact, a red velvet bedspread, a blue carpet and brown wallpaper in her apartment [as in the painting]. What is most interesting for me in this painting is the change of attitude it represents in me over the last 6 or 7 months. The sketch on which it is based, and which I sketched 7 months ago, illustrates this difference. The man [in the sketch] was staring down in front of him, thoroughly depressed. Here [in the painting], his face is resting on his hand, in an attitude of <u>either</u> sadness, a stifled laugh, or simply bored impatience. I also seemed to capture Lena in a nutshell, so much so that even she found the resemblance, both in suggested contours as well as mercurial attitude, astonishing. In my *view, this painting is a first major transitional step towards introducing a more positive and ambivalent approach to paintings as I live them or life as I paint it. You will also note that the point of contact is one of the lightest areas of the painting, as well as being in the very center. Such was not the case in the sketch. Technically, I think this painting has more "depth" than anything I've done before.*

The job situation at KomVux was now looking doubtful. I phoned them on Monday, August 14th to find out exactly when – or if – I'd be starting. They told me in June that they'd be obliged to advertise the position publically, but that they wouldn't be doing so until the week before the term started. That was to give me the best chance so that nobody more officially qualified would apply, but they'd still be obliged to give the job to anyone with a teacher's certificate. Yet they'd gone ahead and advertised it anyway, a week earlier, to my disappointment. Nevertheless I wasn't upset. I was still so euphoric about life, so full of vitality and virility, so excited about painting, that nothing was about to break or even brake me.

Lena apparently didn't come home from Eastbourne alone; she was joined by a whole host of strep-throat-inducing microbes, which didn't show their true colors until that Monday afternoon. When she phoned to let me know all about it, her raspy voice was choking on tears. This of course aroused all my motherly instincts towards her. I was practically on the next bus to Lund to start running all kinds of errands for her – grocery shopping, post office, pharmacy, helping her pay bills (sometimes just paying them), making phone calls on her behalf, making her cups of tea or chicken soup or whatever else she might like to eat, keeping her supplied with cool moist towels, changing her sweaty sheets, taking home her laundry and washing it at my place and bringing back fresh things, holding her hand, buying her flowers, brightening her day, telling her how much I loved her (in case all the aforementioned failed to convey that message), doing everything I possibly could to get her back into shape so she'd be well enough to start the fall term on August 21st. And in between errands for her I was painting.

On Thursday the 17th, the principal at KomVux phoned to ask me if I still wanted the job, which I did, so I was to come to the school the next day for the formal introduction or signing or whatever it was I had to do to become an official temporary part-time employee for just over a month, starting on August 22nd and lasting until October 6th. Unfortunately, in all my endeavors to help Lena get well,

I also managed to assume ownership of many of her streptococcus germs. Just as she was getting over her illness, the broken glass in my throat made it apparent that my attentions had not been without consequences. So what happened when it was my turn to writhe in high fever, unable to swallow or face the outdoors? Well, during those days Lena did stop by *once* to make me some soup. Otherwise, she was "too busy", and I was in danger of missing the start of my own fall term. I didn't let it get to me. She'd become fairly predictable.

On Monday the 21st, Stig Troell phoned again to ask me to come up to Perstorp for an interview, to make some kind of job there official. Fearing that I might not get another opportunity if I turned him down, I agreed to come up two days later (I'd just found out that my part-time KomVux schedule gave me Wednesdays off), despite still feeling terribly under the weather. Also fearing that KomVux might not look favorably on having to get a substitute for the substitute, I went to work on the 22nd anyway.

CHAPTER 7

Perstorp

I parked my bike at the Malmö Central Station on Wednesday morning, got a northbound train to Hässleholm, where I changed to a westbound train to Perstorp, pronounced something like PAIRS-torp – almost like it's spelled, although many non-Swedes I've met have bent over backwards to make it difficult, often pronouncing *torp* as though it were *trop*.

Stig picked me up at the station and took me to the company's head office building, shaped like a thick Y with the three "legs" curved around a central hub containing twin elevators and a broad stairway winding around the elevator shaft. From this hub, which also housed time-card clocks, lavatories, and coat racks for outer garments, three corridors (one for each leg) curved away from each other in directions that seemed designed to confuse all visitors (and recent employees). The exterior of the six-storey construction (plus an exclusive 7th-storey executive boardroom and conference penthouse) consisted of rows of windows separated by cladding of lilac-colored ceramic tiles that reminded me of bathrooms.

There was a hushed, almost reverent atmosphere inside; the higher the floor, the higher the salaries and the greater the reverence. Stig's office was on the 2nd floor. The education department (of which he was the only member until I came along) belonged to the personnel department (as such departments were known until some euphemist thought up "Human Resources"). The occupants of the nearby offices were also engaged in various other aspects of personnel administration, such as recruitment, salary administration, and tasks of an ilk that would have made me weep with boredom.

For my interview, Stig and I were joined by Irene, a personnel manager or officer who was officially authorized to hire me. She and Stig outlined briefly what they were looking for: someone who could provide English lessons for employees, normally 2-4 at a time, during working hours. I rolled my eyes at that one, and told them how ineffective I'd always found that form of language training to be, at least compared to individual immersion courses. They said that the education policy under their latest President, Karl-Erik Sahlberg (replacing Gunnar Wessman, the former President, who in 1975 was booted out or persuaded to "seek new challenges"), so there was nothing to be done about that – at least for now. The job would also include some translation and text-revision work. I was basically going to be the in-house consultant for Perstorp's official corporate language, English.

I brought with me copies of my diplomas and employment records (except from The Emporium). Stig knew me well enough to say enough in my favor so that I didn't have to plead my own case to Irene. It was more a case of them having to persuade *me* anyway, and more a case of what I *didn't* want than what I did – just as it was when they first offered me the job back in 1975.

I still didn't want a full-time job; I needed time to paint. I still couldn't dream of living in Perstorp, so I would need to consolidate all my part-time hours into as few days as possible, and then find some way of getting transportation between Malmö and Perstorp, hopefully without the multi-hour commute that public transportation would entail. And I told them I couldn't start until October 11th (I wanted a few days off after my last day at KomVux).

They calmly offered solutions to almost every problem. Part-time (20 hours per week) would be fine. I asked what we would do about situations that might arise involving such unforeseeable and unplannable things as urgent or big translation jobs, or pupils who cancelled. They suggested that we could make the 20-hours-per-week arrangement flexible – an *average* of 20 hours. *And if it turned out to be consistently more?* They said I could either get paid overtime for the excess or take compensatory time off. My "quota" of 20 hours per week would be calculated as a monthly average, and if I preferred, I could accumulate any extra pay and/or comp time in a "pot", to be settled monthly or quarterly or whenever I felt like it. [*Many years later, I would come to regret not having this verbal agreement in writing! See the Afterword in Book 6,* Perchance to Dream*!*]

The commute might be a trickier problem. They proposed that I spend two consecutive days in Perstorp (I immediately suggested Wednesdays and Thursdays to enable long weekends at both ends for painting and other activities), and they would pay for a room at the local hotel for the intervening night. They also mentioned having heard that there were a couple of full-time Perstorp employees commuting to and from Malmö every day. They would try to procure the names and phone numbers for me so I could see about hitching a ride (travelling by car would entail less than half the commuting time compared to public transportation) instead of staying at the hotel, if I preferred. I said I would try the hotel to start with.

As far as beginning on October 11th was concerned, that was also acceptable, but my employment – and first paycheck – would officially be from October 1st.

Finally, they offered me a fixed salary of 4000 kronor a month. In retrospect, I'm sure they were they were expecting a substantially higher counter-demand from me, but I was never much good at negotiating my own demands, so I just accepted what they offered. I was about to become a Perstorp employee, with employment number 74015 and "Eas" as my *easy*-to-remember employee identity code.

My work at KomVux in the fall was a completely different story from the spring term. I would be an *assistant* teacher. The job was also part-time, not every day, and only a few hours on each of the days when I had anything at all. It felt more like I was substituting a few hours here and there rather than having a proper job. Half of my working hours were at another school across town, to which I cycled. This meant that I only occasionally saw most of the other KomVux teachers, let alone the students (including my former class). And as an assistant teacher, I didn't have my own class, but provided support for another teacher named Ann-Kristin.

At around this time I was trying to discern possible patterns in the chaotic array of relationships I was involved in, that I might achieve a little more clarity. One pattern that seemed to emerge was that Lena, if left to her own devices, would show greater interest in me as soon as I showed less interest in her, and vice-versa, pretty much as Isobel had predicted from the start. (I'd only seen Björn and Isobel once since I came back from the States.) My problem was that cat-and-mouse games felt completely unnatural to me – and I didn't want to play.

Majlis contacted me soon after I returned from the States. She told me that she and her husband had been talking about their marriage. (This was the first bit of concrete information she'd disclosed to me about her relationship status, which I regarded as her business only.) They'd decided to make a new attempt to salvage something out of their dead-in-the-water relationship, so under the circumstances she felt we ought to take a break. Fair enough, I said. I backed off.

Sonja, who'd returned to Malmö after another trip to Stockholm, came over for a while, and we finally had a serious talk about our confusing relationship. As it turned out, to our mutual surprise and delight, we both seemed to have pretty much the same feelings about each other: a warm feeling of friendship, and a fear of hurting the other if the other should happen to be in love. She was afraid that I might have fallen in love with her, just as I was afraid that she might be falling in love with me. Instead, we agreed that neither of us was in love with the other, but that we could be good friends whose friendship needn't always be sexless.

This relieved her of her growing guilt feelings about prioritizing her career over me, and relieved me that she might feel I was leading her on when my heart was with Lena the whole time.

Having completed *Turning*, I was already working furiously on the next painting, *Urban Idyll*,[12] for which I did a sketch directly on a blank canvas back in 1975, with the type of theme I was using back then, but now with my lighter, brighter coloration. The gray masses in the foreground plod their way through their dreary existence with drooping heads, in a kind of ravine that puts out of their reach the equally drab gray buildings beyond the cliffs above them. But on the cliffs is a green pasture, between the ravine and the gray buildings. In the pasture, to the right, is a simple, well-lit white cottage. Although also out of reach, it serves to shed light on those passing by below, particularly on those passing directly beneath the cottage, who are lifting their heads, if only temporarily.

At the same time, having made all the arrangements for securing a sufficient income from work that would leave me time to paint, I began thinking about the future. My thoughts about the *Candide*-based painting I'd made a sketch for in the spring were gestating, ripening and building in my sub-conscious all summer and were now about to erupt. I knew that I had a milestone painting in the offing, possibly on par with *The Midian Children*, but in a completely different direction.

What I wanted to express was an affirmation of life, free of illusion, i.e. not denying the existence of all the misery of the human condition, but not focusing *solely* on it; instead, acknowledging it as a fact of life, then working like hell to develop whatever good can be developed, despite the fact that it won't last and will always be an uphill battle, and taking pride and deep satisfaction in making the effort. This approach to life is in part based on another particularly wise admonition attributed to Voltaire, *"Don't let the perfect be the enemy of the good."*

The painting style would also represent a major deviation from my previous work, reflecting the thematic material. This made me realize that I'd need to "warm up" on a few smaller pieces before launching into the big canvas for the Candide-based work.

To test with a painting having the new thematic direction – the view that effort is required to achieve anything worthwhile, even on a small scale – I chose

---

12 Painting #80 (see Appendix 2)

a motif in which someone (I was my own model) is watering a small potted hibiscus plant (like one I had in the dormer window at the top of the stairs at Korngatan). Outside the window, everything is gray and behind it looms the void. The source of light can be viewed as the person's own efforts. I call it *If You Want a Flower to Open, You Have to Water It*.[13]

Unfortunately, I was continuing to demonstrate my inability not to be vexed and perplexed by Lena's hot-and-cold behavior towards me. [*I was going to write that "she was continuing to vex and perplex me", but it wasn't just her doing;* I was allowing it – *let's take some responsibility here, Stan!*] She'd spend a couple of days and nights with me, then decline to see me again. But since I was no longer hounding her when she turned away, she was obliged to take more of the initiative to contact me when I failed to contact her after she'd told me that she didn't want to see me for a while. That *seemed* to me to indicate that having me running after her was important to her for some reason that perhaps neither of us fully understood. (And I had no basis for claiming that she was even conscious of this "strategy".)

For the past few months (my Stateside trip excluded), whenever she'd take off to carouse with her three Norwegian neighbor students – Øivind, Øystein & Jarle – or whomever else she was seeing and carousing with or whatever she was doing with them, her place in my bed (if not my heart) would quickly be filled by Sonja or Majlis (who now, in early September, was on her hiatus). I *assumed* that Sonja and I were both OK with the "friendship+" relationship since our recent discussion. And Sonja *seemed* to want to increase the friendship part by learning as much as she could about me, so on Monday, September 4th (after having spent Sunday evening and night in bed together), I offered to let her read *The Unparallel Lines* (even though her English wasn't entirely fluent). I figured that if we were to be true friends, we would need to be able to be as open as possible with each other.

That was a *big* mistake. Reading it made her furious. To my astonishment, *she'd* assumed that all my passion for Lena all this time was non-physical, and that where sex was concerned, she – Sonja – was in an exclusive relationship with me. She thus also had to have assumed that her libido was on par with mine. (Good thing I didn't mention Majlis!) She stormed out and told me not to call her, she

---

13 Painting #81 (see Appendix 2)

needed some time to think about it all. I was dumbfounded. What was I to do now?

I remembered that I had a phone number to Marie, the girl I'd met at Pilgården back in February, so I gave her a call and invited her over. To my surprise, she came at once. She hadn't been much more than a listener when we met before – auditing those lively, drunken conversations I had with George – so I didn't know much about her. It turned out she was a cellist pursuing full-time studies at Malmö's College of Music. She was terribly demure, and always seemed to play her cards close to her *extremely* ample chest, volunteering nothing. For quite a number of visits to Korngatan, she flirted seductively with me with her eyes, yet made me keep my distance from her body – even while lying next to me on my bed, talking.

When I told her about how writing *The Unparallel Lines* had an almost miraculously cathartic effect on me since I last met her, she asked if she could read it, so I let her. Mistake *again*! The immediate effect of having read it was that she took off her clothes and had sex with me. *But* as soon as her lust was satiated, she told me that she was convinced that I'd *murdered* Jeanette! It felt like she'd hit me – with a truck. I was utterly baffled, saddened, shocked – and livid. I demanded to know how she could possibly have reached such a preposterous conclusion?! She smugly claimed that her "knowledge" required no rational explanation – her feeling was fact, because after all it was a fact that she had the feeling, and even if the feeling only came from within her and had no bearing on the external factual world, it was true enough for her, and thus a fact. Why bother about rationality?

I was disgusted, outraged, sickened and appalled. I thought her explanation was the product of some kind of extremely warped sense of humor – the only explanation that I could find that didn't have "malice" written all over it. But she was adamant about the inviolability and immutability of her cruel and unfounded feelings, and with the greatest possible speed and abruptness, we parted ways.

A few days after Sonja stormed out, I phoned her to invite her to a birthday party (for my neighbor Tage Thagaard) with me – as my friend – the following Saturday. To my surprise and relief, she accepted. We had a lot of fun, I got plastered, we danced a bit, and she spent the night with me (no sex). We agreed to meet for a drink the next day. I invited her back to Korngatan, but at first she declined, because she was still firm in her wish that we should no longer have sex. After a couple of drinks, however, she practically raced me up the stairs. The next day she was leaving for Stockholm "for a while". We parted on very good terms.

That same Monday evening, while I was resting, I got a phone call from Majlis. She explained that the hiatus simply wasn't working for her, and wondered if it would work for me if she came by on Wednesday evening (I think she lived across town; I never learned where). During the day on Wednesday, both Sonja and Lena phoned, from Stockholm and Lund respectively, to wish me a happy birthday. Lena seemed to be fishing for an invitation that evening, but in fact I was looking forward to an evening and night of losing myself in totally uncomplicated, hedonistic pleasure with Majlis. I could hardly walk the next day.

I could only hope that Bob's geographical distance from me gave him enough emotional distance to maintain a modicum of equilibrium for himself during the seemingly unending, sometimes strangely comical, yet often harrowing trajectories of my life, first through the unspeakable tragedy of Jeanette's death and ensuing year of deep depression that nearly cost me my life, then through the improbable and staccato permutations in the small array of relationships that were causing him everything from great dismay to stunned bemusement to admittedly vicarious and occasionally lascivious pleasure.

Of particular concern to him (for the sake of my mental well-being) was my unforeseen, unforeseeable and mostly one-sided relationship with Lena, which Bob often viewed as an exercise in self-flagellation on my part (this was Bob being very perceptive!), and which his love for me obliged him to discourage as subtly as my unwillingness to listen would allow, which wasn't much. He thus cheered me on every time I informed him of any new encounters with other women – after having ascertained that I wasn't just going to be automatically transferring my can't-live-without-her feelings to someone else.

The fact was that I *did* love Lena, madly, for reasons I could never fully explain. Can any *feeling* ever be fully explained? Wouldn't explaining it take it from the realm of feeling to the realm of rationality, which feelings like love seldom (if ever) are? Must it be explained? Perhaps a feeling must be explained to be understood, but feelings don't need explanations in order to be felt, and perhaps understanding it diminishes the feeling? Or, as Pascal put it, "*The heart has its reasons of which reason knows nothing.*" I couldn't answer my own questions, nor could I shake off the profound feeling of loving Lena, even when there were plenty of rational reasons for not doing so.

Although Bob was my only *confidant*, he couldn't or wouldn't follow me on this one. But there was not another person in the world to whom I felt I could relate nearly anything, which is why I did so to him, openly. He listened patiently, thought carefully, offered rational feedback and advice – as well as emotional appeals – cautiously and diplomatically, and probably hoped that something of the rational would eventually sink in or kick in.

[*Looking back some four decades as I write these chapters in my life's story, I see clearly that the person I'm writing about* was *me, but also that it* isn't *me, to the point that the person I was in 1978 is scarcely recognizable to the person I am in 2016, despite having the memories in my head today. This has not been a ripening from a green banana into a yellow one (or even a black one), but more like a caterpillar morphing into a butterfly (or moth); it's a hell of a lot harder to see the caterpillar in the moth than it is to see the green banana in the black one.*]

Bob had been corresponding occasionally with my mom, especially on the subject of parenthood, with the starting point having been Mom's attempts to play the diplomat for the purpose of resuscitating the non-relationship between Bob and his father Harold. Mom realized that Harold had been a stern, cold, unaffectionate tyrant towards Bob throughout his childhood – Mom even witnessed some of Harold's deplorable behavior first-hand – but she still had some romanticized notions of mediating, supported by cherry-picked Bible verses, of course. Bob told her in no uncertain terms that the wounds Harold had inflicted were too many and too deep, besides which Harold firmly believed that he (Harold) had nothing to apologize for, nor could he ever admit to the slightest possibility that he (Harold) could ever be wrong about anything. He (Harold) was *that* humble.

Sometimes Bob would send me copies of his correspondence to and from Mom, sometimes he would quote them or relate them – and so would Mom (to me). I knew and loved Mom well enough to be concerned that she might be drawing parallels between Harold's treatment of Bob and her own treatment of me as a child, and fearing that she would draw erroneous and saddening conclusions, I wrote to her to assure her that quite unlike Bob, "*I have always regarded my childhood as one filled with love and affection from both you and Dad, and I have NEVER doubted your love for me, even if I may have given you cause to doubt mine for you during my restless years of puberty (a phenomenon which is not at all unusual). But I have, in fact, always loved you and always will.*"

She appreciated my words. I meant them. I have nearly always felt that my parents spurred me to value learning (with some exceptions!) and to strive to treat others with decency and humanity (within certain limitations!), even though the subject matter of the learning I may have been spurred to acquire differed to some considerable extent from what Mom would have wished. Then she wrote something to Bob that absolutely astounded me, brought tears to my eyes – and made me wish she'd written it to *me*: "*As parents we often err in trying to give our children the benefit of our experiences, forgetting to let them think for themselves, and distorting their vision.*" I probably read that remarkable sentence 20 times or more before I could get it through my head that Mom had written it. It was as good an example as any I ever saw of the dual nature of Mom's personality, this having most definitely come from her "good" side, and it was *very* good – one of the more realistic assessments of parenthood I've ever seen.

Another example came after she visited me in September of '77. I'd told her about Gustaf and Magna, the elderly neighbor couple who were among my best and kindest listeners in the months following Jeanette's death. Although Mom immediately started sounding me out about them, so she could try to determine whether they were True Christians or not, she seemed to recognize that these were her old ways, and she exercised unusual restraint – even to the point of not writing them off as human beings just because they by no means professed to love her imaginary friend. I did mention that Gustaf collected stamps, so after she returned to the States, Mom began cutting off the American stamps from the envelopes of many letters she received and sent them all to me to give to Gustaf, which he greatly appreciated. When I later told Mom that Magna had developed a brain tumor, Mom began going to extraordinary lengths to provide Gustaf with a steady supply of stamps.

On Friday, September 15th, when I came home from KomVux in the early afternoon and opened my garage door, I saw that the furthest of my kitchen windows was wide open; one of the panes was smashed. My hair stood on end, and a wave of horrifying memories washed over me. My adrenalin was pumping like *crazy*. I have little doubt that if I'd met a suspicious-looking stranger emerging from my house at that moment, I might have clobbered him viciously until he could no longer move.

The garage door was closed. The back door to the house was still locked. Jeanette and I had specified doors with burglar-proof 7-tumbler locks that required a key to open, even from the inside (which effectively prevented the burglar from removing the TV or anything bulky he couldn't take back out the window with him). I unlocked and opened the back door as stealthily as possible and raced inside, checking everywhere for the presence of an intruder, but he was long gone. He'd left quite a mess, and took key components from my stereo (which I would sorely miss until the insurance payout enabled me to replace them). He also took my best camera, a watch, and a few other baubles and trinkets. (It turned out to be a young man. The police caught him a couple of weeks later, but he'd already sold my stuff to buy drugs.) Like so many had observed before me, the unpleasant feelings of a burglary aren't usually about the stuff – the insurance would cover most of that – but the about the sense of insecurity, of having been violated.

The intense feeling that I might well wreak grievous bodily harm on another person as the result of an adrenalin rush was disconcerting to me. Without the adrenalin, I felt certain that I would try to analyze the situation, look for a solution, seek to understand the burglar's background, help to see that he got help for his drug addiction, and settle the matter as amicably as possible. Clearly, to me at least, adrenalin plays a role in the difference between barbarity and civilization. It should thus be understandable that people acting under duress or panic, their veins full of the stuff, will often behave in ways that society neither can nor should condone. But it should be equally clear that society itself, when enacting laws in accordance with legislative processes, should not allow those processes to be dictated or even influenced by adrenalin.

Two days later, Majlis was back for more of our uninhibited and mutual pleasure (I had recovered my ability to walk in the meantime, which would otherwise have been the only inhibiting factor). But on Monday the 18th I had to take a break, as Rob and Chris came to spend two nights with me. They were "on tour" for a couple of weeks in Malmö and Copenhagen, reconnecting with a number of their old friends from the days when they lived in Malmö, and with Chris's family members in Denmark. They were delighted that I was so dramatically recovered from the rock-bottom state in which they'd last seen me when I visited them in London in February. They could hardly believe the difference; neither could I. They told me that their friends Siv and Harris were having a party on Saturday, at their apartment near Kronprinsen, and that they'd been asked to invite me to join them, which I said I would, with pleasure.

I'd met Siv and Harris a couple of times before, at parties hosted by Rob and Chris when they lived in their apartment near Caroli City in Malmö. Siv was a schoolteacher and was one of those exceptionally warm, extremely kind people you feel you've known all your life within five minutes of your first meeting, but she harbored a deep unquenchable melancholy that always lurked just beneath the cheerful surface of her countenance, stemming from the horrors her mother and other family members had suffered in Auschwitz. Harris was a laid-back accountant from Manchester, with measured speech and dry wit. He lacked Siv's outward warmth and ebullience, but he also lacked her inner demons. (Harris once criticized the US pronunciation of "lever" to me. For the Yanks it rhymes with "ever", for the Brits with "fever"; there's no logic to it anywhere. Harris mockingly asked me whether Yanks say "I have a feh-ver". I immediately replied "No, that's something we nee-ver do.")

There must have been around 30 people at the party. Most of them were friendly strangers to me. It was an Anglophone-style party, i.e. mingling with drinks and snacks. (A Swedish-style party would typically be to seat everyone at tables to eat a more formal dinner.) It was great fun, with lots of drinking, delicious snacks, conversation-permitting noise levels and increasingly enthusiastic dancing. As the evening progressed, I danced with a few of the women, including Chris (while Rob glared at us), as well as with one pretty woman in particular. Her name was Margaretha (her namesake, but not this woman, is found elsewhere in *Hindsights*). She and I began dancing, closer and closer, paying no attention whatsoever to the tempo of the music. Before long, we were dancing so close that it seemed we were trying to get through to the other side of each other. Other interests soon arose, and at about one o'clock we called for a taxi to Korngatan. I'd come on my bike, which we had to load onto the taxi's bike rack. We were giggling and necking all the way. She left the next afternoon when neither of us could move anymore.

On Tuesday morning I cycled to work across town for my half day of assistant teaching with Ann-Kristin. It was my only working time on Tuesdays, but she had a two-and-a-half-hour break until her afternoon lessons began at Fågelbacksskolan. As we were finishing up, I asked whether she'd like to have a light lunch at my place instead of a stale sandwich in the teachers' room at Fågelbacksskolan. She accepted. Her car had no bike rack, however, so she had to drive across town while following me on my bike (I cycled like the wind). We had some lunch in my kitchen, during which she was making impressed comments on my paintings (or were they etchings?). After lunch, we went upstairs to have a look at the rest of them. She later told me she'd been lusting after me for some time.

For my birthday, Bob sent me a subscription to the *New Scientist*, a British publication with articles and news about developments within numerous scientific disciplines. I think he figured I might find or develop some new areas of interest there – and new areas for us to discuss. I typed out a proofread version of *The Unparallel Lines* and made copies to send to Bob, John, Al, and Lee Whitehead (my professor in Vancouver). I decided not to spring it on any more of my lady friends.

On Saturday the 30th, Margaretha came by again for the evening, night, and most of Sunday. We managed to pull our clothes back on long enough to go to the cinema, then went home for more. When I was at Fågelbacksskolan on my penultimate day as a temporary KomVux employee, I ran into Majlis in the corridor. She said she'd be calling me again soon. I invited Ann-Kristin to continue her Tuesday afternoon visits to Korngatan even after my stint at KomVux was over, which she did for a while. That was the kind of thing that seemed to happen to me whenever Lena refused to see me. I consciously (and conscientiously) did my best to assure that I wasn't exploiting or hurting anyone in any way. Perhaps those who find such behavior reprehensible have a problem accepting that a woman can also have an active libido? Besides, it certainly seemed a much better alternative than teetering on the edge of the void!

I got up early in the morning on October 11th, in order to write Bob before taking the train to Perstorp for my first day of work. Although he was cheering me along from the sidelines, I think even he was beginning to find my libidinous schedule a bit confusing, and he cautioned me about the risks of getting burnt again and of not treating the other girls decently. My reply:

> I have learned something from my experience with Lena, namely how <u>not</u> to treat another person, and if I should at any point find myself forgetting that lesson, I'll have it tattooed on my arm. If any emotional involvement on [a woman's] part doesn't develop into something mutual, it will eventually fade away, and during that time, I will treat her with respect, kindness and affection. By the way, I think that if I had met Lena at this point rather than 11 months ago, the chances for something working out would have been a lot better. Desperation, bitterness and confusion are perhaps not the best grounds for building anything on. Whether anything can be salvaged at this point is both uncertain and unlikely, given her present attitude. What the hell...!

I also reassured Bob that he could indeed read *The Unparallel Lines* with completely new eyes, now that my story was just a story, no longer an embellished suicide note. For some months he and I engaged in an enthusiastic discussion on the subject of "Magic Thinking", the incessant and unquenchable willingness of human beings to ascribe magical, supernatural causes and effects to natural, scientifically explainable occurrences. In the same letter, I expressed the view that "*a 'meaningful life' as defined by magic is not free. A freedom from magic entails a freedom to observe, a freedom to formulate values, not bow under them, and a freedom from panic in the face of any unanswered questions. This is fortunate, since the free man is likely to have so many more questions anyway.*" That was before breakfast.

My train ride to Perstorp was boring. As before, Stig picked me up at the little Perstorp train station, but this time he first drove me across the tracks to the Perstorp Hotel so I could check in. Then we went to his office, and he showed me where mine would be – diagonally across the hall from his. My office was larger than I expected, but Stig pointed out that it would also serve as my classroom for as many as four students at a time (as it turned out, I rarely had more than one or two). All the furnishings were tastefully bland beechwood, extremely adequate, and sensationally dull.

The first order of business was the formal signing of my employment contract. Stig would undertake the recruiting and scheduling of my students, who were to report to me in my office for lessons lasting from 45 minutes to a maximum of an hour and a half (double lesson). Stig told me I'd be having no pupils that first week, meaning Wednesday and Thursday. Instead, we'd be using my time for him to introduce me to the company and the company to me.

I was given a binder full of pedestrian policy papers to fall asleep by, as well as some information about the company's history since its founding in 1881 by the wealthy son of a wealthy landowner whose property holdings included much of the beechwood forest that dominated the surrounding area. The son, Wilhelm Wendt, studied chemistry in Germany and returned to Sweden to found the company using clever methods to extract various useful chemicals, such as methanol, out of burnt wood.

In the early years of the 20th century, Mr Wendt came to work with a man named Innanendra Das Gupta, a brilliant chemist from India who'd been working in Germany and Switzerland (at Roche, of all places!). Recruited to Sweden and Perstorp by Wendt, Das Gupta discovered (in 1918) how to further react the company's raw materials into one of the world's first plastics, and Perstorp's profits went from a gush to a torrent, albeit with only a trickle for Mr Gupta, of course. (After Sweden denied him permanent residency in 1919, he left the country.) Perhaps the biggest breakthrough for Perstorp came when the company learned how to use catalysts to react methanol into formaldehyde, a key chemical building block that would form the core of the growing corporation's downstream production for decades.

When I first came into contact with Perstorp on behalf of Hamadi's language school back in 1971, when Perstorp became the school's dominant client, the president at that time, Gunnar Wessman, was leading the company's internationalization, diversification, rapid growth, and listing on the stock exchange, finally making the Wendt family's business a publically traded company. I knew that Wessman had been replaced by Sahlberg in 1975, but when I took my tour of Perstorp that day in 1978, I was unprepared for the extent to which Wessman's name was now practically anathema. The luxurious 7th-floor executive conference and boardroom was hung with the oil portraits of every president the company ever had – except Wessman's. And nobody would talk about it. My questions were ignored and the subject was changed. It seemed to me that Mr Wessman must have committed some mortal sin by taking the staid, conservative "Perstorpers" out of their comfort zone in some inscrutable way. I never did figure it out.

The corporate grounds were spread out over a fairly large area, like a college campus, a layout that perhaps reflected the company's history of trying new things and putting up new buildings to try them in, resulting in an array of vastly different industrial architectural styles, set apart from each other in an almost idyllic woodland setting that contrasted with the many different chemical processes that were taking place.

I thought of a few headline-grabbing disasters I'd read about at chemical plants around the world, and how the chemical industry worked with processes that require an education in chemistry to understand, and how few people among the general public had such an education, and how people tend to fear what they don't understand and to hate what they fear. I realized how easy that made it for anyone (e.g. tabloid journalists) to make a simple, true statement, on the order of "These products contain *chemicals*!" and scare the shit out of that same chemistry-education-lacking general public, while failing to point out that unless the products consisted entirely of energy, theories, values, or other immaterial properties, they would *have* to contain chemicals, atoms being the common feature of all matter in the universe. I was glad that Bob foresightfully gave me that subscription to the *New Scientist*.

As Stig and I went from one building to another, quite a few of the people he introduced me to were people I'd met before, people who'd once (or more times) been my students at the language school. This sped up the process of making me feel more at home in my new job. At lunchtime, Stig took me to lunch at the company's special corporate facility, Persgården, which housed a large cafeteria open to all employees – workers and executives alike. They served pretty good food at highly subsidized prices in a pleasant atmosphere. Every day, starting at around 11.30, rivulets of employees could be seen flowing up the hill to this facility, located on the edge of the industrial campus, like scouting parties of ants returning to the anthill. Persgården included a lounge just outside the cafeteria (for after-lunch coffee), complete with a pool table. There was also a gym for workouts, badminton and volleyball, and there was a top-notch company medical clinic.

Perstorp was organized into a number of semi-autonomous divisions, some far enough away from HQ on the sprawling corporate campus to make Stig feel that we needed to take his car. One such unit, Perstorp Form, manufactured plastic products that included many of the corporation's relatively few products aimed directly at consumers, although the company's decorative laminate – *Perstorpsplattan* – was a household word in Sweden (in the same way that Formica was or is a household word for decorative laminate in the US), and it was now also a prominent feature in my kitchen on Korngatan, in my unique design.[14] Another unit made industrial laminate for printed circuit boards. Yet another made polyalcohols for the paint industry. There was a large lab up on an adjacent hill. And there were several formaldehyde plants churning out the raw material upon which most of it all was based.

Stig invited me back to his home for dinner that night. He lived on a quiet residential street on the edge of the village, of course, as suburban middle class as it could be. Top management openly frowned upon anyone from middle management and upwards living more than 20 km from the company. For many years, this unwritten policy helped to keep the company closely knit and gave it the added benefit of getting innumerable hours of company work done off

---

14 See Appendix 1.

the clock, in the form of neighborly shop talk. Another effect was to make it rather difficult for anyone to leave the company; selling a home in Perstorp could take many months – or longer. That kept resale value low, which helped to keep people in place, while making it attractive for newcomers to settle there. Stig's wife Gurli worked at the company switchboard and kept their home tidy and suitably furnished. They had one child, a son who was about nine years younger than me.

When Stig dropped me off at the hotel after supper, it still felt like early evening to a city boy like me. I quickly discovered that there was absolutely nothing to do in Perstorp during the evening. I went out for a walk to acquaint myself with the heart of the village. There was nothing to do there either. All the shops were closed. There was nobody in sight. It was all very clean, very orderly, very dead. Back in my hotel room a few minutes later, I quickly discovered that the TV offered two (2) channels. The thought of spending one night a week like this made me fear I might go mad. I was, after all, still a big-city boy at heart.

On my second day of work in Perstorp, Stig continued the introductory rounds, which gave him the opportunity to recruit people he was targeting for my services and get them to sign up for a few lessons, or to make use of the opportunity to have someone check the English in their business letters, contracts, pamphlets and sales presentations. In due time, I would take an increasingly active role in *interventions* – scrutinizing the printed matter they hadn't felt the need to have checked, and seeing that it got it corrected and reprinted.

To my naïve surprise, I met all kinds of resistance. (I'd incorrectly assumed that the desire to learn was the default human condition.) Many felt that their English was "good enough", even though they wouldn't have dreamed of sending off a document in Swedish with the number and nature of language errors they were all too willing to send off in their official corporate language. Many argued that the recipient "will understand what we mean," prompting me to ask what would happen if the recipient also understood what they *wrote*, which in some cases was something completely different.

One day somebody handed me a brochure one division had hastily put together for a trade fair, when they felt they didn't have the time or the need to have the language checked. But then at the fair, they noticed customers and prospects smirking. They ended up withdrawing the brochure from further distribution. Among the multitude of grammatical errors, towards the end they wrote "please contact us about eventual problems with our products." I asked if they realized that the English *eventual* means something quite different from the Swedish *eventuell* (possible), that they had more or less *promised* the customer problems farther down the line?! After I pointed out this and scores of other major mistakes, I was asked to completely rewrite the brochure, for which I had to request the original Swedish version in order to understand what the intended messages were.

Soon I was not only looking at things that were brought to my attention; I was bringing my attention to things I wasn't meant to look at. I asked those responsible whether they'd prefer it if their errors caused only *me* to laugh, or their customers and contacts. The majority seemed to truly appreciate this help, but there were a few ostriches – those who resented finding out that they'd made mistakes and found it better to shoot the messenger than to take the trouble to learn and/or to get it right.

And then there was the argument that the recipients in question weren't that good at English themselves. I asked whether they'd pay good money for concert tickets to hear a singer who sang like *they* did in the shower, or if the qualifications to serve as a referee in a boxing match would require the referee to demonstrate his pugilistic superiority by first knocking out both contestants?

At the start of my employment I was actually a bit worried that I wouldn't get enough work to fulfil my 20-hour-a-week quota. Even though the terms of my employment were such that I would get paid anyway, I was eager to start building up a "pot" of comp-time, so that I would have the flexibility to take extra time off now and then. But my terrier-like insistence on raising the bar of the company's written English communications soon started giving results, and I began to dare to hope that I could gradually shift the bulk of my work from teaching to translating and other text work. Text work was something that was in many ways more important for the company. A good salesperson whose English wasn't first-rate could cover many of his or her mistakes with charm, but a printed brochure with linguistic eggs all over its face made a *really* bad impression. And I could do all of the text work more efficiently from home.

For my second Wednesday-Thursday session in Perstorp, my second week on the job, I had my first students. Gunnar and Thomas were fresh out of university and were also newly employed. Their boss, Leif-Arne, once a student of mine at the language school, was the current head of *Formox*. (The name refers to a patented method of producing *form*aldehyde through an *ox*idation process. This division would eventually become my principal client within the corporation.) Formox was responsible for formaldehyde technology, including production for the company's own use, licensing the technology to formaldehyde producers around the world, building the plants for them, as well as manufacturing and supplying the catalyst that made the process work, and long-term technical service.

Leif-Arne also launched a totally unrelated project within his division: to develop *Iodosorb*, a pharmaceutical gel product based on a Finnish chemist's invention of slow-release iodine gel for the treatment of pressure sores and similar wounds. Thomas, a chemical engineer, was hired for the formaldehyde side; while Gunnar, a biochemist, was going to be working on the gel project.

Another of those first pupils was Leif-Arne's secretary, a woman named Marie-Louise Larsson, from Gotland (Sweden's largest island). She reminded me a lot of my sister-in-law Marj, both in her gentle appearance, soft voice, warm demeanor, and the fact that within a few minutes it felt like I'd met a long-lost sister I'd never had – that kind of instant connection and rapport – and someone in whom I could confide when things got a little chaotic in my head from time to time.

[*I should point out that I had very many students over the course of my employment at Perstorp. Most of them were very pleasant and interesting people, but I have limited myself to mentioning those whose work or interactions with me had the most direct impact on my life. This is, after all, my story.*]

At the end of the working day that Wednesday, Stig drove me to my hotel and apologized for not being able to invite me home for supper again. I took a brisk walk into the heart of the village to find a place where I could buy a sausage or something to eat before the entire place closed down for the evening, which meant around 7 PM. (The hotel's own restaurant was only open during lunch hours, from 11.30 AM to 2 PM!) I'd received a small proofreading-editing job during the day, and later that evening I spent an hour taking care of it in my hotel room to alleviate some of the boredom of my long evening.

Perstorp was for me a strange new set of circumstances. I couldn't compare small-town Sweden with small-town America, because I'd never personally experienced the latter (I'd always viewed suburban life as being quite different from small-town life), nor could I know whether Perstorp was typical of small-town Sweden. Yet as in American suburbia, I suspected that peer pressure – the often unspoken, yet not-so-subtle insistence on multi-level conformity – was the power behind everything.

The many close contacts with management, executives and technicians from Perstorp that the language school had given me over a period of six years also gave me a strong impression that Perstorp's company culture was firmly anchored in political conservatism. Many hints and winks I'd observed on every floor of the head office building during my rounds with Stig further reinforced the impression that if you worked at Perstorp's head office, it was not a question of *whether* you held conservative views, but *how* conservative they were. Those who were opposed were likely to be ostracized with ease, swiftness and disdain. The freedom to think as long as you thought like others (or avoided expressing dissenting thoughts) gave me a feeling of suffocating. I understood that I would have to exercise more prudence and restraint than I was accustomed to. But I had no illusions that I would ever fit in, nor did I ever have any desire to do so.

I came to realize that the values behind labels like "liberal" and "conservative", as those terms were used in my native country, were completely different from the values those same terms implied in Sweden. It was my impression, back in the 1970s, that the left wing in the American political spectrum ended roughly somewhere along the right-wing scale in Swedish politics. Even Sweden's conservatives were mostly humane enough to view such things as healthcare and education as universal human rights, and not merely as the privileges of the wealthy. [*Note that this was 1970s conservatism. Swedish politics began a rightward drift in the mid-1980s that has continued to this day and has profoundly changed Sweden's political spectrum.*]

But while Sweden's Conservative party generally maintained a civilized tone and façade, out in the hustings – in small and Conservative mill towns like Perstorp – the office banter could generate a pretty rabid undercurrent, even though it was only expressed in a subtle comment here, an indirect remark there, thinly veiled sneers and snarls. This rabidity was largely directed against the leader of the Social Democrats, Olof Palme, my hero. His outspokenness against the Vietnam War (which began when he was a cabinet minister) contributed to Jeanette's and my choice of Sweden for our exile. He was a thorn in the side of oppressors wherever he could find them: the Soviets for their invasion of Czechoslovakia in '68, the White-supremacist *apartheid* regime in South Africa for their pathological inequality, and the willingness of Sweden's right wing to greedily grab more than their fair share of Sweden's wealth at the expense of those less privileged. To mention a few. For this, the Conservatives hated him. And nearly everyone in Perstorp's head office building seemed to be a Conservative. Fearing the need for some self-preservation, I was less outspoken in those days....

The next morning, I reminded Stig that he'd mentioned something about a couple of daily commuters from Malmö, and I wondered whether he had found out their names. It had slipped his mind, but he made a couple of quick phone calls and got the information. One of these commuters, an eccentric man in his late 40s named Knut (in Swedish, both consonants in the letter combination "*kn*" are pronounced with equal clarity, similar to the "*kn*" in "ac*kn*owledge"). He was known to some as "Smiley Knut" because he tended to respond to any question asked of him with a huge grin that had no obvious connection to the question or the answer, nor did it reflect a cheerful disposition. The other Malmö commuter was a perfectly ordinary middle-aged man named David; the two of them took turns driving to and from Perstorp on alternate days.

I asked Knut whether I could ride with them, and he said yes, as long as I could be standing on Lundavägen near the corner of Vattenverksvägen next Wednesday morning at six o'clock sharp; he and David started their working days in Perstorp at half past seven. I said I'd be there. I found it insanely early, but doable, since the pick-up point was just down the hill from Korngatan, close to where I'd taken the bus to Lund so many times. The pick-up point for the homeward trip would be just outside the security guard station at the gate to Perstorp's industrial campus, also a convenient place for me. For the return to Malmö, the pick-up time would be at 4.40 PM (Knut and David finished at 4.30). Stig said there was no problem if I wanted to adjust my working hours to fit the commuting schedule.

I got up at five in the morning for that first ride with Knut and David on Wednesday, October 25th. I wanted to be awake and alert enough to be sociable during the trip. David's wife dropped him off where I was waiting on Lundavägen a few minutes before Knut arrived to pick us both up, and David told me that Knut lived a few blocks farther along the road. David said he'd ride in the back, if I didn't mind. Just before Knut's old two-door Saab came into view, David mentioned that I might find riding with Knut a somewhat "unusual" experience....

The car radio was playing fairly loudly, mostly news broadcasts or discussion programs, many of them with painfully local news (like the reports on catches from the fishing boats arriving at the harbor in Simrishamn, or farmers' comments on the increase in the price of pig feed). Any time a radio host dared to put on some music, Knut would *instantly* switch stations until he found one without music. It quickly became clear to me that he loathed conversation. When I turned to Knut to make a comment on something just said on the radio (or on the traffic or the landscape), he would hunch over the steering wheel, grin fiendishly, shake his head vigorously, and respond loudly with fierce disinterest, "*Yeah, yeah!*" before I was halfway through my sentence, while simultaneously reaching across with his right hand to turn *up* the volume of the radio until my words were barely audible. (I already *knew* that Knut was no Typical Swede!)

Older Saabs like Knut's featured a "free wheel" function, designed to protect its two-stroke engine, which was unusual in cars. The free-wheel function eliminated engine drag, so that the car coasted like a bicycle on a downhill slope after the accelerator was released. Knut utilized this function like nobody else I'd ever known. He would blast out from a traffic light (pressing me against my seatback) until he achieved the maximum speed for first gear, then release the gas and wait for the force of gravity (not engine drag) to gradually slow the car down. Then he frantically plunged into second and floored the accelerator, blasting us all against our seatbacks again. He repeated the procedure until he ran out of higher gears.

Lest our ride become smooth after that, whenever he was going to pass anyone on the road – another car, a tractor, even a cyclist – he would roar up rather close behind them, then make a comparatively *sharp* left turn into the farthest-left part of the left-hand lane, followed by an equally sharp right-hand turn to straighten out, then roar *well* past the other vehicle, then make yet another sharp right, quickly followed by sharp left to resume his rightful position in the right-hand lane. It felt like *he* felt like he was heroically avoiding a series of head-on collisions. I found it so bizarre, I turned around to catch David's eye in the back seat, but at once I saw that he was quite used to it – and also why he preferred the back seat when Knut was driving.

Knut didn't speed, but he managed to make his vehicle's velocity a white-knuckle experience all the same, every time. He did everything he possibly could to drive at the *exact* speed limit at all times. If the speed limit was 70 km/h, he was going to drive at 70, regardless of the weather or the traffic. If someone in the car in front of him was for *any* reason driving slower than the posted speed limit, Knut would be right up there tailgating, flashing his high beams and audibly huffing and puffing in genuinely unbridled fury, as if the offending driver were committing crimes against humanity by not pulling over *immediately* (whether there was space to pull over or not) to let Knut by. He would display similar behavior if someone tried to pass *him*; Knut was driving at the speed limit, how *dare* anyone have the audacity to drive faster?

I didn't feel at all safe on the mornings when Knut was driving. I asked David whether Knut always drove that way, and he said yes. It wasn't as though riding in the back seat and snoozing isolated him from any interesting conversation. So I quickly learned to stop getting to bed early the night before or getting up early on mornings when Knut was driving; being as sleepy as possible was my only defense.

A mere two weeks into my employment – the source of earning my living, paying my bills, buying my time to paint – already gave me a feeling of panic in connection with getting to and from my place of work, and a feeling of suffocating once I got there. I would have to devise a plan, a way out, a way to earn my living, pay my bills, and buy my painting time without having to spend my time in or at Perstorp. I was aiming to work from home – *only* from home if I could figure out a way. That was now my goal. It was already presumed, right from the start, that most if not all of the translation side of my work would have to be done from home, whether I spent any time in Perstorp or not. So I could strive to increase the proportion of translation work, or I could try to get my students to come to Malmö instead of having their lessons in my office in Perstorp, or both. There had to be a way. And if there was, I was damn well going to find it.

CHAPTER 8

Through the woods

I was glad I'd chosen Wednesdays and Thursdays for my Perstorp days, because for a while I continued to get those two-hour Tuesday lunchtime visits from Ann-Kristin. She claimed I made her feel wonderful things she hadn't felt in many years, which was nice (and soothing for my ego) to hear. I also got a phone call from one of the students from my KomVux class from last spring, inviting me to join them for their fall term party in Copenhagen again, on October 27th, but it was too short notice; I already had other plans.

Sonja phoned me from Stockholm for a chat. She claimed that I had some kind of "animal magnetism" that a lot of women found intriguing, often irresistible. I was skeptical, but I had to admit that I'd never expected the events of the past six months to happen to me. (I suppose, in a broader perspective, I wasn't expecting anything remotely like *my life* to happen to me!) I had no idea how little I understood. [*Sometime I need to take a step back from myself, sigh deeply, and make a general comment like that.*]

Allan Saabye, the son of my Danish car-mechanic neighbor, had been married for a few years to a lovely Swedish girl with long strawberry blonde hair. They had a beautiful little boy with curly strawberry blond hair, and the three of them seemed to be a perfectly happy family. Allan mentioned that his wife was devoting more and more of her time to astrology, but he seemed to dismiss it as just one of those kooky, benign things some people sometimes do. Then one day she came to him and announced, out of the blue, that they would have to get divorced. He was stunned, perplexed. *Why?!* he protested. They'd never even quarreled, she'd never complained, he'd thought they were happy and in love?! All that was quite true, she admitted, but her astrologer had plotted a new horoscope for her and found that her Venus wasn't in the right house, or her Saturn wasn't properly aligned with her Jupiter or in the fourth moon of whatever house or other kind of nonsense that frightened and superstitious Ancients perpetrated upon mankind before knowledge of *astronomy* gradually enabled people to know better and leave the contrived answers behind, in the dust of mankind's ceaseless struggle to understand our universe and our lives. But as a result of her overriding zeal for astrology's magical version of the stars, there were no options; they *had* to divorce, she insisted. And they did. Allan's heart was broken, as was his little boy's home. It was all phony malarkey, but it wreaked real destruction on real people's real lives.

Astrology consists of explanations that ancient civilizations made up because they lacked the knowledge and equipment to find real answers about the stars and planets they could see but whose movements they could not explain. By creating magical links between incomprehensible stellar movements and incomprehensible human behavior and fortunes, for which no satisfactory evidence of any links could be found either, they concocted "answers" they decided to be satisfied with instead. (Astrology also provided employment to quite a few people willing to sell bogus ideas to gullible people for real money.)

Astrology always comes down to accepting, on faith, not on doubting or questioning. Real science – such as astronomy – is based on doubt. *Could this be wrong? What if it isn't true?* Skepticism is what began to bring people out of the Dark Ages, to stop accepting "answers" and keep asking questions. In many cases, science has had to drag out the answers, kicking and screaming. And some people refuse to leave their willful ignorance behind, ever, to this very day.

Many of the discussions I've participated in or heard, especially on the famously "loaded" topics of politics or religion, become derailed because certain key abstractions use the same words to denote very different meanings, and people end up talking past each other. "Faith" is such a word. I've frequently encountered religionist assertions that people have faith in science, just like people have faith in religion – and that faith is thus a shared quality. That, I claim, is utter nonsense. There are two very different underlying definitions of "faith" that could hardly be more different from each other.

"Faith" in the religious sense is believing that something is True *without evidence* (or regardless of the lack thereof). Further, it rejects the *need* for evidence, and *refuses to look* at or for evidence. In its more dogmatic forms, religion actually *prohibits* looking for evidence. ("I have faith in *x* and I need no other answers.")

"Faith" in the scientific sense is believing that the body of evidence currently available most strongly favors certain working hypotheses to explain the phenomena in the universe we experience. Further, it *encourages* doubt and skepticism in order to challenge and test current hypotheses, and it welcomes new evidence that might require modifying or discarding such hypotheses. ("I have faith that this hypothesis provides the best answer available so far, but further evidence is needed.")

In some ways I found myself entering a new phase in my life, or more like a new life altogether. Since my catharsis, or perhaps as the second stage of the catharsis rocket from deep depression into mental balance, my dizzying sex carousel was a principal factor in carrying me further and further from that near-fatal depression. It certainly gave me – as well as a number of young ladies – a great deal of physical pleasure, and it was certainly balm to my soul in terms of giving me the confidence and optimism that comes from having a satisfied libido and feeling attractive to those to whom I was attracted. I endeavored to do my utmost never to exploit anyone, and to avoid hurting anyone. I tried always to be *at least* as much a giver as a taker. Consequently, I didn't feel a shred of guilt about ignoring the contradictory and hypocritical "morality" that my parents and their kind tried to instill in me and indoctrinate me with. I recognized that hedonism has its place; but it also has its limits.

I learned that sex can be an outstanding analgesic. But although it can take away pain, it can't take away longing. Sex felt great, but I longed for Lena. Sonja was fun to talk with, but I longed for Lena. A romp with Majlis took my breath away, but I longed for Lena. Margaretha made me forget the problems of the world, but I longed for Lena. Ann-Kristin was a lovely diversion, but I longed for Lena. All that wonderful sex lifted me up to the top of a cliff on whose edge I could support myself by my elbows and see the next level, but I wasn't there yet; I still couldn't reach Lena. [*And did I even come close to understanding what was going on in my own head, body and heart?*]

Sex is one of the most powerful primal drives throughout most of the animal kingdom. Species endowed with sexual organs are driven by powerful urges to use them. Sometimes our anthropocentric viewpoint limits our ability to imagine that other species might also find pleasure in sex. Apart from bonobos and humans, most sexual relations appear to us as totally pleasure-less disconnection. Think of female salmon dropping their eggs on a riverbed for the males to come along and ejaculate over them. Some sexual relations are even life-threatening: female black widow spiders often devour their sex partners right after coitus. And then there are "slam-bam-thank-you-ma'am" sexual relations (try watching lions mate, or inebriated male *homo sapiens*).

Most species are promiscuous, but a few (e.g. swans) seem to bond with a single partner. In many human societies today, bonding with a single partner is normative, the only socially acceptable way to go, but because it often appears to be out sync with the natural driving force, the bonds are frequently broken. The rules sometimes say one thing and the behavioral drive says another.

One thing that does seem to be unique to human sexual relations is that they are felt to be intimate, and thus nearly always take place in private, behind closed doors. If one were to walk in on a couple of humans (not dogs!) engaging in sex, they would almost certainly (a) cease, (b) cover up, (c) express outrage, and/or (d) feel shame – even if the relationship itself was not in the least surreptitious or unsanctioned by society. (There are a few exceptions to this....)

This is where the power of religion comes in. Building on its intimacy-shame factor, the powerful and universal sex drive can be taken from shame to guilt to the need for appeasement and submission – and the sanctimonious attitudes that result from living by the rules that religion itself makes up. Nearly all religions set up elaborate taboos and prohibitions concerning sex; first you make everyone feel guilty about something universal, then you offer them absolution – at the price of surrendering control over their minds, actions and wallets.

People close to me, with the same smothering Christian Fundamentalist background, have in their desire to keep one foot in the Word-of-God outlook while modernizing by adding more and more coats of whitewash to it (no longer proclaiming eternal torture as a given for non-believers, and living "normal, worldly lives"), still seem to cling to most of the old taboos concerning sex. Some pressure their children into disastrous marriages when the only thing the kids actually want is to get laid. Some have trained their children to practice frustration, and make them want to be "pure" on their wedding night, only to discover sexual incompatibility with their partner later, causing horrible disruption to their lives. And the grounds for the "moral" recriminations against sex – rather than against hurting and betrayal – are taken from the Bible, with its psychotic God who repeatedly slaughters small children, and in which the revered King Salomon had 700 wives and 300 concubines (the latter being women one owns for sex with but will not marry). But that was OK; the Bible tells me so. In fact, if you're an expert enough cherry-picker, the Bible can tell you whatever the hell you want to hear.

Here's another strange bit – "strange" because I couldn't understand it at all: through all my longing for Lena, and all my uninhibited, no-strings-attached trysts with others, I missed Jeanette fiercely. Although the horrific image of her lifeless form hanging there no longer came to me *every* time I closed my eyes, nor *every* night in a dream, it was still always there, lurking. I'd reluctantly accepted that she was gone forever, in a way that I could imagine a double amputee learns to accept that his or her amputated limbs will never be growing back (yet he or she may experience phantom pain), but that acceptance doesn't make everything right or normal again. The gaping void she left in my heart, my soul, and my life was a hole, in the sense that a hula hoop is a large disc with a hole in the middle. Much of the time I felt I was nothing without her, but since I was faced with the prospect of never being anything but nothing until I died, I had to find *something* while I lived.

One of the many things that I couldn't, wouldn't understand back then was that meeting and falling in love with Lena was very ill-timed, at best. I was still far too unstable, far too wobbly in my soul, far too crippled in my heart. I just wasn't ready for *love*. It had blind-sided me, knocked me down before I'd even learned to stand up again. I vaguely sensed, and tried to keep reminding myself, that my vulnerability to Lena was not her fault. Who understands the force that love is? Had I ever understood how much I loved Jeanette? Did I even have a clue? Is hindsight ever useful or is it just cruel? Is that why so many people expend such efforts to suppress so much?

And then there were the guilt feelings, oh how they were there! Those nagging self-accusations that I could have done *some*thing, *any*thing, I should have seen, recognized, warned, taken action, averted disaster rather than my eyes, made everything all right even though it may never have been all right to start with. I berated myself that my love for Jeanette hadn't been enough, that I'd failed to provide enough protection, that I'd dismissed the need to chase away her hobgoblins, and that I'd misinterpreted so many now-obvious signals – *was I blind or something?!* – or even that I was now able to see that which I didn't see then. And then there was a thought that didn't occur to me then, the *deep insight* I absolutely refused to consider but might have or might do later, some day when it was too late: *that my bumbling subconscious would drive me to seek out somebody to love who would <u>not</u> love me back, and who would thus become the perfect embodiment of punishment* for my blindness, my stupidity, my willingness to sweep anything and everything under the rug or proclaim healed that which remained wounded, to declare clean that which remained soiled, to claim absolution for that for which I would never be able to forgive myself. Did I believe that I would heal if I behaved as if I were healing, some kind of self-fulfilling prophecy? Do things work that way sometimes? Ever? Was I through the woods yet? Was I even heading in the right direction?

A Sea of Troubles

I didn't feel there was anybody I could talk to about Jeanette anymore, except Jeanette herself – she was in my dreams (no longer only nightmares) most nights. Friends, acquaintances, and even relatives pleaded with their eyes and body language for me not to keep mentioning her, and their quickness to change the subject if I did anyway left little doubt in my mind. My family didn't exactly refuse to talk about her, but they always seemed to want to pervert the focus, to redirect the topic to their pathetic religion, as if it were even remotely relevant to Jeanette or to me. Jeanette's family, with whom communication had always been limited, became noticeably uncomfortable at the mentioned of Jeanette's name. Rose even wrote to my mom that she found it difficult to write to me. And although I still heard from Marilyn from time to time, she seldom responded directly to any comments I made concerning Jeanette's life – which was probably the only thing we'd ever had in common to begin with. Even Bob seemed to be battle-weary when it came to discussing Jeanette, perhaps because he was so concerned about getting me to look forward. And the idea of seeing a therapist? I was pretty colored – probably unfairly – by Jeanette's having met what felt to me in retrospect like a dismissive attitude immediately prior to her suicide, and by the inane approach I met at the psychiatric clinic in the weeks and months afterwards.

The few times anyone did speak with me about Jeanette, much of the conversation centered on "what she *would have* wanted" – an absurd, totally unknowable and futile presumption. I thought I did know what she *did* want while she lived, but even that turned out to offer little certainty.

By the end of October, I at last got a new stereo, and music was back in my life. Where my relationships were concerned, I was determined to seize whatever positive elements there might be in *any* situation (and I usually managed to find something) and concentrate on them, yet without pretending that negative elements weren't there: I would display openness to everything, but with a conscious will to concentrate on the positive. Formulating this new outlook gave me the idea for my next canvas: a man jogging through a forest. The part of the forest from which he has just emerged is dark and the trees are bare. The forest towards which he is moving and on which he's focusing is light and lush. He's running past an abyss, but it doesn't alter his focus. I call it *Through the Woods*.[15]

---

15 Painting #82 (see Appendix 2)

Out there in the big wide world, others were far from through the woods. Iran, the country to which Jeanette and I might have moved for Jeanette's work for a while, had been in turmoil since early January 1978, when I was too enmeshed in my own turmoil to notice. Young leftists and Islamists had found themselves oddly united in a common cause within an unholy alliance: to depose the increasingly despotic, US-backed Shah, Reza Pahlavi. Their opposition to the regime soon gelled into a full-blown revolution that would force the Shah into exile a year later (January 1979) and the collapse of his loyalist troops a month after that.

The leftists thought the Shah was too far to the right, and in his despotism, he certainly was. The Islamists thought the Shah was too secularist, and by "too" they meant "at all". Beyond their common cause of deposing him, the two forces were completely at odds with each other. That left a particularly poignant question: what, or who, would come after the Shah? The frying pan or the fire?

Meanwhile, waiting in exile in Paris, was the answer: Khomeini, the charismatic (to his followers) Shia Muslim radical clergyman and spiritual leader of the many Iranians who resented the Shah's transformation of the country into a more secular, Western-leaning society, someone who would eventually dismantle and disembowel Iran's reforms and turn the country into a theocracy. *Be careful what you wish for.*

The Shah fled to the US to get cancer treatment and to discuss the situation at home with US officials. The Iranian revolutionaries were demanding his release into their custody, to be tried for crimes against the Iranian people. Talks and demands went back and forth, or more accurately spiraled downwards. In early November 1979, the revolutionaries stormed the US Embassy in Tehran and took 52 American diplomats hostage, creating a nightmare scenario for US President Jimmy Carter. But it was perfect for Khomeini, who returned to Iran as the Supreme Leader, the Ayatollah. The timing was also perfect for the forces supporting Ronald Reagan. After all, 1980 was an election year in the US.

Desperate to showcase "presidential strength", Carter authorized a rescue mission to liberate the hostages on April 24th, 1980, using Special Forces and warships off the Iranian coast. It was a total disaster, a fiasco. Then, a month before the US election, Iraq launched a bloody war against Iran, Sunni Muslims against Shia Muslims, Northern Ireland á la Middle East. Because he was perceived as insufficiently macho, American voters found Carter too weak, something the Republicans took full advantage of. Reagan won by a landslide, accelerated the

A Sea of Troubles

country's rightward drift, and launched the Age of Greed that has continued to impact American politics (and beyond) ever since.

Back to that other reality, back in time to my reality in November 1978. I was still seeing Lena from time to time – whenever she permitted, always on her terms only. It seemed to me that her aim was just to keep her back burner full. But although my feelings for her remained pretty much the same, I was no longer responding to rejection with despair; I succeeded to a large extent in teaching my feelings to be a bit more submissive to rational review, even when rational thoughts were afterthoughts not involved in my first reactions. In those afterthoughts, I told myself that I had no intention of becoming my own (or anyone else's) victim again.

But I couldn't help being puzzled and perplexed by Lena's remarkable fickleness. My curiosity was aroused. I tried and tried to discern a pattern in her mood swings towards me, but I could see no connections with my own moods, her stress levels, her hormone levels, or anything else. Nothing made sense, and I *needed* to make sense of whatever possible, whenever possible.

Did she just turn to me when she was horny? Or when she needed to be adored? She continued to remind me that she was still carrying a torch for Larry (I tried not to let her see how I automatically winced at the mention of his name, knowing that he was crowding my space on her back burner), but there were many aspects of her current and past life that she didn't reveal, so how could I possibly figure out what factors might be involved in how she felt about me from one day to the next?

I let her know countless times that I would be thrilled beyond words if she chose to move in with me, and sometimes she admitted that she was tempted. But why would she? She didn't love me; did I think that my loving her would be enough for both of us? Or did *she* think so? Or did she think it might simply be convenient for her? That I would *do*, for now? She invariably ended up dismissing the idea so emphatically (and sometimes even disdainfully) that I again had to struggle a bit with the pain of rejection. Still, it gave me glimpses [*or should have*] of a sort of indication of how far from reality my aspirations concerning Lena remained. The reality? I might do – till something better came along.

I was soon given a more objective indication. Lena told me that for several weeks she'd been actively combing the classified ads for a proper apartment for herself in Lund. I felt a pang of disappointment since I still harbored a little hope, almost against my will (and certainly against my better judgment), that her next move would be to Korngatan. And yet, why *shouldn't* she get a place of her own? She'd made it quite clear that she felt no ties to me. And I could easily understand that she wouldn't want to remain in her cramped student dormitory room, with no a kitchen of her own. Indeed, perhaps she *had* to move from the subsidized student housing now that she was no longer a student. (Had she been told to move out?) One thing seemed clear to me: investing in an apartment of *her* own was a step away from a life of *our* own. But I tried to remain neutral, i.e. silent.

I'd learned that any form of criticism from me, any questioning of her actions or choices, direct or indirect, whether it was my implication or her inference, would not be well received. But I had yet to learn that she might extend the indirectness of implied criticism to include any response short of enthusiastic and explicit concurrence, preferably augmented by lavish praise.

During one of my lengthy phone conversations with Bob at around this time, I told him that I sensed a "*Harrumph!*" in his tone whenever I mentioned Lena. He somewhat sheepishly admitted that perhaps his feelings on the subject comprised a level of complexity that incorporated elements of a strong desire on his part for caution on my part, insofar as full reciprocation of my feelings towards Lena seemed from his perspective to be an unlikely outcome in the unforeseeable future, which posed the peril that in the meantime, my recent resolve, heartening as it was to him, might be subdued and defeated through the incessant attrition of recurring rejection. He felt that if I were to maintain additional irons in the fire, as it were, until such time as the aspirations of my beloved were to become more closely aligned with my own, he, for one, would experience a tangible reduction in anxiety regarding my well-being, a concern upon which he placed considerable weight. (Those were not Bob's exact words – I didn't run around with a tape recorder – but they do reflect his manner of expressing himself in situations that he felt called for paramount diplomacy.)

Not long after Lena revealed her apartment-hunting efforts to me, she excitedly told me she'd found a place. I did my utmost to disguise any traces of disappointment. I even congratulated her and volunteered to help her move. It was admittedly in a desirable location (apart from the perpetual parking difficulties she would face when living in central Lund), along the tree-lined Södra Esplanaden, on the first floor, about a 10-minute walk to the heart of Lund or to her sister's place (and not more than about 50 meters from the nearest bus stop to Malmö). She would get the keys on Friday, December 1st, but she wanted a little time to fix it up before moving in.

A couple of things at work helped me move a few steps closer to my goal of eventually working entirely from home. At the end of my working day on Thursday, November 9th, one of the bosses came rushing into Stig's office with a report, a 32-page text that absolutely had to be translated into English by the time he left on a business trip to the States on Friday morning – *the next day*. They both came across the hall to my office to see what I could do. I said I'd do my best, but that he'd have to pick up the translation in Malmö on his way to the airport. And I needed a phone number where I could reach him all evening in case I needed further clarification.

The text was complex and in poorly written Swedish, but I got going on it the moment I got home, worked almost non-stop, and completed it at 4.30 AM – in plenty of time for the 9 AM pick-up. All the extra hours I'd put in – overtime hours at that – meant that I needed fewer hours in Perstorp to fulfil my part-time quota. News travels fast in a company like Perstorp; I soon saw an upswing in translation work, and heard quite a few favorable comments on my successful completion of that far-beyond-the-call-of-duty assignment. Moreover, Stig was diligent in letting people know about my capability.

Then I got a request from a guy named Kaj (rhymes with "guy"), the head of Perstorp Form, manufacturers of injection-molded plastic products for homes, offices, workshops etc. It was discovered that one of his newly promoted and thus obviously upcoming young managers, Peter, suddenly required a major boost in his English skills. After discussing the matter with Stig, it was decided that Peter would spend three whole days at Korngatan with me, November 20th-22nd, for a mini-immersion course that could do more to remedy his shortcoming than years of visiting me for an hour a week at my Perstorp office could ever do. I knew that *this* news would also travel.

Ann-Kristin phoned me one day in late November to tell me, with unexpected distress, that she felt she was becoming too emotionally involved with me, and that further trysts would not be advisable for her, and she hoped I'd understand that our time together had been wonderful and would be something she would always cherish, but she just couldn't continue, and she hoped I wouldn't be hurt. I said I understood her perfectly and she expressed profound relief. Then Majlis phoned me with a nearly identical message. It was almost uncanny. I was sorry to say goodbye to them both; but I was relieved that they didn't have to deal with any pain of rejection from me.

My correspondence with Mom was entirely devoid of references to my maze of relationships, of course. Although Mom and I professed to desire more openness, there would always be huge limitations on how much openness she could take. I found it sad to think that the vast majority of children grow up feeling that they are unable to be completely open with their parents, upon whom their very lives once depended and from whom they acquire so much in the form of genes, tastes, shelter, values, food, habits, love, prejudices, health, clothing, neuroses, language and history. The non-openness between us was often a two-way street. But if that was simply the way things were, why did it sadden me?

Sonja and I were still keeping in touch, more openly now than ever, I thought, in spite of her move to Stockholm. She was getting settled into a tiny sublet room on Narvavägen in the extremely fashionable Östermalm district of Sweden's capital city. (It was the district that was fashionable, not Sonja's tiny room!) She was eager to have me come to see her for a few days (I agreed). She even offered to pay for my ticket (I declined). I would arrive on December 15th and spend four days and nights with her.

In the late morning on Saturday, November 18th, while Lena was still at Korngatan, George stopped by unannounced for a friendly visit. He took one look at Lena and started flirting with her, and she flirted right back, right there in front of me. I'm not even sure she knew she was flirting with him (is that my naiveté talking?), but he certainly knew what he was doing. It pissed me off.

In Perstorp on the 22nd, I was supposed to have Kaj as a pupil for the first of many scheduled lessons, but he was too busy to come, so he sent his daughter instead. She also worked at Perstorp Form, and was also named Lena (Lena E, not Lena J). She was young (21), pretty (looked like a young Ingrid Bergman), naïve (even more than me), and knew little English. There was something in our first eye contact, the way she looked at me, that made me sit up and take notice, like a squirrel that hears a sudden noise in its immediate vicinity (or perhaps more like a squirrel that spots a pine cone on a distant tree). Before our hour of tooth-pulling attempts at English conversation were up, I asked her, in the simplest English I could muster, if she might like to come down and visit me in Malmö for the evening on Friday, December 1st, and to my total astonishment, just like that, she said she would probably come. (*You probably will*, I thought, loving her unintended pun; in some areas, I was full of confidence.) Lena J was going to be in Stockholm that weekend with her mother and Eva, visiting her brothers. I had nothing else on.

Sometime that autumn, Bob made a simple, but insightful observation about me: "*You can't stand to be alone.*" My spontaneous reaction was that it was preposterous. He'd previously observed that I was gregarious, but I couldn't see how that implied that I couldn't stand to be alone, although I had to admit that there were many situations that Bob experienced as delightful solitude that for me were outright and howlingly lonely.

I'd begun to realize that the difference between loneliness and solitude isn't in the situations or circumstances, but in how our minds process them. One person reacts with howling emptiness, another with blissful tranquility – to identical external conditions. Is that in our genes or learned in our childhoods? Bob and I had remarkably similar backgrounds, values and philosophies of life, but we were remarkably different in our personalities. Yet Bob had changed dramatically from the nihilistic, pessimistic misanthrope whom Jeanette and I first met in 1970, and while "gregarious" would never be a description of his personality, neither did "nihilistic, pessimistic misanthrope" apply to him any longer. However, the more I thought about his claim about my strong aversion to being alone, the more I felt obliged to agree with it. Could I learn to be alone if I had to? Could I learn to appreciate solitude? Must those two questions have the same answer?

If Bob were right and I did have an uncontrollable urge to avoid being alone – an urge that might be exerting a powerful influence on me of which I might be blithely unaware – it would also mean that I would be terribly vulnerable to forming an unbreakable bond, either too prematurely (before my grief over losing Jeanette subsided, before I was sufficiently healed) or too inappropriately (with someone who did not reciprocate). I'd already experienced how unhealthy that could be. It had nearly killed me. But despite that, I was still on the hook, *her* hook.

One evening on my own I happened to see an old movie version of Somerset Maugham's brilliant book *Of Human Bondage*, on the power of an unhealthy bond. The protagonist (Philip, played by Leslie Howard) is a handsome, young, club-footed medical student who meets an attractive but shallow waitress (Mildred, played by Bette Davis), and his rationality goes out the window. She treats him disdainfully, yet keeps him dangling on the hook, and the bond to her that instantly arose in him becomes a destructive obsession from which he can never free himself, as long as they both shall live.

The human desire to be enslaved and subservient seemed to me to have no limits. On November 18th that year, more than 900 members of a fanatical sect founded by James Jones committed mass suicide in Jonestown, Guyana, having made their minds totally submissive to their leader's crazed will and trumped-up "vision". How many billions willingly submit their otherwise rational minds to ancient superstitions all the time, all over the world, only too happy to believe that even their innermost thoughts can be read and judged by the creator of all diseases? And was I, by dragging up these irrelevant albeit valid examples of human foolishness, just looking for a way to make my bondage to Lena seem harmless by comparison?

In the evening on Saturday, November 25th, Lena and I co-hosted her sister Eva and common-law husband Jan for dinner and the night at Korngatan. It was the first time Lena had ever played the role of hostess on my turf. Despite the fact that she was already moving into her own new apartment in Lund, my hopes once again began to stir. Eva took one look at *Turning* (well over half finished) and burst out, "But it's you and Lena!" which thrilled me, took my perception of Eva to an even higher level, and made Lena squirm. Eva and Marie-Louise had made it abundantly clear to me that they understood my feelings for Lena – and that they were both squarely in my corner. But Lena remained determined not to become emotionally involved with me, even though we'd been spending quite a few nights together again, and I was convinced that she might be softening. [*That formulation, that combination (from 1978)* – "convinced *that she* might" – *says a lot about how accommodating my rationality could be.*]

Exasperating as this situation was becoming to me, I was working hard (and perhaps somewhat desperately) to ensure that while Lena J was in charge of my euphoria, my inner harmony was now strong enough to be merely dampened, not at all extinguished, whenever she had one of her cold spells. I would therefore continue to keep an open door, if not an open mind, to whatever opportunities arose. As Bob wrote to me, "Until your feet are steadier, I hope for variety for you."

In the early evening on Friday, December 1st, 1978, I took the bus to the central station to meet Lena E, my young student from Perstorp. I was still kind of flabbergasted that such a pretty, demure girl had instantly accepted an invitation I more or less just threw out there, presuming she would only take it as a compliment that would make her giggle. But she arrived in the dusky December afternoon, overnight bag and all (I'd only mentioned "for the evening"!), and we took a bus back to Korngatan. I tried to make conversation with her along the way, at first in English, then in Swedish, but she said little – no different from the way she was during her lesson in Perstorp.

I didn't know what to expect when we entered the house. I was planning to make her a nice meal, but it was still quite a bit early for dinner, so I asked if she'd like to have a look around the house. She lowered her eyes, smiled shyly and nodded. After walking through the kitchen and living room downstairs, while she looked around with curiosity but without comment, we headed for the stairs. When we got to my bedroom, she was already entering and I put my hand on her shoulder from behind, meaning to stop her, to indicate that we needn't go in, but she reached up, took my hand without turning around, and led me in, then turned and embraced me. I was *gobsmacked*! We had a lovely evening and night – we even had a meal in there somewhere – which I to some small extent spoiled for myself by wondering why (in my thoughts only!) that other Lena couldn't accept my affection this readily. Then I remembered that she had, *initially*, one year ago.

None of my rational analysis and balanced approach to maintaining stability, nor my determination to keep all doors open until "my" Lena shut all of hers except for me, nor my pre-breakfast mutual passion with Lena E, could entirely save me from that most irksome human bondage to Lena J. So late the next morning, after taking Lena E to the train, I got on another train to Lund, picked up Lena J's car (she'd left me her keys while she, Eva and Marie-Louise were in Stockholm for the weekend), drove to pick up a floor sander, went to her new apartment (she'd left me that key too) and spent the entire day and evening sanding away the dark painted surfaces of her floors to reveal the light and lovely pine. Then I dusted the entire apartment to my masculine standards, and curled up with a blanket for the night. The next morning I got up before it was light (which isn't hard to do in Sweden in December) and started varnishing the floor so that the first coat would be dry and impressive by the time she got back.

She *was* impressed, but I could feel another cold spell coming on – so frustrating. (Were these *conscious* efforts designed to maintain her distance every time she felt it shrinking?!) She didn't have to vacate her dorm room at Ulrikedal until December 22nd, so she was planning to use the intervening time to repaint her new apartment and move her things a little at a time, while also looking around for the necessary bits of furniture she lacked. Lena's dorm room had been furnished, so she hardly had any furniture to move from there, but she had lots of books, papers, clothing, rag carpets, pots and cutlery, wall hangings, and all those other little items that take no space when in place but add up endlessly when you have to move them when to begin a new life in another place.

Before my big brother John got married to Marj and left home in 1960, he was a big fan of the Kingston Trio, a popular folk-country group, thus obviously making me a fan as well. The lyrics of their hit song *Desert Pete*, released in 1963 (the year I graduated from high school), stuck in my mind for some reason, and now suddenly popped back into my consciousness as a perfect metaphor for a message I so urgently needed to convey to Lena:

> *You've got to prime the pump, you must have faith and believe.*
> *You've got to give of yourself 'fore you're worthy to receive*
> *Drink all the water you can hold, wash your face, cool your feet,*
> *But leave the bottle full for others, thank you kindly, desert Pete.*

This was to be my last painting before *Jardin*, and it would be the perfect prelude – thematically and stylistically – to that daunting work. In the foreground there's a pathway of increasing brightness as it reaches the front, i.e. the lower edge of the painting. This path is flanked on both sides by beautiful, bright flowers, and a brightly colored tree (similar to the one I'd be painting in *Jardin*). The flower-lined path is the confluence of two paths from the background, which comprises a dark forest with few signs of life (as in *Through the Woods*). At the fork in the center there's an old-fashioned farm-style pump, with a young man standing on the left grasping the handle with both hands, and a young woman on the right holding a small bucket of water. He's identifiably the same figure as in the earlier painting *If You Want a Flower to Open...*, and she's recognizable as the girl in *Turning*. (Do the math!) The two figures have travelled on the two different paths in the background to reach the fork, the meeting point where the pump is. Beneath the spout of the pump is a large empty pail, waiting to be filled. All she has to do is pour the contents of her small bucket into the pump to prime it, thereby enabling him to start pumping all the water they could ever want. But she hesitates. He's looking at her intently, waiting. She's facing him, but perhaps doesn't see. I call it *Priming the Pump*.[16]

---

16 Painting #83 (see Appendix 2)

My hope was to finish it by Christmas and give it to Lena as a Christmas present, but I realized there might not be enough time. I finally bought a proper box spring for my bedroom (no longer just a mattress on the floor!); I was still helping Lena with her new apartment; Al and Nancy were coming to visit on December 7th-9th; I'd be visiting Sonja in Stockholm on December 15th-19th; Bob would be arriving on December 23rd and staying until January 6th; and I had a quite a lot of work for Perstorp.

Every week, Marie-Louise Larsson, my new *confidante* in Perstorp, inquired eagerly about my ongoing efforts to win Lena J's heart. She was clearly rooting for me. Every step forward (which she could instantly see in my face) elicited a warm smile, and every setback (probably just as obvious to her) caused her brow to wrinkle as she shook her head in disbelief when she understood that Lena had gone cold on me once again. She seemed almost as anxious as I was to solve the riddle: was it possible to discover any trigger factors? In view of the fact that Marie-Louise Larsson always projected an air of greatest propriety and decorum, I was rather astonished when she suggested that I should consider keeping a record of each time Lena and I made love, to see if that might somehow provide a clue. But since nothing else seemed to make any sense, I said I might give it a try, as from January.

The visit from Al and Nancy didn't do me much good. Prior to their arrival, Al asked me whether I'd like them to bring me anything, and I specifically requested a bottle of duty-free scotch. But he didn't bring any alcohol, saying "*We don't drink whisky!*" as if spoken from some jerrybuilt pedestal or pulpit. They met Lena for the first time that Friday. (When it became clear that Lena and I would be drinking wine with dinner, both Al and Nancy joined us.) Nancy mentioned having heard that Lena's late father had been a vicar (I suspect Mom told them; they seemed primed). She immediately set about subtly questioning (interrogating) Lena about her religious beliefs, and being a good, non-confrontational Swede who was unfamiliar with the subtleties that I was all too familiar with, Lena fell into trap after trap. But Lena wasn't feeling well physically either, so our first night in my new bed was an anti-climax. She asked if I could drive her home to Lund on Saturday morning. Al and Nancy came along for the ride. Lena told me I could use her car until she recovered, so I was able to drop Al and Nancy off at the airport bus terminal (the bus drove them to Limhamn, onto the ferry to Dragør, then directly to the Copenhagen airport) in the early afternoon.

On Saturday afternoon and evening, and into Sunday, I painted a bit, then drove to Lund to see Lena, and we moved a few more of her things. She was having problems with the starter on her Datsun, so I dropped her off at her school on Monday morning, drove to a junkyard and bought her a replacement starter. I took it to the Saabyes and had them install it, then picked her up after work. I kept paying for her things; and Lena kept telling me she'd pay me back when she got her paycheck. [*It never happened.*]

On Wednesday, December 13th, Lena and I spent her first night in her new apartment. She was thrilled. I had to fake it; I not only had problems with her telling me she'd recovered quickly and had gone out the night before, I was also upset that she felt she had to tell me that she'd been out with another guy. She sensed that I was faking it (faking what??) and became irritated, claiming that I didn't "own" her. I protested that my feelings for her had nothing whatsoever to do with "owning", they were called "love". That "correction" irritated her even more. A few days later, she said, piano movers were coming to move her piano from Jan and Eva's house to her new apartment. Her slightly haughty tone in the way she announced it made it feel like another nail in the coffin of any residual aspirations that she might someday come to love me and move in with me.

Under the circumstances, my trip to Stockholm to see Sonja was like a breath of fresh air. She seemed genuinely delighted to see me, and she was great fun to be with. Although her tiny one-room apartment (no kitchen facilities except for a miniscule fridge and a hotplate) was part of a large and probably luxurious apartment, it was completely separate and had its own street entrance (it had probably once been a servant's room; the building seemed to be from the late 1800s). The room might have been as large as 15m^2, but because the footprint was dwarfed by the high ceiling (close to four meters), it seemed smaller to me (which I found strange, since high ceilings usually make rooms seem bigger). For Sonja, it was a place to sleep with the advantage of having an extremely convenient location, within walking distance of the theater where she worked.

Sonja had a supporting role in an ongoing Swedish production of Shakespeare's *Othello*, one of my favorites (although also his most troubling), and she had a ticket for me to come and watch her perform one of the nights I was there. Knowing of my love of certain operas, she'd also procured a ticket for me to Richard Strauss's *Der Rosenkavalier*, another favorite. On her days off, we explored the Old Town and the national museums, cozy little restaurants she'd found (including *Fem små hus* in the Old Town), and dazzling views of the water. We had an exciting yet relaxing time. Her tiny room had only a single bed, but we managed fine, thanks to the not-strictly-sexless nature of our relationship. Had she not told me so resoundingly some time before that her focus was on her career, and that she was worried that I might be developing a romantic interest in her, I might have been worried a great deal about hurting her. As it was, I only worried a small deal. But it felt to me that our friendship was deep and our parting was joyous.

With Lena J remaining chilly when I got back to Malmö, with Bob arriving in just four days, and with many of my students in Perstorp taking time off during the week before Christmas, I focused on *Priming the Pump*. I wanted to have enough of it done so that Bob would be able to get an idea of what it was all about. Since I didn't think I'd be able to finish it before Christmas, I decided to complete as much as I could, then take a Polaroid photo of the nearly finished painting, place the photo in the bottom of a fairly large gift-wrapped box with a card promising that Lena would soon be getting the real thing. I wrapped the box in Christmas wrapping paper, and gave it to Lena on the 22nd, to be opened on Christmas Eve when she would be at Eva's place in Lund. As it turned out (according to Eva), Lena was underwhelmed (*"What's this?!"* she said, puzzled, almost sneering). But Eva was in awe.

It was truly wonderful to see Bob, my best friend ever, at the Copenhagen airport on the 23rd, our first physical meeting since Easter. All the transformation – from the suicidal basket case I'd been since Jeanette's death to the daring-to-be-bold, still-naïve, still-grieving-yet-not-succumbing, lovesick, libido-driven, would-be rationalist I was becoming – was to a very great extent Bob's doing. It is probably no exaggeration at all to say that I owed him my life. I wished I could have done more about his! The decline in his physical health hit me between the eyes and between the chambers of my heart the moment I saw him. His movements were significantly slower and stiffer, more laborious, accented by wincing that could only have been due to considerable pain. His voice was weak and shaky. But he never complained. There were so many lessons I had yet to learn from him.

Bob observed that I was a person who, once I decided to approach something (or some*one*), *lunged* at it with passionate enthusiasm – an approach that could be endearing, startling, alarming, repugnant or anything else along that scale to an innocent bystander, depending on who that bystander was, or whether that bystander was, in fact, the "*lungee*". He was anxious to get me to try to keep my heart on a leash, so to speak (there was no chance whatsoever of getting it to "heel"). I knew what he meant; I just wasn't quite sure *how* to get there.

He now met Lena for the first time, a somewhat nervous meeting for both of them. The physical and personality charms that I found so extraordinary in her had little effect on Bob; he was tied to the mast, always looking for something deeper. His principal concern, for reasons he best understood himself, was me and my well-being. I sensed that he strongly disapproved of or (was troubled by) the lengths to which I would go to please Lena. (The lengths she would go to allow herself to be pleased by me didn't even extend to thanking me for *Priming the Pump*.)

Bob's reaction to *Priming the Pump* disappointed me due to its absence. He professed being impressed technically, but he rightly saw the thematic side of it with all the possibly justifiable misgivings and fears he'd been repeatedly hinting at ever since I began relating the tale of my overwhelmingly one-sided romance with Lena. I tried to emphasize the value that this painting had for me as a warm-up for *Jardin*, and that gave him an opening to steer the conversation to that important next painting and to let himself extricate his foot from the immediate vicinity of his mouth.

For the last week of her Christmas break, starting on New Year's Day, Lena decided that she was going to travel on her own to the sun for a week, by which she meant the Canary Islands. She spent New Year's Eve at Korngatan, but a heavy snowfall and severe freezing during the night presented a considerable obstacle to reaching the Copenhagen airport on New Year's Day, particularly since she hadn't thought to bring her passport and suitcase with her to Korngatan. In the morning, the buses had stopped running to Lund or within Malmö, so she and I struggled (*of course* I volunteered – surely that's no surprise by now!) on foot through the snow to the Malmö train station. We waited through long delays on the train, then battled snow-filled streets on foot in Lund to reach her apartment, where we retrieved her things, then slogged our way back to Malmö to catch a ferry to Copenhagen, then a bus to the airport (the buses were still running on the Danish side) in time for her flight. Somewhere during that ordeal, she let it slip that she had to get to a pharmacy to fill her prescription for birth-control pills. She also said, or let slip (?!), "*I guess I would hate to lose you.*" Was that back-door admission of feelings for me just in case her prescription announcement gave me any wild ideas about getting off her hook?

CHAPTER 9

Trying

Even someone as naïve as me *should* have heard alarm bells going off all over the place when Lena made that slip of the tongue about the Pill. But I was always capable of fetching excuses and less painful explanations on her behalf from as far away as necessary. First and most obvious possible excuse: *Hey, I was screwing around, why shouldn't she?* There was, of course, a big difference, as I saw it: I would *not* have been screwing around at all if only she'd love me back and stop treating me like a dildo. Second excuse: *Just because I was totally and madly in love with her, what right did I have to expect or demand reciprocation?* I knew I didn't have any such right, but it felt like she was running some kind of East German radio jamming frequency on my mind and my heart that was trying my patience and my sanity – and the jamming (intentional or not) was disturbingly successful.

Third excuse: *Maybe it was Lena who was hearing all the alarm bells?* My head knew her circumstances well enough to conjecture that she was probably no more ready for a new, serious, long-term, forever relationship than I was; maybe she knew that and I didn't. Or maybe neither of us did, but we just happened to find ourselves trapped in some kind of invisible and powerful eddy current of lust, or a mighty vortex of our inability to understand, to steer or to flee.

I was certain that I was not overestimating the depth of my love for her. It was a feeling I was unable to shake off even when I was keenly aware that it would have been healthier (and more rational!!) for me – and perhaps for her – if I could. But I probably did overestimate the power of my love to break down her resistance to it, and deluded myself into thinking that if I just loved her enough, she would begin to love me. I'd also grossly underestimated how much grief I had yet to process after my loss of Jeanette, how badly crippled I remained. Time is a great doctor, and while it may heal all wounds, it's a lousy plastic surgeon – the scars can remain forever.

Bob was nevertheless largely relieved at the improvement in my state since March. I was full of outward enthusiasm, and displayed a highly visible lust for *life*, but there was still a degree of inward anxiety that kept me fragile and brittle, although I didn't have a clue about that at the time. I didn't allow myself sufficient time for reflection.

I was keenly aware, however, that whenever Lena was affectionate towards me, I felt great; and whenever she turned from me I felt the winds of misery trying to blow me away, and sex became my only temporary refuge. Lena E phoned me one day just after New Year's and asked if she could come down to see me in the evening on January 6th. Since Bob was returning to Basel earlier that same day, it worked out perfectly. I particularly looked forward to seeing Lena E; in addition to being a very lovely and pleasant girl, she seemed to have an astonishingly and inexplicably good stabilizing effect on me.

I really didn't want my moods to be dependent on Lena J's, which were frustrating and incomprehensible. In consequence, in the first half of January '79 I decided to follow Marie-Louise Larsson's advice and start keeping records by making marks and notes in my diary for the purpose of trying to perceive patterns that might give me a clue as to what was going on in that beautiful head of hers, and possibly *why*. [*Ah, hindsight! If only I had seen the implications of what I was writing.*][17]

Björn and Isobel stopped by for a brief visit while Bob was with me. It was the first time I'd seen them in months, and only the second time since they moved to Oxie, which was out of my cycle range. As I recall, they spent more time quibbling with each other than conversing with Bob or me. Bob returned to Binningen on Saturday, January 6th, and Lena E arrived by car, not train, that same evening to help me make it through the night. She seemed to be starting to open up a bit (in the sense of also conversing) and she allowed me to get to know a little about her thoughts and not just her body. She was very sweet, and had an air of almost bewildering innocence that both intrigued me and made me want to take extra care not to lead her on or hurt her in any way.

I suppose I had some Victorian baggage that made it puzzling for me to reconcile her appearance of unspoiled innocence with her totally matter-of-fact approach to having sex with me, how openly she demonstrated her willingness to have sex, yet how dispassionate she remained otherwise, almost disconnected. But getting to know another person is seldom, in my experience, an instantaneous

---

17 I kept that diary daily from January 12th to June 19th, and sporadically thereafter. It was full of insights that I could not or would not see (or both) at the time. It was also full of naiveté, sentimentality, adolescent romanticism, and other modes of garbled thinking. But that was me then, and "me then" contributed to making "me now".

thing. First impressions are occasionally fairly right, but are much more often quite wrong, and they tend to color, distort, warp or even drown out the complexity of other impressions that generally follow. Sometimes the process of getting to know someone offers no shortcuts; and one can only ever *guess* how it would *feel* to *be* another person.

The impossibility of ever completely knowing another person – the unbridgeable void – had been the defining theme of so many of my paintings. It seemed to me that most people I met felt compelled to ignore the void, pretend it wasn't there, refuse to face it or even acknowledge it. When so few people (apart from Jeanette, Bob, and a few others) ever even commented on the central role this abyss played in most of my work, what other conclusion could I draw?

And now I was leaving that theme, or at least its central role. In all my paintings since *Urban Idyll*, I was instead focusing on the necessity of creating whatever good can be obtained, of forging one's own happiness by affirming life. Jeanette was gone, and I could only speculate how she might have seen it. But Bob (who else?!) saw this theme too, before I mentioned it, and he rejoiced in it.

Lena E spent most of Sunday with me as well. We had a great time, with unlimited affection and intimacy, but she was still a fascinating enigma to me – and I found myself wanting to learn more and more.

Lena J returned, well-tanned, from the Canaries in the late evening on Monday, January 8th. I met her at the airport, of course. I told her I'd been watering her plants diligently in her absence, and had bought her a few groceries so her fridge wouldn't be empty. I'd also brought along all her personal mail with me, in case she was anxious or curious about what might have arrived in her absence. As my "reward" (and because it was already so late), she agreed to spend the night at Korngatan.

I reported to Bob that Lena's return made me "*acutely conscious of an independent well-being inside me, the existence of which has no dependence on her, although she provides a major outlet for my expression of it* [...] *even if not everyone fully understands the distinction.*" But Bob did, of course. He probably also understood that what I was describing was how I *wanted* to feel, not how I felt.

The next day, January 9th, a small mini-bus from Perstorp arrived to pick up 10 of my paintings for an exhibition in the spacious company cafeteria in Persgården. My main reasons for agreeing to that exhibition were to get people off my back for a while about never showing my work anywhere, and because Stig (my boss) wanted to make an even bigger splash of me among potential clients for my services. Among the 60-70 people from Perstorp who'd been my students long before I ever dreamed we might someday have the same employer, only a handful ever expressed any interest in my art, despite the fact that I told nearly all of them that I was an artist and many of them had been to our apartment and seen my paintings first-hand. Silence was the usual response; When I asked point-blank, most claimed not to understand art, yet they gave no indication of wanting to (they could have asked the artist himself – he was, after all, right there!); or, if I probed further, they revealed that their own preferences ranged from pretty landscapes to kitschy gypsy children with tear-streaked cheeks, painted on velvet. My expectations for a positive response from anyone might better be called expectorations. Those, at least, were fulfilled.

I was beginning to think that my relationship with Lena E might turn out to have some potential beyond the purely physical. The thought that I might be inhibited from exploring that potential by always being at Lena J's beck and call was worming its way into my highly viscous and reluctant consciousness. So on Wednesday, January 10th, after meeting Lena J's cold disinterest once again the evening before, I phoned Lena E from my office at Perstorp's headquarters to hers at Perstorp Form and asked whether she'd like me to ride home to Klippan with her instead of home to Malmö with Knut that evening, and spend the night at her apartment, then ride back to Perstorp with her the next morning. She agreed without hesitation or reservation, but with poker-voiced inscrutability.

Dusk was already well advanced when she picked me up at 4.30 PM at the same pick-up point used by Knut and David, and drove me the 15 km to the small town of Klippan, my first visit there since December 1969, when Elsa Braun took her Swedish class on a trip to the Klippan paper mill. Lena E lived in a modern two-room apartment on the third floor just off Storgatan, the main street that ran through the town. After she parked her car, she seemed to want me to hurry furtively indoors. She took out something from her freezer for us to eat later, then offered me a whisky. While we were standing there in her brightly lit kitchen, she wondered aloud whether her jealous ex-boyfriend could see that she had male company from his window in the building across the way in the next block, but she made no attempt to close the curtains or dim the lights. We did not, however, remain in the kitchen very long.

She'd never mentioned a boyfriend – ex or otherwise – but clearly someone as pretty as she was would hardly remain single for long. I recall briefly wondering whether she was trying to make him jealous by showing me off, making sure that he *would* see me there. But when she led me into the bedroom, before we'd finished our whisky, I thought no more about it. I did notice a significant increase in Lena E's responsiveness in bed that evening, something approaching the kind of intimacy that was more than purely physical, and I felt myself reciprocating. We parted warmly on Thursday morning near the company gate, and kept the lowest possible profile at the gossip mill where we both worked. I rode home with Knut after work on Thursday and spent a quiet evening at home, alone.

Friday's mail delivery at home brought me a totally unexpected message from Lena E. She'd mailed a little card with a flower on it, and she'd written, "*Thanks for a lovely evening, Lena.*" It touched me deeply, and being who I was, I immediately started revving up my feelings for her, and my brain started trying to work out "where this could be going." I was even becoming emboldened enough to consider escaping from the hazardous bondage of "my other Lena", with whom I more often than not felt like a puppet on a string. [*To understand my frame of mind and of reference, try listening to the lyrics of two popular songs of the 1960s:* Puppet on a String *by Sandie Shaw (1967) and* If You Promise Me a Rose *by Anita Bryant (1960).*]

I was not, however, about to let a few setbacks in my obsessive efforts to win Lena J's heart make me give up yet. We spent Friday night at her place in Lund, but in the morning she told me she couldn't see me on Saturday because she thought she might like some time by herself. Then she said she thought she might spend her evening of solitude with her girlfriend Gun. Minutes later, Jarle phoned, and she invited *him* over for Saturday evening, while I was standing right there just after having turned me down (?!). Then she got angry with me for looking upset. I had the feeling that if I didn't fit her ideal down to the last detail, she'd dismiss me without a second thought. I wondered, in my mind only of course, whether she'd ever get off her ego trip, and whether Dylan's *Don't Think Twice* (or perhaps *It Ain't Me Babe*) would end up being my song to her, when Elton John's *Sorry Seems to Be the Hardest Word* would have been far more appropriate (perhaps as the Swedish national anthem as well). Anyway, fool that I was, I was *still* prepared to go on trying to reach her. I commented on her in my diary that "*it must be hard when one is the most wonderful person one has ever met!*"

But instead of pining for Lena J all day on Saturday, I phoned Lena E in the late morning, and asked if we could meet. She told me she'd drive down immediately but that she could only stay until Sunday noon, because of an early birthday celebration on Sunday afternoon. I asked her whose birthday? "*Mine*," she answered, giggling shyly. As soon as we hung up, I rushed out to the neighborhood florist and bought her 22 red roses. She was moved and thrilled and we had a marvelous time. In spite of my attempts to keep hold of the leash on my feelings, I felt myself lunging with my passionate enthusiasm. I was beginning to feel split down the middle, and was genuinely sorry she had to leave – especially when she indicated that she was looking forward to our next meeting every bit as much as I was! As I wrote to Bob, being with Lena E that weekend gave me my first experience of a two-way-street relationship since Jeanette. And I liked it. [*My analysis was, however, entirely unfair to nearly <u>all</u> of my relationships –nearly everyone <u>but</u> Lena J!*]

In the late afternoon that Sunday, when I was on my own, Lena J phoned me to say that in her efforts not to lose her tan from the Canaries, she'd burnt her face badly under a sunlamp and wanted to tell someone about it (*good ol' Stan, always there when needed!*). But I was fed up with it, and began to do some serious re-evaluation. For the first time I told her something had to come from her, that she was only thinking of herself. She admitted that at times she didn't give a shit about her mother or sister either. (As if I'd feel better about being treated like shit if I knew that she also treated others like shit!) But in fact, it didn't surprise me to hear her say that, considering the many fragmentary sarcastic comments I'd heard from her about them. The fact that she actually *admitted* it did, however, surprise me a lot. She appeared to be wallowing in self-pity, and I knew what that was about! We went to the movies that evening and I spent the night at her place.

When I went home on Monday morning, I felt that *Priming the Pump* was dry enough for me to dare to deliver it, so I framed it. The next day I put some newspaper and a blanket around it and took it with me on the bus to Lund in the late afternoon, as soon as she would be home from school, hoping to overwhelm her. So what happened? A warm embrace and a kiss? No, *still* not even a thank you! Among Lena J's icy observations that evening: that I sometimes "put on airs" (Swedish "*förställer mig*") – this in reaction to my cuddly mood. Then she said that she is "above all criticism"! She really said that (verbatim in Swedish: "*Jag står ovan all kritik!*"), and would not *tolerate* any criticism from me, and that she *never* puts on airs; and that she does so much for everyone. Did she have anything kind to say to or about me or any affection to give? No. And no thanks for painting, nor for the usual flowers, wine, shopping, etc. They were (apparently) her birthright.

Then she announced another obstacle to a future with me: my vasectomy. This was the first time she'd ever mentioned it, although she'd known about it from the very beginning, for well over a year! In one sense, it was a brilliant move on her part, since it was non-negotiable; I couldn't do a damn thing about it. I despaired that she said that. And from my sadness she inferred criticism of her infallibility. She reiterated that it was not "my place" to criticize her in any way! Moreover, it was too much bother for her to come to Malmö that evening (I had to be in Malmö that night in order to get my early Wednesday morning ride to Perstorp). Thursday then? No plans, I could call her then (to give her time to find something better to do?). I left in the early evening and decided I wouldn't be calling.

I was pissed off, and phoned Lena E that evening instead. We chatted for a while – hardly at all dental now – and arranged for me to spend Wednesday night with her in Klippan again. I was also planning to invite her to Malmö for the entire following weekend – regardless of whatever whim Lena J might get about seeing me (it felt like I would only be her back-up plan anyway). *[And I completely failed to realize that my behavior towards Lena E might be seen as a back-up plan!]*

This time Lena E's place was no longer unknown territory for me, and she kept the kitchen curtains closed. She even made me a lovely dinner, which she seemed proud to serve (but eager for me to finish quickly). And not long after we got to bed she threw caution to the winds, and surprisingly uninhibited passion took its place. Afterwards, she seemed to be strangely frightened by the intensity of what she'd felt.

When I got home from Perstorp on Thursday evening, I felt a bit drained, but also euphoric about the development of my budding relationship with Lena E. She told me that morning that she would try to come down to Malmö for the weekend. There was now no doubt that my bonds to Lena J were loosening. I phoned Bob to let him know about this new development and he was jubilant. Then I poured myself a large Ballantine's and sat down to relax and enjoy the fact that I was alive.

A bit later that evening, Lena J phoned when it was apparent that I wasn't going to be phoning her. She wondered why, and I pulled out the stops and told her how tired I was of always having to feel that she was doing me a favor by allowing me to see her, pamper her, love her; that it was breaking me down and that I had no intention of going on like that. Then, for the first time ever, she practically begged me to come out to Lund to be with her. So I did. My brain and my heart were in total chaos.

I took the bus home after an early breakfast on Friday morning, and got a call from Lena E that instantly dashed my surging hopes – like a late frost on budding hydrangeas. She first told me that she was afraid she wouldn't be able to come down for the weekend due to a family get-together. After a pause for that disappointment to sink in, she went on to say that she was afraid she was starting to feel too much for me, that her feelings took her by surprise, that she'd only been out to have a bit of a fling, but now she found herself *liking* me and she didn't want to because I was too old for her (by about 12 years, ouch!) and she was afraid I'd get hurt, which was *not* what she wanted.

She wondered if we couldn't just be friends and maybe spend the night together "once in a while"? Doing everything I could to disguise my disappointment, I told her I felt pretty much the same way – except for the part about being too old for her – and we both laughed. Although I said I agreed that we probably shouldn't let ourselves become involved, I was not convinced that it was the kind of thing one could just decide. Choosing whether to wear a blue shirt or a yellow one is, after all, a different kind of decision. I was resisting the feeling that I suddenly found myself at a fork in the road that I was unprepared to face at this time. Certainly not having two Lenas in my life to focus on would make it less complicated, although I was far from certain that the one who remained would be the one with whom I would truly be happier.

I had another reaction that evening, Friday, January 19th: I started painting *Jardin*. I'd already made a rough charcoal sketch on the canvas. For most of my previous paintings (with the notable exceptions of *Priming the Pump* and *If You Want a Flower to Open...*) I sketched nearly all but a few details directly on the canvas, but these latest paintings were so detailed in themselves that I only made rudimentary sketches on the canvas and kept the details in my head. It was exciting, but also daunting, to be taking this first step on such a huge project, far more intimidating than any other I'd ever undertaken – and *without my muse*. Lena J never showed any interest in my painting, and thus gave me no encouragement either. It was almost as though my paintings didn't exist in her world (or at least not as anything positive).

That evening I was feeling disappointed and rather down because of Lena E's departure, but full of excitement because of having started on *Jardin*. In other words, I was experiencing somewhat more than my baseline level of chaos. I phoned Bob, and as usual he talked some sense into me, which I suppose I needed more than joy at that moment. I was determined not to fall into the trap of increasing my emotional dependency on Lena J just because Lena E felt she had to make her exit. Bob sounded disappointed to hear about Lena E's decision, but he said he was encouraged about how I was handling it. In fact, I was even considering ceasing my hitherto indefatigable pleas for Lena J's love altogether – as usual underestimating the extent of my bondage, and overestimating my ability to remain aloof, even though part of me realized that I could no more remain aloof than Ulysses tied to the mast.

Bob was elated to hear that I'd finally started on *Jardin*, a work that thrilled him unreservedly, both for its philosophical underpinnings and for the graphic expression of them that I described in great detail during his visit. (When I told Lena I'd started painting *Jardin*, her response was something like a timeworn version of *ho-hum*.) Bob pointed out to me, with his usual encyclopedic cross-referencing flair, the manner in which Voltaire's book had inspired Leonard Bernstein's opera *Candide*, particularly the lyrics of the aria "*Make our garden grow*":

> *We're neither pure, nor wise, nor good.*
> *We'll do the best we know.*
> *We'll build our house and chop our wood*
> *And make our garden grow.*

In my somewhat sporadic correspondence with Sonja, who'd become a true friend (without the sex now – easy enough, with her up in Stockholm), I'd been keeping her up to date on the roller-coaster ride that was my relationship with Lena J (I never mentioned Lena E to her), including the latest blow about my vasectomy. On Friday, January 26th, I received a reply from Sonja in the form of an exceptionally thoughtful and insightful letter, with the salutation "Dearest puppy":

> *You're looking for a secure embrace to curl up in. Love. Protection. But you can't force a thing like that. You can't force yourself on another person with all your longing for love, because you'll only make them run or suffocate. You'll just end up sad and disappointed unless you figure out why you want all this love. Start by figuring this out within yourself and don't be afraid of the answer you find. [...] And if a girl were to pull out of a love story with you because you're sterile, that lady is not someone you'd want to have around anyway. Believe me!!*

That was one of the soundest pieces of advice I never listened to, a real gem of insight and understanding, the words of a true, concerned and thoughtful friend! [*But of course I understood nothing of that at the time. I was all but impervious to wisdom.*]

So that evening I went to Lund for another roller-coaster ride, and despite spending the evening at Eva's, in whose presence Lena was invariably kinder towards me, it ended with Lena's irritation at my love for her. The next morning we went on errands in Lund together and her mood improved slightly. In the early afternoon, Eva and little Lina came by. Lina, catching sight of *Priming the Pump* for the first time, was visibly astonished and thrilled. After staring at it closely, she turned to Lena and said, "*Have you thanked Stanley for this wonderful painting?!*" Lena seemed embarrassed and lied: "yes".

That evening, Lena and I went to a party at the apartment of Gunilla, one of Lena's closest girlfriends from her teachers' college days, who'd become romantically involved with Øivind, one the three Norwegian dorm neighbors Lena had at Ulrikedal. Jarle was also there, and Lena was flirting with him so openly that it was becoming embarrassing to him, sickening to me, and perhaps bizarre to a few others.

Jarle was the one Lena was targeting. She even told me so [*why?!*]! For years afterward, I assumed he'd somehow been following Isobel's advice (even though Isobel and Jarle had never met) by unrelentingly playing hard to get, and the more he played that game, the harder Lena seemed to pursue him. [*It wasn't until decades later that Øivind revealed the real reason: Jarle was gay, something Lena apparently never knew either!*]

Those who knew Lena were nice to me at Gunilla's party, almost to the point of being overly considerate, which I couldn't figure out. In the midst of this, a pretty girl named Eva, a friend of Gunilla's, came up to me and asked me to dance. I was glad to have a distraction. While we were dancing, she moved closer and closer until she'd inserted one or her legs between mine, moving along my crotch and making me hard, which she clearly knew and liked. The libido pill worked again. But it was just a dance (and not even the lambada!). I don't think Lena saw it, but she did appear to notice how other people seemed to like me. Perhaps it was group pressure that changed her attitude towards me from the beginning to the end of the party.

The hair-raising ups and downs of my relationship with Lena J were matched by an intense back-and-forth correspondence with Bob (at least 60 lengthy letters in each direction during 1979). Much of the content involved Bob urging me to keep my feet on the ground, while I was using my head to convince him (and myself) that I was following that advice without actually doing so. He was constantly fearing that he was going too far, offending me and provoking me, while I was constantly reassuring him that I could take it, that he needn't feel inhibited or restricted.

He couldn't grasp (and I think he must have pitied) my inability to find living alone an acceptable lifestyle. I countered that I did find it acceptable, just not preferable. And he challenged me to tell him how I defined "love" and "commitment", the two things I was constantly seeking from Lena. I told him I was aware of the difficulty of explaining those two generalities without resorting to other generalities, so I tried to explain through analogy and metaphor, starting with him. He and I loved each other (I told him not to worry – I wasn't going to ask him to marry me!), but it didn't mean that we abandoned all criticism of each other nor that we were dependent on each other for our survival. Rather, it meant a sort of mutual risk-free zone with a minimal need for the role-playing that is an ingredient in nearly all other human relationships; it meant that neither of us would make any real demands without having any real needs; it meant someone to bare one's soul to without having to fear getting one's teeth kicked in; that there would be no exploitation, no taking advantage, no indifference to each other's pleasures or pains; that each would have a shoulder for the other to lean or cry on without concern about the shirt getting wrinkled or wet, someone to laugh with and not at, to bitch to and not about, someone who cares, a sounding board, an island of safety and trust.

I pointed out that Jeanette and I saw Bob's difficulty in responding to our friendship back in the early years *not* as unwillingness on Bob's part, but as his temporary inability to respond, brought on by his deep depression. We recognized that he needed to grow before he could respond, and that was exactly what I was hoping for from Lena.

The storm continued pretty much unabated through February 1979. One day she said she was going to "try" to love me, the next day she was icy (or sometimes hot and cold in the same evening). One day she was thinking of moving in with me, the next she felt out of place in my home. I suggested she could overcome that feeling if she wanted to, but she wasn't sure that she did want to. One night she wouldn't want to be without me, the next she wanted two more years of living alone – *and* she wanted to go out with other guys (she actually told me that!). I told her that if I felt she was just toying with me until something better came along, I'd be off. Her reaction: "Well, I don't know...." [*One might wonder exactly how much clarity I was waiting for...!*] But both Marie-Louise and Eva seemed to like me better and better, and they made Lena aware of it.

Apart from my frequent correspondence with Bob, I was writing my mom about once every 10 days (as long as she didn't start preaching at me) and Sonja about every other week. Letters from Marilyn, which I always answered immediately, were down to about once every six weeks. I heard from her that Rosanne had had a baby, so I sent a baby gift, but got no reply. Exchanges with my brothers were increasingly rare.

Unconsciously, I was keeping my "vacancy" sign turned off, putting all my eggs into a basket named Lena J, and buckling down for the rough ride ahead, in response to her reduced resistance to me. [*Did I just perceive what I needed to, or was I reacting to her mother's and sister's outspoken fondness for me?*] Despite all the protestations I'd made to Bob about maintaining my balance, aloofness, objectivity, independence, mind over heart, readiness for anything, self-control and integrity, I was losing interest in pretending that I could fight or control my feelings for Lena. I would simply *have* to win her love, or else. But to my mom I wrote: "*I'm not so prone to the extremes of gloom and euphoria. Perhaps I'm becoming mature....*"

Knut's usual route from Malmö to Perstorp was the E6 freeway up to Löddeköpinge, then over to Marieholm, on to Röstånga, past Klippan and on to Perstorp. Once when we were passing through Marieholm, I saw a sign announcing auctions there in a community hall every Saturday, starting at noon. At a second-hand furniture store some months earlier, I'd bought a small old solid-oak writing table with two drawers. One of the legs was badly damaged at the base, so I got it for 10 kronor (about $2 at the time). I sawed off the broken part, then sawed off the other three legs to match, sanded it down to remove all the old cracked varnish, oiled it, and had a perfect coffee table. [*We still have it and use it!*] I figured there might be some bargains like that at an auction, so I made a mental note of the site in Marieholm. Both Lena and I were looking for a few pieces of furniture and some bric-a-brac, and we both kind of liked older things, such as furniture made of solid wood instead of veneer-covered chipboard. We also thought it could make a fun outing on a Saturday afternoon.

A Sea of Troubles

It was. We visited those Saturday auctions several times during the spring of 1979, bought small tables and armchairs, old and simple picture frames, old mirrors with beveled edges, antique candlesticks, and patinated flowerpots – for a song. Some of the furniture had to be sanded a bit, some things had to be repainted, and a few screws and bolts needed tightening, but that gave us other projects to work on together. I hoped that at least some of the bonding had nothing to do with glue. I bought a pair of oak armchairs (probably intended for the short ends of a long dining table) for a fraction of the price of one new chair. They didn't look like much because the upholstery on the seats was badly frayed, but after removing the seats, sanding the wood slightly, adding some cushioning and re-covering the seats with soft, tough raw leather, they looked fabulous. (I bought them because Lena said she liked them too, and I was thinking of *our* home some day....)

We tried to make a trip to the Canary Islands together during Lena's winter school vacation week in late February, but were totally snowed in. We made it as far as boarding a ferry to Copenhagen with packed bags, hoping to get a last minute flight somewhere once we got to the airport – anywhere there was sun was Lena's deal-breaking criterion – but the ferry got stuck in the ice on Öresund and had to be towed back to Malmö by an icebreaker. [*Don't get the idea that this was typical for southern Sweden – it was the only freeze-over of the harbor and parts of the Öresund that I've experienced here in more than 50 years.*]

Although all these efforts were about cultivating my garden, and although I was working feverishly on *Jardin* every day or night I could, progress on the painting felt as painfully slow as the progress I was making on winning Lena's heart. My singlemindedness had served me well in some of the other major endeavors in my life: the escape from Oak Park, my pursuit of Jeanette, the escape from the States and the threat of Vietnam, the setting up of a new life in Sweden, the focus on my art until the house restoration took over, and the house restoration itself. In all those endeavors I'd had an exceptional partner struggling with me, pulling in the same direction: I'd had Jeanette (except for the escape from Oak Park, when it was Norm).

At this point, Lena was not *overtly* negative about my art, but neither did she show any support; she was overtly *indifferent*. I was aware that I was not entitled to demand her support for my art in any way. In her world, such a demand would have been tantamount to criticism of her. But at the same I was beginning to experience great difficulty in pursuing my work on *Jardin* without her support. I probably never realized the full extent of the impact of Jeanette's extremely active encouragement of my painting; I'm *sure* I didn't yet realize how dependent I'd been on that intense kind of support – *her* support – to be able to undertake the arduous task of creating the only kinds of paintings that were meaningful for both of us. I did get some active encouragement from Sonja to paint, but that came from afar and couldn't have the kind of impact that carried over to the practical level.

It wasn't that Lena rolled her eyes whenever I said I was going to spend my day, evening, night, weekend, or week painting, at least not at this point. But I think I was realistic in presuming that she would never react with delight as Jeanette always did, quietly seeing to my mundane needs so I could work as uninterruptedly as possible. I told myself it didn't matter, I loved Lena for who she was, just as I loved Jeanette for who she was. Except that now I wasn't being loved in return. And I knew somewhere deep inside me that unless Lena were otherwise occupied, she would want me to devote my full attention to meeting *her* needs and fulfilling *her* wishes, so therefore I shouldn't be painting (or be occupied with anything else). I also knew that whenever she came to Korngatan, I could and should forget about any reaction at all (apart from a yawn) to showing her how far I'd come along on *Jardin*.

As a result, I got into the habit of striving to paint as much as possible (sometimes not even leaving the house for days) whenever I couldn't be with her. It was my time to be with other women that fell by the wayside, not my time for Lena J. I decided not to continue pestering her about whether she would move in with me or not, partly because I couldn't bear the one-day-yes-next-day-no vacillation, partly because I finally realized that if I had to nag about such a decision it wouldn't be worth having anyway. (Having to order someone, like a child, to say *please* or *thank-you* or *sorry* doesn't exactly add to the sincerity of what they say!) And, probably to nobody's surprise but my own, once I stopped asking her, pestering her, the number of yes-days began increasing.

In a letter to my mom on February 26th, I mentioned for the first time that I was fond of Lena, that she was special to me, but that she couldn't make up her mind about me. In reply, Mom of course wanted me to send her a photo.

I remained unable to discern any patterns in Lena's mood swings or in her hot-and-cold approach to me. (Marie-Louise Larsson's suggestion proved fruitless in solving the mystery, but it was interesting anyway, so I continued.) I tried to focus on our shared interests, but it remained a one-way street. I took the initiative for taking her to the Tuesday evening classical music concerts in Malmö (I always invited *her*, of course), and to Saturday auctions in Marieholm (where I usually bought *her* something). [*Although my almost daily diary entries made it perfectly clear to me – but only many years later, with the benefit of hindsight – that Lena would tolerate no criticism from me or anyone else, without a disdainful, withering or furious backlash, and that I was the only one pursuing this one-way relationship in which my love for her had to be enough for both of us, I refused to see it because I couldn't bear to see it.*]

Another measure of my acquiescence was my enthusiastic purchase in early March of a trip for both of us to the Canary Islands for the Easter vacation week in April, the kind of destination Jeanette and I always shunned, partly due to the vacuous cultural life, partly due to the irritating ability of our skin to burn rather than tan. And although I was disappointed to break with the tradition Bob and I had had since 1971 of spending the Easter week together, when Bob had extra days off work, Lena made it clear that the sun (and the free ticket?) was what it would take for her to make a trip with me.

Passionate fondness of a friend or lover often carries with it an intense will to project one's own imagined responses on the friend's circumstances; how I *would* react is how you *should* react, regardless of the fact that I am no more you than you are me. This became clear to me regarding how I was seeing Lena, how my mom saw me, and on several occasions how I saw Bob (mistakenly thinking that how he would react to solitude should somehow involve *my* dislike of loneliness). But that could occasionally be a two-way street.

Although Bob nearly always seemed to have my best interests at heart, he'd been carrying a lot of ideals around with him since medical school, ideals that I didn't share. His semi-conscious hero-worship of Hugh Hefner – the suave playboy type Bob would never be – was one example. Another was his idealization of the bizarre open-marriage relationship of Jean-Paul Sartre with Simone de Beauvoir. That, he told me, was what he wished for me and Lena. And yet it had nothing at all to do with my aspirations. (If Lena had any aspirations regarding me, they were a well-kept secret.) I knew I couldn't convince Bob that a permanent (or even stable) relationship with Lena would be worth all the effort I was putting into making it come about. Nor could I know whether it ultimately would be. But I did know that I in no way aspired to a relationship like that of J-P and Simone.

At the same time, all Bob's skepticism, probing and harrumphing were instrumental in helping me to maintain my balance, and to avoid losing myself entirely in my devotion to pleasing Lena. Although it took me two months to paint just 15% of *Jardin*, at least I was still painting. And I was planning to get going on the restoration of the little house, another huge building project where one of my main desires was to be able to unpack all my books. Jeanette and I had brought most of them with us from San Francisco to Vancouver to Vårgatan, then repacked them into the 70 or so cartons we'd moved to Korngatan four years earlier, and where they'd remained since early 1975.

By mid-March, Lena and I were spending at least part of nearly every day or night together, and for the first time she expressed (at least in my presence) a positive view of me to her mother and sister. I took the opportunity to reflect on a major milestone in my life in a letter to Bob:

> *It amazes me to think back to a year ago now, when I was at my lowest, and all of the changes that have taken place since then. I was just finishing* The Unparallel Lines *at this time last year! I can probably never adequately express my gratitude to you for all of the efforts you have made with what for a long time must have seemed like a hopeless case. You took my lack of receptivity into account the whole time and gave me every encouragement and support at the slightest fumbling in the right direction, always saving your salvos until you were sure I could handle them. If I have been "reborn" in the last year, you have been my parents. More than that: you are a true friend! And your patience and concern have followed me through my new "adolescence", from which I would like to think I am emerging. I continue to value your balloon-bursting. You never tell me, "do this, don't do that", only "yes, but one could also consider such and such", knowing that I will at least make a half-assed attempt to do so as my maturity allows. You have always respected <u>me</u>, no matter how appalling my gropings may have been. And you have never tried to draw my conclusions for me, but only aided me in expanding the bases on which I draw them. I'm telling you all of this, not because you are likely to be unaware of it, but because I want you to realize that I am aware of it.*

At some point in early March, Lena stopped taking the Pill. She also said that it might be fun to make an extended, several-week trip by car down through Europe together in the summer, possibly including Basel. I hoped that Bob would also find it fun. (The significance of this escaped me at the time, of course.)

Bob was having another source of "fun": a revived and intensive correspondence (which he shared with me) with Kathy, who was experiencing problems and frustrations in graduate school in the humanities. That ignited some ruminations on my part, after my less-than-totally-gratifying experience at graduate school at UBC. I came to realize an essential difference in graduate school based on what discipline was involved: that graduate students in the sciences nearly always go on to become scientists, while graduate students in art and literature seldom go on to become artists or writers (perhaps teachers, cultural analysts or critics instead). And thus, while advanced studies in the sciences were likely to become fulfilling to students with a scientific temperament, advanced studies in the arts would offer little to those with an artistic temperament.

On Saturday, March 17th, Lena and I didn't go to the auction as planned because there was a blizzard, and besides, Lena wasn't feeling too well due to stomach cramps. In spite of that, Lena told me she tingled all over when I looked at her, that she couldn't resist me, that she was falling in love with me. Then she finally came out and said it – "*I love you!*" – for the first time ever. And I truly thought that my trying time was over, a thought that wasn't a thought because it was far too much of a feeling, a wish, a hope.

CHAPTER 10

Attrition

On March 26th, 1979, two days before the second anniversary of Jeanette's death, and less than two weeks before Lena's and my departure for the Canary Islands, I jotted down a few reflections in a letter to Bob:

> *As you might imagine, I'm having a bit of a struggle with myself to keep from getting down at this time of year. I'm not really in any danger of depression, though. But sometimes I just feel so damned sad and can't help missing and wanting Jeanette. I suppose "getting over" something like that means getting over the depression, which I have done, and the rest, that little alcove of aching emptiness, I will never "get over". That part of me has not diminished at all, and seems to be entirely disconnected from the depression. Maybe that is the only realistic approach, i.e. maybe "getting over" that would in fact entail suppression of it, which wouldn't be "getting over" at all. It's not reasonable to expect that so major an injury would not leave substantial scar tissue no matter how well the wound itself healed.*

On March 31st, Lena and I drove up to Barkåkra at noon and went out shopping with Marie-Louise. I bought her some flowers, put up the rods for her shades, and helped with a little garden work. Eva, Jan and Lina arrived in the afternoon. In the evening Marie-Louise asked Lena if she knew how good she had it. Lena looked embarrassed.

On Monday we went to Jan and Eva's in the evening to celebrate Lina's birthday. Jan corralled me for my "expert" advice on how to rebuild his kitchen. I managed to come up with a few ideas he liked. I volunteered to help him with some of the work a bit later in the year.

I decided not to tell Mom about the trip to the Canaries until it was *fait accompli* (I wrote her just before we left, so she wouldn't get the letter until we were already there), so as to prevent the risk of a phone call pleading with me not to bump my body against Lena, something she was probably allowing herself to assume we hadn't been doing right from the start anyway. And Mom could hardly rejoice that I was now going monogamous since she wouldn't allow herself to believe that I was ever "gamous" at all, let alone polygamous (or at least polyamorous). When Mom got my letter, she wrote me that she immediately got out her atlas to look up where we were, and then, only after hours of anxiety

A Sea of Troubles

"*...I was able to relax my full heart into loving Hands, and sleep.*" I wondered how a cardiologist would deal with that. When I told Bob what she'd written, he diagnosed her condition as "geocardiac displacement".

(Ever since I was a teenager, I strongly suspected that Mom's sighings, quakings, tremblings, eye rollings, quaverings and bun-fixings were at least 90% histrionic methods of manipulation. I'd learned to ignore their content for the sake of self-preservation, while carefully regarding each performance in order to be ready to present her an Oscar when her performance so merited.)

My year of polyamory served one important purpose: to rebuild my shattered ego from the repeated crushing blows of Lena's erratic spurnings just as I was finally clambering out of the black hole of my depression. And my carousing was, at least, an enjoyable way to achieve the positive impact it had on my mental stability at that particular juncture in my life.

As soon as Mom caught a whiff of the seriousness of my intentions in my relationship with Lena, she wanted to know about wedding plans and what wedding gifts to get, and she informed me that she was prepared to love Lena – "*as my wife*" – once I provided the legal documentation that would magically allow her deep feelings for Lena to erupt into existence. (I suppose I should have been grateful to her for not subjecting Lena to the gantlet she'd unsuccessfully tried to make Jeanette run! But my gratitude didn't stretch quite that far.) I decided to disabuse her as quickly and unequivocally as possible of her notion that Lena and I had any intention of living up to Mom's notions of sexual norms, by removing the bandage with a swift tug rather than making a long and potentially painful process of it. I just told her that I thought it would be "some time" before Lena and I even started looking at any plans for marriage, and that we both felt there was no point in rushing things. I sent her a postcard from Playa del Inglés on the southern end of Gran Canaria, where we stayed at the apartment-hotel Strelizias.

Playa del Inglés was about as touristy as a place can get: full of bars and restaurants, gaudy discos and kitschy junk shops, all serving one high-rise hotel after another like dominos set up for a cascade. The streets and cafés were full of the sounds of German, English, Swedish, Danish and Dutch – but almost no Spanish. We did, however, have a wonderful time, pretty much splitting our days and nights between the beach and the bed, mostly on her and my initiatives respectively. Despite my dark hair and Lena's blonde hair, I'd always found it as hard to get a tan as she found it easy, so I had to make maximum use of a parasol, while Lena turned brown before my eyes (my eyes actually remained blue and still are). But one day, on the sand dunes of Maspalomas, where the bright tropical sun is masked by brisk but balmy ocean breezes, we both managed to get burnt. In my case, I had second-degree blisters on my thighs and chest and couldn't bear contact with so much as a sheet for a couple of days, despite severe chills.

Marie-Louise and Eva had been to the Canaries many times and were eager to hear about all the touristy things we did, and were amused by how little we could report. Marie-Louise then teased Lena about how stand-offish she remained towards me. It felt good to have Lena's mom and sister "on my side". [*But it didn't occur to me to wonder why there had to be a "side" at all.*] All the initiatives – for love or sex or both – were coming from me, as was all the appeasing, cajoling, humoring, pleading, wooing and funding. [*Since I was certain to make a clear, written note of the slightest positive response from her, which would send me over the moon, the fact that I never had any such things to jot down makes me feel certain that there never came a single spontaneous hug from her that was not merely returning mine. Yet I allowed that to suffice, and continued to do so for years to come.*]

The roller-coaster ride seemed to have no end. One day she loved me. The next day she was not sure. One day she thought we might get engaged. The next day such a development was a *long* way off, if it were ever to happen at all. *What was she up to??* On Thursday evening, April 19th, she told me not to come to her place in Lund until 11.15 PM because she was hosting a "hen party" there. I arrived (obediently) at the designated time, but Lena seemed displeased to see me because her friends were still present [*as if I had any way of knowing that – this was long before the age of texting!*]. I offered to go back home, but she sat me on a chair to read until they left at around 1 AM.

The next morning I stayed after she left and did all her dishes from the previous evening's festivities. Late that afternoon, after a rough day at school, she called to thank me for doing the dishes, and asked me to come over. But when I got there, she was clearly *not* pleased to see me, which made me a bit put out, which enraged her. My love meant nothing to her, she said. All her feelings were gone, it was just as well to call the whole thing off, she didn't want to see me anymore. And so, on Friday evening, April 20th, 1979, I left her apartment at 21.45 and went across the street to the bus stop, *hoping* for the speedy arrival of the 22.00 bus that would take me back to Malmö.

I'd finally had enough!!

[*At that moment, I was mentally and emotionally convinced that I'd left for good at last, fully prepared to stand on my own, come what may! I don't think I was fully aware* at the time *of the extent to which this final straw* could *have been the seminal moment, the watershed.*]

What happened instead was this: The bus didn't arrive until just *after* 22.00. And *one minute* before it rounded the corner, less than a block from where I was standing, Lena walked up to me at the bus stop, took my hand and coaxed me to come back. It was the closest thing to an outright apology I would hear her utter for decades. And I was right back on the hook, but I convinced myself that I would henceforth exercise a bit more caution. [*Seems to me I've heard that song before!!*]

The next day, Saturday, although we didn't get up till quite late, we decided to go to the auction in Marieholm after all. Lena was a little crabby again and bought herself two armchairs for her apartment. I realized, to the extent I was capable or realizing anything while mesmerized by her, that there was no point in counting on her moving in anymore. I would just have to try to enjoy life as much as possible, which was made more difficult by her apparent ease in thinking of no one but herself, especially if there were any problems at all, e.g. if she had a slight cold. I noted in my diary that sometimes she seemed to be so much in her own world that she was incapable of realizing that I had feelings and might also be sensitive. Perhaps just allowing me to see her was all the effort she felt she needed to make. Passive acceptance was the extent of her active approach.

I'd now completed nearly a quarter of *Jardin*, which had come to represent to me the profound shift in my attitudes and philosophical outlook over the previous year. The painting is without a trace of cynical detachment from life, nor of overwhelming nihilism – which may never have been my own anyway. But *Jardin* does not overlook the negative aspects of life; on the contrary, I examined them actively and rejected them on their own (de)merits. The vital importance of a zest for life, with the acknowledgement that such zest may need to be worked at, to be maintained if it is to endure, is the message of *Jardin*. The great detail (compared to all my previous paintings) serves to amplify the notion of a studied, feet-on-the-ground joy, not joy that falls like a blob into one's lap, not the joy of mindless euphoria, but joy that is the fruit of what one has toiled for.

It now seemed to me that nihilism could be compared to an attempt to apply mascara with a broom or to uncork a bottle of wine with a sledgehammer. I saw it as the disillusionment that results from having unwarranted expectations of finding something of absolute or objective value without realizing that "value" is in itself, by definition, relative and subjective. Instead of coming to realize this, the nihilist stops after a fruitless search for the non-existent. *Life has the pleasure and meaning you give it because you are living; <u>life</u> has no objective meaning of its own, but <u>living</u> has meaning, even if "only" subjective.* This view, however, is profoundly unsatisfactory to most of human society, who feel compelled – particularly as urged by their religions – to try to imbue life with objective meaning, even (especially!) beyond the grave, to subject themselves to the dictates of gods and traditions in order to obviate the need to think for themselves, and in so doing they jeopardize the possibility of making *this* life good, in the manner of making the perfect the enemy of the good.

There is no evidence, no indication, not even the vaguest hint, that any other species is so enamored of its own existence that it cannot accept the finality of death. The individual human being is presumably unique in its desire to "leave a mark" or "make a difference." There is nothing to suggest that humans – as a race or as individuals – leave any marks on the planet (beyond the perishable marks they may leave on those whose lives they've touched or influenced) that are certain to turn out positive, *except* to mitigate the even more negative and disastrous marks our species leaves: pollution, mass extinction of other species, wasteful depletion of resources, and the unique capability to render our entire habitat uninhabitable, not only for the human race but potentially for all species. Contributing to this is the incessant urge to reproduce, to *over*-populate the earth to the extent that humankind is already wallowing in its own DNA, devouring everything it can come across. In the year of my birth (1945) the world population was about 2½ billion. Today (2021) it is nearly 8 billion. I rest my case.

And yet it is that same unique desire to make a difference that is so urgently needed for our survival, for the survival of life and resources on our planet, and makes it so important *not* to be overcome by mankind's capacity for evil, but to get out there and cultivate the hell out of that garden, *to <u>make</u> it good. Screw the perfect*, it can be there as a goal. In my garden, my *Jardin*, the man *grows* things, the things he wants; they don't and won't grow without help.

This is perhaps what I thought I could achieve in my relationship with Lena: to single-handedly cultivate it without any assurances that it was or would become mutual, that by attrition I could break down her unwillingness to love me, to make her weary of her own refusals, to win her heart when only her body would respond. In fact, on April 6th she said, "*I don't understand why you don't just kick me out. That's weird.*"

I did realize, however, that in terms of my art, Lena was never going to be my muse; she never expressed any interest in my paintings or the thoughts that lay behind them. On the contrary, she seemed almost resentful or jealous of me on those relatively rare occasions when a visitor to Korngatan showed appreciation for my work. Her negative attitude was starting to create a powerful drag on my desire to paint [*subconscious at the time*]. I presume that painting can be a hobby for some, and that the production of works for decorative purposes can yield its own form of enthusiasm or profit or both, but what I was trying to achieve entailed mentally arduous labor, almost to the point of being painful. So far, I still had the momentum of my ideas and of my previous work to shove or drag me onwards.

That Friday evening, April 20th (when I almost "escaped") in some way steeled my resolve to get on with my painting and my work on the house. After the work on the big house was completed in 1978, I'd been on an extended hiatus to pursue Lena come what may, but now I felt I had to start doing something about the little house, where only the downstairs guest bedroom and its *en suite* bathroom were completed.

I had another daunting task before me, and spent many an hour taking measurements, thinking, considering alternatives, weighing and calculating what *had* to be done against what I felt *could* be done, how long it might take (multiplied by four?) – and what I could realistically *afford*. The roof of the little house was the greatest problem. For one thing, it was already too low, even in its uninsulated state. The upstairs ceiling left no headroom. And it sagged. The roof was also rotten. I realized I would have to replace the entire roof, and decided that in connection with putting on a new roof I would have to build up the exterior walls enough to give sufficient headroom as well as space (30 cm minimum) for proper insulation. It would take several months at least, and in a place as rainy as Malmö, having a house (even a little one) without a roof for months would be more than a challenge, more than a high-stakes gamble. It simply wouldn't work.

Instead, I would need to remove the existing roof in sections, as little at a time as possible, then quickly build up the brick wall perimeter for each section, leaving an appropriate gap for each new roof beam, then move on to the next section. This would require a very large and strong tarp to catch any rainwater, not one of the cheap supermarket varieties. It would also require a few thousand more bricks, which I was counting on being able to get for free from demolition sites, as I'd done for the big house. But the roof project sounded so overwhelming to me that I decided I'd need more time to think about it and to prepare; the roof would have to wait another year or so.

In the meantime, there were two internal, non-load-bearing walls upstairs that could come down and give me a clearer picture for planning. The upstairs comprised Jeanette's and my primitive kitchen and living room-bedroom combination, but was eventually going to be one big long room: the library. I tried to consult Lena on her views and possible wishes for how the rebuilt house would be formed, so that she could become a participant in the house I hoped she would come to make her home as well. But she said she wanted no part of it! On Saturday, April 28th, I tore down the first of those two upstairs walls, and the project, *my* project, was underway.

Now that I was taking on more translation and editing work, in addition to holding more and more of my teaching hours at home, my part-time work for Perstorp was evolving in ways that gave me a tremendous amount of freedom. Unless I needed the money, I generally added the extra hours I was accumulating each month to the "pot", so I could take big chunks of time off – several weeks at a time – if the Perstorp work situation allowed it and the home repair situation demanded it. And since I was effectively my own boss, I could to a great extent decide what I wanted to work with, when, and how much. Stig Troell was in effect working as my administrator, rather than I as his subordinate. I told him what I intended to do and what I needed from him or Perstorp to be able to do it, and he saw that I got it – everything but a decent salary.

Time had always been so much more important to me than money. I'd also had a great deal of flexibility with my time at Demaret's and then at Interspråk, which served me well when I was painting full-time and then when restoring the big house full-time, but now I had the security of a fixed minimum salary (albeit low) as well. Fortunately, all the work Jeanette and I had done on the house, and all the good deals on the building materials and craftsmen's services, resulted in exceptionally low living costs. It was literally cheaper for me to live in the 9-10 rooms at Korngatan 12 than in a newly built one-room apartment!

On Monday, April 30th, Lena and I did some grocery shopping, then drove to

A Sea of Troubles

Lund at noon, where we met Lena's brother Lars, his wife, and their children, as well as Marie-Louise. Lars was nothing like his sisters, either in appearance or manner. (I had yet to meet Jan, the eldest brother.) Lars gave me the impression of being ill at ease in his own body, and his voice was greatly strained, such that every syllable he uttered sounded as if he were giving birth to it, and as if he were the last adult on the planet, talking to children who hadn't yet learned how to speak. I found his thin-lipped, strained smile slightly reptilian. But for all I knew and could ascertain under those chaotic circumstances of a first meeting in confined quarters, he might have been a very nice guy. He and his family lived in Upplands-Väsby, a northern suburb of Stockholm, and he worked with accounting at the Swedish State Pharmaceutical Supply Company.

On Friday, May 4th, Lena stayed home from school because of a cold. I went back to Lund at 6.30 PM and went with Lena and Eva to the tennis hall and took a sauna while they played. Shortly after 9 o'clock, Gun and a girlfriend of hers came by for wine and cheese. At 10.30 we all went out dancing at Östgöta Nation. I had to overcome my nausea for the concept of discos that I'd acquired about a year earlier when I'd been in such a miserable state. It didn't help my aversion in the slightest when Lena told me that the previous autumn she'd been out dancing there, picked up a guy and went to bed with him. *Why the <u>hell</u> would she tell me something like that?! What was her point?!* It pretty much ruined my evening. Perhaps I should have said "big deal"; after all, it was before she loved me, but her telling me really bothered me, because it reminded me how much I'd been longing to be with her at that time too.

I got a good letter from my brother John, who'd heard that I'd told Mom about Lena. It was a "normal" letter: no preaching, no sermonizing, no bullshit. Perhaps it seemed good to me because I didn't expect anything from anyone in my family to be that nice.

Lena and I met Marie-Louise that weekend in Lund. She had a lot of interesting things to say to me that showed what a good understanding she had of the situation between Lena and me: that it must be trying for me with our separate cohabitation, that I never tired of looking at Lena, and that Lena still had some growing up to do. Marie-Louise also had a lot of favorable comments about my house and strong hints about which one of her children she'd like to see living there.

On Wednesday, May 9th, I had a surprise (and welcome) visit from Henry and Elsa Carlsson. I hadn't seen them for a long time and I was grateful. Lena was with me, and being the compulsive (and unconscious?) flirt she was, she had Henry under her spell instantly, which made both me and Elsa somewhat uncomfortable. The chronic feeling of uncertainty on my part was exacerbated by the fact that Lena had never given me any clear indication that she was no longer carrying that big torch for Larry, or what she would do if he came back or summoned her.

Fortunately for all concerned, Henry was much more interested in my plans for rebuilding the little house. His unexpected visit gave me the opportunity to sound him out on how to proceed. Once I'd discovered the extent to which I needed to modify it – the significant raising of the roof in particular – I was a little concerned about how much my revised plans deviated from the original building permit. Henry told me not to worry about that detail; the permit could always be updated after the fact. He added that my plan sounded like the best approach for achieving a livable and insulated upstairs space, even though he indicated that it also sounded dauntingly ambitious for one person to undertake. But I wasn't flinching. On Saturday I tore down the remaining upstairs dividing wall.

Lena mentioned that she urgently needed a bicycle. Her birthday was coming up in less than a month. So guess what I did? I went out and bought one for her almost immediately, then cycled out to Lund with it. She was delighted. We had a light supper, after which she preferred to watch one time-killing TV program after another instead of coming to bed, by which time she was tired and joked about how I'd "have to hurry up or it would cost extra." I was already mightily irritated, and her flippant remark turned me off completely. I knew she'd said it jokingly, but was so bloody tired of her not taking us seriously. She admitted she didn't, that she hadn't made up her mind about me yet, and so on and so forth. I began to feel sick – and used. But, as usual, I let it pass.

One evening a week later, after I promised to lend her 2000 kronor more to repay her lunch coupon fund, we began talking about her moving in, but she again said that she wanted "more time". Then she said this would be a fun night to "go out dancing with boys". It felt like a knife in my side (or back). And despite writing all this shit down word for word in my diary, it somehow still didn't register with me. Whoever said that love is blind knew what they were talking about! I wrote: "*She says she's so into her work she can't think about me. Where does that leave me?? What am I to do?? I must be nuts!!*"

A couple of days later, after making love, she again raised the subject of my sterility, which she said was the one big remaining problem for her with me. That distressed me, because it was the one big problem I could do *nothing* about; as far as I knew, vasectomies were irreversible. Then I thought of what Sonja had said about it. The following day, I tore out the stairway in the little house, and then the floor above the part of the cellar I'd walled off, which meant that on opening the door to the little house there was now a void down into the small damp cellar.

Another two days went by. After making love, I told Lena how wonderful it would be if she said "yes" one of these times when I asked her to marry me. She replied coyly that she probably couldn't because she wanted to be married in church and I might not like that. I said I didn't care where we got married. [*It never occurred to me at that time that if this had been a two-way street, the venue wouldn't have mattered any more to her than it did to me!*] Then she asked where Jeanette and I got married, and I said "In church." Lena said "Oh," and went to sleep! The next day she told me she was thinking of going to teach in England again the next summer. Would the shit never end? I wondered how she would react if I treated her with her brand of indifference. She'd probably be gone in two minutes!

During 1979, my work at Perstorp continued to shift to work with texts. I was hired the year before primarily to teach English to selected employees, with only about five percent of my time devoted to translations and editing. By the summer of '79, I was probably up to 30-40% textual work, and that work began to branch out in two ways. One was the result of my never being content to translate what a text *said*, but to figure out what it *meant* and what its purpose was. Was it trying to clarify something, like a manual? Trying to sell something by making it sound attractive? And who was the intended reader? An expert technician? A purchasing manager? A company owner? A consumer? I was always asking questions, and making sure my translations were more faithful to the *purpose* of the original text, not necessarily to the words. Most of my clients appreciated that; so did I, because I found creative work so much more stimulating.

Some of the texts I translated or edited were for brochures that were being created for various Perstorp businesses by advertising agencies (such as Andersson & Lembke in Helsingborg). Occasionally one of those agencies would find a way to get in touch with me directly so they could ask me if I could help them with texts for their other clients. But I didn't want to freelance or start my own company, for two reasons: one was my aversion to having to "sell myself", to make cold calls to build up a client base; the other was that I found all the administrative work, tax reports, financial statements, bookkeeping, VAT reports, accounts payable and receivable, etc brutally boring and terminally tedious. So I spoke about the situation with my boss. Stig told me that if I wanted to, I could report any work I did for external (non-Perstorp) clients on my weekly time sheet. He would then invoice them for my work, and I could add the hours to my "pot" or get paid for them, as I wished, as I was already doing for my internal clients. I was pleased with the arrangement, as were the external clients. Stig certainly was too; it was great for his budget.

Over time, the number of my external clients grew, particularly every time a former internal ("Perstorper") client left to work for another company that needed help with English lessons, translations or text editing, and the former Perstorper recommended me to his or her new employer. In that way, I gradually built up a list of clients from a lot of different companies (mostly in southern Sweden). This essentially gave me all the extra hours I wanted, and enabled me to build that "pot" even more. And since I was fulfilling my 20-hour-per-week quota for Perstorp by doing work for these external clients from my home, my need to commute to Perstorp two days a week dwindled even further, and my increased independence enabled me to enjoy my work – from home – more and more. Thus I became the corporation's first remote employee. I would eventually have a period during my 32 years on the Perstorp payroll when I didn't set foot in the village of Perstorp for more than six years.

Another significant source of my job stimulation was the diversity. Perstorp itself provided a lot of that, with its many divisions involved in numerous areas of chemistry, plastics, decorative and industrial laminates, seamless flooring, noise abatement, numerous chemicals for downstream applications, and even a couple of pharmaceuticals. I was involved, at least to some extent, in all of them. My external clients worked in entirely different fields, all of which posed new challenges to me every day. In order to understand what I was writing about, I had to acquire at least a working knowledge of new (for me) technical terminology (in both languages) as well as a rudimentary understanding of how things were made or processed and why. My job was thus rapidly evolving towards something far more qualified than the job I'd originally been hired for. The only thing that was not evolving at the same rate was my salary. But I still didn't place a high priority on that. I lived frugally and had a low housing cost, so I didn't bother to make waves.

A Sea of Troubles

Bob sent me a book that spring that would eventually impact my life and the way I looked at science: *The Selfish Gene*, by Richard Dawkins. Bob, as a scientist himself, devoured books on one area of science after another with unbridled enthusiasm. He naturally wanted to see whether someone only vaguely interested in science, as I'd hitherto been, might develop a taste for the principles of being skeptical and *not* knowing, which Bob claimed was the driving forces, in true scientific thinking. Because how can you learn anything if you think you already know everything you need to or if you are prepared to accept whatever information comes your way without questioning it?

Despite my rigid upbringing and indoctrination to believe in the literal "truth" of every word in the Bible, my first real exposure to the principles of evolution, in the 1960 movie *Inherit the Wind*, in combination with my budding rebellion against the increasing suppression of my parents' fundamentalism, instantly struck a chord of common sense. Darwin's theory – he had the humility to introduce it as such – was an open invitation to the scientific community to prove him wrong and a challenge to humanity to grow up and grow out of their fairy tales and myths now that so much more information was available than ever before.

The evidence for the chain of species was far from complete when Darwin first began making developing his revolutionary theory, and the mechanisms of change had not yet been fully explained. The religious fundamentalists ignored what he was saying because it was clearly to threatening to their own Genesis-based worldview (for which there was *zero* evidence and *no tolerance* for explanations, full or empty). Instead they mocked Darwin for reasons *they* didn't understand. I remember the self-appointed biology "experts" of the Meeting ridiculing the notion that an individual monkey could turn itself into an individual human being – a notion that Darwin never claimed and would also have ridiculed. More than a century later, with the fossil record piling up the evidence, with the technology for dating it advancing from conjecture to measurement, Dawkins came along to explain the biological mechanisms lucidly. More than that, it was all based on evidence, nowadays backed by exponential increases in the understanding of genomes, not on ancient texts written many generations after the fact by people who were obliged to fumble in the dark to explain the frightening unknown by inventing stories, and who then chose to proclaim that their wild guesses were Absolute and Eternal Truth.

Bob was thrilled over my enthusiasm for biology, and began sending me other books to help me explore new areas of science – quantum theory, chaos theory, cosmology – that were opening up and capturing his attention, curiosity and imagination, while greatly boosting his zest for life. Perhaps he hoped that if I started demanding evidence for an increasingly broad sphere of activities, I might find myself challenging the premises of some of the courses of action I was pursuing, including some that he found ill-advised, although he could only stand on the sidelines and watch. [*I suspect that some readers will guess which areas Bob was trying to get me to challenge – even though I didn't get it at the time.*]

Bob also sent me numerous amazing books by British philosopher and mathematician Bertrand Russell. Bob had been extolling Russell's clarity of reasoning for quite some time, but I'd never found the time to read any of his works. On reading *A Free Man's Worship* in 1979, I understood what I'd been missing – and what solace Bob found in the writings of somebody who thought with his head and felt with his heart and didn't mix them up.

It must, however, have been extremely frustrating for Bob to hear me going on month after month about how I *now* thought that Lena at last might be showing signs of considering the possibility of eventually returning my love, and oh how wonderful that would be, but that I was *now* definitely no longer going to go under if it didn't work out because I'd made so much bloody progress, but oh if she would *only* agree to move in with me, and I think she's definitely coming around, but it will probably take "some time". [*How did he ever manage to put up with me?!*]

Perhaps observing my continued pathetic acquiescence to Lena's every whim exerted a subtle influence on Bob to stand up for himself in his different but equally acquiescent relationships with Kathy and Tante Lore. He mentioned, in any case, that "circumstances had drastically eroded" his contacts with both of them. Hoping it would cheer him up, I told him that I was eager to see him again soon and was endeavoring to arrange a car trip to Basel for me and Lena in July.

Lena wasn't terribly enthusiastic about visiting Bob with me, but said that such a visit might be included in a trip to the Continent, a proposition that was more attractive to her, possibly for a personal reason. Among the tales she told me about her life with Larry was the story of an investment in a near-perfect one-carat diamond through an agency in London; the diamond itself was supposedly resting securely in a bonded warehouse in Den Haag, and was retrievable through a private Dutch bank, presumably to avoid taxes of some kind. It all sounded kind of cloak-and-dagger to me. Now Lena wanted to retrieve that diamond and sell it to get the money, so she notified the bank there of her intentions and wanted us to drive to Holland to pick it up. I said we could do that on the way home from Switzerland and she didn't say no....

In late May I wrote letters to Jeanette's sister Marilyn and mom Rose that, having heeded their urgings for me to "move on", I'd now met someone. I said that it in no way affected the loving memories I had of Jeanette. I expressed the heartfelt hope that would it would not affect my future contacts with them either.

My correspondence with Mom was less frequent since my trip to the Canaries with Lena (and thus Mom's realization that marriage wasn't just around the corner despite the seemingly unavoidable conclusion that we were "doing it"). In early May she wrote:

> *I'm anxious to know how things are going with you & Lena. My heart is <u>large</u> & <u>longing</u> to do the <u>best</u> <u>possible</u> things I can. I know you know me and love me, and how I value that you've <u>always</u> <u>tried</u> to understand me!! [Her underlining]*

Sometimes after a delay she would mention that she was "too full to write", which always amused the bilingual rascal in me ("*full*" means "drunk" in Swedish).

On Sunday, June 3rd, we drove up to Barkåkra, as did Eva and Lina, and in the afternoon we all went to "Eket" – which meant to an old farm property called Persköp outside the village of Eket about half an hour's drive east of Barkåkra. A better name for the place might have been "Allan's Folly". Despite already living out in the countryside, Lena's father was driven by a desire to have a summer cottage. What he found instead was a cheap old wreck of a farmhouse that reeked of mold and mildew. It was located in a marsh, assuring an ample supply of mosquitoes the moment the weather risked making the unheated dwelling habitable in terms of temperature. The little bastards had no trouble finding me. They left me covered in welts that itched for days. The barn was equally run-down, but it was spacious, and gave Allan unlimited capacity to store whatever seemed to him like a bargain at the countryside auctions he liked to frequent. Most of it was furniture, or at least had been, but some was firewood at best.

After he died, his four children found themselves the beneficiaries of equal shares of ownership of the country cottage, but nobody knew what to do with the damn place. Yet nobody dared to divest it since Allan's authoritarian (according to Lena) role seemed to survive him, and nobody had his permission to take action against that particular sea of troubles. The only ones who were interested enough to spend any more than a day or two there were Lars and his family. Lena and Eva seemed to feel it was their duty to visit the place and air everything out prior to Lars and his family arriving there for a few weeks. Don't ask me why.

Although Lena never showed any great interest in my paintings, Jan and Eva did; they purchased *Regret* from me. Little Lina was even more interested, and every time they came to visit at Korngatan, Lina immediately ran upstairs to see how far I'd come along on *Jardin*. I could never understand Lena's lack of response to – her almost active *dis*interest in – my work. Although it was by no means an unusual response among visitors to Korngatan, people to whom I was close in any way usually tended to comment, if only politely. Some actually asked questions about and discussed them!

In the early days of June, I got a friendly reply from Marilyn, in response to my having told her about Lena. She was full of warm wishes and seemed genuinely and unequivocally happy for me. I felt an enormous sense of relief. I didn't hear from Rose directly, but Marilyn seemed to be speaking on behalf of her too, so I didn't think about it. I continued to write to Rose and Marilyn from time to time, and to send birthday and Christmas presents to everyone in the immediate family. I had no clue at the time, but that one letter from Marilyn in the early days of June was the last I would ever hear from anyone in Jeanette's family for more than two decades.

> *I will take this opportunity to digress from the timeline in order to complete the saga of my first painting:*

Strangely, Rose corresponded occasionally with my mom until Rose's death (in the 90s, I believe) and Marilyn sent Christmas cards to my mom, but nothing to me. Fast-forward to around 2003, when I started to work in earnest on *Hindsights*, and realized I had no good photo image of my first painting, *Guitar & Bottle*, last seen by me on Rose's living room wall. I'd learned from my mom – who'd heard from Marilyn – that Michael had moved from the house on Seville after Rose died, but I could find no address.

After many fruitless internet searches, and many calls to the wrong people, I tried phoning the number of someone whom I suspected or hoped might be Marilyn's son. Marilyn herself answered the phone, and when I told her who I was, she became extremely nervous and ill at ease, but she didn't hang up on me. I tried inquiring about the family, their well-being and current status. Her nervousness only accelerated. So I simply asked about the painting, stating my request for a photo. She stammered that she wasn't sure what happened to it, that it had been in the garage on Seville for many years, but that the house there had been sold, and my painting might have ended up in a dumpster. I was stunned, sickened, and found no words. Then she said she'd ask around and get back to me. I managed to get an email address from her and gave her mine.

About a week later I got an email from her. To my great relief, she said she'd managed to locate the painting. Rosanne's son, who actually liked it, had rescued it when the house on Seville was being emptied. He currently had it in his college dorm room. Where did I want them to send it? I replied that I was *not* asking them to return the painting to me, just to get a photographer to take a high-resolution photo of it and email it to me.

And then I let my curiosity get the better of me, due to my extreme puzzlement combined with decades of emotional dilemma, about the door to correspondence having been slammed shut in my face all those years ago. So I added to my email a question: whether she felt that the silent treatment towards me was what Jeanette would have wanted? Marilyn shot back that my email was "hurtful" (the most hurtful she'd ever received), that she couldn't deal with talking about Jeanette, and that my painting was now in the mail!

It arrived about a week later. It was rather damaged and marred, presumably from having spent years in a damp garage. There were a few parallel streaks, possibly from water having dripped across it over an extended period. About a week or two after that, I received a terse note from Rosanne, which I quote here in its entirety: "*Stanley, I mailed your painting on 2-4-04. Please send me $47.60 for postage. Rosanne.*" No greeting, no signature, nothing personal. It could have been from a bailiff. As I hadn't even received any thanks for the trunk I shipped in response to their request in early 1978 (I never had a thought to ask them for reimbursement for the many times costlier costlier shipping charges), I chose to view Rosanne's request as compensation, and let the matter end there. *Guitar & Bottle* is now hanging on our wall in Glimminge.

End of digression.

Also in early June, I got a totally out-of-the-blue phone call from Lena E, wondering if I'd like her to come down for the weekend. Despite the *strong* temptation (a real road-not-taken moment!), and despite all Lena J's continuing and exasperating vacillations, I'd convinced myself that she (Lena J) was very close to ending her resistance to me. I'd also convinced myself that ending her resistance would be tantamount to enthusiastic acceptance and a spontaneous outpouring of unlimited and unbridled affection, much in the way that turning off the roar of a power saw might be tantamount to playing the andante movement of a Mozart wind concerto. [*I didn't even get that the cessation of grumbling resistance was not the same as passionate acceptance! Is that naïve enough for you?*] In any case, I told Lena E that it was no longer possible for us to see each other, because I was about to be engaged. I seem to recall that Lena E sounded disappointed, but I don't remember any details about her reaction or response. (I hope I wished her well!)

Monday, June 11th was Lena's 29th birthday. I brought her breakfast in bed and gave her 29 red roses, keeping up the tradition my dad started for my mom. (I'd already given her the bike.) I also bought her a bottle of Liqueur 43 (our favorite from the Canaries) and a cake. Back at her place in the afternoon, I helped her clean up a bit, and then we looked through her photo albums. For some reason she wanted me to see – *again, at this stage!!* – and to dwell upon the photos of her "great loves", Ola and Larry. (Yet she would *never* look at *my* slides or photos!) Jan, Eva and Lina came at 7, we had dinner and talked till 10.30. After they left, Lena and I went to bed. She started once again talking about the difficulties between us. She said that I would probably go to Jeanette if she came back (unfortunately impossible) and she to Larry if he came back (unfortunately not impossible). That upset me. Lena couldn't understand how it could make me feel threatened. I didn't feel secure about anything.

That same day, I received another letter from my brother John, about what Lena and I might expect were we to come to the US to visit my family:

> *You would be wrong in insisting that Mom give you the same bedroom. I'm sure you realize that but I just wanted to point it out. I think I could deal with it if you came here – not that I would condone it, since the Christian faith recognizes the sanctity of the marriage relationship.*

The mawkish and condescending nature of his comment, particularly the cliché-ridden doctrinal formulation of his last clause, made me furious, made me want to roar "*Fuck you!*" at him, but fortunately the days of instant messaging had not yet arrived and I had time to calm down before responding.

A Sea of Troubles

Three days later, however, on June 14th, in response to one more of my innumerable requests for Lena to move in with me and marry me, she suddenly said *yes*! Just like that. We agreed to make our engagement official on Midsummer Eve in Eket. When we phoned Marie-Louise to tell her of our plans, she was over the moon with joy and burst out: "Lena got the best there is!"

On June 15th we went out and bought our engagement rings and of course I informed Bob of the impending engagement – and that Lena and I would indeed be coming to Switzerland by car to visit him in early July, so he was pleased, almost certainly more about the latter part of my news. We also informed Björn and Isobel and invited them to Korngatan for crêpes the next day. It was trying. Isobel kept going on about how depressed I used to be, which put Lena in a strange mood and made her hesitant about moving in with me. I could have strangled Isobel! Afterwards, I had to have a long talk with Lena to get her – and our engagement – back on track, and twist, bend, and break down the last of her resistance.

So on Midsummer Eve, June 22nd, at the swamp cottage in Eket, in the company of Marie-Louise, Eva and Jan, Lena and I exchanged rings and were thus officially engaged, and I couldn't imagine being happier. On June 19th I made the last of my daily diary entries. Thereafter I only wrote sporadically, e.g. when something particularly noteworthy took place or was said.

CHAPTER 11

The new life

Two weeks of feverish activity and great happiness followed. We rented a van on June 25th and moved all Lena's things (all but the piano, for which we had to enlist the help of piano movers the next day). Then we got her apartment thoroughly cleaned and ready for the next tenant, whom she found the following day. By the time she moved to Korngatan, she'd borrowed nearly 7000 kronor from me over the past six months, a debt I instantly forgave.

Since the house at Korngatan was so big, there were few problems integrating Lena's possessions with mine. We might, however, have been able to foresee that some friction could arise from our different views on the purpose of horizontal space. I was used to keeping kitchen countertops and tabletops as free from clutter as possible so that they could be used for things like meal preparation and working on projects. Her approach was to cover much of them with stacks of magazines and knickknacks, which would have to be moved elsewhere each time the surfaces were needed for use as worktops. I said I liked them bare. She responded scornfully that I must be crazy, that a home with bare surfaces didn't look lived-in, any fool ought to realize that. Naturally, she put her stacks everywhere. Compromise was out of the question. Questions were out of the question. At first I scarcely noticed the addition to her vocabulary of invectives like "fool" and "idiot". I was so willing to grant her wishes on everything – *nearly*.

But not when the bone of contention was my paintings. "Do we *have* to have so bloody *many* on the walls?" she asked irritably. I replied that I was a painter and that was where they belonged. On that I was not to be budged. But in all other respects, she had a free hand and quickly turned my house into a home. I could only hope that she would start to see it as her home too.

Never having stuck my head into any of the closets she had at her apartment in Lund, I'd vastly underestimated the enormity of her collection of clothing, including evidence of a particular fondness for footwear: heels, sandals, trainers, boots, loafers, open-toes, kitten heels, flats, pumps and others with names that sounded to me more something one might find at a hardware store, all in a variety of colors and materials. I'd never seen anything quite like it, not even at Bob's place in 1970. But there was room for all that too, once I'd put up a few extra clothes poles and made some extra shelves for the footwear.

A Sea of Troubles

She loved houseplants (I did too), so when her considerable collection joined forces with my more modest one, some parts of our new home suggested a lovely leafy conservatory. She was industrious about cleaning (which I found at odds with her apparent love of clutter). I suspect (at the risk of being accused and harassed for harboring gender stereotypes) that that is often the case among men and women living together. My only reason for saying so is that I observed such a pattern among many of the men and women I knew personally, but perhaps my acquaintances were atypical and would thus render my generalization fallacious. (I was more concerned about tidiness.)

I was positively glowing with the pleasure of embarking on a new life together with Lena as we left Malmö on July 9th on our engagement trip to Basel, arriving in the vicinity of Kassel that evening. We reached Bob and Binningen (only the second time Lena and Bob had met, and Lena's first time at Bob's place) the following evening, after a detour along the way, through the Schwartzwald, where Lena and I sat on a meadow and enjoyed a picnic lunch with blueberry wine.

Because I was so eager to please Lena in every little way, I'd quelled my feelings of longing to see Bob after such a long hiatus. Lena's first meeting with him had been brief, I told myself, so she couldn't be expected to share my enthusiasm; she didn't. But when we arrived, both Lena and Bob expressed a level of delight to see each other that only the one person among us three who knew the other two could possibly recognize as largely stemming from deference to social expectations. But with Lena's natural charm constituting the perfect counterweight to Bob's equally natural defensiveness, the initial cordiality gradually became commingled with joviality, probably aided more by the Champagne Bob had purchased for the occasion than by any efforts on my part or anyone else's.

The next day, the 11th, was a weekday, and since Bob had to go to work, Lena and I had time for a lazy morning. After brunch, we took the tram downtown and climbed both towers of the Münster, went shopping, and had a beer at Mövenpick on the Markplatz. Lena said she was favorably impressed with Basel. We went back downtown the next day to look around some more in the old town and go shopping. On the Friday, with Bob at Roche, Lena and I spent most of the day in bed (i.e. the cushions of the sofa that we put on the living-room floor), did some reading, listened to music, and prepared a lovely Friday evening meal to enjoy with stunning views on Bob's balcony in the balmy evening.

Saturday the 14th was Bastille Day, so why not visit France? We drove with Bob across the border into Alsace, where we enjoyed the festive holiday atmosphere in Colmar, as well as a memorable meal of escargots, fine wine, and tournedos. The next day, Sunday, Bob guided us to Arlesheim, ostensibly to see the cathedral and its Silbermann organ. Arlesheim was a place of multiple bittersweet memories for Bob; it was where he and Sigrid lived before Sigrid's growing instability became so extreme that Bob was forced to flee and ended up in Binningen. We also paid a visit to nearby Dornach to see the quirky fungal architecture of Goetheanum, Rudolf Steiner's grandiose anthroposophical palace and the world headquarters of the Anthroposophist cult.

Bob was going to be on vacation the following week. On Sunday evening he revealed that he had a surprise engagement present for us: a little outing, at his expense, to a destination that would be revealed as we drove there (but we should pack a bag…). So in the late morning on Monday the 16th, all three of us drove to Luzerne, as instructed, where we got our first views of the snow-capped Alps, and from there on to Interlachen, stopping for a picnic along the way. I'd been here before and began to suspect where Bob was taking us. When Bob guided us onward to Lauterbrunnen, I knew and was thrilled. The views of the Alps and the valleys from the cogwheel train on the way up to Kleine Scheidegg were simply spectacular. Lena was equally thrilled and impressed. We saw hikers along the way, on good trails that pretty much followed the tracks. When we reached our destination, Bob revealed that he'd booked us into rooms at the grand and auspicious Hotel Bellevue at the foot of the Eiger and the Jungfrau. Over dinner in the hotel dining room that evening, we asked Bob if he'd mind if Lena and I took the next day to hike back down to Lauterbrunnen while he took the train. He said he was all for it, of course; he'd brought along several books to read whenever circumstances might permit.

The hike back down on the 17th took several unhurried hours and was fabulous. Wildflowers were everywhere. At the higher altitudes, there seemed to be both spring and summer flowers simultaneously. The weather was bright and sunny, not too cold for Lena nor too hot for me. We picked flowers for Lena to press and frame (in some of the old picture frames we'd bought at auctions in Marieholm). She hung them on our walls (to dilute the dominance of my paintings?), and they looked very pretty. We also had a picnic in Wengen on the way down.

Bob was enjoying himself reading and was surprised that we made it back so early in the afternoon. We all felt a bit saturated with impressions and beauty, so with me driving, we decided to make it back to Binningen for the night. The three of us sat up talking and drinking fine wine and Cognac in his apartment until well past dawn, so we didn't get up until 3 pm on the 18th; just getting up would have to be enough of an accomplishment for that day.

On the 19th, we were back to normal vacation mode and visited the Basel Art Museum, shopping, and back to the Mövenpick. On the 20th, we wrote Mom – my first letter to her that was also signed by Lena. We were approaching the end of our stay with Bob, and he wanted to take us to Zofingen and Solothurn, a couple of places southeast of Basel that we hadn't had time to stop at on our way to Luzerne. (I wondered whether John and Marj would ever get to see Solothurn.)

Sunday the 22nd was our last day with Bob, as we would be embarking on the next leg of our journey the following day, and he would be going back to work, an underwhelming prospect for him. We spent much of that day seeing more sites in Basel and the rest talking on Bob's balcony. I don't want to speculate about Bob's possible thoughts and feelings towards Lena or hers towards him, except to say that it seemed quite clear to me that neither would have sought the other's company if I hadn't been part of the equation. We said good-bye that night; Bob had to leave his apartment before we got up, and we would be driving to the Netherlands to see about Lena's diamond. We arrived in Den Haag in time for a superb Chinese dinner and our room at a lousy hotel.

We found the bank the next morning, one of those aristocratic private banks where formally dressed people speak in hushed, knowing tones and glide stiffly about with lowered eyes. We were put in touch with one of their clerks, who explained to us that they could not give Lena her diamond because it was not theirs to give. It seemed that the London firm from whom Lena (and Larry?) had purchased this quality-certified stone had sent it to an agent in Den Haag for deposit at this bank, but it was only the agent, not the bank, who could retrieve it, and the agent had moved to Antwerpen and was away on business and had not been answering his phone. (In Lena's correspondence with the bank five weeks prior our visit, the bank failed to say a word about these circumstances!) We requested the agent's phone number and tried calling him ourselves after leaving the bank guy perplexed. Was somebody trying to pull a fast one? How did they know he was away on business if he hadn't been answering his phone? Couldn't they have left a message?

We returned to the bank (I was wearing all black, and wrap-around sunglasses for extra effect!), and were shown to a private room as soon as we appeared. Lena told the clerk that something seemed mighty fishy about it all, while I sat there in grim silence, glaring grimly from behind my sunglasses. The clerk tried to explain that the agent was just away on business and it was no big deal, but Lena pointed out that she'd given them *five weeks'* notice about her intention to fetch the diamond, and that the bank had done absolutely nothing about it in the interim, by which time it had become too late to do anything about it now. The clerk paled and made a phone call, after which we were escorted to the private offices of the bank president himself, who looked as humble as it was possible to do while wearing clothing that probably cost the equivalent of the monthly salaries of an entire team of working men and women. In view of the admitted and unfortunate shortcomings in the actions and responses of the bank, he intoned solemnly, the bank agreed to receive the diamond from said agent once said agent could be contacted, and the bank would further agree to hold said diamond, free of charge, until such time as Lena found it convenient to retrieve it. We allowed ourselves to look appeased, and haughtily announced that it might take a year or so until we returned, which the bank president duly noted without flinching. Then we left the bank, walked around the corner where we had parked the Datsun, the closest equivalent we had to a Rolls, and burst out laughing.

After a Chinese lunch, we drove to Katwijk aan Zee, because Lena had heard it was a lovely seaside resort. So had thousands upon thousands of others. We visited the reception desks of dozens of hotels. All were fully booked. We finally found one which, although it too was fully booked, could offer us an extra single, cut-rate room directly above the kitchen. The single bed wouldn't have been a problem for us if it hadn't been so greasy. In fact, every surface in the room – walls, floors, windows, furniture, fixtures – was covered with a thin layer of slightly rancid grease from the frying fumes from the kitchen below. It was probably a good thing that we decided not to smoke in that room.

The next day, with our treasury running low and our minds as full as my mom's heart, we decided to make one last stop before heading for home: Amsterdam. I felt that we shouldn't leave the Netherlands without having tried a real Indonesian *rijstaffel* (a must, according to Bob). It was delicious. After dinner, in response to the relatively great offering of porn around the city, Lena expressed interest in visiting one of several small nightclubs offering "live shows" – actual sex onstage. I suppose my shocked gut reaction was visible all over my face. In any case, she withdrew her suggestion instantly. I was by no means a prude, but.... Instead, we got in the car and started for home, got past Bremen to Stuckenborstel, where we spent the night at a *gasthaus*, before making the final leg home the next day, the 25th.

There was a letter from my mom awaiting us on our return, in which she expressed her hilarious view (certainly unintentional!) that it was "sweet of Lena to <u>give you new desires</u>" [sic!]. Equally mysterious to me at the time was her next statement: "*Oh that the wall between us may soon be forever broken, and that the <u>love that exists</u> be free to be understood and expressed. I have to <u>hold myself in check</u>, so ready am I to <u>love</u> Lena too.*" (The underlinings were hers.)

I couldn't understood what she was talking about until I reread this letter – three times – in connection with writing a draft of this book in 2017. I presumed that the wall she was referring to was the one of her own making, her self-imposed refusal to love Lena *until* we were officially married. That was her crucial, wall-breaking, ball-breaking criterion. Supposing that she was referring to the numerous and historical differences between her values and mine, I immediately wrote her a reply based on that supposition:

I wasn't quite sure how to interpret what you said about breaking down the walls between us. I know that we differ on a lot of things. I also know that I love you very much and that you love me very much. That we, in view of these 2 factors, find it best not to dwell upon our differences may or may not constitute the wall you speak about, but if it is so it must be a sort of protective wall, since we don't want to hurt each other. There are things that are part of my lifestyle which I know would meet your disapproval. I can see no purpose in discussing such things with you, as they would only cause you discomfort. The point is that they are not part of my lifestyle because you disapprove, but because I'm me. And you might get upset because you're you. So if our differences form a wall, we can at least be glad that the wall is not too high for love to get over – in both directions!!

On the same day, Lena wrote a thank-you to my mom for a personal monetary gift, in which Lena mentioned that

Stanley and I have known each other for quite a long time now and I have received so much goodness and tenderness from him all this time. He is such a considerate and warmhearted person, to whom I want to be the same, and never want to lose. Both of

us [sic] were careful for quite a while [about] making too rapid a decision, but now I'm happy for the engagement, and I will care for Stanley and try to be as good as he is to me. My mother has the warmest feelings for Stanley.

On Saturday, July 30th, we got a visit from Sonja (most definitely *not* my sometime girlfriend!), the final member of Lena's "sexklubb" (the six classmates [*in Swedish, "sex" is the word for six <u>and</u> sex*] from the teachers' college who continued to meet from time to time). Lena had forewarned me that Sonja was an active devotee of astrology. My memories of the tragic, astrology-inspired break-up of the family of my Danish neighbor Allan were still painfully fresh in my mind. I was thus prepared when, true to expectations, the first question Sonja asked me was "*What's your star sign?*" I pretended not to understand the question, so instead she asked "*When were you born?*" I told her my birthdate was April 14th, whereupon she immediately started outlining for me in considerable detail what kind of person I was, my personality traits, preferences etc, all based on the failure of the Ancients to realize that the earth ain't the center of the universe! I'd been looking at her in growing amazement and when she finished, I told her it was incredible how readily I could identify with nearly everything she had said – and "*Aries*" even fit so well with "*Eris*-man"! As she began to swell with pride and smugness, I told there that there was just one small problem with her analysis: I wasn't born on April 14th, but on *November* 14th.

Her jaw dropped in momentary shock, but she immediately recovered with redoubled zeal and triumph. "*I <u>knew</u> it! It's absolutely <u>typical</u> of you Scorpios to play a trick like that!*" Then she proceeded to dissect me again, giving me a whole new detailed profile of myself that matched her Scorpio cubbyhole. While she was doing this, I allowed my jaw to drop and my eyes to widen in amazement. As she once again swelled with pride, her smugness fully restored, I once again told her that there was just one small problem: I wasn't born on November 14th either. Her face darkened and she hissed at me "*When <u>were</u> you born then?!*" I smiled sweetly at her and said, "*You know so much about me; why don't you tell <u>me</u>?*" She turned on her heel and stormed away.

I'd probably also been guilty at times of categorizing people, pinning labels on them, stereotyping them, profiling them, making snap judgments, shoving them into cubbyholes and then disregarding all new information that didn't fit my own ill-conceived initial impressions. It seems to be a human trait, a natural foible. But I don't think it's a *good* trait; it's what prejudices are all about. A lot of people

– and a lot of advertising – seem to equate "natural" with "good" ("100% natural ingredients"), but in fact it says *nothing*. All kinds of things are both natural and bad: tornados, earthquakes, the impulse to clobber somebody who bumps into you (intentionally or not), selfishness, greed, myriad kinds of treachery. I doubt that there's anything on earth that is more *un*natural than civilization!

Where natural-but-bad behavior (including stereotyping of others) is concerned, I think the very fact that it is natural and nearly universal makes it hard to recognize, yet recognition of its existence is a prerequisite to doing anything about controlling, resisting or counteracting it. And if a person is inclined to strive to be a *good* person, the bad – especially the wily, insidious, *natural* kinds of bad – must first be recognized. I didn't think that Sonja was *trying* to be bad by trying to stick me into one of her astrological safe deposit boxes, but I couldn't think that it was a good thing to do, and I wasn't going to stand for having it done to me. The fact that I also reacted to her exceptionally hairy legs, and her slight drooling from a sneering mouth showed me how easy it was to fall into the natural *ad hominem* trap, and how useful it would be to have added *paraleipsis* to my vocabulary.

On Monday, we got a visit from Marie-Louise and from the final member of Lena's siblings, her brother Jan, together with his wife Anita and four of their six kids. They lived in Åkersberga, another of Stockholm's northern suburbs. He was the president of Åkeriförbundet (The Swedish Association of Road Transport Companies). Lena told me a few things about him that she felt I might do well to know before meeting him. One was that he was a dyed-in-the-wool Conservative (*don't rush to judgment*, I thought). Another was that he had firmly rejected religion, which had considerably strained relations between him and his vicar father (*very interesting*, I thought). A third was that those already strained relations had been largely demolished by a devious plot on the part of Jan's parents and Anita.

Sweden had an official state church at that time, Evangelical Lutheran, even though they called their clergy *präster* (often translated as "priests", a term reserved for Catholic and some Eastern Orthodox religions in the limited experience of my Meeting background). Every Swedish person *was born into church membership. (You had actively apply to leave the church!* Fortunately, this didn't apply to immigrants.) Despite the fact that few Swedish people regarded themselves as believers, the overwhelming majority were tradition-bound enough to have their infants christened, to encourage them to interrupt their secular lives long enough to undergo confirmation at the age of 14, and then usually to marry in a church and schedule their funeral there, but otherwise largely to ignore religion. Jan, like me, had come to find the practice of infant christening inherently and abhorrently hypocritical and he refused to subject his children to it. This distressed his tradition- and/or religion-bound parents. And because the practice was so tightly bound to the power of *social* tradition – with much stronger bonds than the religious ones – they were easily able to collude with Anita to have the children christened by Allan behind Jan's back, in connection with a visit she'd made to Barkåkra with the kids, without her husband. When Jan somehow eventually discovered the deception (a few years before I met him), he was livid. (I had no trouble understanding him!) The deception apparently destroyed what remained of his relationship with his father, seriously injured his relationship with his mother, and dealt a fatal blow to his marriage with Anita; he was currently having a long-term affair with his secretary, Gun, and making little effort to hide it or her.

Jan and I liked each other immediately, like old friends, from that first meeting. He was a big guy, very handsome, oozing social confidence. Our instant friendship certainly wasn't because we shared the same political views, but nor was it because we didn't. We could argue our respective and sometimes diametrically opposite positions passionately, forcefully, and yet always good-naturedly, and with a dash of humor. There have unfortunately been very few people with whom I could reason forcefully about opposing positions as amicably as I could with Jan (not that we disagreed about *everything*!). Lena seemed quite pleased to see how well we got along, even if she also seemed a bit surprised. Marie-Louise apparently felt the same way.

Earlier that week I received a phone call from a guy named Leif (pronounced *Layf*), who worked at a company called Frigoscandia in Helsingborg. He'd heard of my work from the people at the Andersson & Lembke advertising agency. Frigoscandia was actually two sister companies, one working with cold stores and chilled transport of food, the other with industrial food-freezing and processing equipment. Leif was the marketing manager for the latter. He wanted to invite me to lunch "at a good restaurant" in Malmö to discuss the possibility of my future collaboration on his company's marketing support material, because he claimed to have been impressed by what his contacts at the agency had told him about the

A Sea of Troubles

work I'd done for their Perstorp clients. Leif suggested the Falstaff steakhouse on Baltzarsgatan, an above-my-budget place I'd never been disappointed with when I ate there a few times with my pupils back in the days of Demaret's Language School. We agreed to meet there at lunchtime on Friday, August 3rd.

Leif was a big tall guy, 40 years old, every inch a salesman, with dark slicked-back hair, and a take-charge attitude about everything. He was wearing a yellow-green hound's-tooth tweed jacket. He made it clear that our lunch was definitely a question of my reading the menu from left to right. He left the left to me and I left the right to him. Leif asked me numerous questions about my background, probing *what* I thought and *how* I thought. It took me a while to discern what his plans for me might be. But then he began explaining about how important it was that market communications should get inside the *customer's* head, to write communications that emphasized the *benefits* more than the *features*. It made perfect sense to me. In fact, I spontaneously found it self-evident, even though I'd never formulated it quite that clearly before. *Of course* it had to be that way!

And he expressed complete confidence it me, that I was the one to whom he could turn to rewrite all the draft texts that *his* agency was feeding him. He wanted me to become his "ghost writer". I was to be the one to whom he could turn to transform a dull textbook description of a freezer into an exciting sales tool that would make food producers worldwide sit up and take notice, then line up ready and eager to buy. He would send me texts – or preferably *bring* me texts, to Korngatan – and I would work my magic on them, and he would take them back to the agency and tell them that *this* was how he wanted it to be. I would be his secret weapon. But he did *not* want me to work directly with the agency, only through him (?!). Not only that, he said he'd occasionally want to enlist my services to *write* the texts – not merely to translate, edit or rewrite them. Everything would be invoiced via Perstorp. At Frigoscandia and at the agency, he would take the credit for the resulting texts, and I would remain unknown, the ghost in the background.

It all sounded exciting enough to me, and I didn't give a shit about who got the credit. I would have an unexpected opportunity to take my writing skills to a new level. I'd be working as a *copywriter*; I'd never even heard that term before! Nor had I ever heard of an *undercover copywriter* before, yet I was about to be one.

One strange aspect of this development in my career was that although I billed my work *via* Perstorp, it didn't come *from* Perstorp. To the majority of my clients at Perstorp, I was and always would be nothing more than Stan the English teacher. To a few I might also be Stan the translator. And to a very few I would be Stan the guy who can really polish up a text. It took an outsider to figure out that I might have even more to offer, which I feared might be indicative of the level of agility of the Perstorp mentality.

During our time with Bob in Switzerland, he mentioned (more or less in passing) that he suspected that he'd developed Parkinson's disease. Nothing much beyond the name rang any bells with me. My impression was that it was "kind of serious", but Bob didn't show any reactions to support that. When I got home, I started looking it up and enquiring in the limited ways one did or could before the advent of the internet. My eyes automatically responded to any mention of the disease in any article I came across, including an article about a Swedish-American research project involving treatment with transplanted brain cells. I understood from Bob's reply that he was way ahead of me; he was devouring everything he could find on the subject, and with his access to Hoffmann LaRoche's research library, it was considerable. But none of it was encouraging.

Bob looked at it in an entirely different way. The confirmed pessimist and nihilist I met in 1970 now saw his apparent Parkinson's as a potential meal ticket to early retirement (disability pension) and the opportunity to forever escape the drudgery of a job he had grown to hate, and to enjoy the freedom to devote his days to what he loved most: reading and listening to classical music. He assured me that little else, apart from spending time with me, truly mattered to him. Fortunately for me, he'd learned to accept and allow for what he described as my "dramatic and impulsive nature" in such a way, or to such an extent, that he didn't view it as an insurmountable character defect, but more as the source of an exhilarating ride that brought him joy, both directly and vicariously. And bringing joy to Bob was something I could never do enough.

Bob was still just over 50 years old, an age I'd never associated with retirement, even though his "corporal age" – his physical capability – might have placed him well past 80. I felt so close to him, the only person on earth in whom I felt I could truly confide, and who felt likewise about me. Thus the knell of mortality that the P-word entailed was too horrifying, too repulsive for me to take on board at once. And yet the thought of repressing or suppressing the fact of it (if indeed it were a fact) scared me even more. What I had to do, I felt, was to make it perfectly clear to Bob that I was both interested and concerned, and that he could feel free

– to the extent he found it necessary, desirable or urgent – to relate to me the details of his condition, its development and the anxiety it was causing him.

We began, by letter, to resume our earlier discussion on the subject of "magic thinking": the predilection of the human race to ascribe magic to and create rituals surrounding events or phenomena that cannot otherwise immediately be explained rationally. We both felt that magic thinking was clearly the backbone of religions and superstitions, as well as any traditions that give rise to strong emotional dependencies, i.e. the kind that lack truly rational explanations but nevertheless generate significant levels of anxiety whenever they are breached or even challenged. The only misnomer about "magic thinking" was that *thinking* is involved at all.

We were, however, conscious of the need to avoid retroactive judgment. Modern science provides the intelligent mind with increasingly realistic and evidence-based starting-points that the Ancients simply did not have. Lacking the microscope, early scientists failed to see microorganisms and thus were by no means to blame for concocting now-debunked notions of spontaneous generation. There is no basis for contempt for one who fails to do something because he or she lacks the means to do it – except when they demand that others accept their guesses as fact. With those who now have the tools to get closer to the truth and ignore them or refuse to use them, however, it's a different story. But we felt it still didn't make the *person* contemptible. There can be all kinds of powerful emotional reasons – fear, guilt, revenge, peer pressure, etc – that can at least temporarily disrupt the ability or the will to make use of rational tools.

Bob had strong desires to visit the US again, partly out of curiosity to see what had become of his homeland during decades of his absence from it, partly to continue to pursue Kathy. She was living in upstate New York, not far from Endicott, where Bob's brother Charles lived. But Bob had no intention of visiting his brother due to Charles's oppression and religious persecution of his sons. About Bob's pursuit of Kathy, I felt a bit of the skepticism Bob clearly felt about my pursuit of Lena, one main distinction being a generation's worth of age difference between Bob and Kathy.

My mom still hadn't responded to my letter trying to understand what she had meant by the "wall" that separated us, and I wrote to Bob that I was taking a cautious approach.

Thus far, our conflict has not reached the level of the Arabs and Israelis. Should I suddenly be strafed with tracts and wake up one morning to find the garage being scaled by wild-eyed Plymouth Brethren with Bibles in their teeth and the Hayhoe Brigade setting up gospel launchers with infrared sights on Korngatan, I would find cause to retaliate appropriately. Seriously, I think my reply to her was sufficient to let her know that the door she may not have fully realized she knocked at is unlocked. If she really wants to enter upon that kind of open dialogue, I will leave the door ajar for her to enter at her own speed.

All was not well between Lena and me. In early August, less than a month after returning from our "engagement honeymoon", I found myself again compelled to use my little diary to try to document the situations that had again begun causing me considerable inner conflict. But I still didn't feel I could or should discuss this particular matter with Bob, in whom I could otherwise confide about everything, for fear of adding to his difficulty in accepting Lena as someone who was interested in treating me well. And I was increasingly anxious to avoid becoming neurotic.

On August 9th, Lena told me (I was so taken aback that I had to write it down) that she could well understand how, even if a person loved someone a great deal, one could want to go to bed with someone new and interesting – almost *because* one loved the other person, and therefore would want to spread the "love" further. In view of my *always* having had to take the initiative for sex with Lena, I wondered what circumstances would make such a meeting with this "new and interesting person" possible for her, or what on earth her premise had been that might lead to a conclusion that seemed so preposterous to me. Although I said nothing, the shock (and perhaps some horror) on my face was clear enough to read (I'd never be a poker player). She immediately changed the subject. I remembered Amsterdam.

The question of our conjugal life was becoming a major source of conflict, both internally and externally. If I communicated, directly or indirectly, my enormous attraction to her, she would say that I was only interested in her "in that way". It made no sense to me why the closer relationship we now had (love, engagement, cohabitation) should lead to *less* sex. When we first went out, we had sex nearly every day, often multiple times, and I couldn't help wondering whether sex for her was more associated with infatuation than with love. So was she just going to use me for security, but get turned on by others? Why did I nearly always have to persuade her? She occasionally admitted that she found me attractive, but it sounded to me like saying how hungry you are and then not eating. It could make a fella wonder! Why had she accepted sex so freely when we first met? It certainly wasn't because she wanted to "win" me. It made me worry about the direction in which we seemed we might be heading. I viewed our sex as making *love*, reinforcing love, celebrating the joy of nearness and intimacy. She seemed to be treating it like favors she could dispense or withhold, like scratching based solely on *her* itching – nothing to do with love at all.

I tried to be open with her and talk about it, but she just got irritated and upset (she took it as criticism, of course). After a brief discussion, she said she was "too tired", and that if we were to make love, it would have to be earlier in the evening. But then she never wanted to come to bed early enough to meet her own criterion.

I began to become aware of other areas of imbalance. Few weeks went by without my stopping at some shop to buy something I'd spotted that I thought she might like. When she spent a day shopping, she'd come home with bag after bag of clothing – only for herself. I made the mistake of jokingly pointing that out once, and she thought I was being a pain ("*taskig*"). On another occasion she announced that *she* usually bought things "*for the one I live with*", which not only made me feel like the latest in a long impersonal line, but also made me wonder anxiously why her principle didn't apply to me. More and more frequently I again found myself inescapably observing that our relationship was a one-way street, that Lena never demonstrated any real interest in making me happy; any contributions she happened to make to my happiness were invariably mere by-products of her efforts to make herself happy. The only other person who suspected that this might be the case was her mother – who told me so!

I didn't want to obsess about any of this, nor even think of it. I wrote in my diary my dark thoughts about ongoing events, hoping to get them off my chest and then banish them from my mind. Lena had mood swings, I told myself. Most people do. Hers were far from the worst I'd had to deal with. *Give her time, let it pass, give her space, all will be well. In the meantime, find something else to focus on.*

With their sons grown up and out on their own, and half their house now a vacated workshop, our Danish neighbors, the Saabyes, told us sometime in August that they'd decided to sell their house and move to an apartment down the hill, across Lundavägen. But they would be keeping their car repair shop across the street from us, at least for the time being.

The new life

Taking their place as our next-door neighbors were a Swedish couple, Bo and Peter, two men in their late 30s. Bo was from Sollefteå in northern Sweden and Peter was from Katrineholm in central Sweden. They'd met more than a decade earlier while both were students at Sweden's University College of Arts, Crafts and Design in Stockholm. They worked as designers at one of Sweden's better-known textile producers in Borås. Bo would be working mostly from home on Korngatan, however, while Peter would live in an apartment in Borås during the working week and come home to Malmö for weekends. Unfortunately, experience had apparently taught them that even in Sweden in the late 1970s, it was still prudent for them to practice discretion regarding their unmistakable homosexuality. Why the hell should they have to hide their love for each other from the public eye? What about the public heart? What gives anybody the right to judge other people for loving each other?!

The house-restoration task they were facing was probably every bit as daunting as what Jeanette and I had dealt with, so they were eager to pick up whatever pointers I had to offer that might help them to fulfil their imaginative dreams. They had about as much practical house-building experience as I'd had – close to none – but they were unafraid to learn, and they had a real flair for design.

I was glad to have the big project on the little house to distract me from my increasing frustration and anxiety about being almost, but never quite able to win Lena's love. Somehow it had already become late August and I'd done so little (and had scarcely touched *Jardin*). After removing the upstairs ceiling (while leaving the roof itself intact), I realized that I wouldn't be able to start taking off the roof until *next* summer, 1980; the whole little house would be far too vulnerable for far too long without a roof. But I could at least undertake the project to replace the garage doors and build a wall above them for the garage-roof deck. Since the burglary the year before – through the insecure garage doors – I'd been living with an undercurrent of vulnerability. At least I could *do* something about this problem!

I'd saved the original garage doors for this purpose, having observed that they were almost exactly the right width to fit the opening for the gate towards Källargatan. The gate was higher than the garage doors, but I'd wanted to put a large old wooden beam across the opening anyway, and by supporting the beam on either end with pressure-treated two-by-fours bolted into the vertical iron beams on which the gates were hung, I would achieve just the right height and width for the garage doors.

A Sea of Troubles

Those old garage doors were not a pretty sight. Now at last, the old beaded wooden paneling that I tore out from the upstairs of the big house would be the perfect solution. There was enough paneling to cover the exterior of both garage doors in a herringbone pattern. Then I stained it dark brown to match the beams, doors, and windows. This work went quickly. I was able to bolt the original long hinges right through the doors. Then I installed a proper lock. The results were great.

Now came the biggest challenge: building that wide brick arch. Tage Thagaard taught me how to build arches over the doors and windows in the big house, but few of those were wider than one meter; the garage doors spanned more than two-and-a-half meters. I first knocked out a gap in the brick wall on either side of the door, just above the level of the wooden beam. Next I lay one brick on each side, protruding slightly from the wall and angled upwards to form the beginning of either end of the arch. After waiting a day or two to let the mortar harden, I took a couple of sheets of plywood having the width of the length of a brick, and bent them according to the curvature of the arch, so that the ends were forced up against the two protruding bricks. To support the plywood arch, I propped up two-by-fours diagonally from the ground at each end, forcing the ends of the plywood up against the two protruding bricks. Then I placed one two-by-four vertically in the middle of the arch. Bo made frequent inspections and asked all kinds of questions.

I made sure I had plenty of bricks close by, ready for laying, before mixing a full wheelbarrow of mortar. The stage was set. I slapped a generous layer of mortar onto one long-side of one brick at a time, tapped it into place against the angled brick, while resting it on the plywood frame and alternating from one side to the other as I gradually but quickly worked towards the top of the arch. When I got to the top, the gap was just what I'd hoped for: the full thickness of a brick at the top of the arch, but slightly less at the bottom. Taking a mason's hammer I chipped away along the two lower long-sides until the last brick was beveled enough to fit the gap on the underside of the arch, forming a wedge, with just enough space to press in some mortar. Then I went back across the inside and outside of the arch, using a tuck-pointing trowel to fill in the worst cavities.

When I removed the supports, I hoped the entire thing wouldn't come crashing down on the sidewalk. There was an almost imperceptible shift, a tiny jolting drop, as gravity forced the bricks a little bit closer together, locking the arch in place. No big thud on the ground. Not even a thudlet.[18] It was going to hold. Tage taught me that the best way to strengthen an arch was to add weight to it, alternating the new rows of bricks from one side to the other to retain the balance of weight distribution over the arch. The thickness of the bricks closest to the center of each row had to be specially modified to accommodate the rise of the arch. Once I'd achieved a completely horizontal row level with the top of the arch, I laid an additional straight row before exhaling. I could almost see a similar arch forming in Bo's mind for their project.

Ever noticed how quickly and radically a person's mood and appearance can change at the sound of a bell? (*Not just dogs, Dr Pavlov!*) Even in the midst of a fierce argument or an outburst of tears, the sound of a phone or doorbell can suddenly transform a raging, howling human voice into one that sounds pleasant and friendly. The arrival on the scene of "someone else" can also have similar profound effects. Perhaps a person has no time for the one they live with and supposedly love, no time for a chat, no time for any warm exchange of words, but if the phone rings or a visitor appears at the door, whether it's a good friend or a casual acquaintance, the available time magically materializes. Is this new mood a role? Or is the original mood the role? Or are both, or is everything everybody ever does a role?

Why had Lena agreed to get engaged and move in with me if she didn't love me? After having she'd said she did a few times, she'd even more often said she didn't, or that she was still "trying". Did she just feel that approaching 30 meant that it was high time for her to "settle down" and that I would have to *do*, as I'd repeatedly demonstrated my unquenchable love for her and my acceptance of all her mood swings (or at least my longsuffering)?

But one day, out of nowhere, she hit a new and vicious low-water mark. She lashed out at me: "*If you're so pleasant to live with, how come your wife killed herself?*" This was no standard phrase that a person might let fly in anger. It was targeted, premeditated, malicious. I could hardly believe *anyone* could say anything that knowingly cruel. I shuddered. I felt dizzy with loss, disappointment, devastation.

---

18 *Thudlet* (diminutive): a small thud, as exemplified by the sound of a pine cone of approx. 5 cm in diameter falling from a height of approx 20 m onto a patch of compact soil without grass (cf. *pecklet*: the pecking sound of a lesser spotted woodpecker [*dryobates minor*] pecking at a dead pine branch not more than 7 cm in diameter)

I'd wrestled with that very question myself, of course. Countless horrifying times. I found no answer; there was none. Bob ascribed my asking myself such questions to self-pity, however understandable the circumstances may have made it. And I felt driven to an inescapable conjecture: *Suppose I did, in my darkest moments, feel that I might have driven Jeanette to take her own life? Is then my choice to try to build a life with Lena – with someone who so often treats me this badly – <u>my unconscious way of punishing myself</u>?*

Marie-Louise was appalled by the things she sometimes heard Lena say to me, as well as by Lena's sneering, disdainful tone. Only on a couple of extremely rare occasions did Lena feel any need to apologize for or excuse her own behavior. And why should she need to? I was always all too willing to make excuses for her! (I kept these feelings to myself, of course; I'd quickly learned that if she suspected that I so much as *thought* that anything she'd done might need to be excused, that too would have been inexcusable to her.) How did I deal with it? I'd tell myself that she'd probably slept poorly the night before, that she might have had a hard day at work, that it had been an exceptionally tough week, that this month was extraordinarily stressful for her. Wasn't I resourceful?

I was scared to death of losing her, so I came to the illogical conclusion that the bonds between us would be even stronger if they were also matrimonial bonds. I suggested that we start to think about getting married next year, as if a piece of paper might have the power to make her love me. Perhaps even stranger was that she was now spontaneously *favorable* to the idea of marrying me. Was it just *comme il faut*? Maybe she thought that having broken off one engagement already, breaking off a second might reflect badly on her? Although she would occasionally tell me she loved me (in response to my having said so to her, never initiated by her), she would more frequently tell me that she was "working on it", *trying* to love me, as if the task of loving the likes of me was the equivalent of all manner of Herculean tasks. I recalled Sonja's words all too seldom.

Remarkably, although my ongoing discussion with Bob on the subject of magic thinking was getting into some exciting territory, led and provoked mostly by Bob, little of it seemed to have any influence on my ability to see my own daily reality with anything like clarity. Bob and I had arrived at the view that magic has a legitimate role in feelings, but not in thinking, and that it's essential at all times to distinguish between the two. Bob wrote:

The predicament of man is caused by his incomplete evolution, resulting in his natural propensity to be unable to separate thought from emotion. This unholy mixture leads him to express his emotions as though they were thoughts, and he himself believes they are. It takes rather prodigious efforts for anyone to achieve a level of consciousness in which this fallacy can be recognized, and since most people choose the easy way out, there aren't many who have taken the trouble to make this distinction. Furthermore, once having made it, it's a constant battle with oneself to maintain it. In times of extreme emotional crisis, the effort may become too much, in which case self-pity emerges.

To this I added:

So what do we have to start with? A lot of genetically-programmed emotional responses from our evolutionary heritage plus a fledgling capacity for thought – a dangerous combination, since there is precious little pre-programming to use that capacity or distinguish it from the emotions. We must program ourselves, or effect our own evolution. What we can hope to achieve is a cultivated garden [cf. Jardin!], for which doubt is the primary tool (at least for the initial clearing). Faith is capitulation; the garden goes to weeds.

It occurred to me that whenever the religious people I'd met (and grown up with) launched into an argument to "prove" the existence of their god, they quickly found themselves unwilling to believe in the existence of a bad or evil god (which would make so much more sense, given the barbarity of the Bible or the Koran, or the existence of diseases and barbarity in nature or the state of the world). They would retreat behind statements like "We humble creatures cannot know the mind of God", or "He moves in mysterious ways", or "He will reveal all to us some day, in His time." Life becomes a crooked casino where the house always wins.

I called it *"the zero multiplier"*, because one times zero is always zero, just like a million times zero is always zero. The house wins. Someone's cancer goes into remission. Isn't God wonderful?! Someone else dies of cancer. God the Wonderful has "called them home". One must accept "God cannot be wrong" as the premise, the axiom, the presupposition, in order for religion to make sense! But only then. And there is no evidential basis for the premise. Given x, one might be able to prove y, but why the hell should x be given?

A Sea of Troubles

I was always, and will always be, grateful to Bob for his compassion and concern, while consistently and gently prodding me with his persistent refusal to allow any bullshit I uttered to go uncriticized and unchallenged, because we both understood that *true support <u>demands</u> criticism*, challenging the other person's premises, forcing them to *think*.

Love, however, has little to do with rationality. Bob's continued passion for Kathy, despite her advanced pregnancy and a generation of age difference, was far less intense than mine for Lena, but that may have been a mere quantitative difference. In any case, he felt compelled to take a week out of his limited vacation time and visit her at her home in upstate New York in late September. He was no more capable of perceiving the one-sidedness of his passion for her than I was in my relationship with Lena.

It turned out that Bob was still carrying a torch for another would-be (or might-have-been) relationship. Decades earlier, one of Bob's friends from Rochester NY married a girl named Althea, whom Bob usually called "Jenny", and for whom Bob instantly developed a great passion – that she reciprocated – when he met her in Paris (late 1950s?), *when she was on her honeymoon* (!). According to the few details Bob shared with me about that encounter, a romantically rainy summery Parisian street was involved, and something that would cause Bob on numerous occasions to recite a well-known poem from a little-known English poet named Leigh Hunt (1784–1859):

> *Jenny kiss'd me when we met,*
> *Jumping from the chair she sat in;*
> *Time, you thief, who love to get*
> *Sweets into your list, put that in!*
> *Say I'm weary, say I'm sad,*
> *Say that health and wealth have miss'd me,*
> *Say I'm growing old, but add,*
> *Jenny kiss'd me.*

He could never get through that brief poetry recital without his voice breaking and tears coming to his eyes. He was, beneath his super-rational exterior, a real softie, and I loved him for that too.

Anyway, Althea/Jenny was now living in La Jolla in Southern California. She'd acquired Bob's Binningen address through friends, and wrote to tell him she'd be coming to see him for a day in early October. I suspected that Althea's forthcoming visit might have diverted to her a lot of the not-entirely-welcome attention Bob was paying to Kathy, although I think he might have benefited more from keeping the memory of Althea intact as his One Great True Love rather than updating it with a whole new "reality". Not all loves (or fascinations or infatuations) age well.

Although I'd decided against tackling the roof on the little house until the following spring or summer, there were still lots of things I could do before the cold and darkness would make outdoor work too difficult. One was to continue building up the brick wall above the garage door to its full height, a bit more than a meter above the level of the future garage-roof deck. The wall, at least once it was whitewashed like the rest of the house, would transform the appearance of the house from its partially industrial look to one that looked more like a castle or fortress, at least the long Källargatan façade. I originally thought to have sloping black roof tiles along the top of that wall, but decided it would exaggerate the fortress effect, so I put flat black metal plate there instead, with brackets suitable for holding flower boxes; not many fortresses are fortified with flowers.

On Monday, October 2nd, I was cycling home from an errand at a store at Värnhemstorget. Along my way, as I was passing Jeanette's and my old apartment building on Vårgatan, I saw that a crew of workers were in the process of removing all the balconies from the entire building that we'd once called home. I stopped immediately to have a closer look and struck up a chat with one of the workmen. After the last tenants from all stairways had finally vacated the building, it was now about to be totally refurbished into modern apartments with triple-glazed windows, central heating, an elevator, the whole works. The street entrances to the building (including 4A, our former address) were being walled up and the doors replaced with windows. The new entrance would be through the courtyard around the corner, on Mellangatan. That entrance would entail a new stairway and an elevator. Perhaps the old stairwell from the Vårgatan entrance would give each apartment an extra room? I was dumbfounded at first. Then I realized that the rent for an apartment the size of ours would skyrocket to a level several times what it now cost us to live at the house on Korngatan.

I looked at the growing pile of wrought-iron balcony railings, my mind whirring. Almost immediately I thought of our garage-roof deck (at Korngatan), and how ideal a couple of those railings would be for fencing off the open side towards the yard. I asked the foreman what was going to happen to them. He said they were going to a scrap-iron dealer. I told him I'd lived in the building they were working on a few years before, and how fantastic I thought it would be to have a couple of those railings. Cutting one section in half and welding it to another whole section would give me just the right length for the deck. The foreman told me I could take a couple of sections. I said I was unsure of how to get them home, even though we lived less than a kilometer away. He said that if I could wait until the end of the working day, he'd be happy to throw two or three of them onto the back of his pick-up and drop them off – provided I'd give him 100 kronor, which of course I did. A few hours later the pickup arrived with three sections of the railings (he'd thrown in the third one for good measure). I was thrilled, but I'd have to wait until the following year to install it, because it would involve some rebuilding of the wall....

By this time I'd accumulated a huge pile of rubble from the walls I tore down in the little house, so it was time for the next $10m^3$ dumpster – the first of four more I would fill that autumn. All this heavy work with bricks, mortar and concrete was adding still more muscle to my frame. Several of my favorite Harris Tweed sport coats (from The Emporium) no longer fit me across the shoulders, as well as the sleeves.

Al came to visit us during the first weekend in October, in connection with a business trip he was making to Switzerland and then to England. We had, as usual, a pleasant time. Al always seemed to me to be a little bit more like his old self (his pre-Thursday-Night-Massacre self) when he travelled alone. It felt to me like he laughed more easily and more heartily (especially at my off-color jokes), and he more readily accepted my offer of an after-dinner whisky. I sometimes got the impression that he and Nancy were always trying to "out-holy" each other, but all these "observations" might have been too colored by my fertile imagination reading things into them, or my being too selective in my perceptions. But he also seemed to wish to avoid any controversial topics – the tabasco of conversation – so cordiality won the day over substance, from my perspective; we could always go to the park and play catch with a football.

My meeting at the Falstaff Steakhouse with Leif from Frigoscandia led to frequent phone calls from him about English words and phrases. Then he began making visits to Korngatan to work through draft texts of brochures and other printed matter. His approach was unlike any I'd heard of before. For example, he'd brief his agency on the content of a new brochure, get their draft, bring it to me at Korngatan, I'd edit it or completely rewrite it, then he'd take it back to the agency with "his" changes. Sometimes this procedure would be repeated three, four or five times before he was satisfied. He kept me completely under wraps; neither his agency nor even his colleagues knew of my existence. New and significantly improved versions would just appear from his desk with no explanation. This pattern persisted even after he changed agencies.

Leif was hands-on, to put it mildly, yet he knew what he was doing. Our combined efforts invariably resulted in printed matter that made powerful tools for the sales force, so nobody was complaining. It wasn't long before Leif began asking me to write a few things from scratch (from his briefing) instead of revising the agency's work, even though he eventually had to turn my copy over to the agency for the graphic work and production. He quickly and categorically dismissed every hint I made about the possibility of more direct collaboration between me and the agency. He seemed to be having too much fun with all the behind-the-scenes maneuvering. In the meantime, I was learning a lot about copywriting, so I was also having fun.

On Tuesday, October 16th, after making love, and three and a half months *after* we got engaged (!), Lena suddenly, out of the blue, told me she wouldn't go back to Larry even if he came back – that she would always stay with me!! If she'd said that to me back in January or even February – *before* she said she loved me, *before* we got engaged, *before* she moved in with me – it would have thrilled me beyond words and allayed all my fears. But now, more than two years since she left him, nearly four months after we got engaged and she moved in with me?! Her timing was disturbingly weird. I was dumbfounded. Why on earth would she make that kind of an "announcement" to me at this time? Sleeping dogs, anyone? (Cf. the Monty Python sketch in which a bored pilot in mid-flight announces to the passengers, "*There is no cause for alarm.*")

Wearily, I thought of the opening lines of Schubert's *An die Musik* ("*Du holde Kunst...*"):

> *Oh wondrous art, how often in ashen moments,*
> *When life's wild storms my being have embroiled,*
> *Have you my heart with warmest love ignited,*
> *And taken, borne me to a better world!*

A Sea of Troubles

And borne me to a better world!
[My free translation]

I decided to take refuge in *Jardin* after the longest hiatus I'd ever had from a painting. I'd only finished about a third of it since starting early in the year. With my work on the garage door and wall finished, four dumpsters filled, and no more building work planned until April, plus weeks' worth of hours in my "pot" at Perstorp, I had the time. I could easily have taken a month off from everything else, just to paint, and with the right encouragement I would have finished it, since once I got going, I could paint day and night, unwilling and unable to put my brush down. Indeed, by the end of October I had progressed from one-third to one-half completed. But that brief period of artistic freedom was not to last.

I wrote to Bob in general terms about the frustration of having all one's attempts to communicate misunderstood or misinterpreted. What I didn't tell Bob was that I was beginning to experience a recurring pattern of miscommunication with Lena. I would say X; she would claim that I *meant* Y. I would say that I said X because I *meant* X. She would insist that I *really* meant Y – and then get angry with me for meaning Y, which I'd neither said nor meant. (A simple question – "*Did you mean Y?*" – might have solved this, but it was never asked, nor was I certain that my negation would have been accepted.) I found no defense against this. It was as though I wasn't even part of the conversation, a dummy with a recorded voice programmed to say whatever she didn't want to hear.

She complained that I wasn't pulling my weight around the house (presumably because I was devoting so much time to painting, my "hobby"). I offered to take over as much of the cooking as she wanted. I liked to cook, and a lot of my pupils said (jokingly?) that they came to my home as much for the lunches I made as for the English lessons. Asian-inspired food had become my specialty, as well as a few European dishes. I tended to leave the Swedish home cooking dishes to the Swedes, not because I found the task of making them daunting, but because of the strong ties they have to Swedish traditions, and I was too much of an experimenter or iconoclast, adding spices that "didn't belong" or frying things that Swedes expected to be boiled. So I told Lena I would leave the preparation of Swedish dishes to her, whenever she wanted them.

The most common and most traditional way of preparing potatoes in Sweden was boiling them, which happened to be my *least* favorite. Whenever I tried to make boiled potatoes, I either boiled them too long or not long enough, neither of which would ever be acceptable to a Swede. As a result, I left the preparation of boiled potatoes to Lena. When she left the cooking to me, I made rice instead, or sometimes pasta, or potatoes that were fried or baked or roast. For Lena, having fried or baked potatoes, or rice or pasta, together with meatballs was simply unthinkable. More than that, it was an outright insult; she told me I was an idiot for suggesting it. I said I hadn't meant to suggest it, just that it was what I knew how to make, and that she was more than welcome to boil the potatoes if she wanted them that way instead. That turned her irritation to fury, her voice to a scream. Her eyes flashed with contempt. I didn't know what to say. [*It's unlikely I would have bothered to mention the "boiled-potato dispute" had Lena not continually brought it up over the years, most recently in 2018, claiming that I "hadn't allowed her" to have boiled potatoes...!*]

But I slowly began to realize that there was at least one more thing that could bring Lena's screaming to a screeching halt, besides a knock at the door or the ringing of a phone. All facial displays of rage would vanish at the raising of a camera viewfinder to my eye; her photogenicity admitted no compromise (although it returned in full force and more the instant the camera was lowered).

I wrote to Bob – couched in the discussion of magic thinking and the deleterious effects that physical deprivations like hunger can have on rational thinking – about sexual frustration (without mentioning a word about the sickening frequency of Lena's rejection of me in that department too). But Bob never seemed to pick up these hints, possibly because he didn't want to have to think about them, or just because I failed to confide clearly enough.

During November, Bob was contacted by the widow of a former colleague from Roche, whom Bob always referred to by his last name only, Heusser. The widow, named Carmen, was perhaps a few years older than Bob and was interested in meeting Bob for social conversation, although Bob developed a theory that she was interested in "pursuing" him, carnally, which seemed both to repel and attract him. In spite of only hearing about Carmen from Bob, I was convinced from what he recounted that she was simply lonely and wanted some company. I became his sounding board on what was to become an increasingly emotional topic for him – a role in which I didn't feel terribly comfortable, especially in view of never having met her.

On Monday, December 3rd, I made my first-ever visit to Frigoscandia's futuristic office building on a hillside on the southern edge of Helsingborg. Some of the functions and technical details of the freezers that Leif was asking me to write about pretty much required my having seen some actual industrial food-freezing equipment up close (and preferably in action). Leif asked me arrive there at 12.30. I later realized that the reason for this time was that nearly all the employees would be out to lunch at the company cafeteria, so nobody would wonder who that guy (me) was, so my (actually his) cover wouldn't be blown. The only ones I met were the receptionist and Leif's secretary (with whom I'd spoken on the phone several times). I wasn't sure whether she was one of the ones Leif liked to brag about having banged at his office.

We didn't stay in the office building, but drove down to the company's big workshop facility where they assembled and tested most of their freezers, including a huge circular freezer with a continuous self-stacking spiral belt that looked to me like the world's largest Slinky. There was no question that seeing how it worked made it a hell of a lot easier for me to write glowingly about how it worked for Frigoscandia's customers. (The glowing part was no exaggeration; it *was* pretty amazing.) The company was already taking the frozen food business by storm.

Sometime that autumn, when Lena and I were visiting the Malmö City Theater, we saw a small exhibition of paintings in the foyer. For years, people had been nagging me about exhibiting my work, but because I'd never been terribly interested in selling, and since galleries are business establishments, and thus more (or at least equally) concerned with selling than with displaying, it seemed to me like an irresolvable dilemma, an unsolvable equation, a conundrum. I would have gladly, ecstatically, exhibited at an art museum, but art museums only exhibit works of known artists, and if one has never exhibited at galleries, one remains unknown, which was fine with me, but not with all my naggers. The theater foyer seemed to be an ideal exception: a public place, one where the cultural interest level of visitors might be presumed to be higher than in the average public place – and there was no requirement to sell. So I thought I might look into it.

On Friday, December 7th, I phoned the theater and asked to speak with whomever was in charge of arranging the art exhibitions in the foyer. I was told that it would be the newly appointed theater director himself, a middle-aged Danish man named Holger Reenberg. When he answered the phone, I told him my name and said I'd seen the art exhibitions in the foyer. I added that I was an artist myself, and concluded by saying that I was interested in exhibiting my paintings there if it were possible. He grumbled that their walls were fully booked for exhibitions for at least a year to come. I told him I was in no hurry at all. Then he asked if I had any photos of my work that he could have a look at. I replied that I had them all in an album. He asked me to show it to him at my earliest convenience. I said I could cycle over to the theater with it right away, and be there in 15 minutes or so.

When I arrived, I was directed to his office, where he was seated behind a huge desk. He looked up at me over the rims of his glasses. I explained who I was while handing him my album, and he motioned for me to take a seat opposite him, at his desk. He started turning the pages, slowly, occasionally pausing, his face the picture of deep concentration. When he'd looked through about a third of them, he looked up at me over his glasses again and said, "*Extraordinary! When would you like to exhibit them?*" I was astonished and stuttered, "But you said..." He smiled cryptically, waved his hand dismissively and asked, "*Next month?*" I gulped and said, "How about February?" He nodded and asked, "*How many of these do you have that we can show?*" I'd counted them before and found I had 67 paintings at home (excluding the unfinished *Jardin*, of course). Then he said, "*There's no way we can put up than many on our foyer walls as they are – so we'll have to get our stage manager to put up some extra partition walls throughout the foyer so you can get them all up!*" He stood up smiling and extended his right hand towards me. I didn't dare to stand up too quickly.

CHAPTER 12
The show

Bob had hoped to spend the Christmas holidays with us in Malmö, but his "duty" to be in Garmisch delayed his arrival until December 29th. Consequently, Lena and I spent Christmas alone with Marie-Louise in Barkåkra. I asked Lena about her family's Christmas traditions, and had my suspicions confirmed: I would be served *lutfisk* for the first time in my life.

When I was a boy, Mom – whose grandparents were born in Sweden – frequently told me stories from her childhood home in Des Moines, where her parents spoke Swedish with each other and observed a number of Swedish traditions. On several occasions she spoke of *lutfisk* being served at Christmas. She couldn't mention the word without a shudder and grimace of disgust, although she'd never been obliged to eat it herself. When Jeanette and I were moving to Sweden in 1969, Mom warned me again about this awful dish, but by this time I was in my 20s, and had acquired the ability to take a more critical and selective approach to the things she had warned me about; in quite a few cases I interpreted her warnings as recommendations.

Lutfisk literally means "lye-fish" – because of its chemical preparation. It has a long tradition in Scandinavia (not just Sweden) as a method of preservation of fish (some would say unsuccessful), dating back to the 1400s, whereby certain types of white fish (e.g. cod, ling, etc) caught during the summer are hung out to dry in the wind in order to secure a supply of fish for the Yuletide. Shortly before Christmas, the dried fish are soaked in an alkaline solution of soda (sodium carbonate) and lime (calcium hydroxide) for over a week, then soaked in water to remove those chemicals once they've done their job as preservatives. Finally, the fish are cut into smaller pieces, baked or boiled, and served in a high but perhaps diminishing number (less than half) of Swedish homes on or around Christmas Eve. The Johannisson home was one of them. *Lutfisk* was *de riguer*.

When I taught conversation-based immersion courses in English – only one pupil at a time, sometimes for hours, sometimes days, even a couple of weeks – we covered all kinds of topics, and I generally took the opportunity to ask my pupils what they thought of *lutfisk*. About half of them stated that they abhorred it; some grimaced when they said so, much like my mom had done. The other half stated that they liked or loved it and couldn't dream of Christmas without it. Only a few were indifferent, undecided or neutral. Of those who said they liked or loved it, well over half said it was because of the delicious sauce. Either of a couple of different traditional sauces accompanies *lutfisk*, depending on what part of Sweden one is from. Peas were also included. (I always skipped them – too.) This made me curious. Wouldn't a good sauce with a good fish be preferable to a good sauce with an otherwise disgusting fish?

In the 10 years I'd now lived in Sweden, I'd never had the opportunity to try the stuff, so I was actually looking forward to it – or at least to stilling my curiosity. In Lena's family, *lutfisk* was served in the evening on Christmas Eve, everyone having spent much of the early afternoon stuffing themselves with the traditional dishes of a Swedish Christmas buffet: baked ham (usually made the day before and served cold), multiple varieties of pickled herring, several types of bread, boiled eggs, boiled potatoes, smoked salmon, meatballs, fried *prinskorv* (tiny wieners) and other sausages, a variety of cold cuts, cabbage (white, red, brown or green, depending on which part of Sweden), beet salad, pâtés, Jansson's Temptation (a casserole made with scalloped potatoes, onions, cream and anchovies), as well as numerous things I've forgotten or suppressed. All this is accompanied by beer and schnapps. The meal is rounded off with rice porridge served with jam or fruit sauce, pastries (some served with whipped cream), and lots of candy. Some claim that the alkaline nature of *lutfisk* serves as an antacid to all that has gone before.

The Christmas ambience in Barkåkra was hearty, and all three of us were still a bit stuffed when we sat down to *lutfisk* in the evening. In spite of the none-too-alluring, dishwatery odor, and the exceptional quivering blandness of the appearance, I was determined to keep an open mind, and to give it my best shot. After all, taste is often acquired, certainly so for me with respect to beer, wine, whisky, cognac, certain cheeses, most vegetables – the list is long.

The dish of *lutfisk* was placed on the table before me, as were the sauce and the potatoes. I took some potatoes and sauce. Then I cautiously took an even more cautious portion of the slightly trembling *lutfisk*, noticing its unusual gelatinous consistency. I thought of a casserole made from jellyfish and wallpaper paste. I speared a piece of the *lutfisk* on my fork, added some sauce, put it in my mouth, not knowing what to expect. I didn't gag. Nor did I experience pleasure. I found it edible, in a pinch, but little more than that. I couldn't [*and still can't*] imagine how anyone could claim to *love* it. I finished my portion, but declined seconds.

I did have some extra potatoes (boiled ones at that!) with plenty of sauce; after all, I was almost hungry.

After Christmas, Bob's visit was most enjoyable – certainly so for me – but to my dismay I noticed a further marked decline in his health, which took the form of tremors, stiffness in his hands, and somewhat greater difficulty in walking. He told me that he'd been to a neurologist (he'd chosen to wait and give me this news in person) who confirmed the diagnosis of Parkinson's. Bob was now on medication to help alleviate the symptoms; nothing could be done about the inexorable progress of the deadly disease. Although he was a doctor and well-read on the subject of his latest illness, he seemed surprisingly cheerful about it, or more likely in spite of it. He was by no means in denial about his condition and its ultimately fatal prognosis. Instead, he was looking beyond the initial gloom to the longed-for benefits of early medical retirement, and a number of years of sufficient functionality for him to live a meaningful and rewarding life, which absolutely thrilled him. What an amazing man!

[*It seems so obvious that it should be that way. After all, nobody gets out of here alive. We are all mortal! You can decide to bemoan that fact, and by so doing spoil every chance of enjoyment of what remains of your life. Or you can refuse to let the perfect become the enemy of the good – like Bob.*]

Lena had had a miserable autumn semester teaching in Lund. Early on in the term, a number of the parents of her pupils demanded a special parent-teacher meeting to protest what they felt were Lena's draconian methods of holding tough current events quizzes every week. Some of the pupils were feeling stressed about it. Lena and I thought the parents might have rejoiced that their kids were being stimulated to learn something about what was going on in the world around them besides sitcoms. I joined Lena at this "crisis" meeting to lend my support. It didn't go terribly well, which perhaps I might have suspected, given Lena's difficulty in dealing with almost any form of criticism from any source. The fire was put out, but the embers continued to smolder, and by the end of the term, Lena decided to give her job the heave-ho, and work part-time as a substitute teacher in Malmö instead.

Mom phoned during the Christmas holidays, so she and Lena got to speak for the first time. Following his visit to Korngatan, Al told me he'd spilled the beans, intentionally or not, regarding Lena's and my sleeping arrangements, but Mom made no mention of it. She did mention going to Florida with Ralph and

The show

Maxine, who were now quite serious about moving there. Living in Florida was most emphatically *not* of interest to Mom, but neither was losing the neighbors on whom she was dependent for getting just about anywhere she needed to go.

In January I noticed signs of a distinct thawing in Lena's mood, particularly towards me, which encouraged me greatly. She was less irritable, less inclined to start complaining, bickering, yelling and fighting on an almost daily basis. Maybe her frequent bad moods during the autumn had had nothing to do with me after all, but were only shock waves from her negative work situation? Maybe she was finally starting to love me? One can always hope – and I always did.

At around midday on Friday, February 1st, my sculptor neighbor Fred came by with his small van to help me get my 67 paintings to the theater for the exhibition. A custodian was awaiting our arrival and helped us get them all indoors and up to the spacious foyer, which now, after some frustrations and misunderstandings, included all the free-standing partition screens I needed to be able to hang all my paintings (using both sides of the screens), complementing the walls ordinarily used for exhibits. I had pretty much worked out in my mind where I wanted each painting to go, and the custodian assisted me until everything was set up.

It looked rather impressive to me, but more surreal and weird than real and wonderful. I felt like a shy person entering a nudist colony: out of place, exposed, embarrassed, vulnerable, threatened. But there was no denying that it was exciting as well. Returning home felt awful – our completely bare walls looked so desolate. It no longer felt like home to me. This bare and barren look would be facing me for an entire month. Why was I doing this? Was it just to show that I could?

At least I could now defend myself against accusations that I was refusing to share my work with others, that I was hiding it away where nobody could ever see it. Some 30,000 visitors went to the Malmö City Theater during a typical month, the director told me. Surely that would get off my back the people who claimed I was hiding them from everyone?

Bob was off to London again, his favorite destination after Malmö. I longed to go there again too, but Lena showed no interest in going to big cities with me, no matter how much culture they offered. Sunshine was her thing. And in February, the only choice, the only sunshine certainty, was among the destinations and hotels in the Canary Islands, a five-and-a-half-hour flight away. In fact, shortly after my exhibition got going, she suddenly announced that she wanted us to make another trip there – to the Canaries, for more than two whole weeks this time – right in the middle of my exhibition, from February 8th to the 23rd. I was so eager to please her or appease her in any way, to make this upswing in her mood and attitude towards me a more permanent thing, that I readily agreed to her impulse.

There was no "opening day" for the exhibition. It was, after all, a theater foyer, not an art gallery. But Lena and I went to the theater that Friday anyway, just to see people's reactions. Whenever I saw people going up to the paintings for a closer look, then turning to each other to make knowing comments (or inane ones), it gave me a small thrill. But the big disadvantage was that people had come to the theater to see a play, not paintings, and there was far too little time to see 67 paintings, even for those who arrived early and took full advantage of the intermission. I presumed that I would get no other response than what I was able to overhear, and being in the Canaries for half the time would seriously cut into that. Ultimately it didn't bother me; I wasn't terribly outer-directed (apart from kowtowing to Lena!).

As I wrote to Bob, "*Fortunately, my motivation to paint is not a factor of other people's interest in buying, and I don't find it any great inconvenience to have the studio floor partially occupied by stacks of paintings.*" Then I drew a comparison to the many letters Bob had written to the editors of TIME (only a couple were ever published). "*You express yourself meaningfully, with a certain desire to communicate ideas, and you express yourself well. A response to what you have to say would be gratifying, but you probably realize that none will come. At the same time, the writing itself gives you some measure of satisfaction – a kind of philosophical masturbation.*"

Lena and I had a wonderful and relaxing time in the excruciatingly balmy and numbingly boring Playa del Inglés. The temperature was comfortable, in the lower 20s. Based on my experience from the previous year, I knew better than to try to spend more than a couple of hours a day in the sun. Even Lena was more cautious this time. Lest I become too bored and would want to spend all our time in bed the next time we went on a trip to the sun, Lena bought me a snorkel set for Christmas (had she already known we'd be going in February?!), and in the Canaries I had my first underwater viewing experience since Malibu with Keith Sartorious in 1961. I was wild about it. My mask did not leak.

Mom was already planning to move from her house in Knoxville. She was busy getting rid of possessions, sorting out what furniture to keep or to divest –

without having anything more than a vague idea about where she would be going, beyond that she would like to live "somewhere out West", i.e. closer to John or Al, and thus farther from her sister Maxine and her dependence on Ralph. Since John now lived in Northern California, in an area almost as ill-suited for a person without a car as Knoxville, I urged her to consider Seattle, where the relatively good public transportation network would give her almost as much independent mobility as the Chicago area had once provided. I reminded her that since there were direct flights between Copenhagen and Seattle, the travel time between me and her would be considerably *less* than to Knoxville. And the climate was so much milder. (I also had a strong feeling that John would appreciate my efforts to lobby for Seattle.)

I was surprised to receive a letter that February – in perfect but somewhat antiquated Swedish – from my mom's Aunt Marie, the youngest of my Grandpa Larson's nine siblings, born in 1896. Although I'd only ever met her a few times, most of which were when I was a little boy, I remembered her as by far the most ebullient one in the family, always fun-loving and laughing heartily (she never joined the Meeting). She probably wrote to me on a whim, in order to see whether she could still write in Swedish, which indeed she could. Mom gave her my address and a brief and highly selective update on my life. It was fun to hear from Marie, and I wrote her back (in Swedish, of course). I got one more effervescent letter from that delightful lady, with a check to "buy some flowers for Lena," which I did.

It seemed that Mom couldn't write us a letter without pushing for news of a wedding date, which was becoming a bit irritating to me. Even if Lena and I had started talking about it, surely it was our decision? I wrote her that "marriage is, of course, a somewhat bureaucratic and symbolic confirmation" of two people's love, but has no real effect on the love itself. [*But was I secretly (even to myself) hoping that it* would *have an effect, like a self-fulfilling prophecy?*] I *loved* being married to Jeanette, but I really *hated* our wedding! Lena's resistance to saying she loved me seemed to be fading now, and the idea of marriage was perhaps more attractive to her, but she made it abundantly clear that the church in Barkåkra was the only possible venue. (She loved giving me choices!) I thought I could live with that easily enough, but I shuddered to think what demands for unknown Swedish wedding traditions would start mounting up in one big compulsory pile.

My love for Lena was in fact continuing to grow, and as soon as she stopped shoving me aside so she could go out with others, I became unconditionally monogamous. I'd just heard a new song on the radio, by Billy Joel, called *All for Leyna*, and I couldn't stop humming it to myself. The only part of the lyrics I'd paid attention to were those in the refrain:

> *There's nothing else I can do*
> *'Cause I'm doing it all For Leyna*
> *I don't want anyone new*
> *'Cause I'm living it all For Leyna*
> *There's nothing in it for you*
> *'Cause I'm giving it all to Leyna*

Perhaps I should have paid some attention to the other lyrics as well [*q.v.*]....

My month-long exhibition at the theater came to an end, and on the last day – February 28th – I got a phone call from somebody on the staff at the theater informing me that there was a man there making inquiries about my paintings, and that this man would like to speak with me about buying a few of them if I had time to come to the theater? I said I'd be there in the time it took to cycle from Korngatan, around 15 minutes.

A middle-aged man in a suit was waiting to greet me. He was accompanied by his wife. With an enthusiastically rapacious smile he told me he wanted to buy four of my paintings, and he wanted a good price on them, since after all he was buying *four*. (Was he thinking "Buy two, get one free!" or had he calculated the number of square meters of canvas?) He and his wife had been to the theater every day to see them, he claimed, which was flattering, but I felt mostly alarmed on hearing the word "buy", and I may have turned pale as he was removing his checkbook from the inside breast pocket of his suit. It felt more like he was pulling a gun on me.

But I composed myself and asked which four paintings he was interested in. As soon as he pointed out the first (*The Funeral*), I immediately began to relate the story and the thoughts behind it, what it meant, what its message was, and how it made me feel. He looked annoyed. He clearly didn't want to be bothered with a bunch of details (like what it meant). He gestured dismissively at me and turned to the second (*A Red Horse*) before I'd even finished explaining the title of the first. He interrupted me again and began talking about what a good investment he thought they'd make and how important it was to assure a healthy return on capital nowadays, and how *nice* it was that my paintings would also offer him *nice* decorations in his nice home in the nice meantime.

I froze. I focused my attention entirely on trying to ascertain whether or not this guy was for real. Did he truly think that my motivation for painting, my driving force for putting so much of myself, my soul and my energy into creating these works, was to give him bloody investments and fucking decorations??! He demonstrably had zero interest in what the paintings meant. Was he the kind of person who buys beautifully bound books solely to show off meter after meter of leather spines on his shelves (or buys the leather spines only!) and never reads any of them? If his only real interest in my paintings was to make himself rich some day, then he'd presumably start wishing for my death, because anyone knows that the value of an artist's work tends to rise or soar after his or her death. What a complete asshole!

But I said nothing of that aloud. I only looked at him calmly as he continued to ignore everything I was trying to tell him about my paintings. Then I smiled, interrupted him and said, "I think perhaps you should put your checkbook away for now and think about this a while longer." He looked at me wide-eyed, as if I'd gone mad. (And I *was* mad!) Then he snorted, mumbling something about what a fool I was, put his checkbook away, turned his back on me, grabbed his wife by the arm and the two of them scurried off and left the building. I felt a profound sense of relief. Fred helped me bring my paintings – all of them! – back to Korngatan the next day, and my house became our home once again.

That same weekend, our lovely neighbor Magna Jeppsson died from her brain tumor. She and her husband Gustaf had been so fond of Jeanette and so supportive towards me in my grief. I knew what it felt like to lose a spouse, and began visiting Gustaf regularly to let him talk or be silently with him or just understand that I was one of those who had cared about Magna and also cared about him. He would have a long dark road ahead. Beyond being there for him, all I could offer Gustaf was stamps and my ear. Mom and Bob were both active stamp contributors, but it would take a while before Gustaf could bring himself to haul out his stamp books and philatelic tools.

My trips to Perstorp were now down to about one day a week on average. The infrequency of my presence there put me on the periphery of office politics and the conversations about national politics that had been growing in intensity and dominating the coffee breaks since the autumn, specifically about the national referendum that was to be held on atomic power in March. Sweden's various political parties all took official stances in the debate, despite atomic power not being a truly political issue in the sense of a left-center-right issue. After all, there were countries with right- *and* left-wing governments that were on *both* sides of the nuclear power debate.

As I see it, the only truly political, left-or-right issues are those that ultimately have to do with the distribution of wealth. Nevertheless, *all* laws – even politically benign ones like traffic codes – are made by lawmakers, and lawmakers generally become lawmakers only by first becoming politicians, and their political parties take positions on *all* laws, whether they concern *true* political issues or not. And therein lies the risk that politics will make cowards of them all.

Nearly everyone in Perstorp's personnel and payroll department, where I was formally employed, was right-wing (or in a few cases ultra-right-wing), and thus politically bound to be strongly *for* atomic power. Sweden's anti-nuclear Center Party had only one supporter in the department, a personnel manager named Sören. Everybody knew it, and as the referendum was approaching and the debate was heating up, Sören (who was also one of my pupils from time to time), was becoming more and more ostracized. People – his own colleagues – would stop talking when he entered the room. There were dirty looks. It was acceptable for them to expound their views publically, but not for him. [*I know how that feels!*] Being who I was, during one of our lessons I asked him directly (in English, of course) about the ostracism. He was acutely and painfully aware of what was going on. It spurred me even more to work as much as I could from home, and it spurred him to find another employer in another town far from the Perstorp gossip mill.

Another of my pupils in Perstorp was Tomas, a middle-aged man from the finance department, who was also the mayor of the village of Perstorp (Conservative Party, of course) – and an avid Freemason. During one of our lessons, he told me he was going to be traveling to the US and was intending to visit some Freemasonry lodges, and wanted my help in translating some ceremonial greetings. (He made it clear that I wasn't going to be made privy to any of the secret stuff!) My first mental reaction, while trying to keep a straight face, was "*Don't these people ever grow up?! Didn't they get any secret-agent code rings in their cereal boxes when they were kids!?*" Then, on reflecting on how much power the Freemasons wield in many parts of the world (both now and in Mozart's time and before), it felt scary to realize the juvenile mentality of those wielding it. But I played my cards close to my chest, kept a poker face, played the hand I was dealt, and did the translation. Then I started innocently asking a few questions, like how one becomes a member, and was told that one had to be "suggested". Suddenly he wondered whether *I* would like to be suggested. (He clearly didn't know much about me!) My love of Mozart's *Magic Flute* had spurred me to learn a little about its background and the role of Freemasonry in it. I asked Tomas whether belief in god might be one of the criteria. "Oh, yes, of course!" he exclaimed. "Then it's not for me," I replied, and he looked as if I'd hit him with a dead fish. (I didn't mention any of the other reasons why it wasn't my thing.)

Taking my mom to task for harping at us about marriage paid off at last. The letter from her that arrived on March 11th was for the first time addressed to Stan *and* Lena. In it, she claimed to love Lena *already* – no longer contingent on our being married, or on Lena being cross-examined to determine that she "belonged to the Lord". [*I can only guess that my parents tried their extortion shit with Jeanette because it had worked so well with Nancy.*] And there were no questions at all about if or when we were getting married. I was proud of her. She even wrote a totally non-preachy letter to Bob, which he enjoyed receiving. Could she already be moving away from Maxine in her mind, from that undeclared and unholy "holier-than-thou" competition between the two sisters? I wrote John that if we three brothers were having such a competition, I was pleased to know that I'd be taking the bronze unchallenged – and that I was sure he would *not* be getting the gold. I wondered whether he would see that as a compliment (it was so intended!) or as an insult.

Perhaps my mom felt that all her prayers and efforts to nag us into getting married had paid off, however, because a week later I wrote her that we were planning to marry three months later, on June 20th, at the church in Barkåkra. Lena and I spoke about it with Marie-Louise, and she was *thrilled*. To my relief, Lena said she was also interested in "keeping it simple", which turned out to mean "a lot simpler that she might have been inclined to have it", but not nearly as simple as I might have chosen. No matter. But we were going to do as much as possible ourselves. Lena was going to make her own wedding dress. I was going to make the invitations. I refused to wear a tie (I wore an ascot instead). The ceremony would be short and simple in the church, followed by a dinner in the next-door parish house, followed by a garden party reception at Marie-Louise's place, for which I would construct a temporary plastic roof in case it rained. We'd make an audio tape with all our favorite songs to dance to or to ward off silence, and a large vessel of elderflower punch spiked with wine *"that maketh glad the heart of man"* (Psalm 104:15). It would be low-budget and fun.

Although I no longer felt I had to fear that Mom would make a scene about the drinking and dancing if she came to our wedding, I nevertheless advised her not to. I was careful to explain that it wasn't because we wouldn't want her there, but unlike the other guests, she'd have to make an intercontinental journey, only to find us terribly busy with preparations just before the wedding, then off on our honeymoon shortly afterwards, so wouldn't it make more sense to come and visit us properly when all that chaos had settled? She understood perfectly, and was grateful for our consideration.

Lena and I took the train to Basel to see Bob for a week at Easter (late March-early April). He was happy to see us, and somewhat to my surprise seemed genuinely delighted to hear that we were planning to get married in late June, plus maybe going to come back to Switzerland by car for our honeymoon. Then he announced a huge surprise: as a wedding present (he would not be coming to the wedding due to his increased immobility), he wished to treat us to a week in a lovely vacation apartment in the village of Zuoz in the Engadin Valley in the canton of Grisons/Graubünden in southeastern Switzerland, not too far from the famous resort town of St. Moritz. He'd sent for some brochures about the place and it looked both unpretentious and amazing. It was an old (but fully modernized) two-bedroom farmhouse in the heart of the village, just off the small central square, with a fully equipped modern kitchen. Lena and I were beyond thrilled; we were overwhelmed.

Bob explained that he'd stayed in that village many years ago with Sigrid, and loved it. Mountains rose steeply up on both sides of the fairly narrow, nearly flat, verdant and relatively isolated Engadin Valley, and kept rising above the tree line and right up to the snow level. It was here in this valley, Bob told us, that Switzerland's fourth language – Romansch – was spoken, in seven dialects that were often mutually incomprehensible. Towards one end of the valley lay St. Moritz, the playground of the people whose chief problem in life seemed to consist of the arduous task of finding ways to spend more money, and finding ways to assure themselves of an even bigger slice of the finite pie of the world's resources. At the other end of the valley was Zernez, the gateway to the Swiss National Park.

The show

Lena and I had developed a taste for Alpine hiking the year before near Jungfrau, so this looked like the perfect place to continue. We could take trails up one side of the valley one day, up the other side the next, then the national park – absolutely fabulous. But since we'd then be out all day every day, we wondered whether Bob couldn't consider joining us and reacquaint himself with Zuoz? He could take the other bedroom, and spend the day enjoying the amazing Alpine air and views while reading on the balcony and seeing that we got his money's worth out of the apartment. He could also enjoy the highly scenic ride to and from the Engadin and explore Zuoz on his own. (I hoped he might be able to exorcise any residual troubling memories about his previous stay there with Sigrid as well.) No further persuasion was required.

Our Easter trip to Basel included an excursion for the three of us into Alsace – the Vosges Mountains and Colmar – and, as usual, delicious meals and fine wines. After sounding Bob out about his ever-growing need for shelf space for new books, I took measurements for the new bookcases I would build for him during our summer visit. He was acquiring a dozen or so new books every week; they were piling up everywhere. He usually read at least eight books at a time. He had a good supply of bookmarks.

My anxiety level about Lena's feelings for me was now close to zero. With our wedding in the early planning stages, she seemed to be firmly committed to the idea of *us*. Although many people seem to question professed love in a relationship without *formal* commitment, does it occur to anyone to question whether commitment or marriage can be a *substitute* for love for some people? But Lena did write to my mom, on April 21st, that I was "*...a good life companion for me and I hope that I am for him too.*" I was now convinced that she loved me. Perhaps she'd convinced herself as well.

Lena and I were regularly engaging in more *public* physical activities as well: swimming, jogging and tennis. All this harmony – the major improvement in my relationship with Lena, the wedding plans, the good vibes with Mom, our work situations and finances under control – was giving me tons of energy, some of which I directed at work on the little house. Before starting, I got the name of a new electrician from a neighbor, had him come over to assess the situation, and agreed to give him the job for the little house.

In April I got going in earnest on the downstairs floor, first by removing the last of the old cracked concrete floor, then by filling in the remainder of the walled-off part of the cellar and levelling it out. Before pouring the new concrete,

A Sea of Troubles

however, I put down a thick layer of compact insulation, then a number of electrical conduits, then contacted the electrician to prepare the wiring. But he was unavailable, so I postponed further work on the floor of that room until after our wedding and honeymoon. I did complete the wooden floor above the cellar, so it was again possible to open the door to the little house and walk straight in without having to confront the void and do a balancing act on the joists.

The new-found harmony between Lena and me unfortunately didn't extend to Björn and Isobel; their marriage was clearly on the rocks. Each time we saw them, whether at Korngatan or in Oxie, they seemed to be quarreling all the time, full of contempt for each other. It was ugly and sad to see, and made it hard to understand the sincerity of their congratulations on our forthcoming marriage. Isobel always took so much credit for our relationship (at least when it was going well), when all she could legitimately take credit for was our first meeting, the result of the fluke of her having had Lena as a neighbor and me as a colleague.

Mom had pretty much decided she'd be looking for a condo in the Seattle area, with Al's help, of course. A couple of her old friends lived in that area, and there was a Meeting. But she ran into a major snag. The demand for isolated homes, far outside the already isolated village of Knoxville, Illinois, turned out to be almost non-existent. She would probably have to accept any offer she got, even one far below what she and Dad had paid for the property. She was prepared to do that, but there were still no offers or any kind.

Marie-Louise generously said she wanted to pay for our wedding, but we convinced her to let us pay for half of it. Then my mom said the same thing, so we ended up agreeing on three equal shares. We were planning a tasteful wedding, but by no means an extravagant one; our preliminary total budget was just over $1000.

On April 28th we picked up our marriage license, and the following weekend we went up to Barkåkra to start discussing some of the details together with Marie-Louise. I knew next to nothing about the rituals and traditions of Swedish weddings (I'd never been to one), a fact that became painfully clear once the discussion got going. And my experience from American weddings was pretty negative (except for John and Marj's).

I had to explain a number of differences between Swedish and American weddings to Mom. Unlike in the traditional American wedding, Lena and I would enter the church together; nobody would "give her away". Only the bride receives a wedding ring, but both receive engagement rings (and thus we'd already had those for a year). We wouldn't be having any best man, bridesmaids or ushers; just us, and little Lina as a flower girl. Even though Lena had decided to take my last name, it wasn't an automatic thing in Sweden. Nearly all Swedish couples live together, often for years, before getting married. Tiered wedding cakes were virtually unknown in Sweden. What would Lena's reaction have been if I'd suggested following any or all those American traditions? (Not that I had the slightest inclination to do so!)

It's *not* that I have a problem with traditions *per se*. My problem is with the *imperative* to follow traditions *blindly*, without understanding where they come from, why they still exist, whether they're merely nonsensical commands from the past asserting themselves on the present for reasons that are no longer there, whether they actually bring joy to *per*form or just stress to *con*form. My spontaneous reluctance to subjugate myself automatically to the "sanctity" of anything anyone chose to label a tradition might, in certain circles, have been regarded as enlightened and even enlightening. But thinking for oneself seems to be widely regarded as onerous, defiant, unscrupulous, suspicious and rude. This may account for the utter contempt with which thinking for oneself is frequently greeted, equal to the contempt towards those who fail to follow blindly.

With Lena and her mom planning "we'll do this and then we'll do that, and then that, of course" and me in the background interjecting "why?" over and over, I succeeded in arousing Lena's ire and Marie-Louise's confusion. Remembering my previous wedding experience, I figured that gender equality was off the table and I had better shut up and pretty much do as I was told. But whenever I was unable to suppress my questions (like why married couples could not be seated next to each other at the dinner, which I genuinely could not understand), Lena told me my question was idiotic and strident, while Marie-Louise became embarrassed and nervous at her daughter's tone. Both said it was a *tradition*, supposing that I'd accept that as a valid and complete answer to my question, perhaps only because they knew no other, nor were they interested in finding out where the tradition came from or whether the reasons the tradition got started in the first place had anything whatsoever to do with today's reality. Lena made it clear that I was just being a trouble-maker for asking. But our basic harmony seemed to remain intact.

Over many years, I've tried to discover the origin of that tradition of separating married couples at dinner parties. It has never made much sense to me. One reason (?), I've been told by many, is to assure that the husband and wife will have different conversation partners than those in their daily lives, and will thus meet new people. I call that nonsense! Here's what usually happens: the wife talks to a strange man, the husband talks to a strange woman, and in the car on the way home they relate the stories of these two strangers to each other's total boredom. It's not as if he'd say to the strange woman, "Hey, this was nice, let's do it again sometime!" On the other hand, if a husband and wife were seated together, opposite another couple, and conversed with them, they all might very well find the beginning of a new friendship.

Further digging into the origins of this pointless tradition led me to the only reasonable explanation I've ever found: that it all started among the French aristocracy, when such stratospheric people didn't marry for love, but only to amass fortunes, procreate the requisite heirs to those fortunes, and then live more or less openly with their lovers and mistresses. Having to sit next to one's *spouse* at a dinner would be close to an insult. So people adopt this "*fine*" French tradition from "*fine*" French people and never ask why. Forgive this my digression.

Lena completed her wedding dress by late May on the fairly old sewing machine she'd borrowed from her mother, which gave me an idea for the perfect wedding *and* 30th birthday present for her: a real top-of-the-line zig-zag sewing machine. I had her come with me to the shop to pick it out herself, since I didn't know a bobbin from a hole in the ground. But the prospect of thrilling her made me so excited.

[*Unfortunately, my mind-numbing excitement and love-is-blind enthusiasm for Lena made me totally forget one important step in the plans: getting a pre-nuptial agreement. It never occurred to me, despite reluctantly realizing even then that Lena perhaps didn't love me, that perhaps I conveniently adored her at a time when she felt it urgent to "settle down". This unfortunate and potentially devastating mistake would fortunately be offset by an equal and opposite mistake some years later....*]

Lena's friend Gunilla was going to marry Øivind in Bjärred a week before our wedding. We were invited to theirs. Gunilla came from a relatively wealthy family (who were funding the affair), so their budget was an inverse fraction of ours. We'd exchanged visits with them a number of times, and I found Øivind to be particularly sociable, vivacious and funny. I thought he closely resembled the popular Swedish singer Björn Afzelius (except in his politics). He was also a highly talented and natural musician on the piano and guitar.

I hardly knew anybody at their wedding (nor did Lena know many more very well). To me, their wedding felt so bound by traditions others had invented that it could have been *anyone's* wedding. Øivind told me just beforehand that for the wedding dinner they'd decided to seat me and Lena in close proximity to his elder brother Jan [*have I mentioned that* Jan *is pronounced like* YAWN*?*] and his wife Grete, who were driving down from Oslo for the occasion. Øivind told me he was concerned about Jan's lack of social skills, saying that he had few friends and was painfully introverted. Øivind expressed the hope and desire that I could "draw him out" a bit from his isolation. I found it a strange request, but I was always glad to meet new people, and what Øivind said intrigued me.

Jan was a big, barrel-chested man, with strawberry-blond hair and a ruddy complexion – a stereotypical Viking, except for his somewhat awkward nervousness and a slight stammer that contradicted his potentially intimidating appearance. Grete, with her long dark hair and pale complexion, looked more Irish to me than Norwegian. Her personality was warm and nurturing, but I found it very difficult to understand her Norwegian, which bore no trace at all to Irish (which I wouldn't have understood either). But her handmade traditional Norwegian folk costume gave her all the Norwegian credentials she needed.

When Swedes and Norwegians meet (Danes as well), each generally speaks his or her own language (more slowly and clearly than normally perhaps, particularly if they are genuinely interested in a conversation). But not having grown up with any exposure to those similar yet different languages, I found myself frequently struggling to follow what Jan was saying – and impossible to follow Grete. Fortunately, Jan could speak "Scandinavian" – a kind of hybrid – and he didn't mind occasionally switching to English, which I knew somewhat better.

It quickly became clear – particularly after a few glasses of wine – that Jan was a real Norwegian patriot, proud of expounding on his countrymen's accomplishments. Pursuing this theme to its darker side, after some further glasses of wine, he revealed that he was not at all pleased that his younger brother had chosen to marry a Swede. He also told me that he shared my disdain for royalty. What he would really like would be for both Norway and Sweden to cast off their monarchies and form a new union (Sweden and Norway have been unified several times in their history) to be called the Republic of Scandinavia. I thought it sounded like a superb idea. But in what sounded to me like a complete contradiction of this idea, Jan said he was embittered that Øivind was planning to make Sweden his permanent home, thus forsaking Norway.

I pointed out that I'd also left my native land to settle in Sweden, but he waved away my comment with a bitter laugh. There was no comparison; I hadn't left *Norway*. In spite of his agitation about this, all I had to do was change the subject and Jan's joviality returned in full force, possibly aided by the wine. Perhaps Jan also wanted to find an escape from his endeavor to turn my admiration of The Republic of Scandinavia into full-blown patriotism for a country I hadn't even yet visited. In the meantime, Lena and Grete were carrying on their own conversation and seemed to be getting along well – and also seemed to be amused by how well things were going between Jan and me.

As the party was winding down in the late hours of the evening and night, and a few of the guests were moving about or beginning to leave, Jan told me that they had two young boys back home in Oslo, where he worked as a nurse. All his lifting of heavy patients had contributed to his obvious muscularity, he claimed. Not to be outdone (not on the wine either), I claimed to have acquired some muscles too, from my work on restoring a house. With the unspoken, unthrown gauntlet down (and the guests thinning out considerably), we proceeded to clear the table between us and engaged in arm-wrestling. Jan won (with right arms), to his obvious pride and pleasure; then I won (with left arms), to my equally adolescent joy and his surprise. We continued drinking, began telling jokes, laughing our heads off. The next time Øivind stopped by our table, he hardly recognized his newly (even if temporarily) extroverted brother. Before we parted, Lena and I promised to come up to Oslo sometime to visit our new friends.

Lena and I drove up to Barkåkra a couple of days before our wedding to take care of the final arrangements. I was going to be free from Perstorp for eight consecutive weeks that summer, which pretty well matched Lena's summer vacation as a teacher. All that free time helped to alleviate the stress of our wedding plans, the honeymoon and whatever else we might get up to. Practical preparations for the wedding were largely undertaken by Lena, Marie-Louise and me (they did the arranging, I did the heavy lifting and carrying). Such tasks included setting tables for the wedding dinner, carrying china and glasses from Marie-Louise's house to the parish house, picking and arranging flowers to place on the tables, ordering Lena's bridal bouquet, making place cards for seating, buying food, preparing mushroom-filled *vol-au-vent* for starters (the main course of salmon, new potatoes and sauce was catered) and fresh fruit and ice cream for dessert – polishing silverware, and arranging things for the after-dinner party in Marie-Louise's driveway.

I also designed the invitations and a temporary jerrybuilt plastic canopy (plastic film stretched over a few boards) above the driveway, primarily the part between the main door on the side of Marie-Louise's house and the out-building where Lena and I would be sleeping on our wedding night (literally *sleeping* – Lena *never* allowed any sex at her mother's house, no matter how remote we were from Marie-Louise's not-very-acute-and-uninterested-anyway ears). We also went to the church for a brief rehearsal.

Despite having to marry in a church again, and vowing – to a god I regarded as a human invention and a cruel joke on mankind – that I would love, honor and cherish the woman I *already* loved, honored and cherished, our wedding in Barkåkra was a major improvement over the one at the Church of the Epiphany in San Francisco nearly 14 years earlier, especially in terms of venue. But I was nervous about the symbolic auspiciousness of it all, and thus I remember little about the actual ceremony except trying desperately not to *look* nervous, at least not to faint, and to say the right words at the right time. I wasn't used to saying such words with an audience present. It was like being on a stage with stage fright (yes, I'd zipped up), reciting lines that came from a book and not from my heart, like a show or a charade. But Lena looked absolutely lovely and happy in her white dress, and I considered myself the luckiest and happiest man on earth.

My happy daze continued throughout the dinner in the beautiful old single-storey timber-framed parish house. I remember little about it – almost nothing about eating or drinking, nor how many people were there (30-40?), nor what most of the speeches were about. Some of the guests were total strangers to me. I do recall that both Marie-Louise and Eva made short and heartfelt speeches welcoming me into the family and wishing us a long and happy marriage. One thing that does stand out in my mind was Björn's speech, in which he chose to divulge (or remind us all) of the torch he used to (?) carry for Lena. But what made his speech memorably awful was his apparent need to make several sneering references to his "Irish wife" who was sitting right there, with no place to hide. It wasn't his words that were hurtful; it was his sneering tone. I had seen plenty of signs that their marriage was on the rocks. This was a tasteless public execution.

Following the mid-afternoon dinner, some of the guests dispersed and some – mostly the immediate family and closest friends – continued two doors south to the party at Marie-Louise's home, and the big "punch bowl" I'd made by cutting the top off a 25-liter plastic jeep can that I'd decorated with drawings of festive flowers and wedding motifs. We filled about two-thirds of the decorated plastic "punch bowl" with white wine, elderflower juice and a little vodka. There was music and a little dancing, as well as a little rain, as well as lots of laughter and happy faces of many sizes and ages.

At one point during the festivities, Lena's eldest brother Jan buttonholed me to ask me a question as seriously as he could muster in view of his (and my) intake of the punch. "*Tell me something, Stan,*" he said, trying hard not to laugh, and clearing his throat to try to achieve a tone of something resembling mock fraternal authority. "*You had it all. Already! Why the hell would you want to get married?!*" His question appeared to have the most sobering effect on his own ears, while I could hardly believe mine. I looked closely at him, puzzled. He looked back at me and, as if our different gazes and perspectives had assumed the character of a staring contest, he suddenly broke into a bitter laugh, waved a hand and said, "*Don't mind me! Congratulations!*"

Lena and I stayed in Barkåkra for a day or two after the wedding to help Marie-Louise get her house back in order. She kept saying how happy she was to have me as a son-in-law (*svärson* in Swedish, literally "swear-son", although "son by oath" renders the literal more accurately), a feeling that was entirely mutual and genuine. And she was now my *svärmor*.

When Lena and I drove home to Korngatan to unload a car full of presents, our new neighbors, Bo and Peter, were waiting for us with one of the most fantastic presents of them all. We weren't expecting *any* present from them, let alone an amazing one, since we still didn't know them well. We did know they were textile designers, but when they presented us with an exquisite and colorful 65x45 cm hand-stitched mosaic "quilt" beautifully depicting the front of our home, we were bowled over – by their workmanship, by their exquisite tastefulness, and by their generosity. They must have been working on it for months, and here I thought they'd only been studying our house to get some ideas for restoring their own!

The next day, June 23rd, 1980, was full of newlywed sparkle. We left for Basel in Lena's dark-green Datsun. Like the previous year, we again made a scenic detour through the Black Forest along the way, but we were especially eager to get to Bob's place, because I had a building job to do: more bookcases and cabinets. I'd sent Bob a detailed shopping list for the materials to order from his local lumber supplier, so my work would be literally cut out for me to try to have it all finished in time to leave for our week in Zuoz five days later. Bob was working that first week, so Lena and I were on our own every day, but even though carpentry had to settle for our number-two priority spot, I managed to get it done, to Bob's delight.

The trip to Zuoz through the Alps was spectacular and the weather was sunny and warm, but exhilaratingly fresh. In the higher altitudes at the passes, Bob and Lena pulled on sweaters. As we crossed the Julier Pass and headed down towards Silvaplana, the whole Engadin Valley spread out before us like a bright green velvet ribbon between the mountains, dotted with villages, all the way up to Zernez. Zuoz was one of the smaller villages along the way, about midway between Silvaplana and Zernez.

It was everything Bob had promised, with a few unexpected features. One of these was that among the many bottles lying in a display barrel by the check-out counter at the small and totally unassuming local convenience store, was a bottle of Chateau d'Yquem – and not at any bargain price either. This astonishing juxtaposition led me to guess that we might be in a part of the world where the wealthy came to slum in hand-crafted hiking boots, pre-soiled designer jeans and high-end flannel.

To reach the apartment Bob had rented, we parked in the little town square and walked up a narrow street just off one corner of the square, past small village farmhouses with chickens and cows. There was nothing about the appearance of the building that suggested anything but the most primitive living, but inside, everything was well-appointed, and we quickly noted (with a lot of relief, at least on my part) that the two bedrooms were at opposite ends of the apartment, separated by the open-plan kitchen-dining-living area and the modern bathroom. Most of the walls and most of the furniture were of the local unfinished wood, which had a warm, pleasant sheen. We loved the place, and Bob was visibly relieved that his – and our – expectations had been fulfilled. There was a comfortable armchair where he could sit and read, as well as some comfortable benches outdoors, not far from the apartment, that offered the crisp, fresh mountain air and spectacular views of the mountains and valley without requiring him to walk any further than he could comfortably manage.

Lena and I immediately went out foraging for supplies. In addition to the small grocer's, we found a well-stocked butcher shop and a bakery with mouth-watering fresh breads and rolls. We bought all we'd be needing for meals for two evenings, breakfast, lunch for Bob, and sandwiches and water bottles for Lena and me to take on our first hike the next day. The air was so still, so incredibly pure, and despite the valley's only main road passing right through the heart of the village, there was almost no traffic. Most of the time, except perhaps when cars were passing through, the distant sounds of cowbells could be heard from numerous points along the slopes on both sides of the valley. The idyllic location was as close to magical as any I'd seen, and it was easy to understand why Bob was eager for us to get to know it.

The next day, Lena and I started our first hike, up the western side of the valley from the village. The trail zig-zagged straight up the slope, and after an hour or so, we were feeling exhausted but proud of ourselves, convinced that we'd undertaken something that few could match – until a young family of hikers whizzed right by us, as if they were walking on level ground, laughing and chatting cheerfully. We realized that the Swiss must have some genes we lacked, and we laughed at ourselves. But we continued upwards for quite a while.

Apart from our hike down from Kleine Scheidegg the year before, neither of us had ever undertaken anything like Alpine hiking before. We soon discovered a core principle: when you see the peak of the mountain ahead of you, as soon as you get there, there'll be a new peak beckoning, with another even longer long climb to get there, followed by another, and another, and another. To avoid feeling the discouragement and frustration of Sisyphus and to assure yourself that you've made a little progress, you need to look back down at where you started from time to time. [*This is perhaps not dissimilar to the experience of writing books about one's life?*]

We also realized that we'd brought far too little water in our small backpacks; we were running out, which is not a good thing to do when you're still climbing. So we stopped for a while to rest and just soak up the breathtaking views before heading back down to the village and Bob, fully intending to try a hike up the east side of the valley the next day. Bob claimed to have had a most enjoyable day reading and relaxing. He'd even gone for a short walk around the village.

We woke up aching the next morning, but were determined to work it off by walking it off. The eastern slope of the valley was greener and lusher, with more trees at the lower level. It took about an hour or so of hiking before the aches from yesterday's hike were gone, and we continued on with great enthusiasm – and an improved water supply. As we got higher, there was a lot more space between the trees, which gave us even better views than the day before. It also gave us an appetite, so we sat down under a larch, high above the tree line (as I described it to Lena), to have lunch. She doubled up with laughter at my description of our location. She looked at me with tenderness.

We were *happy*. I felt a release, a profound and exuberant sense of relief and joy flooding over me, as if I'd at last won Lena's heart at last. The long struggle, the long and arduous climb was completed. *She loves me too!!* I was standing on top of the world, wasn't I?

We climbed even higher that day, and didn't feel much pain, but by the time we returned to Zuoz in the late afternoon, our legs were wobbling. That evening we decided to take a break from hiking the next day, and instead took a short tour by car along the valley, so Bob could see something too.

One of the places we visited – to see what the fuss was all about – was the renowned village of St. Moritz. The percentage of luxury cars (Rolls-Royces, Bentleys, Ferraris, Aston-Martins, Lamborghinis, Maseratis, Monteverdis, etc) parked casually along the streets was one clue. The muted but pompous entrances to palatial hotels was another. But there were other, "subtler" clues of the opulence of the super-rich that told a much clearer tale. While the three of us were strolling along one quiet street, looking in shop windows, I spotted in the window of a camera store a Nikon camera that stood out from all others I'd ever seen: the camera house was made of 18-karat gold. Clearly that material added considerably to the weight, as well as making it more likely to cause undesired reflections. But at least it was colossally, vulgarly, obscenely *expensive*, and that was obviously the whole blasted point. And thus the 18K Nikon became for me an ikon of obnoxious wealth, the nutshell of an argument for why the world can indeed afford to do a better job of fighting poverty.

It was hardly the fault of the locals that the world's wealthiest people had discovered that the Engadin was a perfect place for skiing. After all, it has ideal slopes everywhere for the Alpine skiers, as well as a broad flat valley perfect for the cross-country variety – and for landing private jets. Even in the summer it was a grand place for Alpine hiking, with spectacular views one could visit after drooling over the hundreds of millions in one's Swiss bank account. What I found hardest to understand was that so many people seemed to think that this was OK while so many languish in extreme poverty.

Some of those I talked with felt that maybe those fat cats had *earned* it. The dictionary offers two definitions of "earn": (1) to acquire money in return for labor or services; this would not be the case if the actual labor or services in question were being carried out by others; and (2) to deserve rewards or remunerations in return for highly commendable behavior or achievements. It seemed to me that rewards or remunerations that went so far beyond the recipient's needs – at the expense of creating or failing to meet the most basic needs of others – could not reasonably be considered commensurate with commendable behavior. Then there were those who'd *inherited* great wealth and lived totally unproductive lives that contributed nothing to the greater good (are the idle rich and playboys anything more than bums with money?). Or the outright criminals and dictators, who robbed their people for personal greed, or gangsters who lived in withering luxury by exploiting, extorting, and terrorizing others.

I was extremely disgusted and agitated by the whole equation, but I was determined not to let it destroy my ability to take in the magnificence of the mountains and our honeymoon, and in this endeavor I had the help and cooperation of Lena and Bob. The next day, Lena and I decided we'd take our hike a bit further afield. We drove to the other end of the valley, to the small village of Zernez, and onwards to the Swiss national park. The weather was sunny and warm, and most of the time we had the incredible trails all to ourselves – with the exhilarating exceptions of sighting a number of antelope, deer, marmots, and even a couple of *steinbock* (a.k.a. Alpine ibex), the wild Alpine goat that can clamber over just about anything – even the most uneven rocky slopes – as if it were walking on a flat meadow.

Bob seemed to enjoy thoroughly his days of solitude in that magnificent setting, and his evenings in our company listening to accounts of our day's exploits, just as Lena and I enjoyed being alone together in mountain meadows and shady trails, our evenings with Bob and our nights of passion. I couldn't very well tell Bob that I felt loved at last, could I? In any case, Bob's euphoria matched my own. He suggested that we should do this again sometime. When we readily and enthusiastically agreed, he suggested another week in Zuoz the following year, at around the same time. We heartily agreed to that as well.

CHAPTER 13

Landing

After Zuoz and the Engadin, Lena and I spent close to another week with Bob in Basel and Binningen, filling his new bookcase in accordance with his instructions, getting the last of his books and records in order for him, tidying up whatever we hadn't had time to do before Zuoz (including his cellar compartment), and conversing into the early hours of the morning. Bob was now more open and relaxed about discussing his Parkinson's, and being able to talk about it seemed to relax him and better enable him to deal with his apprehension and fear. He told us that he'd be undergoing a thorough review with a neurologist in a few weeks, which was a considerable threshold for him. As a doctor, he said he knew it was imperative. As a member of the human race, he of course realized that he was susceptible to his own psychological defense mechanisms, of which denial is invariably among the most powerful.

The sudden thaw in Zuoz in Lena's manner towards me – no longer holding me at arm's length, no longer recoiling from my love for her, but responding warmly – continued unabated in Binningen for that last week. My joy was boundless. Bob went to bed at around one in the morning, but seldom got up before noon, so Lena and I had the night and morning to ourselves.

We also spent those last days together enjoying good food and wine. One of the wines Bob had picked up – on a hunch – for our visit was a Bordeaux called Chateau du Têrtre, a fairly young 1976 vintage. When we'd each taken our first sip one evening, we all looked at each other, wide-eyed, as a big smile broke out over all three of our faces. "*This* is how wine ought to taste!" we all exclaimed, almost in unison. The next day, Lena and I took the tram to the Markplatz and went to the food department of Globus, where Bob said he'd bought it. We were armed with the heavy-duty two-wheeled shopping cart that Jeanette and I had bought for Bob some years earlier, and tested its capacity to the hilt, coming home with two cases of that incredible wine. We put one of the cases in Bob's cool cellar for him to retrieve a bottle at a time at his convenience. The other case we brought home, even though it put us eight bottles over Sweden's import limit.

We drove home by way of Den Haag again. This time Lena's diamond was ready and waiting for her. The pick-up took around 10 minutes and was undertaken completely without drama or fuss. I didn't even need my black outfit, sunglasses and snarl. The trip home was free of snarling and condescension, and I didn't have a care in the world. When we arrived at the Swedish border, it was raining. The customs officer asked us if we had anything to declare. I told him, "*We have a few extra bottles of wine...*," while he stood there dripping and looked as if he'd *love* an excuse not to have to deal with it, while I casually added, "*...from our honeymoon.*" And he just smiled and waved us on through.

It was at last time to get back to work on the little house, which Lena encouraged me to do, rather than get back to work on *Jardin*, which she didn't. Picking up downstairs where I'd left off for wedding preparations, I persuaded the electrician to spend an hour or two drawing pull wires (or was it pulling draw wires?) through the conduits so I could pour the new concrete for the floor.

A few days later, once the concrete had hardened, I put in the new staircase. Actually, it was an old, steep staircase, one that our neighbor Lennart had ripped out of his renovation project at the house diagonally across Korngatan from ours. It was currently in our garage, awaiting something firm to stand it on. And with the concrete floor now ready, I started putting up studs and insulation, at least once I'd opened up the wall and closed up part of the doorway for the new windows towards the yard. My goal was to have the downstairs finished by Christmas. But the upstairs – including the new roof – was a project for 1981.

Mom was still having house problems of her own, and her desire to leave Knoxville and get on with a new life in the Seattle area was greater than ever. But the sluggish house market persisted, and only a few prospective buyers even bothered to come out to take a look. Of those who did, not one came back for a second look. On the advice of the realtor, she decided to have new siding put on the house in the hope of priming the pump. I tried to encourage her not to lose heart, and reminded her that all it would take was one buyer and she could be out of there.

In other respects, she seemed positive, and she reacted with great pleasure and enthusiasm to my detailed account of our wedding (which included honorable mentions of the champagne toast and the dancing!), and to the photos we sent her. It was often difficult to predict how she would react – whether her response would come from the sword-wielding Evangelist Mom or from my fun-loving Mom – but I sensed she was becoming aware on some level of consciousness that her sword shut doors, whereas the fun and the love would always be openly reciprocated.

Bob's neurologist was reluctant for him to commence taking strong anti-Parkinson's medication. Apparently there was no medication that could treat the disease itself, only the symptoms, and the medication had a few nasty side-effects. But the neurologist's main reason for urging a delay was that the medicine's power to alleviate symptoms would only last for a few years – and the progression of the disease itself would continue unimpeded all the while, underneath the effects of the drugs. There was some "strong stuff" that could then be used, but it came with the risk of even more severe side-effects.

Bob knew that the prognosis was ultimately death, after a long and inexorable decline into debilitation and dementia or derangement. I wondered how it was possible to face such a fate with the profound equanimity Bob always displayed. He told me several times that his work at Roche enabled him to obtain some pills (he never said what they were or where he kept them) that would enable him to "pull the plug" if he felt that the disease was rendering his mind incapable of functioning. He also joined Exit, a Swiss organization that offered legal assisted suicide if and when suffering became permanent and unbearable. He asked me to promise him not to allow him to be placed on life support against his will. I had a clear and chilling memory of when Jeanette made that same request to me, albeit not based on any discernible degenerative physical condition. I understood Bob's request and how he felt and why. I did not oppose him, but I had no clue how or when I might be called upon to act.

None of his contingency plans was in any way related to depression. He was full of enthusiasm for life, bursting with intellectual curiosity, receptive to all the joys of music and any other sources of delight that he could find. He was also exceptionally free from sentimentality, which he abhorred and sought to root out in himself and recognize wherever it turned up. He was determined to suck out every drop he could from however many years might remain of his life, and not waste any of them wondering or bemoaning why there wouldn't be more.

From our first-ever meeting, in Malmö in 1970, when he was in such awful shape, there was something about him that shone through the layers of misery that made me determined to uncover it. What he revealed was an intellectual drive and an encyclopedic mind unlike any I'd ever encountered. His exceptional intellect was matched by a powerful humanistic and humane outlook, free from superstition and sentimentality, full of concern for the human condition and sympathy for his fellow human beings. The fact that we shared an extraordinary background of indoctrination that we had both managed – in different ways and by different paths – to escape, and that we alone among our greater family had landed in Europe (in the two European countries that Americans are most likely to confuse with each other!), only broadened and deepened our mutual spontaneous understanding, cementing a kinship of our souls far stronger than the genes that once led us to meet.

About a year and a half had now elapsed since I began painting *Jardin*, but I hadn't done any work on it for about three months. The large, half-finished canvas stood on the easel in my studio, untouched, a constant reminder of the arduous road I was no longer taking, the road I nevertheless longed to take, needed to take, so as not to lose my way. Although Bob was in so many ways my patron, it was not for him to be my muse. But as my unrivalled *confidant*, he was also my sounding board, particularly in the philosophical underpinnings of my art.

He had of course observed the sea change that *Jardin* (and the paintings leading up to it) represented and was curious as to the direction I thought my future work might be taking, and specifically its relationship to the void. I wrote:[19]

> *I think the void will continue to have a part in my future paintings, as it does in* Jardin, *with a slightly different emphasis, but still the same symbolic content. Earlier paintings had it as something to be discovered, more or less, which I think was necessary for me to do. Now (e.g. in* Jardin*) it is more something to be overcome – but not suppressed. The "basic denial" would be not to paint at all, not to live at all (in the active, conscious sense), to leave the entire canvas empty and black. What is happening in* Jardin *is a conscious creation of non-apathy, a defiant affirmation of life. The <u>living</u> of life is its own counterpole to the void. The consciousness of it makes it affirmation rather than acquiescence, and the awareness of the void raises the level of this consciousness.*
>
> *Despite the overtly positive theme of a painting like* Jardin, *the willful creation of an idyllic garden would be worthy of the cover of a women's magazine if it were not portrayed as a conscious creation of a counterpole to the void. Far from a need to deny, it is a very acute need to create, a conscious need that achieves its consciousness only through a simultaneous consciousness of its antithesis.*
>
> *I think the main difference between the use of the void in my paintings and the use of it in* Unparallel Lines *is that in the former the void serves as a contrast to the subject matter, a frame of reference, but never as a <u>desired</u> goal. The only possible*

---

19 The long quote is compiled from my letters to Bob of August 6, 12, and 19 (1980).

exceptions to this are Competition *(in which void-as-goal provides the satiric edge),* Departure *(but here hardly a desired goal) and* Despair *(but here as an unwitting goal). Perhaps also* Turning, *but here void-as-goal is from the man's point of view. Where the void plays a more active role than simple frame of reference, it is a foe, the bridge to be conquered, in my interpersonal-communications-difficulties paintings (e.g.* Discussion, Hate, The Unexpected Meeting..., Tables for One, Dialogue*). In* UL, *the void is frame of reference and supreme goal, where the other subject matter serves as the background for it. This reallocation of its role was, as you have been able to see, fortunately a temporary aberration. The role the void is now taking in my paintings is, as I have described with reference to* Jardin, *more consciously as the enemy, actively fought through awareness of it as such.*

I suspect that the great majority of Picasso's paintings would also produce a how-can-you-live-with-that reaction were it not for the fact that the world art market has provided the primary answer for most people: investment, thus status symbol, thus the question is rarely asked. The same is true for Francis Bacon (the 20th century painter, not the other one), and certainly for a great number of other painters. Partly because the paintings that attempt to say anything serious stand as a greatly contrasting minority to the general public's view of Art as decoration/illustration, and partly because the general public avoids engaging or being engaged in dialogue beyond the superficial level in any other context, it is not at all surprising that a painting which fairly screams out from far beyond the superficial level to the supposed existence of such a place within the viewer would be met with a how-can-you-live-with-that reaction. They react like small children would to Hennessey X.O. They are thrust into confrontation with levels of which their only previous experience is platitudes, used to keep them out of such levels, and here it doesn't work. Even when my paintings grow on people to the point where they can fully come to terms with them, I get the feeling that they just couldn't have them because they just couldn't do a thing like that to their friends/guests. You get what I mean.

By mid-August, I was back to work at Perstorp and faced a huge backlog of translation work, requiring me to work long hours and even a couple of weekends. Lena had a good new job as a permanent support teacher, going around to various 4th to 6th-grade classes in Malmö where a teacher was needed temporarily, or to help out as an assistant. The ambulatory role freed her from nearly all the planning work she'd had with a class of her own, but there was uncertainty as to where she'd be working from one day to the next. It kept her busy, but she seemed to enjoy it. At mid-term, however, she accepted an offer to take over a 4th-grade of her own in Rosengård.

With Lena and me "safely" married, Mom could now talk of coming to visit us in the spring, and we responded enthusiastically, suggesting that she stay with us for two or three weeks in late May and early June. In late August, with the work to replace the siding on her house underway, she at last got a prospective buyer, which encouraged her a great deal. But the contractor who built the house with the defective siding (supposedly guaranteed) seemed in no hurry to complete the replacement work, so the prospective buyer left for greener pastures and Mom's frustration returned full blast.

I found myself too underwhelmed by lack of support on the home front to get back to *Jardin*. Taking on a challenge like that only to be met by indifference, even on one's home turf, was like climbing a steep hill carrying a 50-kg sack of stones. At the same time, I was too restless to do nothing, and I was still too happy about life to allow frustration to turn into bitterness. I'd been planning to wait to complete the downstairs of the little house until I'd given the little house a new and higher roof, but I realized that would mean rebuilding the upstairs brick wall too, so it could be a good idea to have a structurally sound downstairs wall first.

There had been no windows in the south-facing downstairs wall of the little house (towards the courtyard), only two doors. One was from the old garage into the downstairs room that had been a workshop, the other was the entrance door that led to the stairway. In the latter case, it was "simply" a matter of replacing the old battered door with a Dutch door identical to the others facing the courtyard. Instead of the door to the workshop, I rebuilt most of the brick wall on either side of it, eliminated the door altogether, replacing it with *three* windows along that façade, each with a brick arch. Construction work had proven to be a good way of channeling my creative energy before, and so it was now.

For the first time, however, I began to sense signs of a different kind of problem arising between Lena and me. Too many visitors were lavishing too much praise on me for my work on the house (both the completed work and the ongoing work), and Lena was showing subtle (subconscious?!) signs of envy: irritated looks she couldn't completely hide when guests were clearly impressed by the magnitude of the restoration. She said nothing directly, but she again began to talk about "*your* house", and I would correct her and say "*our home*".

Sometimes, out of the blue (it seemed to me), she would make some reference to "your wife", meaning Jeanette, and I would immediately respond with "*But you're* my wife!" I understood what she said, but I didn't understand what she was getting at, nor what she wanted me to do or say. I therefore tried not to think about it, tried to tell myself it was my imagination, or some kind of paranoia – on *my* part. Then, incongruously, in a letter to my mom on September 22nd, Lena wrote that "…our house is so comfortable and nice." (Go figure!!)

The best news in September was that Bob's neurologist had suggested that Bob start a Parkinson's medication after all, and he was responding well to it. He enjoyed increased mobility, as well as reduced stiffness and tremors, all of which made his spirits – and mine – soar. Another serendipitous side-effect was that Bob was now more open to my arguments that he should allow himself a bit more social life. I pointed out to him that in my experience he always tended to use his prodigious intelligence and knowledge as a resource for others to enjoy, never as a weapon with which to belittle anybody, and that this made him a pleasure for anyone to meet, and he should therefore stop hoarding himself. (I saw no possible parallel to my art; otherwise I would have mentioned it.)

Over the past few months, Bob had spoken of a married couple at work who had invited him to their place several times for a meal. But after two or three times, Bob was reluctant to accept further invitations without inviting them back, and yet he didn't feel at all comfortable about doing that. I insisted that he didn't need to invite them for a meal – he could just say "for a drink". He finally did so in mid-September and gushingly reported having had a wonderful time.

I was, however, greatly surprised when Bob told me he hadn't told anybody but me (and thus Lena) that he had Parkinson's, let alone that he was responding to treatment. I felt certain that most of the people he met would have been able to guess that something in that direction was going on, and I found it difficult to understand that he didn't realize that too, and why he would bother about the charade.

In early October, I got a letter from Al in which he mentioned (to me!!) problems he and Nancy were having with their eldest son, Michael. Al made some vague references to Michael's rebelliousness and questioning of Christianity. Then he expressed the hope that Michael would soon "wake up and discover what an intelligent guy he is." I couldn't help replying that if Michael was questioning Christianity, he'd probably already begun to discover just that. It was a while before I heard from Al again. My prowess as a diplomat knew no limits!

My boss's wife, Gurli, who worked at the head-office switchboard in Perstorp, told Stig that the switchboard had just installed a new device called a telefax, a kind of telecopying machine that enabled documents, drawings, photos – anything not larger than the A4 format – to be sent from one location to another via the phone lines. Stig went up to the switchboard to see for himself, and immediately thought it would be perfect for me and all the translation and text revision work I was doing, much of which tended to be quite urgent, and sometimes had to be sent back and forth via courier. He asked me what I thought, and I instantly saw the potential for further reducing the number of visits I would need to make to Perstorp, always a good thing in my book.

Before the end of the year, I had a fax (only the second such machine in the entire corporation). It was bulky (something like 60x60x40 cm), and it took up to six minutes to send or receive a single page, but six minutes was a lot faster than at least a whole day by post or hours by courier (not to mention the expense), so it was a big improvement.

The autumn rolled by, and Britain's "Iron Lady" – the ultra-conservative Margaret Thatcher, who took the helm as Prime Minister the year before with a successful mission to make the rich richer and the poor poorer – was now being joined in the corridors of power by Ronald Reagan in the US, who was aiming to institutionalize greed (add a ton of spin to get his term for it) in America as well, all backed by the rabidly cheering Moral Majority who were hell-bent on imposing their strict middle-class "Christian values" on the Land of the Free. It was disheartening. Now if they had started with a few of *Christ's* values – caring for the poor, the sick and the elderly – that would have been fine by me. Something seemed to have got lost somewhere between "Christ" and "Christian".

My work on the new room downstairs in the little house was now finished. It had originally been my intention to use it as a more spacious guest room than the tiny room next door (which could be for storage), but Lena wanted to move her piano as well as the black leather sofa into the new room. She'd never played the piano more than a few minutes during the year and a half it had stood in the living room, because she said she felt too self-conscious, since the living room windows (triple-glazed, fairly soundproof) were right on the little street. Although I couldn't see why that should matter, we hired piano movers to come and move the heavy upright piano across the courtyard and into the new room. It wasn't easy for them. The piano had to be raised onto one short end, then simultaneously rotated and tilted to fit in through both doors (one from the courtyard into the entry of the little house, the other from the entry into the new room). It was an extremely tight fit, about 2 (two) cm to spare. But by extraordinary effort and creativity, they made it.

During the first weekend in November, Lena, Marie-Louise and I took the train to Stockholm to visit Jan and Lars and their respective families. We had a great time in Åkersberga with Jan. In the evening, he and I and his teenage son Henrik went down to the basement to play poker and drink whisky (or vice-versa, except that Henrik was too young for the booze), tell an awful lot of jokes, and create strong bonds of friendship. We had lively, raucous debates about politics, he being the true-blue Conservative and I the dark-red Social Democrat, but our differences didn't matter a bit to our friendship, nor did they dampen our laughter. Unfortunately, they didn't dampen our sobriety either, and I ended up having a long conversation on the Great White Telephone, retching my guts out in the early hours. I believe it was the last time I ever allowed myself to get that drunk, so perhaps I learned something from it after all.

In a letter to my mom in late November, Lena told her that she was proud of me for my building work. [*If I'd known she'd written that, I might have found it odd that she <u>never</u> said so to me. I didn't see the letter, which my mom had saved, until I was writing this, in 2017!!*] Instead, I was back to hearing more and more snarling complaints about the ugly way I looked, the awful way I sounded, the disgusting way I smelled, as well as the horrible things I did or failed to do, many of them being the *same* things. [*I believe this was my first damned-if-you-do-damned-if-you-don't experience.*] All of the blissful "Zuoz effect" was gone.

On the last weekend in November, we had a visit from Charlotte and Kent, our friends from Karlshamn. She was a teacher (one of Lena's former classmate-friends from the teachers' college) and Kent was an engineer working for Ericsson. We were just starting to prepare dinner when we discovered that nothing on the stove was getting hot, just slightly warm, and that lamps with 60W bulbs were burning at about 5W – a real brown-out. I went to have a look at the fuse box and when I reached up to check whether the main fuses were properly screwed in, I nearly burnt my fingers. Kent, being a computer engineer who knew a whole lot more about electricity than I did, advised me to phone the power company at once, which I did. (I hadn't even known that they had a 24/7 emergency hotline.) Since it was a Saturday evening, however, I doubted we'd get anyone to come to check it before Monday. Ten minutes later they knocked on our door.

It turned out that the problem I described posed an immediate and clear danger to us and possibly others, and that the electrician who'd done all the wiring in the big house had failed to tighten many of the screws in the outlets, and had even failed to ground the fuse box itself. The guy from the electric company, together with our new electrician who also came running when we called, worked until two o'clock in the morning to check and correct the wiring in every outlet in the house. They told us that our first electrician's shoddy workmanship might have caused a severe electrical fire, among other things, and that the electrician would be cautioned and even risked losing his certification. He had only risked our lives, and the house. They also told us that the first electrician would get their bill.

Just when it seemed to me that Bob might be on the road to breaking his extreme reclusiveness after having explicitly enjoyed a social evening with a couple from work, he suddenly changed his position. He'd apparently spent some days analyzing what had happened that evening and reached the conclusion that nearly all social contact is a form of using people, and role-play, and he doubted he wanted to have anything further to do with it – or with anybody. I challenged him: "'*I enjoyed myself. Why did I enjoy myself? I can find no reason for having enjoyed myself, ergo, I did not enjoy myself.*' Something of this seems to have crept into your analysis of the prospects of further social contact."

Bob felt that the need for role-play prevented him from calling a spade a spade, which was more important to him, but would alienate everyone. I countered that it would only alienate half the people, and that while saying "*You're an asshole!*" would probably alienate most, saying "*That idea is asinine!*" would only alienate those who couldn't or didn't want to see the difference. I told him that social contact needn't be more *meaningful* than walnut ice cream (Bob's favorite), and who the hell cares *why* walnut ice cream tastes good if it brings pleasure?

But I realized that what I'd said could be interpreted as facetious, that social contact is about so much more than bringing pleasure. There were many social situations that I also found distasteful and sought to avoid. For me, most of the distaste involved formality – strict, blind conformity with traditions – and most of the social contacts involving formality also involved groups – the larger the more formal – in which the important thing seemed to be to display one's ability to conform to convention, to cede one's *self* to convention, to avoid "being oneself" at all costs, and thus to avoid all *real* human contact. Such situations seemed to me to be more like contests in playing the affectatious roles stemming from our heritage of some bygone aristocracy's way of dealing with *ennui* and one-upmanship, where anyone who behaves "naturally" is considered coarse, gauche or bizarre.

Landing

Faced with the awkwardness of getting to know another person, many people are more insecure than they would like to be or would like others to realize. Donning the mask of formality by conforming to tradition provides the security of a learned, preset social role or mask – while unfortunately defeating the purpose of getting to know whoever is hiding behind the mask; the only thing one gets to know is how well they are playing the role. No wonder masquerades were so popular for so long in High Society!

Bob opened up this topic by telling me that he was feeling isolated, and was even noticing pangs of loneliness, but was insecure as to how to initiate social contacts, and had thus sought my advice. Now he'd somehow turned it around completely, as if I were trying to convince him to be dissatisfied with his life of solitude, rather than trying to help him solve a problem he'd told me he was experiencing. I reiterated this forcefully, but also told him that *"what you have to offer others in the way of companionship is more than what most people have. Whether you want to offer it or not is your decision."*

Bob arrived on December 20th to spend two weeks with us and was thrilled to see the new, completed room next to the guestroom, downstairs in the little house. He could, in fact, hardly believe his eyes. He was clearly a bit disappointed to see that *Jardin* was still not much more than half finished. I certainly shared that feeling, and was determined, now that there'd be no more building work until April, to get back on track and finish it in the early months of 1981. I felt in some way that I'd been betraying myself – and Jeanette's last wish for me – by having done so little on it for so long.

Lena, Bob, and I drove up to Barkåkra for Christmas Eve, where Jan, Eva and Lina were also spending a couple of days. It was Bob's first exposure to a "real" Swedish Christmas, and a whole list of Swedish Christmas traditions, as opposed to the cherry-picked observance or non-observance (mostly non-) that Jeanette and I had chosen.

On that list was *lutfisk*. This year, however, Marie-Louise apparently felt that she couldn't subject Bob (who could not be presumed to be as immersed in Swedish ways as she'd presumed I was) to *lutfisk* without offering an alternative, so she served boiled cod as well. And thus I at last got to conduct the experiment I'd been hypothesizing about for years: to see which I would find better: a mildly disgusting fish with a good sauce or a reasonably good fish with the same good sauce? The answer was crystal-clear to me after one bite of each. Bob, who tended to like everything he was served, glanced around nervously after taking the first bite of the gelatinous wallpaper paste known as *lutfisk*. He was visibly relieved when Marie-Louise assured him that he needn't finish it.

Despite all my glowing reports to Bob on what a warm and wonderful person Marie-Louise was, it took a personal encounter for him to make a certain instantaneous association that I never could. She reminded him – almost like a *doppelganger* – of our mothers' mother, Bob's beloved *mormor*, who died a few years before I was born, but who had given Bob living and ample proof that our family didn't consist *entirely* of religious lunatics.

During 1980, my work situation at Perstorp had given me even greater freedom. With the emphasis shifting more and more towards translations, writing for external customers, and teaching pupils one-on-one at home, I was now commuting *less* than one day a week, on average. And by being able to accumulate my extra hours to take time off when it suited me, I'd enjoyed 19 weeks off (including my four vacation weeks) in 1980!

My building work had gone well, and Lena and I had had a good wedding and a lovely honeymoon. But my frustration was keeping pace with Lena's growing irritation with me. I'd heard the old jokes about whether one should believe in sex *after* marriage, but they were no longer as funny to me as they used to be. Perhaps my insatiability was my problem only, but it wasn't *my* desire that was changing. And that was becoming a problem.

CHAPTER 14

Clutching for hope

In connection with Perstorp marking the centennial of the company in 1981, they compiled a slim but attractively bound book called *Att göra pengar ur rök* (*Making Money from Smoke*), an illustrated history of the company's development from its humble beginnings under a less-than-humble entrepreneur. I was assigned the task of creating the English version. In my usual manner, I endeavored to understand the content of what I was translating, not just the words.

I've often found that texts can take on lives of their own, and those who write them may be unable to see the words for the trees. [*The possible applicability of this phenomenon to what I am currently writing has in fact occurred to me.*] When I read in the original Swedish text about how the company founder created conditions that brought misery to the workers, who responded by going on strike, and were met with violence and scabs, I felt compelled to consult those who'd given me this assignment as to whether they were certain that this was the kind of material they wanted to include in a book promoting the company's solid foundations. They hadn't thought about it in that light before, and seemed a bit embarrassed to see what they'd written, but concluded that the extra expense of rewriting the already-printed Swedish version would be too exorbitant, and told me just to proceed, as if I were likely to disconnect my brain while making the English version, just because they'd…. *Aw, never mind!*

Perstorp was the epitome of a mill town: a hamlet that grew into a village largely thanks to an eponymous company. It had many of the vestiges of mill-town mentality. A high percentage of the residents were company employees. That figure could be multiplied by around four when all the family members of the employees were counted. Add to that the people (and *their* family members) who worked at the shops, schools, clinics and other peripheral services offered to those who worked at the company. Not many villagers were without some form of relationship to the company.

The company culture tended to be staid. The first company president who was unrelated to the founding family, and the only one to venture outside the narrow restraints of tradition, was Gunnar Wessman (whose role had been hugely downplayed in the book I was translating). Ostracism of mavericks was encouraged, although never officially; people like Sören were obliterated.

But although the corporate culture was wrapped in gray flannel, there were fortunately numerous exceptions as well.

I remained on the outside looking in. As the first corporate employee to telecommute, and someone whose role did not fit anywhere in the hierarchy, I was an anomaly. But I did my job, and I did it well. I was fiercely loyal. I developed my job myself and delivered increasingly more value than they were paying me for and I didn't complain. I got to meet people as individuals, the level at which I find people most open and most interesting, and I enjoyed what I was doing – especially since it gave me so much time to devote to so much else that interested me even more.

In January 1981, I finally got back to painting *Jardin*, after a hiatus of nearly seven months. It was crazy. No painting had ever taken anywhere near this long. During the daytime, when Lena was at work, I was free to concentrate all my efforts on this painting, in my well-lit studio, one of the reasons Jeanette and I bought the house six years earlier. How much had changed since then! It felt like a lifetime ago, and in a very real sense it was exactly that.

I couldn't quite settle into anything remotely like my old Vårgatan painting rhythms, when I'd practically abandoned all considerations of time and space, listened to Bach and forgot hunger, the clock, my clothing and the world around me. But now, if my steam were up when the weekend came, I had to suppress it if Lena wanted me to join her for shopping. If I said I needed to finish a bit more, she would call to me from the foot of the stairs after half an hour, wondering whether I was ready to come shopping *now*?

I would always join her when she insisted, but it began to be important to her that I not only *consented* to do as she wished; she would become irritated if I failed to convince her that I *wanted* to do as she wished, that I preferred to do her bidding above all else. [*I was not conscious of it at the time, but in hindsight I suspect that this was where the first conscious aspects of the gave-her-my-heart-but-she-wanted-my-soul nature of our relationship might have begun; it probably did in me.*] I quickly learned that standing my ground was tantamount to criticizing her, which would not be tolerated. The lack of toleration was expressed by her raising her voice at me, flinging at me accusations of wishing to be "difficult", selfish, hostile. Any attempts on my part to defend myself against such unfounded accusations were met with scorn spiraling rapidly into screams heading in the direction of hysteria. I began to find myself struggling to prevent panic from erupting beneath my feet like toadstools in damp autumnal mulch.

I was desperate to find a solution, and felt I'd first have to find some explanation, some cause. Then she mentioned that she was finding it difficult and disturbing to feel bound to me – to *me* – to the one who would be unable to give her children. And was she to go through life childless, and why had she ever agreed to marry *me*, of all people? Such comments – and they were frequent and escalating in harshness – blew away all the remaining harmony that had at last arisen in Zuoz.

And then that mood would pass, and she would again *accept* my love for her without returning it. These feelings seemed to me to come in waves, swells, following some unseen and unknowable pattern, possibly monthly. I again noticed that her behavior towards me was perceptibly improved in the presence of others – friends, family, neighbors, anyone – so I naturally encouraged us to have an increasingly active social life, as active as possible. The presence of others had become the catalyst that allowed me the only possibility of hearing from her lips any kind words at all about myself.

One day I read (possibly in the *International Herald Tribune*) about vasectomy reversals being performed with an increasing success rate, and it made me gasp. I'd thought a vasectomy was unconditionally permanent. Of course I phoned Bob about it, knowing that if he didn't know already, he would quickly find out through his contacts at Roche. He was surprised, and mostly delighted, to hear of my interest in undergoing such a procedure. If he suspected that it might be an expression of my desperate hope to save our marriage, he concealed his suspicions well. He had, after all, quite a few other things on his mind.

He was again having problems walking, due to his Parkinsonian legs. Having tasted the relative freedom the milder medication gave him for a time, he became more amenable to what he called "the hard stuff". Despite the greater risk of side-effects, he contacted his neurologist on returning home from Malmö. The neurologist agreed that it would be worth trying. The benefits appeared almost immediately, and made him so happy that he booked a trip to London to prowl the bookstores on Charing Cross Road (principally Foyle's and Blackwell's), and to take in as many theatrical performances as he could squeeze in.

He mentioned having heard rumors in the wind at work about a major restructuring of the research organization, and was uncertain about what it might entail for him. What he was hoping for – *deeply,* but with all the restraint he could summon to avoid disappointment – was that he might be offered early retirement in the form of a disability pension. He also mentioned that he'd found out that vasectomy reversals were becoming increasingly common and safe, and that I should probably contact the urology department at our local hospital to find out how the procedure was viewed within Sweden's medical community.

Before doing so, I discussed the whole thing with Lena. I needed to make very sure, before undergoing a surgical procedure with such potentially life-changing consequences, that it was something she also *really* wanted – that she wanted to have *my* child if it turned out to be possible. I also wanted to confirm something that we'd agreed on before (when talking about her brother Jan): that if we got lucky and managed to have a baby, we would *not* begin its life with a lie: we would *not* have it christened. But I didn't need to present arguments; she said she felt the same about it as I did on that particular matter.

By the end of January, my work on *Jardin* was coming along fine, and there were moments – sometimes hours at a time – when I felt like a painter again. I would generally rush about tidying up as soon as Lena left for work in the mornings, then paint furiously all day, and finish in time to get myself deep into translation work before she got home in the afternoon, so it wouldn't be obvious that I had "wasted" my day at my easel. I had by now developed enough skill and acquired enough experience to plow through a translation in a fraction of the time it had once taken me, so nobody was likely to assume that I could accomplish what had once been a full day's work in a couple of late-afternoon hours. I never mentioned my progress on the painting to Lena when she got home from work, and she never looked or noticed.

Even though I was working feverishly and almost furtively on *Jardin*, I hadn't lost sight of the tremendous joy that had inspired it – Voltaire's story of gradually awakening from extreme naiveté to liberation from the superstition of old unfounded beliefs. Candide would probably never change his name, never shake off his predisposition to naiveté, but he had learned to question and to doubt. [*Am I still talking about Candide here…?*] To underscore his underlying nature, I introduced some elements of naivism my painting, in the form of idealized bluebirds and butterflies, and even a bunny half hidden in a field. My optimism was struggling within me – and still prevailing.

The facial expression of the protagonist in *Jardin* (Candide or me – I was my own model) was of paramount importance to the message of my painting (and possibly Voltaire's), which centers on the phenomenon that shrewd people have invented gods (or at least shrewdly exploited gods invented by their innocent forbears), to whom gullible followers are willing to give all credit for everything good that happens and no blame whatsoever for any of the evil that happens, even while those gods clearly don't give a damn what happens to mankind. In *Jardin*, the protagonist is *facing the void with open eyes*, yet he is smiling, even if wanly. How can this be?

Understanding and accepting as reality the totally uncaring mix of objectively random events that we subjectively label "good" or "bad" (and most people seem to prefer to use only one of those two labels, the more accurate continuum of grays being too confusing to handle) that the universe presents to us, empowers us to create our own subjective good. This is a good that brings real and deep joy – not euphoric or ecstatic joy, nor the pseudo-joy that may arise from the abnegation of the need for evidential legitimacy. But because even a temporary, open-eyed victory over the odds stacked against mankind by the uncaring universe brings greater permanent value than blind faith in the good will and benevolence of a conjured-up "divine" force that is so self-evidently misplaced. Shit still happens and will most likely always happen. One can be *wrong*, time after time, but being wrong is how one *learns*, and being wrong is no reason to resign. On the contrary, it's a call to roll up one's sleeves and fight self-pity, resist cynicism, struggle and forge whatever good can be forged, to become the engineer of one's own spirit, however temporary the good may be, like life itself. What the protagonist in *Jardin* is cultivating is no selfish act, but is on a scope that goes far beyond his own needs, because *creating value for others – even when others are unknown and/or nowhere in sight – gives a fruitful landscape of the mind and the heart.*

In retrospect, it seems odd that Lena and I invited Björn and Isobel to our place to try to talk some sense into them about the imminent break-up of *their* marriage. We made no progress at all, however; hostility towards each other seemed to be all they had in common, even though little Patrick was sitting there looking confused and forgotten.

Al and Nancy also seemed to be clutching for hope regarding their rebellious son Michael, and expressed interest in sending him to stay with us for a month in the summer, ostensibly to help me with the rebuilding of the little house. Although I was interested in helping them all – Michael with channeling his rebellion into something constructive, and his parents with some anxiety relief – I was also wary of accepting the guardianship of someone I didn't know that well (not at all, to be honest), and who might see coming to Sweden as a jumping-off point for things I couldn't handle. I wrote Michael a lengthy letter outlining what ground rules would apply (e.g. absolutely no drugs). His interest in coming here faded quickly, whether coincidentally or as a reaction to my list of restrictions.

I got a letter from my brother John who, in response to some direct questions from me, expounded upon his feelings of revulsion for the popular televangelist Jerry Falwell, and John's view that the so-called Moral Majority had little to do with what John considered moral. I felt relieved, and hoped that this might be an indication that he was beginning to question more than he'd ever dared to question before.

For Sweden's "winter sport holiday" in the second half of February, when schools are closed for a week to enable skiers and other winter sport enthusiasts to hit the slopes and rinks and trails, Lena and I took an overnight boat from Copenhagen to Oslo to stay with Øivind's brother Jan, his wife Grete, and their two boys Preben and Carl-Victor. Øivind and Gunilla were also going to Oslo for that week, by car, and would be staying with Jan and Øivind's parents. Lena and I would return to Malmö by car with Øivind and Gunilla.

It being February, most of the 16-hour boat trip took place in darkness, but in the late dawn the next morning, cruising into the Oslo fjord was a stunning sight, with the bright snowy city stretched out like crystals falling over the steep hills that plunged into the dark and undulating icy shoreline. Towards the top of one of these hills, towards the west, rose the graceful sweep of the landmark Holmenkollen ski jump.

Jan, looking so much more the Viking now that he had the proper winter attire to fulfil the stereotype, met us at the ferry terminal in his little Fiat, to take us up to his family's apartment on Olav Aukrusts vei, not far from that landmark.

I felt immediate and strong rapport with Preben and Carl-Victor, six and three years old respectively. I'd always loved clowning around with kids, letting loose the kid that continued to reside in me, since I'd never been fully persuaded it was necessary to force it into submission or oblivion. I could hardly understand a word the boys said in Norwegian, and had to frequently consult Jan for help. It wasn't long before my head was spinning. I found Norwegian tantalizingly similar to Swedish, but there was always a time-lag between when they said something and when I figured out what it meant. That alone would have been tiring mentally. But the Norwegian intonation, with its sharply rising tone at the end of a sentence, made even the most banal statement sound like to my ears the world's greatest, most alarming surprise. "*The milk is on the TABLE!!!*" made me jump, only to find that the next casual observation carried the same terrifying weight. And the next, and the next. Even banalities can be exhausting when they are expressed as serial alarms.

Øivind had warned me that Jan was a stern disciplinarian towards his kids; we only noticed that they were extremely well-behaved at the dinner table, and that he never had to tell them twice to do anything. It never penetrated my naiveté that the kids might in any way be suffering under despotic rule. Whenever I made them laugh, which was not infrequently, Jan only smiled tersely and impatiently, as if I were frivolously interrupting something having a graver dignity than I could comprehend.

As the elder of the two boys, Preben probably had to bear the full brunt of the insecure desires of his first-time father to mold the behavior of his offspring, which may have accounted for his added shyness and flinching obedience to his father. Carl-Victor couldn't walk; he could only run. Even if he was in no particular hurry to get anywhere, or hadn't even yet decided where he was going, he always ran there, as if escaping from some unseen explosion. The two boys were so endearingly sweet; perhaps there were other reasons for my willingness to reconsider my aversion to parenthood?

Grete was the one to whom the boys always turned for comfort, never Jan. But Jan and I got along well. He took us all on the tram to Vigelands Park in central Oslo, full of the works of the eponymous Norwegian sculptor (very impressive, but in a style that was a bit too heroic for my taste), and I began clowning around with the sculptures, getting Jan to pose with me to mimic some of them, to the delight of the boys.

Coming to Norway in the winter invariably involves skiing. The Holmenkollen ski-jump tower that identifies Oslo from afar also identifies the Norwegian mind. They all (including the kids) seemed to be good skiers – experts by most other nations' standards. (Some have claimed that Norwegians are born on skis; even the trams in Oslo are fitted with ski racks.) I was the only total novice in our group; in fact, although I was pretty athletic, I'd never had an occasion to stand on a pair of skis in my entire life. And we were all going to Holmenkollen, which was not only a spectacular ski jump, but a complete ski center. There were a couple of slalom and downhill runs – infinitely beyond the skills of a novice like me They were, in fact, designed and built for the world's top-notch skiers. Instead, I was told we'd be taking the cross-country trail. I pictured a nearly flat course on which I could learn to balance and propel myself forward, at my own pace.

The Holmenkollen cross-country course was nothing like that. My first-ever experience on skis was on what I was certain was one of the world's toughest courses. The tracks were deep ruts – well prepared with ice – on steep hills (OK, not as steep as the downhill or the ski-jump), with sharp curves, and full of disciplined, high-speed Norwegian experts. After giving me a three-minute lesson on how to stand up on my skis and move slowly forward, Jan and Øivind apparently felt that I was ready for the world's most terrifying cross-country course. They guided me to the starting point, got my wobbling legs and hostile skis deep into a pair of icy ruts, without ever having assured themselves (or me) that I could do anything at all about things like slowing down, stopping, turning, changing ruts, or meeting the challenges resulting from coming to the bottom of one slope and finding that gravity was no longer pushing me forward twenty-seven times faster than I wanted to go but was now trying to push me over backwards instead.

On the first part of the first downhill stretch, I managed to retain my balance initially, but my concern was growing as fast as my speed. There was a stranger on the course ahead of me, a *Norwegian* stranger, going nowhere nearly as fast as the speed I had now attained. And he was in *my* ruts! Somewhere in the rushing wind in my ears I heard Jan and Øivind shouting at me to *Change TRACKS!!* but I was completely unable to lift my ski-outfitted leg out of the rut I was in. I ended up having to throw myself to the side, into a snow bank, so as not to run my skis up the Achilles tendons of the Norwegian skier ahead of me. When I crashed into the snow bank directly behind him, I thought I caught a glimpse of him looking indifferently over his shoulder, then skiing on with a slight shrug at the commotion I was making behind him.

The course went on and on, down and down, faster and faster. Every time the tracks turned, I couldn't. I went rushing straight ahead and crashed (or threw myself) into the next snow bank. (I hoped for left turns only, so I could crash into the snow bank without first crossing the other tracks.) At last we reached the bottom and were going to start heading back – *up, steeply up* – on skis, in icy ruts. I understood the gravity of the situation. Except that now, when there was no other option, Jan and Øivind thought now – with me struggling frantically not to slide rapidly backwards – would be the proper time to give me a lesson in climbing a hill. "*Never keep your skis straight or you'll just slide back down!*" they intoned solemnly. "*And never cross your skis!*" they said even greater emphasis, as if *my* skis had the slightest intention of *ever* doing anything I might want them to. I was told to have them wide apart, like a duck's feet, and use my poles to help out. And after showing me how it's done, they were off. As soon as I tried sticking my left ski out on an angle, the back end of it came to rest on top of the back end of my right ski, so that when I tried to angle out my right ski, I fell down. *"Don't cross your skis!"* Jan and Øivind shouted back helpfully.

I ended up placing my skis firmly into the ruts, bearing down with all my might on my poles, and *thrusting* myself up that goddamn hill on pure arm strength, in rapid-fire bursts of adrenalin-fed energy that ran out – completely – the moment I reached the summit. Both Jan and Øivind said they'd never seen anybody climb that hill with straight skis. They made this observation with no more admiration than if I'd managed to open a tin can with my teeth just because I couldn't figure out how to work a damn can opener.

The next morning I was bruised and aching all over, but instead of Holmenkollen, we all headed out in two cars to Jan and Grete's cabin in the mountains in Norefjell, a few hours' drive northwest of Oslo. Their place was a small, beautiful, rather primitive log cabin with fabulous views of the old, snow-covered, rolling Norwegian mountains. There were many similar cabins sparsely distributed over the mountainside, all seemingly positioned so as to give each one both privacy and unrestricted views. Our primary business in being there was to ski.

This time, however, there were no steep slopes and no icy ruts, just breathtakingly beautiful pure white powder flowing over gently undulating ground as far as you could see in every direction. We spent most of the daylight hours out there on skis, and I didn't fall once.

Jan and Øivind's parents, it turned out, were strict, straight-laced, old-school religious people. This clearly had an impact on their sons, who got about as strict an upbringing as a more fanatical offshoot of the Norwegian State Church (also Lutheran) could offer. I never saw their father smile. He reminded me of my dad's father, except that Jan and Øivind's father hardly ever said a word in my presence, so I was unable to ascertain any comparable predilection for pontification. Perhaps Jan's father had treated Jan with similar stern discipline to what Øivind claimed Jan was doing to his sons? Was the fact that Jan and Øivind were as different from each other as Preben and Carl-Victor just a coincidence? The family was also marked by political conservatism, which had also rubbed off. Jan told me that he'd undergone several rounds of molting to arrive at the conclusion some years earlier that if there were a god, He would have to be a sadist. Beyond that, Jan generally avoided discussing politics or religion with me. But the seed of strong friendship had germinated and was sprouting well.

It was clear to me that there was no love lost between Jan and his new sister-in-law. It was also clear that Jan and Øivind competed fiercely with each other in everything they could: homes, careers, stereos, skiing. One area they didn't seem to compete in was music, which I mentioned to Øivind in the car on the way home to Sweden. I knew that Øivind was one of those lucky people who are musically gifted and can sit down at a piano and make it sing any song they want to, in any key and tempo and style. Jan didn't even have a piano. Øivind snorted in surprise. *"Jan is a <u>much</u> better musician than me – he could have been a professional pianist!"* I asked Øivind why Jan never played. *"Because he's a perfectionist! He'd rather not play at all if he can't be the best in the world!"* I thought of Voltaire.

When I phoned the urology department at the Malmö hospital, I was connected to a surgeon named Sverker Hellsten. I got an appointment to see him on March 12th, to discuss the possibility of a vasectomy reversal operation. He told me that he and a colleague of his, Bo Husberg, had been interested in trying out some new microsurgical equipment that he felt would enable them to perform a successful operation of this kind.

First I had to provide some semen samples to make sure I needed such an operation, and not just more sex. (I *always* needed more sex, while Lena appeared not to, but I said nothing about that.) And since she was rejecting me more frequently than ever, causing me increasing problems with frustration and anxiety, I'd often been obliged to take matters into my own hands. I was thus well accustomed to the procedure for providing semen samples. I was also a curious person, so I purchased a microscope to be able to look for sperm cells myself, both before and as soon as possible after the operation (scheduled for April 23rd), so as not to have to wait on tenterhooks or any other kind of hooks to get the answer.

On Saturday, March 14th, at four o'clock in the morning, I finished *Mais Il Faut Cultiver Notre Jardin*, some 26 months after having started it, and after a 20-hour non-stop final push through the ambient disapproval. I was exhausted, thrilled, drained, hopeful and desperate. It was the only painting I'd made during that entire 26-month period. On completing it, I again reflected on a thought

I'd had many times during the arduous process: if I'd made my livelihood dependent on selling my work, *I could never have afforded to paint* Jardin*!* Would anyone be prepared to pay a price equivalent to more than two years' salary for a single painting by a not-very-productive artist, even if I hadn't been completely unknown?! Not bloody likely!

Lena seemed relieved that it was over (for far different reasons than I was!), but said nothing about the result. A couple of weeks later, she grimaced as I enthusiastically hung it up on our living room wall. She expressed no congratulations. Bob was all the more enthusiastic about the prospect of seeing it at Easter, the time of his next scheduled visit to see us.

At the end of March, Bob received notice – or confirmation of what he suspected and hoped – that he was going to be placed on disability pension, officially effective four months later. He was not yet 53 years old. He had a progressive, debilitating, and ultimately fatal disease. Yet he was thrilled, and would have been even more thrilled had he known that he would have 18 more years to live, all but the 18th of which would be filled with his beloved books and music, and intellectual stimulation of a degree that few are endowed with the capacity to enjoy. And I was thrilled to have more time left with him, more than either of us dared to expect, during which to develop our singular friendship so much further.

Certain circumstances at Perstorp gave me the opportunity to point out to one of the company's directors that some of the company's "English" brochures were glaringly sub-standard, and that this was painfully embarrassing for the company. I backed up my claim, of course, with numerous examples from the printed matter in question. He promised to take it up with the various department heads, which might mean opening floodgates of additional work for me. It wasn't that I was looking for more work; I really was thinking of the best interests of the company and its communications to the marketplace. There was an added benefit for me: the fact that my textual work could all be done from home, which might bring me nearer my goal of not having to travel to Perstorp *at all*.

Lena and I continued to exchange social visits with Henry and Elsa Carlsson, and Henry pursued his English lessons with me, now with a bit greater urgency due to a forthcoming work-related trip to the US. As before, I welcomed any and all social life, as Lena's level of disdain for me (whether conscious or not) was rising by the month, and thus the contrast between her increasingly distressing attitude towards me when nobody else was present, and the sweet charm she turned on to showcase for others feelings towards me that I rarely saw glimpses of when we were alone. [*Pardon my belaboring this point; it certainly was belaboring me!*]

Correspondence with Al revealed his ongoing desperation concerning what to do about Michael; and Bob – responding to my accounts of our correspondence from a base of his own direct experience with his brutal father and indirect experience of the brutality of his brother towards his boys – found it hard to understand why I seemed to be defending Al by responding to him more gently than Bob felt the situation called for. I told Bob that I wasn't defending Al's actions and the indoctrination of Michael's upbringing, but was trying to understand Al and where he was coming from, including the tragedy of the Thursday Night Massacre. I wrote to Bob that "*I have always cared for him [Al] a great deal and felt sorry for him since I was 16,*" which was why I didn't see any benefit to jumping all over him in a crisis, and making him even more defensive.

Although I had some other ideas for paintings, a couple of them sketched out in charcoal on the already-stretched canvases, I was so artistically debilitated by Lena's total lack of support for my work – and still nary a comment from her on *Jardin*! – that I could hardly bring myself to face the empty easel in my studio. That entire room, the largest in the house, was a constant reminder to me of the difficulty of pursuing my vocation further, like trying to thread a needle while falling from a diving board.

In lieu of painting, I again turned my attention and energy to the little house. I ripped out all the wallboard upstairs (there was no insulation to remove) to prepare for the huge summer project of replacing the roof. The amount of rubble was again enough to fill up the yard, which was still mostly covered by the cracked concrete slab that used to constitute the original garage floor. It had been convenient to leave that slab intact for the time being, since it greatly facilitated collecting, sorting, and removing all the new rubble, one wheelbarrow at a time, to the continuing series of dumpsters that were frequently parked on the sidewalk outside our garage door. I was fortunately able to bury myself in that kind of work.

At least Bob was going to spend eight days with us at Easter. He arrived on Saturday, April 11th. On entering our home, he immediately turned right, into the living room, to gaze at *Jardin*. He stood there for several minutes, peering, squinting, scrutinizing, occasionally leaning forward to catch some detail, occasionally shaking his head in amazement. Lena watched his concentration briefly, then left the room without comment.

Bob and I spent a lot of time at the window in the living room nearest the front door, talking and playing chess at a small round oak chess table (about 60 cm in diameter) that Marie-Louise no longer wanted in her home. The table had a wooden intarsia chessboard and a glass cover. Lena wasn't interested in chess, but preferred to sew and read. She sometimes sat in the living room with us, sometimes upstairs. One day she told me she found the English-speaking atmosphere uncomfortable, which surprised me. She'd told me before that a few years earlier she'd spoken mostly English with Larry, her American ex-fiancé, and had no problem with it. Bob gave no indication that he'd sensed any discord.

Two days after Bob's departure, I went for a pre-op examination at the hospital, then went back two days later for the operation itself. My surgeon briefed me on what would happen. He also told me it would be the first-ever vasectomy-reversal operation using microsurgery to be performed in Sweden. They were going to reconnect just one of the vas deferens, and then wait some months before deciding whether they needed to reconnect the other. I hadn't been expecting a "monoballular" approach, but they seemed to know what they were doing, or at least they knew what they were intending to do.

The only painful part of the operation itself was getting the spinal anesthetic (it felt like my back was being broken). Lying still for 44 hours post-op was difficult for me, and after the anesthetic wore off, the feeling of having been kicked in the groin was unpleasant. But I tried to maintain a positive attitude, grit my teeth and persevere. Another indirectly painful aspect was that a few weeks after my operation, Lena was obliged to get a rubella vaccination. My doctors advised this, just in case she got pregnant sooner than expected after my operation. And since the vaccination itself produced all the symptoms of the disease, we were advised against having unprotected sex for two months. Lena seemed not to have heard the word "unprotected" in that piece of advice.

In late April, just before her first trip to see us in Sweden, Mom finally sold her house in Knoxville, to her great relief and joy. We had a wonderful, exasperating, humorous, loving three weeks with her, except at the outset, when we had to prevent her from her spontaneous inclinations to manipulate. Lena and I had wine with every dinner (normally we might have had wine only on weekends), and we watched the news on TV afterwards. Some of the news reports were in

English (with Swedish subtitles), which Mom was able to follow. One report in Swedish involved an interview with Sweden's Minister of Industry, Nils G. Åsling. When Mom saw him she gasped audibly; his resemblance to Dad was striking, almost uncanny.

The first evening she was with us, the news was followed at eight o'clock by *The Onedin Line*, a British TV series about a family-owned shipping company in the 1860s. Lena and I had been following the series, and since it was in English, I saw no reason to turn off the TV. At first, Mom watched it with apparent interest, until a verbal altercation at quarter past eight caused the main character, Captain James Onedin, to burst out, "*Damn you!*", whereupon Mom shot straight up from her seat and stood there glaring back and forth at Lena and me. I knew what was going on: a none-too-subtle attempt to make me turn off the TV. But I did nothing. Then she announced that she was going straight to bed. I calmly asked if she was tired. "Well, no," she sputtered, "but I didn't raise you to watch such filth!" I told her I didn't consider it filth, but an interesting dramatization of a historical period from around the time her grandparents had emigrated from Sweden to America. Then I wished her a good night's sleep, told her I understood that she might be feeling some jetlag, gave her a hug, and let her huff off to the guestroom in the little house.

Her first comment about *Jardin*, which dominated one wall of the living room, was that she liked *that* painting, that it was "nice". Since nobody calls my paintings "nice" and gets away with it, I later had occasion to tell her where I got the idea. Apparently "Voltaire" was a real buzzword for her, because as soon as I mentioned his name, her face dropped like a lead balloon, she hurriedly looked away and hardly even glanced at *Jardin* again during her stay, or at least not when I was present.

When she began telling me that this or that Meeting person had asked her to send me their "love", I wasn't having it. Some of them were people whose names gave me zero association with a face. None of them knew me at all, not ever having seen me for at least 15-20 years, and they certainly didn't love me. I told Mom I didn't believe they could reasonably claim to love someone they didn't know, and that it was far from certain they would love me if they did. I said she could send them my regards for *her* sake, but *not* my love. She replied, "*Do you have peanut butter in Sweden?*" [*Changing a subject that had become uncomfortable, and changing it so abruptly that your eyebrows might fly off, was one of Mom's characteristic behaviors. She mastered it like nobody else I've ever met.*]

Clutching for hope

During her visit, she surprised me by pulling off her engagement/wedding ring (she'd had them soldered together years before), and said that now that she was a widow, she'd love to give it to "Stan's loving wife". That gave me some mixed feelings, but I told Lena and she seemed happy to wear it.

One day we took a drive up to visit Marie-Louise in Barkåkra for the day. Mom concurred with Bob's impression of Marie-Louise's resemblance (in looks and demeanor) to my *Mormor*. Apart from the minor conflicts during the first days of her stay, her three weeks with us were far less conflict-filled than any others had been for quite some time, since Lena's insults and screaming at me were suspended throughout her stay, and I was happy. But Mom seemed so lonely, frightened, confused and insecure about all the disorienting aspects of her forthcoming move and the new people she would be meeting. I felt genuinely sorry for her and was sad to see her go.

As soon as she left (May 30th), I got to work on the long southern upstairs wall of the little house, facing the yard and garage roof. After getting the lengths of the balcony railing from Vårgatan cut to size and welded by Gert, our neighbor, I drilled three holes in the wall of the big house in which to insert one end of the completed railing. Then I removed the half-rotten window in the wall of the little house, even with the edge of the garage roof, and with the other end of the railing propped up in the window opening, I walled it up, thus walling in the other three free ends of the railing. (I'd picked up several thousand more free bricks during the spring from demolition sites, to be prepared for the big roof-raising project.) Now that the railing had given us a garage roof without a precipice, I was basically ready to tackle the existing rotten roof of the little house when we got home from Switzerland in the first half of July.

I was hoping that Lena and I could find some of the magic that our honeymoon trip to Basel and Zuoz provided the year before, and maybe give Lena some of the feelings of something close enough to love for me that I could believe. It wouldn't, however, be the same cozy car trip. The main gasket in the Datsun had blown, and although Saabye fixed it before out trip, we didn't trust it on a trip through Germany and into the Alps, so we took the train on June 21st instead.

Bob was effervescent about some news he'd just received: it was now official that he'd retire at the end of July. He'd booked another week for the three of us at the same apartment in Zuoz, and we drove there in his little Renault instead (he finally let me drive it). Now that the mountains were less of a mystery to us, Lena and I undertook somewhat more adventurous hiking, even crossing a glacier at a higher altitude. It was incredibly beautiful, and we saw so many wild animals that we lost count. Lena was in high spirits and unusually affectionate towards me; I was once again sitting on top of the world. Our week in Basel getting Bob's apartment ship-shape was also relaxed and fun, and included a few more outings to Alsace and some additional attractions near Basel.

To my surprise, Lena wrote Bob a lengthy and friendly letter on our return home by train. She told him about my mom having written from the Puget Sound area, but made no direct reference to a new place. She did write about the death of Harry Hayhoe, one of the real patriarchs of the Meeting, whose demise Lena described to Bob as having "gone to that great Meeting Room in the sky"! Mom wrote in her next letter about finding it difficult to settle in – that her temporary accommodations with Al and Nancy felt like a motel. The apartment hunt was on, and it would be the first time she'd lived in anything but a house (except for a couple of short, temporary, transitional stints in apartments) since she was a newlywed in the mid-1930s.

One sequence of events, sometime during the summer of 1981, that I am unable to pinpoint in my memory, is the move by the Saabyes from their workshop in the building opposite us out to Fosie, an area of Malmö zoned for businesses and small workshops. But regardless of exactly when they moved, we remained in close contact, assured by the constant need for repairs the Datsun represented and by the continued camaraderie between us.

The vacancy in the house directly across from us on our narrow street – Korngatan is less than six meters wide, plus sidewalks of about half a meter on each side – was immediately filled with new tenants, another team of auto mechanics who were expanding their car repair business from its original premises two blocks away, down the hill on Torngatan.

The new tenants were an unruly bunch led by a somewhat corpulent, roughshod but muscular guy named Sven. At the end of a day's work (not always waiting for the end), they liked to drink themselves into belligerence, then vent their anger at the world, demonstrating their lack of civilization by their lack of faith in it. Cars had to be driven into the workshop through the same sliding wooden garage door (directly opposite our kitchen windows) that the Saabyes had used. But the Saabyes' always took great care never to gun the engine when driving in (due to the fact that the tailpipes faced our kitchen windows), and to leave as much free space as possible in front of our house for parking any cars that were waiting their turn to enter the garage. (Parking regulations prohibited parking 10 meters from the corner, and our corner property was only ten and a half meters long, which should have precluded all but half a meter of that problem anyway.)

Our new neighbors were less considerate. We smelled the fumes and heard the roar of just about every car they drove into and out of that garage. And they filled up the narrow street, including the last 10 meters, with their clients' cars to the extent that if we wanted to get in or out of the house with a piece of furniture, we would have to ask them to move whatever car they had parked squarely in front of our door. They didn't apologize. They just smirked and sneered.

While Lena was whitewashing the big house (it was already time for another coat), I tore down big sections of the southern wall of the little house, the part overlooking the yard. The little house had a shed-roof construction sloping towards the yard from the alley. In order to avoid having exposure to the elements any more than absolutely necessary, I tore away a three-meter-wide strip of the roof, then supported the roof beams with trusses on the upstairs floor, while tearing down a section of the brick wall and building it up again, this time with arches for three new windows (which had been part of the window supply I'd purchased some years earlier for the whole property), and making the new wall about 70 cm higher than before, to improve the ceiling height by 30 cm while also allowing space for 30 cm of insulation. I borrowed from a neighbor (Gert) a huge red heavy-duty tarp to catch any rainwater that would follow the slope of the roof towards the opened roof and keep it flowing into the yard. I really hoped it wouldn't rain for the few weeks I'd calculated it would take me to get a new, watertight roof in place.

Nobody was listening, except me. It rained like hell a couple of nights, and that kept me awake like a trapped animal. I was out of bed every half hour to check the huge quantities of water that were collecting in the tarp, which sagged into the opened part of the roof like a hammock, between the new, higher wall and the old slope of the roof. It was gradually forming bulging vats like huge, heavy bathtubs with nowhere to go. I realized I'd have to get up in the middle of the night and push on the tarp from beneath, in order to empty the collected water down into the yard in monumental cascades. And all the while, the tarp kept refilling with more rainwater. I tried to get a little sleep, then got up at first light to carry on rebuilding the wall. The section overlooking the deck was going

A Sea of Troubles

to have one of the four Dutch doors, as well as a window, both with arches of course. I was exhausted; I'd never worked on bricklaying so fast and furiously before, and never under such pressure.

We got a visit from our new friends from Oslo for a few days during the last week in July, giving me an excuse to take a much-needed break to reinforce the bonds of friendship – with the boys (Preben and Carl Victor) too. I was about to start back to work at Perstorp after the vacation, although there wasn't much work *in* Perstorp anymore, just Wednesdays at most. Everything else was from home, and I could always do the translation work in the evenings if I needed the daylight for the work on the house. In fact, I didn't go to Perstorp at all until August 26th.

By August 5th, the entire southern wall was at its new and final height. The upper part of the north wall, which I'd presumed was *clad* with boards, turned out to be *made* of boards, so my need for bricks was going to be a lot greater than I'd originally estimated. I removed the first few meters of the boards, nearest Källargatan, and began laying bricks as fast as an inexperienced amateur bricklayer like me could manage, especially when mixing all the mortar with a shovel in a wheelbarrow, by hand, and carrying it up the stairs one heavy bucket at a time. When I began to reach the new full height, I could adjust the height of the short east wall (by August 10th) and start putting the new roof beams into the gaps I'd prepared for them in the new north and south walls.

The end was in sight; I could almost smell it. But a week later the rain returned and I had a couple more nightmarish nights of emptying the huge build-up of water from the tarp down into the courtyard. By August 16th I'd collected another thousand bricks and finished nearly half of the 10.5 meter-long north wall.
On September 1st, with the walls completely finished and the new roof beams aligned and in place, I started putting on the new roof boards. It took two more weeks to complete the boards and get two layers of roofing felt down. I'd finally achieved a watertight structure. I realized very clearly that if rebuilding the walls and raising the roof of the little house had been my first renovation project, I'd have given up long ago. Now, with so much work requiring so many skills behind me, I understood how far I'd come and that I was no longer afraid to tackle practically any project I could imagine.

By the end of August, Mom was becoming acclimatized in her new apartment in Kirkland, and Bob was starting to truly enjoy his freedom from the tyranny of

Clutching for hope

Theiss, Roche, office politics, alarm clocks, and the early bedtimes the alarm used to compel. Bob was also expecting a visit from Kathy and her baby. They were coming to stay with him at his expense for a couple of weeks in late September, but his anticipation was rapidly turning into apprehension, partly due to the mental instability Kathy was increasingly displaying in her letters. [*I'm unable to verify Bob's assessment, since I never met Kathy, nor had any direct communication with her, all part of Bob's tendency to compartmentalize his contacts.*] Apparently she waited until the last minute to confirm to Bob that she was coming to see him. That delay, that uncertainty, caused him no end of anxiety.

Another factor seemed to be that Bob was taking it upon himself to arrange for a cot, a crib, a stroller, diapers, baby food, a babysitter – all of which would have been a considerable undertaking even for a healthy, mobile, practical person, but for Bob it was a major and mostly self-inflicted ordeal.

I was also concerned about Bob's increasing difficulties to walk. Although he spoke fondly of hiking in the mountains in his youth, I'd never seen him walk anywhere that he could get to by car (including the Coop grocery store a block and a half away from his apartment), nor voluntarily go anywhere he couldn't drive to. All his activities were sedentary (almost an oxymoron there), and now that he had Parkinson's, the lack of pre-existing muscle tone didn't seem to be serving him well. I urged him to get out walking more, to push his limits as far as possible. I suggested that he get a cane to assist him, and he winced. He presented intricate theories why a cane wouldn't work for him, and I wondered why he didn't think it could be worth a try. I reminded him of Aristotle's wife's teeth. (Bob and I enjoyed tears of laughter on reading Bertrand Russell's account of how Aristotle reasoned that because of his perceptions of female weakness compared to males, that females must therefore have fewer teeth. And then Russel's commented that all Mr Aristotle would have had to do was open Mrs Aristotle's mouth and start counting, and he would know he was wrong!) But apparently canes were strongly symbolic of old age to Bob, something he didn't want to admit. Perhaps vanity was the real culprit.

I'd been requested to submit a semen sample to the hospital lab to check for sperm cells, but they found none (either; I'd already checked under my microscope!), so the doctor wanted me to come in for a chat and an appointment for a second operation, in mid-December. I couldn't understand Lena's return to "rationing" her intimacy with me since we returned from Switzerland, but I knew I needed to bite my tongue. Any questioning, wondering, complaining

A Sea of Troubles

or expression of my unfulfilled desires would be interpreted as criticism of her behavior, and that was a trigger for her rage. I'd strayed down that road too many times already.

I had a visit one day from Bodil, the daughter of my recently widowed neighbor Gustaf. She was in the company of her husband, his brother Bengt, and Bengt's wife. They wondered if they might possibly get a closer look at my paintings, which they'd glimpsed through the windows along Korngatan and heard a bit about from Gustaf. Bengt was enthusiastic about them, for all the right reasons (he was actually interested in learning what the message was!), and that qualified him, in my eyes, to be allowed to purchase *A Red Horse*. Not long after, Bodil bought *Imagine Our Surprise* on behalf of the art club at her place of work, the Swedish Customs Authority, where it was raffled off. [*I had no further contact with Bengt for some 35 years, when I tracked him down for the purpose of obtaining a high-resolution photo of* A Red Horse *(painting #36) for my album. He was proud to show it to me, prominently displayed on his wall. Unfortunately, I have been unable to trace the whereabouts of* Imagine Our Surprise *(#58). I can only hope it's found a good home!*]

Kathy's two-week stay at Bob's in late September and early October turned out to be pretty much of a disaster. After venting her displeasure at how her friends and acquaintances in the States were treating her badly by failing to recognize her genius, and were utterly negligent in expressing their unending adoration for her talents, she spent most of her two weeks at Bob's reading a book she'd brought along. She pointedly declined to engage in conversation or discussions with Bob. Why she came halfway around the world at his expense to use Bob's apartment as her reading room was a mystery to Bob. Nor did Bob find it terribly admirable when she made repeated comments to and about her toddler son to the effect that she could have accomplished so much more without him. (All this was according to Bob.) [*Many years later, he admitted to having tried to grope her, so that might have been at least part of the explanation for her coldness towards him.*]

Lena and I spent another enjoyable evening at the home of Henry and Elsa. Henry was full of curiosity about the progress on the little house, and kept nodding and smiling in his avuncular way as I related all the details. He told me he'd be wanting some more English lessons in November.

Our widower neighbor Gustaf struck up a friendship with Agnes, his new next-door neighbor, a fastidious and elegant widow (or divorcée). Their relationship seemed to be quite sexless, at her insistence (probably not by mutual agreement!), although she flirted with him coquettishly and incessantly. Her tiny house gave me the impression of a museum dedicated to an author of quaint old children's books: full of frilly artifacts, lacy curtains, fringed lampshades and an abundance of various shades of pink and gold. It would have been difficult to imagine an odder couple than the elegant Agnes and the down-to-earth, gruff, straightforward retired telephone lineman Gustaf. We invited them to dinner at our place and had a lovely evening, during which they announced that they'd also like some English lessons from me – together. I gave it a couple of tries, but in this, too, they were just too mismatched. As a result, it quickly degenerated into a social hour (not that there was anything wrong with that).

During October, one of my regular pupils from Perstorp Form, a middle-aged man named Pelle Lundholm, wanted us to go through the company's catalogue and talk about their products in English. I readily agreed that having a topic of great relevance to him would be an excellent idea. Most of the products from Perstorp Form at that time were injection-molded plastic systems of bins and trays for use in workshops and industries, to enable convenient sorting and picking of parts, screws, bolts etc, when assembling or repairing all kinds of things. I was enjoying our discussion as well, since I found I could learn a lot about how such things are made and how they are used. When we came to the end of the catalogue, there were also a few small trollies with racks for holding a number of the small plastic bins. The trolleys had a flat working surface on top, so that the unit essentially comprised a mobile workstation. The company also sold some wall-mounted cabinets, both for bins and for locking away expensive tools. As I looked it over, I thought that surely the end-users who worked with power tools would benefit from being able to lock them up on the spot, without having to bring them back to the lockable cabinets, and since there seemed to be room beneath the working surface of the trolley for such a lockable cabinet, why not combine them? Pelle was intrigued and delighted to hear my suggestion, and said he would take it up with their design department as soon as he returned to Perstorp.

The next time he came to Malmö for a day's lessons, I asked him about the response to the combination I'd suggested, but he said that the designers rejected it "for various technical reasons". A year later, when Pelle again came to me in Malmö, he had a new catalogue with him, and there it was – the trolley with the lockable cabinet! I was astonished and exclaimed, "Hey, you used my idea after all!" Pelle averted his eyes and sternly claimed not to know what I was talking about. He claimed that the idea came from their design department, that it was a new best-seller, and that I was not a little cheeky for insinuating that the idea was mine. And for some reason, I lost interest in giving Pelle any more English lessons.

Although the performance of Mozart's *Marriage of Figaro* at Covent Garden thrilled Jeanette and me, as did a few other operas like Strauss's *Der Rosenkavalier*, I'd never been that big of an opera fan. Eva's partner Jan was a real Wagner buff and tried to enthuse me about it (he also tried unsuccessfully to enthuse me about golf), but I found Wagner far too rich to enjoy in anything but small quantities, like a quadruple-chocolate cake. Then we heard and saw Joseph Losey's film version of *Don Giovanni*, and it blew my mind. The beauty of Mozart's music, amplified in wonderful harmony with Losey's dramatic flair, opened an entirely new door on the operatic genre to me – a door that Bob was quick to encourage me to explore further.

That was, to me, one of the most amazing things about Bob. His vast knowledge in such widely varied fields enabled him to provide the services of a guide in almost any area, to *point out* so many doors lurking in the deep shadows of the unknown. And this was his supreme approach: *to point out, never to force-feed*; to hold the doors open to let you look in, but never to shove you through any door you didn't want or feel ready to enter. I told myself that if Lena and I ever succeeded in having any children, I would make it my task, my mission, to open as many doors as possible for my children, but never to push them to explore any they didn't wish to.

On October 6th, we were horrified and saddened to hear the news of the assassination of Egyptian President Anwar Sadat, who since 1970 led Egypt on the road to becoming a modern democracy with a multi-party system. In spite of Israel's annexations and land-grabbing occupation of its neighbors' territories, Sadat felt that peace was paramount, and he willingly entered negotiations with Israel, resulting in an important peace treaty that won him the Nobel Peace Prize. This, and his efforts to make a separate peace with Israel, without first gaining the consent and consensus of the other Arab states, incurred the wrath of the fanatics who murdered him. Another significant voice of peace and reason was silenced.

Bob continued to agonize over Kathy. She sent him a post-visit letter (which he forwarded to me for comment), in which she basically said "you're welcome" *to Bob* for her having granted Bob the privilege of giving her and her son a free trip to Europe! She apparently left Bob a copy of some of her efforts at *"free verse" poetry* (or perhaps that should be *free verse "poetry"*), and as a gesture of appeasement, Bob found an expert bookbinder to turn them into a slender, elegantly leather-bound volume. I felt so sorry for Bob. And I predicted that Kathy would return the book to him. She did.

On the subject of free verse (for the sake of clarity, I'm using the definitions wherein "verse" is defined as poetry that uses both a meter and a rhyme scheme, "blank verse" uses a rhythm scheme but is unrhymed, and "free verse" uses neither. Perhaps, apart from W.H. Auden's "exceptional cases", like Walt Whitman (or e e cummings?), free verse *might* also mean "free *from* talent"?), I wrote Bob about my skepticism, starting with a quote from Auden, who, by the way, was one of my favorite poets:

> *The poet who writes "free verse" is like Robinson Crusoe on his desert island; he must do all his cooking, laundry and darning for himself. In a few exceptional cases, this manly independence produces something original and impressive, but more often the result is squalor – dirty sheets on the unmade bed and empty bottles on the unswept floor.*

I compared free verse to totally abstract art, which I saw as the equivalent in that artistic medium. It offers little in the way of criteria by which to assess its merits and opens the door to used toilet paper as art, not to mention the crap that gets dumped on a general public too afraid of appearing Philistine to call a spade a spade. (I find the association with Hans Christian Andersen's *The Emperor's New Clothes* unavoidable.) In some cases, an "artist" can bully the public into regarding *anything* he or she does (including their dirty toilet paper) as art, and the poet's every word as poetry. (The effect is greatly enhanced when it is read aloud slowly, with the utmost supercilious reverence and histrionic affectation.)

I don't think
that
just because I lay
it
   down
      cleverly
on paper like
this
 that it is therefore poet
ry.

I was, however, convinced that a great many people would be inclined to view the above "poem" – especially if they were told it were from a great poet – as "a masterful statement of the human condition, full of subtle overtones of sexual-social-psychological symbolism, a concise prism of words at once capturing, collecting and dispersing the essence of life itself, providing the human spirit with the insight for coming to terms with the darker side of the soul; in short: a jewel."

Expanding to music, which of the following composers or "composers" may be called artists? Mozart? John Cage? The Beatles? Punk rockers? J.N. Darby? A cat walking across a piano? A baby pounding on the piano? John Cage pounding like a baby on the piano? John Cage pounding a baby on the piano? Some of these are obviously art, some should equally obviously not be. One problem is that there can be no borderline cases because there are no borders, no clear-cut lines, only general and diffuse border *areas*, a continuum.

In early December, Lena and I went up to Eket to pick up a table. Lars had announced to his siblings that he was proposing to buy out their shares of the place – which all of them readily accepted without persuasion – and that if anyone wanted any of the furniture, now was the time to retrieve it. The slightly battered oak table had caught my eye because it could be made nearly six meters long (using six or seven extra leaves). Without the leaves, it was no bigger than the oak table Jeanette and I already had and fixed up. I thought it would be a great addition to my studio; I still harbored a little hope of someday continuing to paint after *Jardin*.

I'd now completed all that I could complete on the house for 1981. Upstairs in the little house – the future library – all the wallboard was in place, the paneling was in the ceiling, the windows and door were in place, and the pine board floor was sanded and oiled. All that remained were the bookshelves (which I would make of old floorboards), the railing around the stairs, as well as the puttying and painting.

Now I had to take a break, because on December 13th I had my second vasectomy-reversal operation, this time under general anesthetic (the doctors probably didn't want to repeat my painful spinal experience either). I was to do no heavy lifting for a week or two afterwards. This was a big deal. The first attempt, on ball #1, didn't succeed; after the second operation, on ball #2, I'd be out of balls to work on. It *had* to work.

Bob was going to spend Christmas with us, as usual (I hoped), from December 19th to January 9th. We welcomed him to stay much longer, but he may have found it difficult to escape the former habits from his working days (he was definitely a creature of habit), and we were unable to persuade him to stay longer.

A few days before Christmas, I took it upon myself to go out and find us a small, not-too-tall Christmas tree. Most of the little squares throughout Malmö had temporary stands selling them, but most of the trees on offer were too large for our living room. (I should mention that unlike in English, the Swedish word for Christmas tree, *julgran*, specifies the *type* of tree: *gran*, meaning spruce. Close to 100% of Swedish household obediently used nothing but spruces as their Yuletide trees.) Bob had already been with us for some days, so I was speaking (and thinking) mostly English, and therefore lacked that culturally and linguistically imposed definition for my Christmas tree selection. When my search led me to a tree stand at St. Knut's Square, I spotted a lovely little pine among all the big spruces, and thought it would be perfect. Pines have longer needles and don't shed them all over the place (it often took months to find and remove all the dried spruce needles after each Christmas) and pines have a nicer fragrance. Moreover, a pine was no more expensive than a spruce, so I bought it.

When I got home with it, Lena took one look at it and was outraged, livid. *"How could you do such a thing?! Is this some kind of sick joke?! Are you trying to <u>ruin</u> my Christmas?!"* Before I could begin to defend my evil actions, she'd already retrieved her garden shears and was snipping off the branches to use for wreaths. *"Go back and get another one – a <u>proper</u> Christmas tree this time, you idiot!!"* I'm not sure where Bob was during this exchange, but I surmise that he could hardly have been present; it would have affected him deeply, and given him insights that I'd been shielding him from. (Even though Lena was railing at me in Swedish, her message and the fury of her body language were quite clear). The secondary effect of this outburst was to ensure that our home conformed to Swedish traditions this year as well, but the principal effect was to sadden me deeply, and launch me once again on the road to depression – clutching at the straw of fertility.

A Sea of Troubles

CHAPTER 15

The end of an era

Following my second vasectomy-reversal operation in mid-December 1981, Lena seemed only too happy to use my recovery period as an excuse for the kind of abstinence I knew (and hated) all too well. In the spring, she was going to be taking a break from teaching to study history at the university in Lund, while receiving 75% of her teacher's salary. I, the unflagging optimist, hoped that she would experience less pressure from not needing to do so much diligent preparation work for her pupils, and that it would make her less irritable, and that we could find something to build on, something in the direction of mutual love.

Around New Year's (Bob was still with us), a heavy snowfall covered our street with a thick layer of slush. Our hostile garage mechanic neighbors, led by the stocky, burly fireplug called Sven, were working and drinking hard, particularly the latter. Nearly every time they drove a car into their workshop, they gunned the engine and sprayed our kitchen wall and windows with dirty slush and exhaust fumes. They'd been doing this for weeks. I had repeatedly and politely asked them to stop, but they just laughed. My patience ran out, so on January 2nd, while performing my legal obligation to keep a path clear to our door for the postman, I piled up the shoveled snow along the curb directly outside our kitchen windows. The pile was about a meter high, and had the intended effect of preventing our neighbors from coating our windows with the dirty slush every time they wanted to get a car indoors for repair. I hadn't made it *impossible* for them to drive in, just quite a bit more difficult.

Guess what? They didn't like it. They smoldered and scowled for a week. On Saturday, January 9th, their displeasure was accelerated by uncontrolled consumption of alcohol, and they seemed already to be simmering with fury when I returned from taking Bob to the airport bus at the Central Station in the middle of the day. By the time Bob reached home that evening, my neighbors' intake of alcohol had piqued [*sic*], and our end of the short and narrow street was seething like a faulty and overloaded pressure cooker.

As the brief and gloomy winter day turned to dusk in mid-afternoon, Sven staggered out of the door of the workshop, his face ruddy and bloated, yet not swollen enough to conceal his wild eyes. He was holding a water hose by the nozzle. He proceeded to spray *hot* water on the pile of snow, occasionally "missing" and spraying our windows instead. Two or three of his friends could be seen watching and lurking in the steamy windows of the workshop, snarling, sneering and laughing. After a minute or two, Sven rejoined his friends so they could make further contributions to the alcohol content in their blood and the reduction in their judgment.

Sven repeated this procedure several times. Each time, he was drunker and more belligerent than before. Rational conversation with him was never an option, and was certainly never going to happen that day, which rapidly turned to evening in the December mid-afternoon. Meanwhile, instead of melting, the pile of snow seemed to be turning to ice, and Sven cursed it as though it were taunting him, like Moby Dick. Then he started beating his fists on our front door, swearing and shouting threats.

All this while, Lena and I were watching anxiously through the narrow gaps in our venetian blinds, with mounting uncertainty about how to deal with Sven's burgeoning ethanol-fueled temper, and with rising apprehension about what he might do next.

After a further few drinks, we saw Sven approaching our front door with the hose in his hand, seething with frustration. He'd bent the hose and was holding it tightly, ready to release a torrent of water. He stuck the end of it the through our mailbox, intending to flood our entrance hall. The moment the water began gushing, I shoved it back out again. Fortunately, our mailbox was not at all flimsy, but was a heavy-duty wrought-iron model with a tightly coiled spring mechanism for the flap. (Jeanette and I found it in London back in 1976.) But Sven's attempt to cross a line, to break the perimeter of our domain, so to speak, signaled that the booze had shattered his remaining inhibitions. At that point we found the situation sufficiently alarming to phone the police.

While waiting for the police to arrive, our phone began ringing. Thinking it might be the police phoning back for some reason, I answered, only to find myself on the receiving end of a series of ten increasingly violent threats (*seven* of them were death threats!) from Sven and his cohorts: his henchmen would be coming to mutilate us; our house would be blown up with dynamite; we would be annihilated. Bo and Peter, sensing the escalated level of belligerence, had witnessed the hose incident and hurried over to join us, as did Lennart from the house diagonally across the street from us – and next-door to the workshop.

The five of us kept vigil in our darkened living room until the police came. When they finally arrived on the scene – it probably took them 15 minutes, but it felt like five hours – two of them came in to speak with us, while two or three other officers entered the workshop to see for themselves and try to dial down the drunken chaos. They told us that we'd handled it well and that we'd done the right thing. They advised us to maintain our vigil for a while. (Apparently Sven and at least two of the others had criminal records for assault and other offences, and two of them were already on probation.) The peace was temporary; there was a new incident with renewed death threats from Sven on Saturday, January 23rd, and another on the 27th. Both times Sven and his pals were drunk, disorderly and hostile.

The incidents attracted a lot of attention in the neighborhood, of course. The general view was that everyone should unite behind a petition to the zoning authorities to issue a new zoning plan focusing on the preservation of Kirseberg's few blocks of 19th-century homes, most of which were now in various stages of restoration. (Malmö, unlike many other towns in Skåne, had a miserable track record of preserving its historical buildings and neighborhoods, so here was a chance to salvage something.) I drafted the petition, with the help of Bo, Peter and Lennart. Nearly everyone in the neighborhood signed it.

The confluence of several seemingly unrelated conditions – the workshop incidents, my second vasectomy-reversal operation, and Lena's deteriorating attitude towards me – was deeply troubling to me. I expected (in view of Lena's pronounced strong desires to have a child) or at least hoped that our sex life would again become a source of joy and pleasure for both of us, particularly once the dust settled after the last face-off with Sven and his crew. Instead, the solidarity she showed me during the incidents quickly turned to disdain afterwards.

There seemed to be no limit to her loathing of me. As far as sex was concerned, she complained that I was always there with my desires and thus never gave her a chance to express her own, so could I please wait for her to want to? I waited. More than a month went by. I thought that masturbation was for lonely single men, having mistakenly and naively assumed that married men would not be lonely. I felt signs of my old depression returning, and I fought desperately against it. Nor did I feel, for the same reasons as earlier, that I could enlist Bob's help as my *confidant* this time. It would be too upsetting for him to bear. And here I'd been hoping that having a child might effect a miracle, the miracle of love.

In my growing desperation to find an explanation, I wondered whether my responses to Sven's belligerence were to blame. Wasn't I macho enough? Maybe Lena was measuring my passive resistance against what she thought Larry the Black Belt's might have been? A fist through the door? A fist through Sven's face? Violence just wasn't me. But Lena's burgeoning contempt for me felt like an unpluggable leak in a rowboat out in the middle of a deep lake in utter darkness.

The little house was now complete. The upstairs was one long, narrow room (about three by ten meters), with five south-facing windows (including the window half of the Dutch door to the garage roof) and one small east-facing window overlooking Källargatan (the only east-facing window in the entire property). All along the fairly high north wall were bookcases up to a height of about one-and-a-half meters. I took thick old tongue-and-groove floorboards (sanded and oiled) to make the bookshelves, joining two boards together (I sawed off the tongue on the outer one) to achieve the desired shelf depth. For the uprights I held the boards together with laths screwed into both boards from both sides. The laths then also served as the shelf supports. I should mention that there were two main reasons for building the bookcases this way: they were sturdy and they were cheap. And there was plenty of room for all the books that Jeanette and I brought with us from San Francisco to Vancouver to Vårgatan to Korngatan, which had been gently aging in the wine cartons for close to seven years.

I hung eight of my paintings above the bookcases, two more on the east wall, two on the west wall, and three on the south wall between the windows, 15 in total. The floor, like the bookcases, was of old pine boards, sanded and oiled. The ceiling was of beaded wooden paneling. I made a railing around the stairs using old dark-stained beams. There was a dark-stained desk and two chairs at the top of the stairs, in the eastern third of the library. I would be using this part of the room as a classroom on the days when I had pupils. In the larger western portion of the room we placed two short pink-and-white-striped sofas (they looked classic but they were from IKEA), with a small old coffee table between them. It was a bright and beautiful room.

Now that the little house was finished, every room could be used to its full potential. But in the downstairs room, Lena's piano continued to languish in the autumn of 1980. I asked her why she still never played. She said that the downstairs room was too dark. (Sigh!)

I had to keep busy to keep depression at bay. I felt unloved, unwanted, unworthy. On Sunday, March 21st I flew down to Basel to spend an intensive week building Bob an "office" in his bedroom. I assembled drawer cabinets and built bookcases on top of them. I worked feverishly to avoid the risk of allowing Bob to discover the real reason for my growing stress and anxiety; I couldn't burden him with that, and I was fairly certain that the slightest hint would have been a huge burden for him.

The week after I got back, I had a backlog of pupils to deal with, followed by a visit from Rob and Chris the following weekend. Then on Monday, April 5th, we took off for Oslo to visit Jan and Grete and the boys. We took a tour to their mountain cabin, stopped off to visit friends in Tanumshede on the way home, and Barkåkra on the Saturday, Easter Eve. Eva, who was now nearly seven months pregnant, was also there with Lina. Both Eva and Marie-Louise gasped in astonishment several times at Lena's surly, sneering comments to me.

In late April I took delivery of the pressure-treated wood for the garage-roof deck. For drainage, the underlying roof was designed to slope sufficiently in two directions, diagonally from the southeast corner down to the northwest. This made it a bit tricky to achieve a flat deck floor on the sloping substrate, and required a lot of spatial concentration – all of which helped me to suppress the inescapable conclusion that the woman I loved, and to whom I was married, not only didn't love me but was increasingly contemptuous of everything I did. I could hardly bear to think of painting.

It went better with the deck floor. The garage roof was transformed into an oasis of sun-drenched privacy [*maybe "sun-drenched" is a bit of hyperbole – this is Sweden we're talking about – but there was sunshine from morning to evening on all the non-cloudy days*], easily accessible from both houses, big enough for parties, with room for plenty of tubs and pots for bushes an flowers, overlooking Källargatan as if from parapets.

The petition that we and our neighbors submitted to the authorities about permanently removing the car-repair workshop from our street apparently came to the attention of *Sydsvenskan*, the Malmö newspaper. On Friday, May 28th, they sent a reporter to Korngatan to talk to us and to Sven (separately), then ran a six-column article in the Saturday paper. It didn't please Sven and his pals, who must have begun drinking by noon. They appeared more and more frequently out on the narrow street to rage incoherently and shake their fists at anything that moved, including clouds.

By mid-afternoon the situation had deteriorated to the point where their fists were now holding hammers, with which they pounded on our door as well as on Bo and Peter's, then on our Datsun, leaving dents and screaming barely intelligible drunken threats and insults. Bo went outdoors to meet them and was shoved up against a wall for his trouble. We had no option but to call the police – as they'd instructed us to do. When the policemen arrived on the scene, the activities and threats emanating from the workshop were so rowdy that the policemen entered with dogs and drawn weapons – a *highly* unusual measure in Sweden at that time. Sven was taken away in handcuffs. He was plastered and aggressive. All this was again reported in *Sydsvenskan* as "*the culmination of years of a neighborhood feud*". [*It was actually no more than five months, but perhaps "years" sounded better to the editor.*]

In the early evening on Sunday (the sun hadn't come close to setting), Lena and I went next door to discuss the situation with Bo and Peter. We were joined by Lennart. While we were sitting there talking, a stone suddenly came through their living room window, and we heard two young men running away. Peter and I immediately shot up from our seats, ran outside and gave chase, following the sound of the retreating footsteps. We caught up with them at the corner of Vattenverksvägen and Solgatan; we were close enough to get a good look at them and hear their Olduvaian remarks, but we decided that this was a matter for the police, so we returned to our "crisis meeting".

In the middle of the night, Lena and I were awakened by the sound of a big bang – not the beginning of a new universe, but of Håkan, one of Sven's pals, swinging a wooden club viciously at our triple-glazed living-room and kitchen windows, together with a few of his equally inebriated friends. He broke six windowpanes, but Lena got a good look at him while I was again calling the police. We were able to give them his name, assuming they would pick him up, but they didn't. After further percussion practice on our house by Håkan and his gang that night, Lennart, Bo and I decided to set up a nocturnal watch in Lennart's car the following night. We were joined by Allan Saabye, who'd read about our plight and came around to help out. (Maybe he figured he could pretend that Håkan was his ex-wife's astrologer.) Allan supplied each of us with a 50-cm length of heavy black-rubber-coated electrical cable (about 35 mm diameter) that he said would help us ward off evil, or at least not be entirely defenseless.

We sat there in the car, in the darkness, in almost complete silence, for hours. The tension was palpable. But nothing was happening. It felt far beyond weird, one of the most unreal, bizarre feelings I've ever had. We were listening nervously to every sound, watching every shadow. Every car that passed by along Vattenverksvägen behind us made us freeze and hold our breath, as if we shared a single pair of lungs. There were only a couple of cars that turned into Källargatan, immediately unleashing a flow of adrenalin, only to gradually subside into mere tension again. Then, at about 2 AM, a car pulled just into Källargatan after turning off its lights and then its engine. It stopped just a meter or two behind us, in the street. We could scarcely breathe. Four guys got out. One of them was Håkan. They were whispering as they headed towards Korngatan 12, brandishing clubs (perhaps pieces of two-by-fours). They passed our car without seeing us; they were too focused on sizing up our darkened house. One of them looked around nervously, and suddenly spotted the human silhouettes in our fully loaded car. He hissed at the others that they weren't alone. They froze momentarily, then tried to swagger as they made their way back to their car and took off. This being the time of Margaret Thatcher's Falklands War, our house was quickly (and temporarily) dubbed "Fort Stanley", complete with the parapets.

Sven, Håkan, and one other guy were eventually charged and tried. They pleaded that they were too drunk to remember. Only Sven got sentenced to prison – for a duration amounting to the one month he'd already spent in custody. The other two were fined, but faced certain consequences for probation violations. The workshop was shut down permanently during the summer, and the city planners eventually rezoned the property as residential only.

On June 8th, I received confirmation from Sverker Hellsten that a normal sperm count had been achieved. (I already knew, thanks to my trusty microscope!) The reversal of the vasectomy was successful. Although I underwent the two operations primarily to please Lena, it was my understanding that pregnancy was to be achieved by our "doing it", not by my jacking off into a test tube. I also naively hoped that my valiant heroics in the face of tremendous neighborhood adversity would move her heart, kindle her ardor, and that at last true and reciprocated love would be ours forever. But her contempt only grew. The only antidote was once again having other people around us, as frequently as possible. The strangest thing was that I began to realize that other women, quite a few of them, seemed anything but contemptuous towards me. For some reason, it made me a bit nervous, so I tried to ignore it.

Jan, Grete, Preben and Carl-Victor came to stay with us for a few days in late

June. On June 29th, Lena's sister Eva delivered Emil, a darling little boy. For about a month following Emil's birth, Lena was relatively receptive of my affections. Was there a connection? Who knows?

The neighborhood ordeal brought us closer to a number of our neighbors, including Ole and Birgitta, a couple about our age who lived at the other end of the block behind us. Ole, half Danish, was two or three years older than me. He wore dark-framed glasses and had a Chevron mustache. If he'd had a larger nose, he might have looked a bit like Groucho Marx might have looked if Groucho had looked normal, which he didn't. Ole worked at the University of Agriculture and Horticology in Alnarp, just outside Malmö. His wife Birgitta, a teacher like Lena, was a couple of years younger than Lena and was kind of pretty; she squinted when she laughed. They'd just found out that Birgitta was pregnant, and seemed thrilled about it. We found them to be pleasant company, and began spending some enjoyable evenings together over dinner, alternating venues between our two homes, only about 50 meters apart.

We were thinking of visiting Bob in Switzerland again, but mostly due to residual anxiety about the risk of another neighborhood flare-up, we decided not to go. So Bob came to spend 15 days with us in the latter half of July. We had beautiful weather, Swedish summer at its best: clear blue skies and temperatures in the 20s nearly all month long. It was Bob's first-ever summer visit to see us, and it was a pleasant change for him from the usual short, slush-filled days. Bob really enjoyed sitting out on our new garage-roof deck on a sunny day.

But Lena seemed to feel that fine weather could not be fully enjoyed anywhere but at the beach, preferably in Höllviken, so the beach in Höllviken is where the three of us spent nearly every day during Bob's visit. Lena stayed in the sun, Bob in whatever shade he could find. I had no particular desire to alter the color of my skin, not that it was great in any way, but I loved spending my time at the sea *in* the sea, snorkeling if possible, then in the shade with Bob to talk. We also had Jan and Eva for dinner at our place, together with their kids of course. All of them were fond of Bob, as was Marie-Louise, whom we also visited. We enjoyed many of our evening meals on the new deck that summer.

Since Bob tended not to get up at the crack of dawn, I filled my early mornings by laying bricks as part of a new project to turn the ground-level passageway between the two houses into a kind of corridor under the garage roof, while giving added support to the part of the roof that hung out beyond the wall of the garage. I obtained a couple of charming old arched window frames of cast iron, originally part of a now-demolished barn, to be placed on either side of an open archway out to the yard. The yard itself would be my project for the autumn.

In addition to our growing friendships with Bo and Peter, as well as Ole and Birgitta, Lena and I continued socializing regularly with three members of Lena's "*sexklubb*" – the six former teacher's college classmates. Gunilla (and Øivind) and Mai (and Lars) both lived in the Malmö-Lund region, while Charlotte (and Kent) lived in Karlshamn, about two hours' drive to the northeast. Most of those meetings were with one couple at a time. A new and unifying theme was varying levels of desire to start a family. Maj, who seemed very skeptical about having kids, couldn't stand the thought that young parents couldn't seem to talk about anything but their children. Lena was happy to spend time talking with her girlfriends, and fortunately for me, their partners were all friendly guys, so we had fun. But why did I seem to see a trace of pity in the faces of Lena's girlfriends when they looked at me? What was she telling them about me? Or was I becoming paranoid too?

By this time I'd acquired a number of "regulars" among my pupils – pupils who came to Korngatan for a full-day immersion course 2-6 times a year, which meant that I was getting to know each of them well, both as colleagues and as people, individuals. Since the small (60 or so employees) but highly successful Formox division of Perstorp had only one customer in Sweden, Formox was heavily dependent on global markets; and since they were highly customer-oriented, most of them needed well-developed skills in English. As a result, nearly every one of them came to Korngatan for a one-day course from time to time. Moreover, they frequently faxed their English correspondence to me for review and correction, so as not to inflict sub-standard English on their customers. Their technical reports and presentations also tended to cross my desk, requiring me to develop a rudimentary understanding of some of the chemistry and engineering related to formaldehyde production.

One of my frequent pupils was Harald, a bright young man who sold catalyst to Formox customers throughout Asia. One of his visits to me in Malmö came just after an unsuccessful sales trip to a new potential customer in Indonesia. His self-confidence was shaken by how badly it went. He told me that when he entered the customer's conference room and had just begun to talk about the exceptional performance of the Formox catalyst, they kept interrupting him to ask about his family, what sports he liked, what this or that was like in Sweden

– everything *but* catalysts. In reply, he mentioned that he had two infant sons – twins – and they immediately asked to see photos, but he had none with him. Then they just seemed to lose interest in further discussions.

I told him I suspected that they were trying to *calibrate* him. He didn't know what I meant in such a context. I pointed out that Sweden was an exceptionally homogeneous country (it certainly was in the early 1980s), where any Swede from anywhere in the country already "knew" every other Swede, shared similar values, reference points, language, customs, behaviors and background knowledge. With other Swedes, business meetings could get right down to business, but that was not the case in other countries. First you had to find out what kind of *person* you're dealing with. If he or she says "We'll deliver in six weeks", do they *mean* six weeks and not twelve? Is "six" a guess, a belief or a promise? How can you know?

One way to learn how he or she thinks is to weigh the responses to simple, ordinary questions, like about sports and family – questions that Swedes would normally regard as distractions in business meetings among each other – or as unnecessarily personal and private. "If you and your wife invite friends over for dinner at 7.30 PM, I suppose you know which ones are likely to arrive at 7.30 sharp, and which ones are more likely to arrive a little later or a little earlier?" I asked Harald. He agreed. "So then you're calibrating, and you wouldn't prepare a soufflé for the non-punctual ones. As long as you know what to expect, there's no problem – just like with what you mean when you say a delivery time or any other important point in your negotiations."

I then asked Harald if he'd asked any of his Indonesian contacts about *their* families? No, he hadn't. About Indonesia? No again. I suggested that his inability to produce a photo of his twins rendered him as extremely *odd* in their eyes, as if he were someone from another planet, a wild card with whom business could prove risky indeed. And that his failure to ask them the same types of questions made him appear self-centered and arrogant. So what could he do to remedy the situation? I suggested that any question they asked him about Sweden should be his cue to ask a similar one about Indonesia. That simple. "And put some family photos in your wallet!!"

When I met Harald a month or so later, he was grinning and his face was glowing. He'd gone back to visit the Indonesian prospect again – they'd given him a second chance. One of their first questions was about his twins, and this time he produced a photo or two, which they passed around the table, laughing and making comments, creating an amicable atmosphere. They discussed differences between the two countries, sports, food and climates. Only after discussing such topics with him – *calibrating* him – did they feel confident enough in him *as a person* to show interest in hearing more about Formox catalysts. And Harald came home with a signed sales contract.

Another of my most frequent Formox pupils was a guy named Max Henning, about seven or eight years older than me. Max spent around half of his time traveling all over the world selling formaldehyde plants. His English was never the best, but his communication skills were exceptional, and he seemed to be highly respected by every Formox customer he met. Over several years, we got to know each other well, and we became good friends on many levels.

I often helped Max draft and rehearse various speeches and presentations that he was called upon to deliver at various conferences. I did the same for the former head of Formox, Leif-Arne, who was much better at English than Max, with one exception: he *could not* pronounce the word "negligible" to save his life. It came out as *negiblible, nebligigible, nebliglibliglble* – and he'd used the word numerous times in his written draft of an important speech he was to be giving at a prestigious conference somewhere in Europe. After several unsuccessful attempts – I asked him to pronounce each syllable, one at a time, before trying to string them together, but it didn't help – I suggested *writing* "negligible difference" in the text on the slide he would be showing, but *saying* "trivial difference" instead. Problem solved.

A radically different person among my frequent pupils was a woman named Siv, from Hammarplast, a company based in Tingsryd that Perstorp had recently acquired. They primarily made plastic kitchenware (making this one of Perstorp's few consumer-oriented businesses), and Siv was the purchasing manager. She was tough as nails,[20] but had a heart of gold. Being on the purchasing end of things, her need for business diplomacy was not as great as for the sales people. We always got along fine; sometimes bluntness can be refreshing.

I still had a few non-Perstorp pupils from time to time. One of these was Göran, the head of the big but aging Kockums shipyard, whose huge harbor crane had dominated the Malmö skyline for decades. Göran never had time for a whole day of English, but seemed to enjoy impressing me with the view from the executive suite atop the company headquarters overlooking the construction of some of the world's biggest supertankers ever built at that time.

---

20 Cf. John Zon, final chapter of *Natural Shocks*

And then there was my old avuncular friend Henry Carlsson, still struggling valiantly and gracefully with his English, calming my fears about the building authorities, bemused by how his crazy American friend set out on a cataclysmic course of complexities, disastrous plunges, daredevil undertakings, and somehow persevered – in no small part with Henry's help. Henry and I would always be so different from each other, but there was always an incredibly strong bond. That bond was mutual (except that I left the avuncular part to him).

I finished the outdoor "corridor" in late August and was filling what I hoped would be the last of the dumpsters with the accumulation of rubble in the yard, in preparation for turning that space into yet another oasis. My mom had a fall on August 31st and injured her arm. We were counting on an extended visit from her the following May, and I hoped that her fall wouldn't jeopardize it. Lena wrote her a sweet letter on September 1st, expressing our wishes for Mom/Francys to visit us. The letter contained not a single trace of Lena's disdain for me, and I knew that any length of time Mom might be able to spend with us would give me an equally long and sorely needed respite from Lena's contempt.

During the last weekend of August, we visited Barkåkra. Marie-Louise asked if we could take her out to a place called Glimminge Plantering, where a German couple rented a cottage for a couple of weeks every year after Sweden's tourist season was over. Marie-Louise and her husband were old friends of the man. He'd lost one arm in the War. He was about 30 years older than his blond wife, and was now an ordained minister. Lena told me he was always making flattering comments about her legs. He spoke no English; Marie-Louise used her broken German to communicate with him. Glimminge Plantering seemed like a rather pretty place with a rather odd name.

Lena resumed her history courses at Lund University in September, and I began working a bit more for Perstorp to make up the shortfall in our household income. At the same time, I began my big autumn yard project. Along the north wall of the yard, i.e. along the little house, which got the most direct sunlight in the summer) there would be a flower bed, dug out 60 cm deep and filled with rich compost soil, on the professional advice of Ole. Before I could begin any of that, I had to dig out a narrow 70-cm-deep trench along the north and south walls, then build frames for casting concrete bases or plinths to protect the foundations from the moisture and pressure of the soil and the growth of roots. Once the concrete was thoroughly hard and dry, I coated it with tar before filling the trench with soil.

The main surface of the yard would be covered with granite cobblestones in various muted shades of gray, brownish, and reddish. In the corner nearest the back door to the big house, I dug down an 80-cm-diameter, 60-cm-deep precast cement well. I drilled a hole in the perimeter for a hose that ran underground to the garage, where it I connected it to a pump, from which another hose pumped water under the yard to the far side.

Along the entire far wall (the wall we shared with Bo and Peter's house), I built a raised flower bed, about 70 centimeters high and half a meter wide, also filled with compost soil. The wall was protected from moisture by a high-strength waffled plastic mat. The height of this bed was achieved by a stone wall of naturally rounded granite boulders 10-30 cm in diameter, held together with mortar. The opening of the heavy-duty hose from the pump in the garage protruded slightly from the third of this wall nearest the big house, and allowed water to trickle down stones in the wall of the raised flowerbed, across a slightly lowered pathway (prepared to prevent leakage) of cobblestones to the well, into which the water splashed, then circulated back to the pump and back to the wall. The well would be a home for few goldfish, although I wouldn't finish all this until the spring. Between the "babbling brook" and the wall of the big house, there was a narrow flowerbed for plants that didn't mind constant shadow; Ole provided expert advice on our choice of plants for the whole yard.

In the meantime, Bo and Peter were hard at work clearing out the half of their downstairs nearest us (on the other side of the shared wall of our kitchen) in preparation for putting down insulation and casting a concrete slab, as Jeanette and I did in our house about six and a half years earlier. When they heard I was also going to be casting some concrete for the base along the two walls in the yard, Bo offered to come and help me with that, so that their floor slab wouldn't be his first-ever experience of wet concrete. We did that on September 17th. Our yard remained a huge pile of dirt until the 23rd.

One weekend in early September, Bo and Peter joined us for a trip up to Barkåkra, where we picked up Marie-Louise and drove out to Eket. All five of us – plus Bo and Peter's little bulldog Cedric (who for some weird reason was always trying to fuck my shin) – somehow managed to squeeze into the little Datsun. Our neighbor friends were looking for a pair of old doors that I'd spotted in the barn in Eket, doors that they felt would be just right to use as the main entrance to their house. We all also went mushroom picking up there.

The Social Democrats, led by Olof Palme, were returned to power in Sweden's September election, and although I was largely pleased, I was becoming worried that too many of them were becoming overly pompous, in the special way that only politicians seem to have. The fundamental democratic idea – that elected representatives hold office thanks to the will and consent of the governed, that they are there to serve the people, not to receive obeisance – is so easily lost (in *both* directions). After 13 years in Sweden my capacity for critical thinking was more developed. And yet, all things being relative, I couldn't come up with a country that better stood for the values I'd consciously been evolving.

Certainly it is a good thing to keep thinking critically, about everything, all the time, never resting, never letting one's guard down? Relax for a year or two and the forces of evolution, progress, regression, boredom, apathy and disintegration will have shifted or obliterated what once was solid ground. Critical thinking is about living deliberately – and screw the autopilot! – because you only get this one round of life. Will your life be more meaningful, more worthwhile, if your main pursuit is money? Power? Advantage? Conformity? Is the world too much with us? Why not give kindness a chance? And knowledge for its own sake? Think it might make the world a better place?

I was suffering from feeling that I couldn't paint, that my painting was a painful, pointless burden to the woman I loved, that I was betraying the memory of my muse, that I could find no resolution, no way out, no peace. I had some ideas for paintings, but I'd been suppressing them, struggling to contain the chaos gradually building up within me due to the lack of support, encouragement, love, understanding, recognition and reason to go on. I even made a sketch on one of my blank canvases – of a bus, a special bus – but couldn't find a way forward in the face of so much domestic hostility.

Yet I went on building. By early October, the yard was beginning to look like a garden. The stone wall was completed. That would have to suffice for fulfilling my creative needs for the time being. On the 12th, a truckload of compost soil was delivered, and I just kept hoping that something somewhere somehow would tip the scales, make Lena realize that all this was for her, to make her happy, to make her love me. What a naïve jerk I was capable of being!

On Friday, October 17th, a cement truck arrived early in the morning and parked in front of Bo and Peter's house. The three of us were in the starting blocks. Bo and I filled one wheelbarrow each, ran it into their house and tipped it into the frames, where Peter was frantically pulling the concrete out with a rake between the parallel boards set up to pull along to assure a level floor, just as Tage showed me how to do. Soon Bo and I were outpacing Peter, and since I was going to be taking about three or four wheelbarrows of concrete for my yard project, Bo and I ran those around the corner, through our garage and tipped them where I needed them. As soon as we were finished we both went back to help Peter and to run more wheelbarrows.

When we arrived back on the scene, I nearly screamed. Peter was stomping around in the wet concrete, *barefoot*! He clearly didn't know (how could he? – nobody told him, including the guy with the cement truck!) that wet concrete is dangerously corrosive to the skin, wet Portland cement being *highly caustic*. Peter innocently explained that his clogs kept getting caught in the wet concrete, preventing him from moving, so he'd just taken them off. I urged him to rinse off his feet immediately, and keep rinsing, but it was too late; he ended up having to rush to the hospital with severe chemical burns. Meanwhile, Bo and I had to finish the floor on our own, and were ready to collapse.

By the end of October, the yard was finished, cobblestones and all. It looked amazing. Ole, our horticultural expert, offered us plenty of advice about what kinds of plants and flowers to have in different locations, depending on the amount of sun that would reach them down in the gorge-like atrium yard. Lena planted a total of 70 plants and some 400 bulbs, the first step in transforming what had never in the history of the house been a pretty place into a niche of beauty. We even beautified the front of the house, along Korngatan, with a climbing red rose on either side of the front door, as well as a wisteria vine close to the end of the house nearest Källargatan.

Lena was doing well in her history course, and was planning to take a one-term course in the spring to qualify as a teacher for special-needs children. For that course, she would continue to be on a leave of absence from her teaching job, but this time without pay, so we would have to live entirely on my meager salary. Unfortunately, our Datsun was better than ever at devouring our money, so we began considering living without a car. Since the building projects were no longer taking any of my savings, I hoped we might be able to manage. And since I was by now working almost entirely from home, I persuaded Stig to get Perstorp to pay me a small sum for rent each month. It wasn't much, but as long as we kept our expenses down, we might be able to cope.

Mom was managing fine in the Seattle area, and was thrilled that she could get around fairly easily on public transportation, and thus didn't need to "burden" any of the people who would have been more than willing to help her. Mom was so eager to have Lena and me come to visit her that she kindly offered to pay for our tickets. But Lena expressed no interest at all in visiting the States. A trip of that magnitude would hardly be just for a week or two, so perhaps she didn't seem to want to forego that much sunbathing time to see my family, especially when she could hardly spend any time with me without finding more things to complain about than words to express them with.

Against awful odds, in early November I began painting again. I used a canvas on which I'd already sketched the motif. Far from rejoicing with me, Lena growled and sulked, but I felt I'd been such a good, hard-working boy, finishing the little house, the garage-roof deck, and the entire yard, so now maybe I'd earned the right to do another painting.

All those times in 1978 and early '79 that I'd walked down to Lundavägen to get the bus to Lund to see Lena had made a big impression on me. The Malmö buses were green and cream-colored, but the inter-city SJ buses were orange and cream-colored, and the people I observed sitting on them as they went by (to Lund and other destinations) always seemed to be sitting alone, staring blankly out the windows, not communicating; in fact, doing their best to avoid communication. The passers-by were equally non-communicative. I was never a great believer in the joys of non-communication. It took me less than two weeks to complete the painting. I call it *Bus*,[21] and it would turn out to be my penultimate painting. Lena's only response was to reiterate her view that we already had enough goddamn paintings on our walls.

On November 15th, after an excruciating (for me) hiatus of 13 days, Lena took her hand off the emergency brake long enough for me to get her pregnant, although we had no idea or conscious intention that pregnancy might be the result at the time (and thus qualified as sinners according to Catholicism).

On November 27th, we were dinner guests at Ole and Birgitta's little house at the end of the block behind us. They were expecting their first child soon and were elated about it. Perhaps some of that excitement rubbed off, because Lena was at least temporarily less inclined to keep her figurative doors closed to me.

Bob arrived for his two-week Christmas stay with us on December 22nd, and

---

21 Painting #85 (see Appendix 2)

was both surprised and pleased to see the new yard and my new painting. The following day, however, Lena experienced some pain and bleeding and had to make an emergency visit to her gynecologist. That's when we discovered that she'd already been about six weeks' pregnant!

We both had mixed feelings – sorry about the miscarriage itself, of course, but also thrilled by the fact that it showed that we *could* get pregnant. Lena experienced some aching for several weeks, but neither of us felt particularly low. With a little more diligence (and frequent attempts, I hoped), we could succeed. Hope was now a realistic concept for us. But were we hoping for the same things?

Bob said he experienced similar mixed feelings about the miscarriage. He reminded me of his longstanding desire to have children – *many* children – which seemed to me so incongruous with how I perceived his character and outlook. All I was hoping for at this point was that children would add a dimension to our marriage whereby Lena would love me. I must have been purposefully unaware of the *non sequitur* such a wish entailed.

On Sunday, January 16th, Lena and I became godparents to Ole and Birgitta's daughter Sara. According to the church certificate, we were "Lena & Stanley *Eriksson*". That wasn't the only mistake I perceived. When Jeanette and I unwittingly became the godparents of little "Andos" just weeks after arriving in Sweden back in 1969, we knew no Swedish and didn't even realize that we'd just become godparents until the deed was done. This time it was different. As we stood there promising to see to it that little Sara would get a Christian upbringing should anything happen to her parents, my mind was screaming *"Wait a minute here!! This is not at all what I believe, this is totally against what I stand for!"* I suppose it could only be hypocrisy if I'd been aware of it beforehand, but I certainly became aware of it at that moment and it felt hypocritical.

I remembered the outrage and sense of betrayal Lena's big brother Jan felt when his wife connived with Jan's parents to christen his children against his wishes. Starting off a child's life with promises in the name of the Father, the Son, and the Holy Ghost? Why not Mickey Mouse, Zeus and Elvis? Most Swedes I spoke to about it said I was overreacting, that it was "just tradition", that it didn't at all mean that you had to believe that stuff, and that few people in Sweden did. But then why cheapen the momentous moment of the beginning of a child's life by making insincere pledges to an outworn belief, all in the name of "tradition"? I reminded Lena that if we were successful in having a child, there was no way I would agree to carrying on that particular tradition. She assented.

Apart from the Christmas and other concerts that sometimes brought Swedes to church, there were normally only four other occasions in life that would cause most Swedes to attend church: christenings, confirmations, weddings, and funerals. The first two, I felt, were explicitly and essentially about church membership. Weddings, on the other hand, were about two people deciding to spend their lives together, so there was a significant non-religious aspect to them as well, even though making this commitment in the name of a trinity of gods seemed to me a dishonest way for a non-believer to begin married life. Funerals were also a way of saying goodbye, for the sake of any grieving survivors, even though I had yet to experience a funeral where the officiant didn't resort to preaching some of the self-deception that is inherent in religious beliefs. (I've also experienced funerals where the officiant pontificated about the life of the dear departed without having known him or her at all.) On the basis of all this, I concluded that I could, without hypocrisy, attend church weddings and funerals, but not christenings and confirmations; the latter two were solely about religion and for the religious.

Lena visited her gynecologist on January 25th, and was advised to keep a temperature record for six weeks, in order to establish her ovulation cycle, and determine the most probable days when she could get pregnant. Perhaps the gynecologist assumed that we were having sex regularly. Unfortunately (for me), Lena seemed to think that we were supposed to have sex *only* during ovulation, thus indirectly arousing in me a tremendous interest in thermometer readings.

Now that they had a baby, Ole and Birgitta found their tiny house near us to be too cramped, so they bought a lovely house in the Rostorp district of Malmö, a 10-minute walk from our place, and right across the street from Beijer's park, bordered by beautiful old beech trees. The two-storey houses in that neighborhood were from the 1930s, with light, spacious rooms, and big gardens full of fruit trees and flower beds – a paradise for them, and great fun for any horticulturalist. They wanted to make a number of changes in the house, including a structural modification or two, and wanted to hire me to help them.

I spent the first two weeks of February going there every morning with my tools and returning to Korngatan every evening. Ole was usually there assisting me, and I got to watch their little baby, Sara, growing and changing every day.

They were highly satisfied with the work I did and Ole found a number of other small jobs for me to do (e.g. building a bicycle shed). The extra money came in handy due to Lena not having any income at all that term.

Despite Lena's active discouragement of my painting – and of me – I was still determined to go on. I painted a couple of canvases in the first few months of 1983, but became dissatisfied with them and destroyed them. And yet there was one more painting – one *last* painting – I felt I just had to do, a final statement. But I hadn't yet made up my mind how I would do it.

At some point during the early spring, Lena's brother Lars sent a formal letter to his three siblings, confirming his wish to purchase their shares in the property in Eket, and to sound out Jan's, Eva's and Lena's willingness to sell at a price corresponding to one-quarter of the market value each, to be determined by an assessor from the local bank that Lars had contacted. Since Lars and his family were the only ones who ever spent more than a rare weekend at the rundown place, there were no objections whatsoever. (Jan may have driven this action by suggesting to Lars that he would be pulling out of the joint ownership if no action was taken; he *never* went there.) Lena and I saw it as a way of financing some kind of replacement for the similarly rundown Datsun. The question was *when* all this would happen. Lars' letter sounded a bit urgent, but that turned out to be a conclusion based on excessive jumping.

Lena and I flew to Stockholm for the Easter break (March 27th to April 4th) to see her brothers. The good connection between Jan and me was reinforced by a reprise of our previous meeting in Stockholm: copious quantities of whisky and increasingly humorous games of cards in his basement, with Jan's teenage son Henrik and pre-teen son Olof joining in the fun (not the whisky). I seem to recall that Jan and his wife were separated by this time. In any case, Jan's long-term relationship with his secretary was a very open secret. He seemed to have little to do with Lars and his family. The two brothers were polar opposites in personality and amicability. Lars said little about Eket, except that the wheels would "soon be in motion".

I wondered whether the visit to Lena's siblings might make her more amenable to the idea of visiting my family in the US, but Lena seemed not to draw any such conclusions. However, there was always going to be the question of a possible pregnancy, and a possibly legitimate reason for avoiding transatlantic travel should that come to be. But with my mom urging us, we did make some tentative plans (for June and July), and I even made preliminary flight reservations.

In the meantime, I decided to visit Bob on April 11-17 to build him some more bookcases – he always needed more. The time was right – between ovulations – and I realized by now that I wasn't going to be getting anything but frustration anyway. Bob consumed books like no other, and remembered them, in detail. Moreover, in his mind he synthesized them, cross-referenced them, wove their contents into a fabric of contextual understanding, and could impart whatever wisdom he found in them to anyone who cared to listen. In 13 short years (and counting), the times I spent listening to Bob's ruminations had taken their place among the greatest high points of my life.

When I arrived home on April 17th, it turned out to be Ovulation Day, which had the magical and unusual effect of making my beloved willing, which in turn made me hornier than ever. I realized that just one sperm actually causes fertilization, and that a single ejaculation normally contains 100 million of the little fellas, and that twice that equals 200 million, and yet just one is all it takes, all it *can* take. But no thoughts of hundreds of millions went racing through my mind, only thoughts of *"maybe she will start to love me now??"*

Within a week or two after returning from Basel, from the singular (or dual) unknown moment of immaculate conception, I finally abandoned the record-keeping that I began on January 1st, 1979. The direction our "love life" was taking was now too glaringly obvious, too inescapably pessimistic, too heart-rending. My record-keeping felt too much like Don Giovanni's flipside: in 1979, 220 times; in 1980, 127 times; in 1981, 103 times; in 1982, 79; and in 1983, just 24 times in the first five months. It was far too depressing for me to go on recording. But at least I was eating more, smoking less (I was down to about a pack a day), and drinking little. Lena and I pledged that we'd both quit smoking altogether the moment we found out that she was pregnant.

I hadn't set foot in Perstorp for more than a year at this point. My plan had succeeded. I started painting *my last painting: Self-Portrait with Tulips*.[22] This final painting is split vertically, subtly, right down the middle, as though through different colored filters, reflecting my inner dichotomy, my feelings of being torn apart by how I perceived my life to be versus how I perceived it *could* be. I show my cheerful, optimistic side (the left-hand side of the painting) and my dark, gloomy side (right-hand side), enhanced by red and blue "films" respectively

---

22 Painting #86 (see Appendix 2)

A Sea of Troubles

(seen as such only against the background void), covering each half of the face. The films also affect the "reality" in the foreground – making things look lighter or darker than they "really" are. (My dark side would soon assume an increasingly dominant role for close to five years....) Does the background slope down to a precipice or up from one? The tulips, as in some previous paintings, make a counterweight to the void.

The central character (similar to the central character in *Jardin* – using same model might explain it) is one person, but is equally valid as more than one. Both sides of me are realistic; my hope is as real (or as unreal!) as my despair. The overall "real me" is the combination, the sum. My point was to suggest a plurality, not a dichotomy, even though I used a dichotomy to portray it. Of course there can be many sides, overlapping sides, self-contradictory sides, a veritable maze of facets and aspects. The two-way split is merely symbolic of the multiple split.

By the time I completed *Self-Portrait with Tulips*, I had a strong feeling that it was going to be my last painting, quite possibly my last ever. After onescore years of painting, all the currents that drove my creativity into that medium had been turned awry. In my first eight paintings, done in Oak Park in 1963-64, I fumbled around in a fog of innocence, searching for something or someone or someway to impart meaning on a world that was so hard to understand. The last of those eight paintings (*Man with Guitar*) turned out to capture the curiosity and heart of the one who would be my muse – Jeanette – the one who bore me through the 70 paintings that followed, forming the core of my work.

Without Jeanette, I found myself struggling against a swift and merciless current, through the final eight paintings, during which Jeanette was practically a banned topic in what had almost been her own home, and all my efforts to rebound were being trampled underfoot, perhaps unconsciously (to cede the benefit of my doubts). Everything I undertook (not just painting) was being assailed, as was everything I failed to undertake. Every aspect of who I was – my physical appearance, the sound of my voice, how I smelled, what I thought – seemed to serve as triggers for the wrath of the woman I loved. Depression had once again begun wrapping its coils around me.

But there was another factor in my decision to put away my brushes: the public factor. "*The arts are related*," Professor Walsh told our class in San Francisco back in 1964. Perhaps the arts even overlap. Think of literature and music as two artistic media primarily occupying either end of a continuum of abstraction, from less to greater, with painting overlapping both, from the realistic to the totally abstract.

I felt that my own work in this continuum – never totally abstract nor totally realistic – was shifting more and more towards a commonality with literature, reaching towards the limit in *Jardin*. Now it felt to me like my future creativity, if I could find my way back through my sea of troubles to develop any new creativity at all, would have to be in literature. Maybe someday I would write....

On May 10th, after having been to the doctor for tests, we received the eagerly awaited results via a phone call: "*Mrs Erisman, you're pregnant!*"

END OF BOOK FIVE

A Sea of Troubles

APPENDIX 1
Laminates

The unique Perstorp laminates in our kitchen on Korngatan

The design of the laminates, from bottom to top is shown here:

1. Here in the lower cabinets, the little pink people play and hide among the **roots**, which form shoots that become…

2. …the **stems** on the countertop, some of which continue on up to…

3. the splashback, where they become **flowers** and buds. Some of the stems continue on to…

4. the upper cabinets to become **exuberance**, as personified by the little pink men, no longer hiding.

Appendix 1

The design of the laminates shown in a single laminate for the door of the tall cabinet (right):

4 in full bloom; no longer hiding

3 flowers and buds

2 stems

1 roots and shoots

A Sea of Troubles

I drew this during the awful summer of 1977.

Man listening to tape recording of his late wife's voice. Laminated drawing, 1977.

Appendix 1

The laminated photo collage I put together in the summer of 1977, with Jeanette's farewell letter.

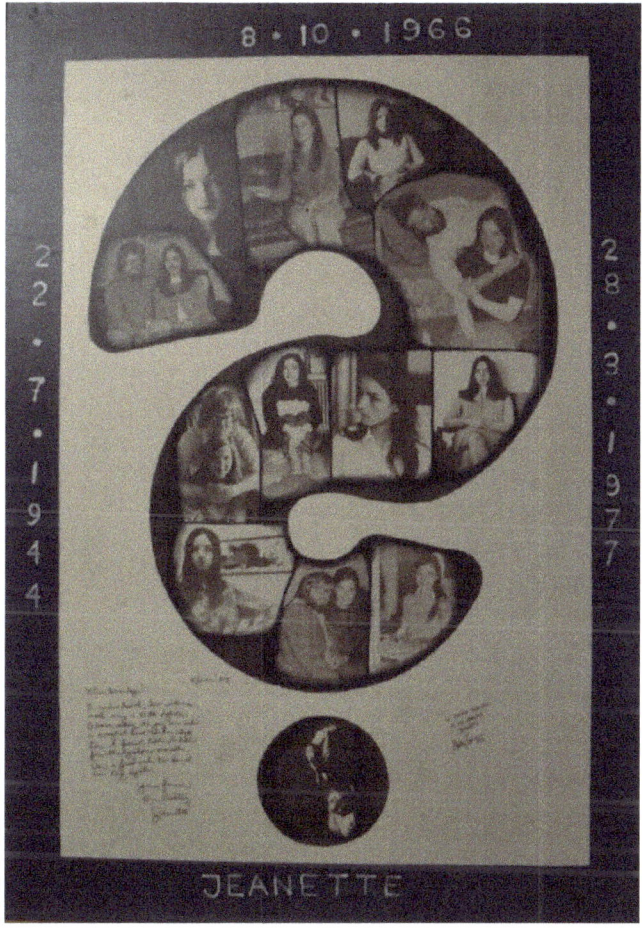

APPENDIX 2 – paintings 79-86

These were the only paintings I painted after Jeanette's death. All were painted at Korngatan.

#79 Turning

#81 If You Want a Flower to Open, You Have to Water It

#80. Urban Idyll

Appendix 2

#82 Through the Woods

#83 Priming the Pump

A Sea of Troubles

#84 Mais Il Faut Cultiver Notre Jardin

Appendix 2

#85 Bus

#86 Self-Portrait with Tulips

Hindsights
the six-part autobiography of an unknown artist

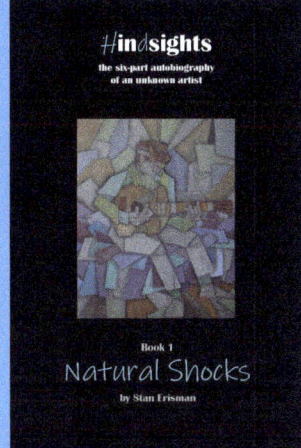
Book 1
Natural Shocks
by Stan Erisman

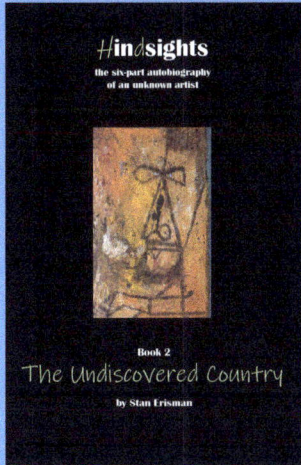
Book 2
The Undiscovered Country
by Stan Erisman

Book 3
No Traveller Returns
by Stan Erisman

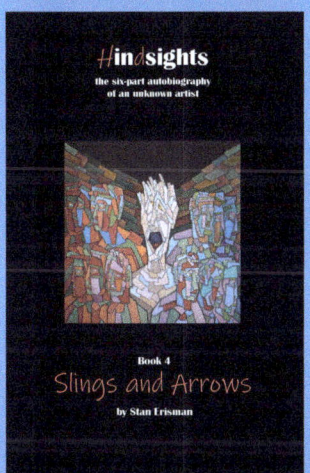
Book 4
Slings and Arrows
by Stan Erisman

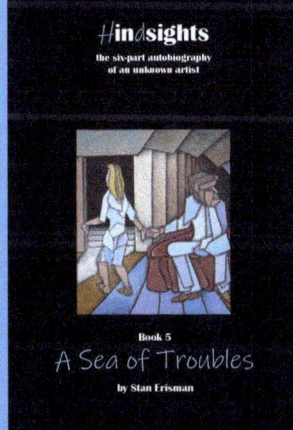
Book 5
A Sea of Troubles
by Stan Erisman

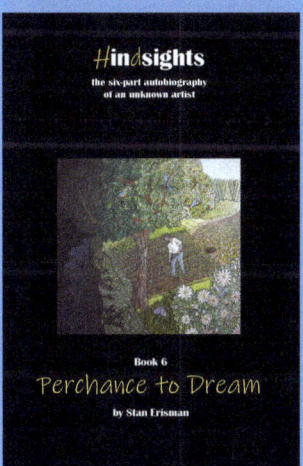
Book 6
Perchance to Dream
by Stan Erisman

www.ingramcontent.com/pod-product-compliance
Lightning Source LLC
Chambersburg PA
CBHW061246230426
43662CB00021B/2440